PERFECTION SHE DANCES

PERFeCtiON SHE dANCES

A True Story of Love, Drugs and Prison in Modern China

robert h. davies

MAINSTREAM
PUBLISHING

EDINBURGH AND LONDON

To my parents, my wife and all those who stood by me.
Also to all those whom I met along the way and especially those who
continue to suffer unjustly.

First published in Great Britain in 2001 by
MAINSTREAM PUBLISHING COMPANY (EDINBURGH) LTD
7 Albany Street
Edinburgh EH1 3UG

ISBN 1 84018 416 7

A catalogue record for this book is available from the
British Library

Typeset in Adobe Garamond
Printed and bound in Great Britain by
Butler & Tanner Ltd, Frome and London

AUTHOR'S NOTE

Because of certain circumstances and in order to protect certain characters
described in the narrative from retribution, I have altered identities and changed
names where necessary. Other than that, this story is true.

Foreword by Howard Marks

Autumn was falling heavier than usual. An army of small multi-coloured leaves had paralysed the railway network; billions of tiny drops of small rain had drowned the roads; and the water in the rivers, lakes, forests, and fields was filthy dirty. The windscreen was opaque with condensation and its wipers squeaked to the beat of last night's techno lullabies. Drizzle and mist threw sheets of spectral gauze over damp shoppers and muddy sheep. I was in Wales, taking my one-man show there on tour for the first time ever.

The Cardiff gig had been good, with hellraisers like Gruff of the Super Furry Animals and Kelly of the Stereophonics in the audience. The Swansea one had really kicked off, thanks to droves of magic-mushroom eaters from nearby valleys descending on the flowing bars of Twin Town.

'Howard, them English had no idea what getting caned was all about until the Scots and Irish showed them a bottle whisky, did they?'

'That's right – and I think the Welsh probably invented that, too, when you think about it. Even St Patrick was Welsh, so we probably had something to do with discovering Guinness as well. No one gets out of his mind as much as a Welshman does. And they have the bloody nerve to call us sheep shaggers.'

'Well, they don't understand the ancient mythology, see Howard, about Mary fancying the Welsh dragon – the only animal that smokes – Merlin getting jealous, and Mary having a little lamb. The English always get their religion and nursery rhymes mixed up, every time.'

And the Porthcawl show went ballistic. All were off their heads, but to such an extent that the local neighbourhood watch group council publicly withdrew future support of the venue's acts. This heralded the usual media pronouncements of outrage and disgust at the idea of a drug dealer being entertaining to the country's youth. Such publicity was always good for ticket sales, as long as the local authority didn't force the venue to cancel.

Tonight's show would be at the Arts Centre, Aberystwyth – owned by the council but, fortunately, organised by the students' union, which whipped up substantial local interest: Ottakar's arranged a book signing and Maldwyn Radio and Ceredigion Radio wanted to interview me, as did Golwg, the Welsh national entertainments magazine.

I took the stage and did my usual showing off about the exotic places I had been, the big dope deals I had done, the years I had spent in maximum-security prisons, and my relentless crusading for the legalisation of marijuana. The question-and-answer session was lively, intense, interesting and exhausting. I hobbled off, my work done. The dressing-room was crammed with beautiful people and large personalities: a fiercely intellectual and exotic lady from Pakistan; the Professor of History at Aberystwyth University; the sister of an author self-exiled in Moscow; nephews and nieces of my old Oxford contemporaries; and individuals who were so independently crazy they would never get insane. Smoke clouds and animated conversation swirled around each other. Another set of potted life histories. More and more questions. They were getting harder to answer. I was flagging. A gentle voice almost whispered in my ear:

'I'm Robert. Can I ask you a few questions on behalf of Radio Maldwyn?'

I didn't know if I could handle any further questioning.

'Our lives have been a bit similar, actually, full of the most remarkable coincidences.'

I knew I couldn't handle another life story. I looked up, slowly and painfully, at my latest interrogator. Immediately, I knew I was gazing into the eyes of someone who was either much smarter than I was, much stronger, had suffered more, or had been around for a lot longer. One learns.

'I too did seven years in prison for dope, Howard.'

'Where?'

'Shanghai.'

'Jesus Christ. How were you busted for dope there? How the hell did you survive? How did you manage to be released? Are you okay?'

'Well, you know what it's like: make every experience work for you, help people and don't take yourself seriously. It is amazing how strong you become. But let me ask you some questions for the radio.'

'I'd rather ask you some, Robert.'

'I'll send you the manuscript of my life story, if you like.'

He did. And it answered every question.

PART ONE

Outside the Mouth

Picking Up the Trail

It is good to be out on the road, and going one knows not where,
Going through meadow and village, one knows not whither nor why.

John Masefield (1878–1967)

IT was June 1988, and after working in London in the construction business, I felt that it was time to move on. I decided to head on down to Australia and maybe join a shearing gang, taking in a bit of overland travelling on the way. While planning my trip I read a book called *To the Frontier* by the well-known travel writer Geoffrey Moorhouse, and in it he described the journey that he had made through Pakistan. I'd never read anything so exciting. I wanted to do the same. My first port of call would be Karachi, and I would follow Moorhouse's trail through the wild and formidable land of the Baluch and the Pathan, and up into the Hindu Kush. As I read more, I soon realised that it was possible to go one better than my hero. I could cross the Karakoram mountains and slip into China and visit the fabled Silk Road city of Kashgar (or Kashi as it is sometimes known). Afterwards it was my intention to spend three or four months touring India, before flying to Thailand and working my way down the archipelago to Bali, from where it would be just a short hop to Oz.

Two and a half months later I was on the Chinese border with Pakistan behind me and the most mysterious and exotic country in the world ahead. The gateway that straddled the road in front informed me that I was now crossing the Khunjerab Pass, known to the Arabs as Bam-i-Dunya, 'The Roof of the World'. At 4,800m above sea-level, it is the highest border crossing with a surfaced road in the world. I couldn't imagine being three miles above the sea, but there I was, in the most dramatic mountain area on the planet. It is the confluence of six of the highest ranges known to man and there is nowhere else on earth to compare. The Greater Himalaya, the Karakoram, the Kunlun, the Hindu Kush, the Pamir and the Tian Shan ranges all meet here.

The bus stopped and all the Pakistanis got off to stretch their legs, have a piss and take photos. There were no guards, no machine-gun posts or barbed wire, no passport control or customs. An inscription on the modest-looking marker-post read: 'Sino-Pakistan Friendship Highway. Completed 1978. Welcome to China.' The other side said the same, only in Chinese, and with 'Welcome to Pakistan'. Another plaque honoured all those who had lost their lives during the construction of the 800-mile-long road. Nearly a thousand men had perished, most of them Chinese. But for China that hadn't mattered: they had used a convict labour force, expendable and easily replaced. This feat of man's determination to prove himself against nature had taken twenty years to complete, using 30,000 labourers.

Back on the bus, we trundled off down into a wide, open valley. An army post, instantly recognisable as being Chinese by its squareness and the red flag flying above it, was dug into the hillside and served as a reminder that even up here Big

Brother was watching. In the rolling tundra, huge sheets of ice sparkled in the sun, and dry yellow grasses bent in the wind. These were the summer pastures of the Tajik nomads, and reputedly the best mountain grazing in the world. A herd of hairy black yak crossed the road, taking their time. Marmots sat up on their hind legs on small mounds, surveying the countryside like sentries. Clouds appeared and disappeared in the blink of an eye as shadows raced across the landscape like pedestrians at rush hour.

The customs post at Pireli could not have been in a bleaker place. There was nothing at all to shelter it from the driving winds and powerful blizzards that swept across the mountains. As we pulled over to the side of the road, everybody was ordered off the bus and our luggage was unloaded, ready for inspection. Another bus which had arrived before us was still waiting to have what looked like tons of cloth checked, and it appeared we were in for a long wait. The customs building itself was another square affair, with a glass door leading into a VIP reception room on the one side, and a little shop on the other. Through another door was immigration and passport control.

I filled out a simple form and presented it to a young Chinese woman dressed in a uniform three sizes too big for her. Scanning my passport, she said something that could have been anything. I nodded my head in a yes and no fashion and hoped for the best. She stamped my passport, ignored my bag, and that was it. I changed a fifty-dollar note at the money exchange counter and got some sort of monopoly-money stuff called Foreign Exchange Certificates in return. I had been warned about this by travellers I'd met along the road, and had done a deal with a guy who was leaving for the equivalent of a tenner in the real local currency, renminbi ('people's currency'). The theory was that foreigners were only supposed to spend FEC, but that had no chance of working, especially when you could exchange 100 FEC for 190 renminbi or rmb on the black market. Anyway, I headed for the shop where I'd seen beer on the shelf – six cans of Tsing Tao to be exact, and no more. I took the lot, and immediately quaffed down my first beer in two months. It was delicious.

To pass the time, I crossed the road to a wooden shack that was trying to convince me it was a restaurant. The smell of food did make me feel hungry, however, and I ordered the same as a bloke sitting next to me: thick, chewy noodles with some sort of chunky stew-like stuff over it, in a chipped and cracked bowl covered in grease. That was nothing: I still had to deal with the chopsticks. You could choose your own from a selection of worn wooden specimens standing in a glass of oily water. I was more than surprised when the first mouthful tasted really good – better than that bloody dal I'd had to suffer in Pakistan.

My next introduction to China was the toilet facilities adjacent. It consisted of an enclosed wooden platform built out over a rocky outcrop with six slots in the floor. It wasn't only the icy wind that shot up through the holes. Five generations of frozen human excrement, two metres high like stalagmites, poked their noses through as well. It was impossible to crouch down fully for fear of sitting on it. Thank God my giardia had cleared up and I could wait.

The bus that went on from Pireli was Chinese and about as uncomfortable as it possibly could be: wooden benches, dirty windows jammed half open and a cloud of exhaust fumes bellowing out from underneath the engine cover.

Everything rattled, and when the bus hit a pothole I slid off the seat. Drinking my beer and watching a herd of two-humped camels grazing in the twilight, I contented myself with the thought that this was *real* travelling, and that the experience outweighed the discomfort a hundred times.

The road left the plain and started to drop down, passing through gorges that caused the temperature to fall so much that I was shivering. The region was notorious for the huge contrasts in temperature between direct sunlight and the shade. One nineteenth-century traveller claimed to have recorded 38ºC in the sun and -10ºC in the shade.

At about eight o'clock the charabanc groaned its way into the courtyard of what seemed to be a hotel in the first town in China, Tashgurgan. By the time I'd got my rucksack down from the roof of the bus, the hotel was full. The only other hotel in town was unfortunately still only half built. I was tired and hungry and decided to deal with the problem later. If I had to, I'd roll out my sleeping-bag in the lobby and kip there.

Two thousand years ago, Ptolemy had named Tashgurgan, the gateway to Seres, the Land of Silk, but that was far too exotic a title for what I saw. Marco Polo had also stopped here after crossing from Afghanistan.

Tashgurgan had a main street and a side street. Dark, dingy little restaurants puffed out steam from bowls of hot noodles, and barbecues shone cherry-red and the smell of roasting mutton drifted through the air. Little shops sold a hundred different brands of cigarette, bottles of serious-looking spirits and big green bottles of beer. After the enforced abstinence of Pakistan, this was heaven on earth.

Looking about the town I could see very little that could be called Chinese, though. This was Xinjiang, a land populated by Turkic tribes, little changed from Polo's time. The townsfolk were a mixed bunch, all red-faced, strong and healthy-looking, and could all be distinguished by the different hats they all wore. There was supposed to be a total of 28,000 Tajik people, each of whom, it was said, had a hectare of land. Three-fifths of the population lived in and around the Tashgurgan area. There were also Uighur and Kirghiz people there, as well as a pocketful of Han Chinese who maintained a presence in order to keep an eye on things.

This was where the ancient trade routes from India and Persia met, and it had been a resting-place for the famous Tang Dynasty monk, Xuan Zang, when he made his trip to India to acquire the Buddhist scriptures.

Many Tajik believe they are descended from an ancient European race who long ago came and settled in the high, rich pastures. It was only in the eleventh century that the name Tajik, which means 'crown', was generally accepted as the collective name of these mountain herdsmen. Remaining loyal to their traditions, nearly all are nomadic, rearing animals to provide an income, and considering business a dirty way to make a living. They say that you can count the number of Tajik shopkeepers on the fingers of one hand.

Apart from the Han Chinese, Xinjiang is well known for the fourteen different minorities that it is home to. There are Hui, Dongxiang, Tu, Salar, Bonan, Yugur, Uighur, Kazak, Kirghiz, Xibie, Tajik, Uzbek, Russian and Tartar. The majority are Muslim Turkic-speaking peoples while the rest are Buddhist and of Mongolian origin. Xinjiang, meaning 'new dominion', is the largest of China's provinces, over six times bigger than the UK. The total population is about 14 million divided roughly half and half between minority and Han. Due to forced migration and the expansion of the provincial capital Urumchi, however, it is the Han's numbers which are now increasing at a faster rate.

After a good hot meal and a few beers, I decided not to bother confronting the hotel staff. Instead, I went back to the bus and climbed in through the window and stretched myself out on the back seat. The next morning, with the valley bathed in an eerie fluorescent light, I saw that the town lay in the shadow of a huge cliff of black rock which seemed to stand there like a prison guard. It was claustrophobic to say the least.

I was up early enough to listen to a propaganda broadcast in Chinese pumped through tinny little speakers that were tied to the trees in the main street. Since most locals only spoke Tajik, a language similar to Farsi, I couldn't see what purpose this served. I had thought of going to see the remains of the old stone fortress from which the town got its name, but by the time I'd had some hot fresh bread and a bowl of tea, the bus was already revved up and ready to go.

Very soon after we left, the road disappeared in a mound of rubble and the driver was forced to take us down into a dried-up riverbed. After about an hour he found the road again, and we were off at full speed. Fifty or so miles from Tashgurgan we came to Karakul, meaning 'black lake' in Turkic, a reference to the colour of the water when the clouds block out the sun. When I was there, though, it was a pure blue, reflecting the 7,800m-high Muztag Ata in its waters, powdery snow billowing from the peak.

To the left was another huge snow-clad mountain, the 7,719m-high Kongur, also known as Tagharma, with its thirteen glaciers racing each other down to the shores of the lake. Chris Bonington, the British climber, had led the first expedition to reach its summit in 1981, but I'm sure he didn't stay in either of the three 'tourist yurts' that now sat beside the road. This was Kirghiz country, a name that supposedly means 'forty virgins', from whom the tribe of this region is said to have descended. Mainly nomadic, they are famous for playing what the Chinese call 'sheep chase' or what we know as *buzkashi*, a forerunner of polo, but with bare hands and a live sheep instead of mallets and wooden balls.

On the other side of the lake, as the road left the valley, twenty or so gnarled, scruffy Chinese in blue uniforms laid kerb stones on the side of the highway. It was obvious that they were prisoners, and their accommodation, built from stone walls and covered with tarpaulin sheets with pipe chimneys poking through the top belching smoke, sat in a gully to protect them from the wind. These were not volunteers, that's for sure, but I guessed it was better than a bullet in the back of the head.

We made our way through deep canyons, dropping steeply every minute. Boulders and razor-sharp outcrops lined the route. Then, as if we had reached the bottom of a topographical stairway, we ran into an army checkpoint, its red-and-white pole barring our path. A boy who looked about fifteen, dressed in a green uniform and canvas shoes, boarded the bus and almost vomited the word for 'passport' in Chinese at us, and then held out his hand. I thought of shaking it, but knew it wouldn't be appreciated.

Moving on, the gorge began to open up until we came out on to a wide flood plain. The right-hand side was lined with the most bizarre corrugated ochre-coloured cliffs I'd ever seen. It was as if there was a fire causing them to glow from within. Losing yet more altitude, I was suddenly aware of trees, grass and other signs of life. We passed the odd donkey-cart and from then on the traffic increased. Enclosed compounds, with flat-roofed sun-baked mud-brick houses, each with its own little orchard, came into view. Tall, silvery desert poplars started to line the road, and we crossed a bridge over a gushing mountain stream. Suddenly there were horses and carts with jangling bells and children playing in the dusty verge.

Xinjiang has had a variety of names in the past, including High Tartary, East Turkestan, Chinese Turkestan, Kashgaria, Altyn Shahr ('the land of the six cities', a local name) and Serender ('the silk route').

The Tian Shan mountains divide Xinjiang into two desert basins, Dzungaria, the home of the Western Gobi in the north, and Tarim Pendi, the home of the 800,000km square Taklamakan desert in the south. The region is regarded as the most physically inhospitable place on earth. The desert was named Taklamakan (meaning 'He who enters will not return' in the local dialect) as a warning. Svin Hedin, the famous explorer, one of the few Europeans ever to have crossed it, called it 'the worst and most dangerous in the world'. Sir Percy Sykes, the one-time British consul-general in Kashgar, called it 'a land of death' – and with good reason. Its 100m-high shifting dunes and fierce sandstorms known as *kara-buran* ('black hurricanes') can whip up in a minute without warning and dash a man to death with a blitz of sand and stones as big as your fist. Locals are said to have found skeletons stripped of all flesh by the ferociousness of the wind, while others lie lost and buried forever under tons of sand.

The first Uighur settlement we came to was a small town called Upal. As we all piled out of the bus it was time for a kebab and a bowl of *chai*. Sitting down at one of the stands, I was immediately surrounded by about fifteen locals who stayed there the whole time to watch me eat and drink. It was extremely disconcerting but I was so hungry I managed to ignore them. It crossed my mind that for most of them it would have been the first time they'd ever seen a westerner in the flesh. The KKH had been open for just two years as a route for entry into China for foreigners, so there couldn't have been many chances to spot a live one eating before.

Kashgar was only two hours or so away now, and I simply couldn't wait to get there. I felt exhausted. I needed a rest, and I'd heard that there was a restaurant there which catered to foreign tastes, serving up egg and chips, spaghetti bolognese and apple pie. It wasn't that I didn't like trying out the local grub – I loved it – but there was a craving building up in me for something familiar. It was to the Oasis Café that I wanted to go.

Oasis

A sinful city full of thieves and gamblers, no-hopers, wasters, charlatans and true nuts.

From the movie *Wild Bill*

THERE are many cities in the world whose names evoke mystique and conjure up exotic images of remote, dusty towns sitting on the edge of nowhere, where conspiracy, intrigue and cloak-and-dagger goings-on abound: Tombouctou, Marrakech, Istanbul, Baghdad, Buhkara and Samarkand are just a few. The mere mention of their names is enough to carry you away on a magic carpet to a land where time has stood still and where the genie is more than a superstition. But there is another city which has all these ingredients and which has also managed to keep its reputation intact: Kashgar. Situated 1,290m (4,232ft) above sea-level, Kashgar is said to mean 'land of jade'. It is also known as 'a pearl on the Silk Road', the rich commercial route that linked the Middle East and Europe with China. Kashgar's legendary glory lasted for ten centuries, from the Han Dynasty (206BC–AD220) to the end of the Song Dynasty (AD960–1279) when maritime routes opened and the expansion of the Mongol tribes disrupted overland travel. A vital watering-hole, supply centre and trading-post for merchants, dealers and the drovers of huge camel caravans, it also attracted bandits, criminals, hawkers and other flotsam and jetsam from all over the continent, giving it a gloriously seedy reputation.

Ptolomy included it in his map of the world in the second century as being in the area of 'Horse-eating Scythes, Cannibals and Terra Incognita', and it has become the intrepid traveller's ultimate destination. Further from the sea than any other town on earth, trapped on two sides by the most rugged mountain ranges on the planet, and on the other two by 'the land of death', only the brave dare even to attempt to reach such a far-flung place. In the past, many came to a sticky end, one way or another, without ever reaching their goal, and those who did make it were not guaranteed a safe return. It was only in the 1860s that the first travellers started to come back to Britain with news of Kashgar, Yarkand and Hotan. The rediscovery of these cities was the greatest of challenges, and rivalled darkest Africa in excitement and reward. Interest quickly mounted, and geographers and explorers were dispatched to map the mountains and rivers and discover new routes.

The British were not the only ones with an interest in East Turkestan. The Russians, boosted by conquests in Central Asia, regarded expansion into Xinjiang as a natural progression. The Indian Mutiny of 1857 had indicated to the Russians that the British might not be able to trust their Indian soldiers, and that given time the Raj would destroy itself from within. As such, Xinjiang would be the perfect spot to wait for such a demise.

But when the Chinese Muslim Uprising of 1860 finally caused the Muslim population of Kashgaria to rise up and kick the Qing Dynasty rulers out of the whole Xinjiang region, the revolt's principal leader, Yakub Beg, became a much sought-after character. He was invited to St Petersburg for talks, and the British sent an envoy to Kashgar with a letter from Queen Victoria. The British were eager to support Beg, hoping to establish another buffer zone like Afghanistan, and they even promised to supply him with 30,000 guns. The idea was eventually scrapped because of fear that the Kashmiris would hijack the cargo *en route*.

The Russians, meanwhile, hedged their bets, and when Yakub Beg was murdered in 1877, and the Chinese walked straight back in, it was they who came off best. In 1882 the Chinese allowed the Russians to establish a consulate in Kashgar, but it took another eight years for similar permission to to granted to the British. A man called George Macartney, the son of a Scots father and a Chinese mother, took the post of consul-general, and ended up staying there, in Britain's most remote listening-post, for twenty-eight years. Macartney's adversary for many of those years, while the intrigues of the so-called 'Great Game' unfolded, was the notoriously imperious Nicolai Petrovsky.

The Great Game was not only about gaining influence and a foothold in the region or stifling the opposition's advances, it was about robbing the area of valuable antiquities, books, manuscripts, Buddhist scriptures and whatever else could be dug up from the lost cities deep in the Taklamakan. Over the years, Macartney played host to an endless stream of archaeologists, gravediggers, adventurers, opportunists and spies. Had anything changed, I wondered.

Located on the Kashgar river delta, it is today one of the richest parts of Xinjiang. The huge oasis is fed by fresh-water springs that bubble to the surface some three miles to the west, and water from the Tooman River and the Kizil Darya that is diverted through a complex system of canals and channels to irrigate the fields and supply drinking-water. The old city, with its houses built of clay and mud bricks, retains much of its ancient charm. Intricate networks of back streets turn into small lanes with projections spanning overhead connecting one side to another, and the cleverly carved wooden multiple-arched corridors with hanging eaves and balconies are a vivid indication of the passion of the people.

The bus drew up at the gates of the Chinibagh Hotel, the former British Consulate, at about seven in the evening, and was greeted by a colourful throng of money-changers and cloth-dealers who swamped the vehicle in search of business. Luckily I had my rucksack to hand and was able to get clear of the chaos straight away. Chinibagh, meaning 'Chinese garden' in Uighur, was still recognisable as the residence described by Mrs Macartney in her book, *An English Lady in Chinese Turkestan*, although the famous gatehouse had long ago been replaced by a far less ornate kiosk selling cigarettes. A tree-lined driveway led up to the old administration building, which was a mud-brick copy of a seventeenth-century manor-house. With its parquet flooring still in place, it was now the hotel reception.

An arch on the right led through to a courtyard which was overlooked by the main building of the former official residence. To the left ran a line of barracks that had been the expeditionary force's officers' quarters, and on the right, in front of the reception, were three other slightly less comfortable barracks for the ordinary soldier. Without any renovation, or any expense, these were now hotel rooms. The main building was also used for accommodation, thus making it possible to stay in the consul quarters themselves, with their balconies overlooking the garden and the back streets of Kashgar. The Pass of Torugart, visible between the snow-topped peaks of the Pamir on the skyline, some 100km away, was a constant reminder of the closeness of the border with Kirghizia.

The dormitory, in what had once been the consul library, was now where you could find the cheapest bed in town, a refuge for the budget traveller. There were no showers or baths in the rooms, only an enamel bowl on a stand and a thermos flask. The toilets, in what had once been the stables, were a long line of squat slots in the corner of the compound, and were a defrosted version of what I had seen in Pireli. The showers, in a newly constructed block behind the officers' quarters, were divided into male and female, and were open at six o'clock every evening for two hours, or as long as the hot water lasted.

I paid the equivalent of a pound for one night, and was shown to a room already occupied by a young Frenchman. It didn't take long for him to tell me about the Oasis Café and the existence of another hotel on the other side of town known as the Semen Hotel or *lao bing guan* ('old hotel') which was the former Russian consulate. François was already a regular at the Oasis Café, and had clearly been impressed, describing each dish in mouthwatering detail. The very thought of cream of tomato soup, Kashburgers and chocolate cake made me ravenous, and in less than five minutes we were striding off down the road in search of the place that I was sure would save my life.

Turning the corner on to Semen Road, I noticed that the 6m-high mud walls of the old city were shamefully crumbling into disrepair. Horse-cart taxis, with their jingle-jangle bells and red awnings, clip-clopped up the street, overtaking donkey-carts driven by small boys in flat caps cracking whips and cursing, '*Keerch, keerch, anang eski.*' Big green trucks were blowing their horns and carving a path through the traffic, stirring up clouds of yellow dust that settled on everything in sight. Women in floral headscarves and brightly patterned silk dresses sat on the horse-carts next to others veiled by thick chocolate-brown yashmaks revealing pink bloomers and stockinged legs with folded banknotes slipped under the garters.

'It's over there,' said François, pointing to a Chinese-style building with 'Friendship Hotel' written on the roof. 'It used to have a veranda with arches, but Tahir put glass windows in and made it into a café. It's in all the guidebooks now, and he's packed out every day. Whichever direction they come from, people are tired. They need this place to help them build up the strength to carry on,' he told me eagerly.

As we walked by the five high arched windows I looked in and saw two rows of tables in a long narrow room. A group of people sat around one of the tables, but apart from that it was empty. We were met at the door by a grey-eyed young man with dark shoulder-length hair, wearing a T-shirt and beads. I'd heard the place was run in a sort of a college bar way and assumed he was a Portuguese traveller who was helping out.

'I'm sorry but we're closed today,' he said apologetically. 'There's been a death in the family. Sorry, but we'll be open tomorrow.'

Disappointed, we nodded and walked away.

'That was Tahir, the owner,' said François.

'Doesn't look very Chinese, does he?'

'He's Uighur. Let's go to John's Café in the Semen Hotel. It's good too.'

The Semen was further down the same road. Just across from the entrance, behind a line of tall dusty poplar trees, I could see two cafés with loads of foreigners sitting outside on rattan chairs under an awning.

'That's the Limen, and that's the Semen Restaurant. Good for Chinese food. They also do a great schnitzel.'

I was amazed. There were more travellers here than I'd bargained for, and I was beginning to think the place wasn't as remote as I'd imagined.

The gateway to the Semen was blocked by four or five seedy-looking blokes in suits, wearing stacked heels and acting as if they were going to sell me a dirty postcard. One sidled up to me furtively and, in a loud whisper, said: '*Wai hui barma?* FEC, FEC, one hun'red eighty-five.'

François brushed them aside and said, 'They're giving one ninety-two in Chinibagh and probably more down in front of the Id Kah Mosque. Some reckon it'll be two to one very soon, which is good news if you intend to hang around for a while.'

John's Café was a shady arbour under a trellis swamped with grapevines. A big painted sign on the wall welcomed the visitor and listed the services John provided: minibus and car hire; international phone calls; sightseeing tours to Karakul, Hanoi (not to be confused with Vietnam, this is the site of an ancient city in the desert) and the Caves of the Three Buddhas; bus tickets to Urumchi, Turfan and Pakistan; and bicycle hire. It was cool, comfortable and clean, and the Chinese waitresses were pleasant and polite. I suddenly realised that in Pakistan I'd hardly seen any women at all, and to have these pretty young women flitting about was nice. The beer was cold and the vegetable omelette and chips was the best thing I'd eaten in weeks. It seemed as if it was all happening here, so the next day I switched hotels.

The Semen Hotel was much the same as when the Russian consulate had occupied it. It had been set in gardens among trees with high-ceilinged rooms that were built to last. It was a nice shady place, relaxing and quiet, and in nearly every flowerbed there were dope plants growing, which relaxed me even more. My room was a dark, musty-smelling affair with three beds and a bathroom, with cold running water that argued with the pipes every time you turned the taps on. Nevertheless, it was better than Chinibagh, and at least I had some privacy for the moment.

I decided to have breakfast at John's and then saunter up to the Oasis for lunch. Halfway through my egg and tomatoes, I was joined by an English student who introduced himself as Tom Wells in a way that suggested I should have known who he was. He explained that we were close to the fiftieth anniversary of the closure of the British consulate in Kashgar and that he was organising a fancy-dress party in room 701 of the old residence to commemorate this tearful episode. Was I interested in dressing up and joining in the fun? It would mean sticking around for a week, but I thought it was a cracking idea, and agreed to spread the word and invite everybody I met.

An hour later I walked into the Oasis and managed to find a seat at a table for two by the window. It was by any standards quite a neat place, with rattan chairs, a wine-coloured carpet, floral tablecloths, large mirrors on the walls and a grape trellis running the whole length of the ceiling. The wooden bar's shelves were stacked with Napoleon brandy and whisky. A sound-system pumped out Fleetwood Mac's *Rumours*, and the scene was set. Inside the café you could have been anywhere in the world, but when you looked out the windows you knew differently.

By that time of the morning it was starting to get hot outside, and the short walk had given me a thirst. I needed a cold beer. A young woman wearing tight jeans, trainers and a T-shirt glided up to my table with a menu and a smile. I did a double take and focused on her eyes. I had never seen anything quite like them. They were two sparkling sapphires, electric-blue, demanding my attention. Almond-shaped with large black pupils, they hypnotised me, and insisted I take notice of the fire that burned within. Her gaze seemed to penetrate my skin. I felt as if she had read my mind and assessed my character, all in a matter of seconds. Her skin was olive and her hair was black. I struggled to place her. Where was she from? Brazil? Maybe she was Lebanese or Egyptian? Perhaps she was Cleopatra reincarnated? Suddenly I was nudged back to reality. I took the menu and ordered a beer. Even though I'd had breakfast not all that long before, the list of dishes (including cream of mushroom soup, vegetable tempura, Kashgar pizza, quiche and apricot nut bread) tempted me to eat again. I'd lost at least ten kilos in Pakistan and now saw a chance here to put some of it back on.

'Spaghetti meat sauce, please.'

Fifteen hours later, I was still there. I had eaten four meals and drunk beer solidly the entire time. The young woman had told me her name was Sharapet Sharif and that she was Tahir's sister, but I was unable to understand anything more. She spoke only Uighur and Chinese. I spoke neither, apart from *yige pijiu* ('one beer') which I'd learnt in a *Lonely Planet* guidebook. I was fascinated by this Turkic language, though, and during a quiet period in the afternoon I persuaded her to join me and teach me one to ten in Uighur. I listened to Sharapet and the other waitresses talking and was enthralled by its musical tones. It was the most beautiful language I'd ever heard. I had to learn more.

It was time to go. Seeing me a bit the worse for wear, Sharapet offered me her bicycle on which to go home. I couldn't work out if it was more hazardous to ride it or not, but in light of her obvious generosity, I accepted. I wanted to kiss her to thank her but, remembering that they were Muslims, I thought it might offend her and I didn't want that.

The next day I was back in the Oasis again, quite content to sit there for another day, eating and drinking, shooting the shit with other travellers and just watching the world go by. And what a world it was. Huge, hairy camels hauling massive loads of rock salt into town in preparation for the Sunday market, hundred-year-old men with long white beards balanced on little donkey-carts trundling by with the crack of a whip, and the odd local galloping by on his horse at full speed. I could already feel a deep attraction, and knew that I was falling in love with the place. I looked at the faces as they passed by and seemed to recognise them. They were the same faces that I remembered seeing in Oswestry livestock market, and I felt at home, almost as if I had been born there.

The Uighur had a special quality about them, a spirit which set them apart from their Han oppressors. They were Muslim, but unlike in Pakistan women were visible and the majority went about unveiled. The menfolk liked to drink and dance, and I was soon hearing that the women liked to drink and dance too. It was plain to see that these were a proud people, intent on maintaining their identity at all costs.

Every day I met different people from all over the world, most of whom were obviously not your average traveller. Aussie Kim had been on the road for ten years and Mexican Tony seemed to want me to believe that he was a gold smuggler. A little Jewish girl from New York who played the flute rather badly tried to convince me that she was a Buddhist priestess, and a hairy Japanese told me that his father had built the Bullet Train. We all swapped yarns, told jokes and gleaned scraps of information from each other. I soon learned that Kashgar was a unique place, and that the people who came here were a different breed.

A few days before the fancy-dress party, Duncan, a guy I'd met in Pakistan, arrived. He was looking rough and complaining of giardia, but when he heard about the party his spirits rose. Tom had gone to the trouble of making little Union Jacks which he then tied to a length of string. On the night of the party they were hung like bunting around the room and over the balcony. About twenty-five guests turned up in the end, dressed as explorers, Arabs, Chinese and tarts. The old residence hadn't seen anything like it for years. The old residence hadn't seen anything like it for years, it was almost like stepping back in time. According to the account of his stay with the Macartneys in his book, *Buried Treasures of Chinese Turkestan*, the famous explorer and treasure hunter Albert von le Coq had stayed in that very room but had found it far too homely and ended up dossing down on the balcony with a saddle for a pillow.

Just as the party was reaching its peak of alcohol- and smoke-induced debauchery, we were raided by officers from the Kashgar Gong An Ju (public security bureau). They had been informed that there was an anti-Chinese gathering celebrating 'colonialist thought', and, fearing that we had come to Kashgar to stir up trouble, five PSB officers had burst in through the doors with a video camera and halogen lights in an attempt to bust this cell of free-thought and expression before it got out of hand. They demanded to know who had organised the party. Tom confessed and the officers tried to drag him off for questioning, but then Duncan stepped in and also confessed, so they took the two of them away in spite of strong protests from the rest of us. We were told to take down the Union Jacks and wait until they returned.

None of us was able to take such a thing seriously, and dismissed it as a typical blunder. We turned the music back on and carried on as if nothing had happened. After about an hour, Tom and Duncan returned, having managed to convince the authorities that it was not a political meeting trying to drum up anti-Chinese feeling, and that it was just a bit of fun. The police were finally satisfied and gave us permission to continue on one condition: we had to remove the Union Jacks. How pathetic, I thought. It was like being back at school and getting caught smoking behind the bike sheds. Anyway, we ripped them down, waved goodbye to the cops and got back to rolling up.

The days passed and I continued with my Uighur lessons with Sharapet. The more I learned, the more interested I became in her and her language. It felt as if

I was the only foreigner in the world learning that strange tongue. I was being allowed into a world that few tourists ever enter.

Sitting in the café all day also put me in contact with more and more travellers. A New Zealander who had spent sixteen years in Nepal and India converting himself into a Sadhu monk claimed to have spent seven years in a vow of silence. It had taught him to use his body to convey his thoughts and his eyes to see into others' hearts. Trixie and Susan were two twenty-five-year-old 'Essex gels' on their way to Japan to become escort girls. They had heard it was possible to make thousands of dollars pandering to the needs of randy Tokyo businessmen, and that if they worked a double act it would be worth thousands more. It seemed as if they had been practising their routine along the way, picking up innocent young men and giving them a night they would never forget.

There was a fifty-five-year-old German who ate his every meal at Oasis dressed up like David Attenborough. When he wasn't in Kashgar, he was in the desert wandering around looking for lost cities for days on end. There was Eduard, a Peruvian, and his Japanese-American wife Orashi. They had met in India and got married in Ladakh six weeks later. They took six showers a day together and bought soap by the carton.

There were two customers at the Oasis who were as regular as me – an English couple by the name of Peter and Cynthia. She was in her late thirties and he was in his fifties. Wearing a green *dopa* (a round embroidered hat worn by the locals) with a long pointy white beard and a nose like a hawk's beak, Peter would hold court at one of the tables near the bar. He would be surrounded by young travellers listening in awe to his tales about life on the road. The pair of them had left good jobs back in Britain fifteen years before, and headed out on the old hippie trail to India. They had spent time teaching English in Iran while the Shah was in power and then in Afghanistan before finding a home in Goa. They were almost theatrical and reminded me of a travelling magician and his assistant. They were well educated, well read and more than willing to take on the role of resident experts. It was their third time in Kashgar, and they loved it. They had a room at the Chinibagh where they always stayed out of fondness of the old place and some distant sense of patriotism. It was their intention to stay in Kashgar for at least three or four months before heading back to India. They had once been antique-dealers in Britain, and now liked nothing better than searching the bazaars for rare trinkets that could be sold in Hong Kong at a handsome profit.

Peter and Cynthia knew everybody worth knowing. They knew money-changers, horse-cart owners, various Pakistanis and other travellers who were return visitors. They had known Tahir and his sister when they ran the original Oasis opposite the Semen, and it was from Peter that I heard the story.

Tahir was an example of a new breed of entrepreneur in China. The relaxation of certain laws had allowed him to run his own business and make a profit. He had studied electronics and made his initial capital repairing TVs and radios. With a pocketful of money he decided to leave Kashgar and go to Guangzhou with a dream of making it big. He ended up getting ripped off by Triads and had to find work in one of the big hotels. It was while he was there that he got the idea of setting up a restaurant, because with Xinjiang due to be opened up to foreign tourists, there was a definite opportunity beckoning.

Returning to Kashgar, he approached the people who ran the Kashgar youth hostel, opposite the Semen Hotel, for help in setting up a business. The hostel was a front for a government body which placed graduates in employment. It had the power to authorise loans and locate premises. As luck would have it, there was a vacant shop next door, ideally situated near the hotel. Tahir borrowed some money and signed a two-year lease. The Oasis Café was born. His only aim was to capture the tourist trade, so in every spare moment he studied western cuisine, spending hours poring over recipes and practising in his little kitchen. Within weeks of opening, the Oasis Café was known from Rawalpindi to Hong Kong. People couldn't believe that such a place existed in this far-flung corner of the world. Tahir was doing a roaring trade, probably on his way to becoming one of the richest twenty-year-olds in Kashgar. But his success was not going unnoticed. Running any sort of private business in Kashgar presented difficulties, but a restaurant for foreigners like Oasis was a minefield. For health and hygiene alone there were three different departments: for the kitchen, for the restaurant and for the food served. There was the tax bureau for purchases, the tax bureau for sales and the tax bureau for income. There was the trade licensing bureau, the restaurant trade licensing bureau and the liquor licensing bureau. As if that wasn't enough, there was the beloved PSB, which thought that he was a spy. Each department made a visit at some time or another to do a check. A proprietor was normally expected to wine, dine and charm in order to obtain the necessary certificate to allow him to trade. Usually the heads of departments would very thoughtfully come alone so as to give prior warning of the raid and let it be known that they were doing him a favour – a favour, naturally, which needed repaying. Bottles of spirits or cartons of cigarettes usually did the trick. If the favour was ignored, the visiting stormtroopers from the bureau would find any excuse to withhold the permit, effectively closing the business down. It was an expensive game, but it was more expensive if you didn't play.

It was the PSB who eventually found an excuse to put Tahir out of action. They attempted to charge him with black-marketeering when they discovered his collection of foreign banknotes on display under the glass top of the counter. The customers were up in arms about it, and immediately lodged a petition in support of Tahir. It was signed by nearly fifty tourists and handed in to the local PSB. Some threatened to expose the dastardly deed to the world's press, and eventually, more out of embarrassment than anything else, the Oasis was allowed to reopen.

The youth hostel had watched Tahir's business blossom, and figured that seeing as he was doing so well, he could easily afford a rent increase. When the time came to renew the contract, the rent had doubled. Tahir told them to shove it and said he'd look for somewhere else. He found a new location in the Uighur-run Friendship Hotel, and after a major refurbishment, Oasis II opened in April '88. In the meantime, a Chinese translator working at the hostel had also seen the potential in a western-style café. He approached the Semen Hotel with an idea which the Chinese management jumped at. John's Café was up and running within weeks and soon became Tahir's main rival.

Business was booming. If you didn't get in early, there was a good chance you wouldn't get a seat for dinner. Tahir had overhauled his menu, adding dishes he'd picked up from visitors. He'd learnt to make real pizzas from Italians, real quiche from a Frenchman and real apple pie from an American.

Peter went on to talk about Sharapet, revealing that she was in fact married and had a daughter, but that Kang, her husband, supposedly a right bastard, was in jail in Urumchi. I was eager to learn more, and quizzed Peter at length. Sharapet had had a rough time of it recently, and the reason the café had been closed when I arrived that day was because her grandmother had died. Tahir and Sharapet had been brought up by their grandparents and it was a great loss to them both.

One afternoon Kim came into the Oasis totally revved up and excited. He told me that he had discovered the whereabouts of the remainder of the books of the once-famous Chinibagh library. They were down some hole at the back of the main building, and if I wanted to go and have a look, I would need a rope and a torch. Duncan came in and we decided to wait for dusk and then go and check it out. Apparently when the Chinese were converting the building into a hotel they took the books from the library and dumped them in a tin shed. Two inquisitive British travellers had, by chance, found them lying there in a heap and had made an offer to buy the whole collection, but the Chinese refused. The British decided that the books were in effect property of Her Majesty the Queen and that it was their national duty to break in and rescue them.

They sifted through each book carefully, and only took first editions and those with dedications to Macartney from the likes of Peter Flemming, Ella Maillart and Sven Hedin. All the books were stamped on the inside cover with 'British Consulate General Kashgar' and would surely be worth a bob or two to the right people. Eventually, word got around and a few others tried to get in, but the Chinese got wind of it and moved the books out of the shed to a better hiding place.

Duncan and I slipped through the dormitory and out onto the roof. Making sure that nobody was following, we dropped over the side, onto the roof of room 701. To the far left was another drop into a closed alcove. A small hole led to a dark, dusty room some nine feet below. Leaving the rope tied to the beam so that we could get out after, we dropped into the darkness as quietly as we could. Turning the torch on, we saw cases upon cases of the books all stacked up. You could smell the decay immediately and I knew that it was only a matter of time before these relics were reduced to dust. In the middle of the room there was a trap door and another drop down into the dark.

One at a time we squeezed through the opening into the murk below. I landed on yet more books that had obviously been thrown there by philistines. It was unbelievable that the Chinese could treat such a valuable collection with so much disrespect. We convinced each other of the righteousness of our mission and carried on. The space we were in was not a room as such, more of a hole really, hacked out of the ground by hand. I spotted a small tunnel leading once again down and off to the right. If we crawled on our bellies there was just enough room to get through. Down and down we went. In some places there had clearly been cave-ins, but I dug through easily with my hands and carried on. After about 30 metres the tunnel came to a dead end and there was nothing else for it than to crawl back up the hole feet first. This was what was left of the tunnel that had been built to allow supplies in during a siege situation – or to escape if things started looking a bit sticky.

Back amongst the book cases, Duncan and I searched desperately for something of value and in good enough condition to take away. I hadn't heard of any of the titles that I took, but the mere fact that they had the stamp on them was all that really mattered. *The Way of all Flesh* by Samuel Butler, 1903; *Essays of Elia Lamb*, 1902. One book I did manage to find, though, had a different stamp. It spoke volumes about the colonist mind and indeed the whole Great Game itself. The stamp read, 'British Consulate General Kashgar India'. This I knew was my prize.

*

I went away on a trip to Lake Karakul with my friend Duncan. When I got back a few days later Sharapet (whom I now knew as ShaSha) looked as though she'd missed me – or was that just my imagination running away with me? The number of long-stay visitors had increased, and we were all getting to know each other fast. Parties every night on the upstairs veranda cemented our friendships. ShaSha would get her guitar out and sing Uighur folksongs in the most beautiful lilting voice any of us had ever heard. She was a natural performer with perfect timing, and she could make you laugh or cry three times in the same song. I could feel myself falling, being swept along on a course that it was impossible to turn back from.

I went to Oasis every day solely to see her. We would spend hours gazing into each other's eyes searching for a truth. Behind a sadness I saw laughter and a thirst for life burning like hot coals. The language barrier meant that we had to use more than our tongues to communicate, so Uighur lessons became an excuse to play footsie under the table.

Sitting on the horse-cart, on our way back from a staff and 'most favoured customers' picnic in the countryside, ShaSha put her hand on my leg. It felt electric. I was out of control. I wanted to touch her, rip her clothes off then and there, but there were eight other people sitting next to us. What could I do? A mixture of hash, happiness, booze and messing about caused us somehow to fall off the cart, tumbling over and over on the tarmac as the driver brought the horse skidding to a halt. We weren't hurt at all and instead just laughed, because we had not only fallen off the cart, we had fallen in love.

That night was the first of many that I was to spend in Oasis. As Heigua, the old Japanese night watchman who had spent twenty-five years in a jail in the desert, lay asleep on his camp bed, ShaSha and I kissed, fumbled, giggled and gripped each other under one of the tables. Partly to do with the religion of the locals and mostly to do with the Chinese making sure that their presence was felt, there were strict laws relating to sex out of marriage, so there was no place else for us to go. I couldn't take her back to my hotel, because if she was spotted there with me they'd call the police and for her that could be dangerous, especially since she was still married.

ShaSha lived in a room above the bar which was also used by Reyhan the cook, a waitress called Lanlan, and Nana, ShaSha's ten-year-old daughter. So that was a no-no. But it was all okay: our feelings dictated events, and we would always find a way to be together.

The next day I decided that it might be best to talk the situation over with Tahir. I wasn't sure how Muslims went about courtship and maybe, since I didn't know where her father was, I should ask Tahir's permission to date his sister.

'Can I have a word with you in private?' I asked Tahir nervously.

'Sure. What can I do for you?'

'Well, it's about ShaSha, actually. You're probably aware that we are pretty good friends, right? I'm not very sure how you go about things here, so . . . do I have to ask you or your father's permission to go out with her, or what?'

He smiled at me, and suddenly I felt like a right idiot. 'We are not like Pakistan here. I mean, ShaSha's a grown woman, she's old enough to make up her own mind about such things. But my advice to you is that if you want to go ahead with it, be careful. There are many spies who might inform against you. The Chinese do not like relationships of this sort, and they can make life very difficult for us. That's all.'

I thought a moment and then asked, 'What about her husband?'

'She wants to divorce him because he is a bad man, but he's not here now, so it shouldn't be a problem. Don't worry about it.'

Despite the warning, I was relieved. It was like a green light, and I immediately went to tell ShaSha the news. That evening we went for a walk together for the first time, out in the open like lovers do, but we were careful to keep to the small lanes in the suburbs of the north side, where there was less chance of being noticed.

My Uighur was improving now, but there was still a long way to go before we could have a proper conversation. It didn't matter, though. I broke a branch from a tree and scratched a diagram in the dust to explain my home and where I had come from. We used our hands and made funny noises to describe things we had no words for, and we knew exactly what we were talking about.

The lane soon came out at the city limits and a little road lined with tall poplars. Women and children were working in the corn fields, throwing the heads up into the air to separate the chaff, and old men cycled slowly down green lanes. It was quiet and peaceful, and there was harmony.

ShaSha was taking me to the *mazar* (graveyard) to see where her grandparents were buried. I realised, of course, that had they been alive, it would have been her intention to take me home to meet them. As that was not possible, this would have to suffice. She was admitting me to a very private, and personal part of herself and I felt honoured – privileged even – and realised that it was a very special moment for both of us.

I had never been to a Muslim cemetery before, and didn't really know quite what to expect. As it turned out, it was not much different from cemeteries everywhere except that there were no flowers and the headstones were made from dried mud. With a small brush ShaSha swept away the dust, and then threw a few handfuls of rice grains over the grave before kneeling down to pray and speak to the two people who had been so important to her as a child. Without asking, I joined her, knelt down and said a prayer – something I had not done for a long, long time.

Happy People Productions

Just to the windward side of the law.
Charles Churchill (1731–64)

THE Pakistanis never seemed to go anywhere without taking something along to sell. The buses that arrived every day were loaded to the gunnels with all sorts of weird stuff, from garishly coloured bolts of cloth, shining gauze, cheap headscarves, ladies' make-up and Lipton's Tea, to Arabian jewels, Indian joss-sticks, necklaces and henna. And that's not all. Smuggled down their trousers were packets of strange pills which they tried to sell off as aphrodisiacs and anti-impotence drugs to anybody with a problem and the money to pay for them.

The Kashgar traders and money-changers waited for the buses to arrive at the Chinibagh Hotel, and the dealing would begin through the windows before the bus had even come to a halt. The Kashgaris could be heard shouting, '*Eh brader, rech bar ma?*' '*Eh Pakstan, dollar bar ma?*'

With flailing arms, a clap of hands and a slap on the back, the deal was made. Huge bundles of money flew in all directions, rupees, dollars, FEC and renminbi. It was chaotic. Cloth was measured by the arm, bags of stockings were being counted and Pakistanis and locals were running off in all directions to talk behind trees and walls.

It all looked friendly enough but once each had got what he wanted, that was it. The Kashgaris had an intense dislike of the Pakistanis and the feeling was mutual. The Pakistanis believed themselves to be more devout Muslims than the Uighur, and the Uighur thought the Pakistanis were the scum of the earth. Pakistanis complained about all the women on the streets without *chador*, and all the men drinking in bars when they should have been at prayer. The Uighur claimed the Pakistanis were two-faced when it came to religion. They accused them of drinking alcohol they couldn't handle, trying to get off with their women, assaulting little boys and pushing heroin.

The thousands of Pakistanis who invaded Kashgar every year congregated either in the Chinibagh or the Friendship Hotel. Some brought their mothers along to cook on smelly oil stoves in the doorways and wash their clothes for them, which were then hung up to dry in the corridors, out of the windows and in the toilets. There was nothing sacred in a hotel. If it was not welded to the framework, it was removed. Thermos flasks, bicycles, glasses and clothes were easy pickings. One Pakistani even nicked the doors to the showers in Chinibagh and used them to make packing cases. Having crossed the Karakoram, they acted as if God was unable to see what they were up to.

In every small bar they could be heard shouting, 'Hello, hello, bruder, one bek whisky.'

'Hanim, give me XO, one bek XO.'

For the most part they didn't know the difference between cola, beer and whisky, so they drank everything at the same speed, necking treble whiskies like water. The result of all this debauchery was usually seen outside the Chinibagh gates, spewing in the gutters and crashed out under trees.

Others liked to go and ogle the western girls who wore skimpy vests in the tourist cafés, or sit down uninvited at the same table. It was quite common to see a group of six order one can of Fanta and six glasses, and spend two hours trying to catch a glimpse of bare flesh. Some even tried to get away without paying, and I had seen Tahir on more than one occasion feel the need to wield a meat cleaver to encourage the settlement of a bill.

Of course, to say that all Pakistanis behaved badly in Kashgar would be wrong, and especially unfair to the Pathans and the Hunza. The Pathans were solely business-minded, and practised their Islamic faith to the letter. The Hunza men, on the other hand, loved a drink or two, but no matter how oiled they got, they always paid their bills and showed good manners.

Many Pakistanis seemed incredibly generous, though, and loved to give gifts, no matter how worthless. The local kids cottoned on to this fast, and chased behind every Pakistani they saw shouting, '*Oi, Bajistan, sorhrat bar ma?* – Hey, Pakistan, you got a present?'

Despite the acrimony, business was brisk and, apart from the official trade in grain, sugar, machine parts, tools, bicycles, hand-woven silk, cotton, canned fruit, carpets and thousands of cheap radio-cassette players, there was a huge amount of illegal business.

Poorly paid customs officials in the remotest of posts were easy targets for unscrupulous businessmen. A $2,000 bribe equalled more than two years' wages, and they might get countless such offers every day. Contraband, therefore, was flooding in and out in vast quantities.

The tenacity of Pakistani smugglers, added to the fact that the country not only produced its own drugs but also acted as a staging post for world export, made it 99 per cent certain that huge amounts of drugs were shifted along the KKH. Heroin, for example, was clearly coming into Kashgar from somewhere, and it was unlikely to be from the Golden Triangle (where Myanmar, Laos and Thailand meet) because what would be the point? It'd be easier to take a short trip to Hong Kong and make twice the profit than take it all the way to Xinjiang.

I'd heard on more than one occasion that the Pakistanis bought cannabis pollen on a yearly contract basis from producers in Xinjiang and smuggled it over the border to be processed. That would explain the scarcity of top-class hash in an area that was supposed to be awash with it.

Gold smuggling was good business, too, and it was mostly destined for sale in India. Antiques of all sorts were sought after, especially carpets, porcelain, silks, clothes, furniture and books. Groups of Pathans went from house to house in search of old rugs to buy, and they didn't mind what condition they were in either.

They all thought they were God's gift to women, but since 1986 when they had been allowed access to Xinjiang *en masse*, only two had managed to find local women willing to marry them. But that didn't deter the others from having a go. The customers at the Oasis were sick of it. Tahir did not want that sort of harassment in his restaurant and in the end he banned the Pakistanis, except the Hunza 'Tajik Magic' crowd and one or two exceptions like Ibrahim Beg, the chairman of the Gilgit Poetry Society, Muzafir Malik, a government minister from Islamabad, and Khawaja Farouk Majid, the managing director of a large export business who did not come to stare at protruding nipples.

I had been in Kashgar for six weeks by this time and hadn't even been to the Sunday market – the only reason many tourists came to Kashgar. I'd been too busy getting involved and, unlike all those with schedules to keep to, I could take my time. However, to help me get out and about a little bit, Peter invited me down to one of his favourite 'hole-in-the-wall' drinking establishments.

Just down the street from the entrance to Chinibagh was Li Jiangping's, a tiny bar-cum-shop affair. It could seat four people comfortably, six people uncomfortably, and eight people all squashed up together – all right if it was cold, but downright awful in the heat of the summer.

Li Jiangping herself was a pleasant Chinese in her early fifties who loved ballroom dancing and killing flies – a trait no doubt implanted in her psyche by Mao Zedong in the 1950s. The most important thing in her favour, apart from a ready smile, was that she had learnt the art of serving cold beer. A little window allowed one customer, usually Thundernose (Peter's nickname), who got there first, to look out at the passing donkey-carts and drunken locals. If you felt peckish, she could rustle up a boiled egg or some *dadou* (roasted broad beans in salt).

After the first session, it soon became a ritual for Thundernose and me to meet at Li Jiangping's in the early afternoon for what we called aperitifs. Then, at four o'clock, we'd grab a horse-cart and rip down to the Oasis for a spagbol or a Kashburger. Then we'd just drink and drink until we were kicked out.

Sometimes I would go round to room 508 in the old officers' quarters of Chinibagh for morning tea and listen to stories about 'milk runs' to Korea and Japan. It had been a big thing in the early 1980s for businessmen in Hong Kong to employ destitute travellers to take cameras, calculators, watches and the like to Korea and Japan, where they were sold for twice the price. The trips sometimes (but not always) bordered on the illegal, but it was worth the risk for a thousand dollars. Soon, though, the travellers realised just how much could be made and started organising their own trips.

There were always plenty of interesting characters in room 508. Very often there'd either be a money-changer sitting there grinning, totally stoned out of his head, or some old friend that Thundernose and Cynthia had met in Kashgar the year before, or a new arrival looking for a toke. For example, there was Willy, a German with a Hong Kong girlfriend, who had been on the road in Asia for ten years. He smuggled gold and hash, and made no bones about it. He also happened to be a fine handicraftsman too, making beautiful bags from leather and Kirghiz saddle blankets, which he sold to Japanese tourists for three hundred dollars apiece.

There was Scottish Andy, who taught English in Korea but came to Kashgar to buy his stash. There was Tom, a London schoolteacher who was retracing the steps of his grandfather, Sir Francis Younghusband, the nineteenth-century explorer who led countless expeditions through the Pamirs and Karakoram, and who in 1904 was the first Briton to visit Lhasa in Tibet.

Another modern-day explorer and regular visitor to Kashgar, the Oasis and room 508 was John the Map. He was a cartographer who travelled around Asia with a foldaway bike, mapping every town he came to. This was not a problem in most places, but in China it was a different story. The authorities had spotted him pedalling around Kashgar, taking compass-bearings, making notes and photographing buildings, and quickly came to the conclusion that he must be a spy. To make sure, they put a tail on him. At first they were hardly difficult to spot because they were in the plainclothes disguise of green trousers with a red line down the seam, white shirts and sunglasses. These guys melted into the background like a roast pig at a bar mitzvah. But knowing they were there was not necessarily a comfort. John got more and more paranoid, but he was determined to finish his map of Kashgar before he was kicked out of the country.

When Thundernose was boozing with me, Cynthia would hire a horse from one of the taxi boys and go riding off into the Kashgar countryside. I had seen Tahir riding a horse once or twice, and when he invited me along for a ride I jumped at the chance. It had been ten years since I'd last ridden, when I had worked on a sheep farm on the Brecon Beacons and used horses to do the gathering. Tahir found two beautiful black stallions, standing about sixteen hands, for us to borrow, and while ShaSha, Bridget, Thundernose, Eduard and Orashi cradled the beer and the meat on a horse-cart, Tahir, Cynthia and I rode out onto the Kashgar plains to a rendezvous under a tree on a bend in the river. We had the freedom to gallop as fast as we wanted, and were always racing and playing games, just like the young Tamerlane, Tahir's hero, and his friends would have done six hundred years earlier on the vast plains of Central Asia.

As we passed through villages, the locals would run out to look at us, often giving a helping hand with the crack of a whip. By the time we found the cart, the beer was already lying cold in the river and the barbecue was smoking. We ate and got drunk and stoned, and then ShaSha and I lay down on the grass in the sun, holding hands and listening to the nearby springs bubbling up, watching the plovers and larks soar and dive over the steppe. Time stood still on such warm autumn days. Life was good and getting better.

During our long debates and discussions on life, sitting in Li Jiangping's watching the world go by, it became clear that it wasn't only antiques that Thundernose and Cynthia dabbled with. Both had for some time been talking about the imminent arrival of 'the Germans'. These, apparently, were old friends from Goa, and in the same line of business. It didn't take a genius to work that out what that meant. My curiosity grabbed me firmly by the balls and I wanted to know more. Smuggling hash intrigued me. It was daring, sort of romantic, and somehow didn't strike me as really breaking the law. It was doing the rest of us, the smokers, a favour.

It wasn't long afterwards that 'the Germans' arrived in town. They shacked up in the Kashgar youth hostel, just across the road from the Semen. There were much better hotels in town with more privacy and certainly more character, but these guys wanted a suite and only the hostel could offer such accommodation. It was no different to any other Chinese-run hotel anywhere in China: nondescript, square and concrete. It had big bulky radiators that creaked even when turned off. It had bare, carpetless corridors, a large foyer, miserable staff supplied by the Gulag Training School, and a curfew. The only thing good about the place was its proximity to the Limen Restaurant (which we called Fat Mamma's) where they could order a good rendition of a schnitzel and plenty of cold beer.

These Germans weren't actually all German. Two were, but there were also two Austrians and a New Zealander: Marius, Gerhard, Arno, Don and Lucas. From a distance they looked like any other bunch of travellers, but on closer inspection there was something decidedly suspicious about them. No rucksacks, no guidebooks, no interest at all in their surroundings. They liked drinking, smoking and gambling – oh, and women. They were in Kashgar on a mission, and nothing more.

The Schemer. Marius was in his forties, looked like Jack Nicholson, and had the same smile Jack had used to such good effect in *The Shining*. There was something Rasputin-like about him, almost evil, and he believed that he was a scammer *extraordinaire*. His humour and morals betrayed a side to his character that could have been summed up by Rasputin's motto of 'sin that you may obtain forgiveness'. But, for all that, you couldn't help liking the guy.

The Worrier. Gerhard, also in his forties, wore glasses and a grimace. He was tall but he stooped to conceal it. He looked depressed, sounded depressed, and actually felt depressed most of the time, but worked hard to change all that with constant supply of booze and drugs. He loved music and carried a briefcase full of cassettes and a huge boom box.

The Joker. Arno was short, about fifty, and wore Woody Allen glasses, Hawaiian shirts and disco shoes – just the thing for trekking through the Taklamakan. Arno was the founder of a company, if that's the right word, called Happy People Productions, which promoted events that involved dancing to loud techno music and taking LSD and ecstasy. He had stickers with the HPP logo and stuck them everywhere he went.

The Cool Box. Don was also short and quite good-looking. They called him Don Juan, but he didn't chase. He had been locked up in northern India for eighteen months for the possession of a large amount of hash, and had only recently got out. I expected to see some sort of effect from such an ordeal, but he was totally together, which was completely different to . . .

The Deviant, Lucas, who had shared a cell with him. Lucas was younger than the others, tall, dark and somehow always looking as if he'd just climbed out of bed. He was turned on by every woman he passed. He was so obsessed with sex that many questioned his sanity, but he was also obsessed with drugs and alcohol, so that made him okay.

Thundernose introduced them to the Oasis, and they loved it. Without it, they would have found it very difficult to pass the time in Kashgar. It wasn't long before they were spending all day and night there with the rest of us, and the parties got wilder and wilder. It was as if we had constructed a cocoon in which we lived in a Freaksville '88, while on the other side of the tall arched windows, donkey-carts trotted through the dust in a world unchanged for thousands of years. Listening to Talking Heads, Tracy Chapman, Ruben Blades, Miles Davis, John Coltrane and Yello, eating vegetable tempura, Hungarian goulash, *coq au vin* and chocolate cake, knocking back as much beer as we could, smoking the tastiest hash in the world, and watching men with 150-year-old faces saunter by holding eagles on their arms, camels wade up the street hauling huge loads, and little kids with bare arses and black caps chase metal wheels with sticks. Who could not but fall in love with Kashgar?

It was already the end of September and my visa was all but expired. I had to make a decision. I had to go back to Pakistan whatever the weather, but was I then going to head for Colombo to meet a friend who'd be there till December, or was I going to get another visa for China and come right back to Kashgar to be with ShaSha?

In the end I realised there was no contest and no decision to make. I was already totally smitten and couldn't bear the thought of saying goodbye. We had only just started to get to know each other, and it was as if I had just popped the cork on a magic lantern. To walk away now and not wait for the genie to appear would be a sin.

Moreover, I had also spent weeks listening to stories about how easy it was to take a piece of hash out of China and sell it at a good profit. If I made some money I could stay within reach of ShaSha for longer, and the more I thought about it, the more appealing that idea became.

Arno spent every day turning me on to the delights of the Philippines: great weather, beautiful beaches, beautiful brown-skinned girls, great parties and great nightclubs and discos. According to Marius, Goa was finished: the package tourist was taking over and the police were getting heavy about all the drugs. The government had changed the visa laws, meaning that people who had been living there for years without hassle now had to get out and get another visa every six months. The 'in place' to be now was Borocay Island. A lot of the Goa freaks had moved there and the place was really buzzing. 'You gotta go there, man!' I had to admit it was an interesting idea, and if I could make a few dollars into the bargain, Borocay for winter R&R was perfect. I could get a new visa, come back to Kashgar for a few months, then pop over to the Philippines for the winter, and head back to Xinjiang for the summer. If not, I could always get back on track later and head on down to Oz. For the moment I decided to just ride the wave.

I packed my bag with a load of river pearls and Chinese silk and headed off back down the KKH to Rawalpindi. It was a gruelling trip – eleven days to Pindi and back – but it had been an experience. I got a nice three-month stamp in my passport and, after selling off the pearls and silk, I was barely out of pocket. Anyway, I was glad to be back in Kashgar. I felt good, and, to make me feel even better, Tahir invited me to stay at his house in Gul Bagh Yol, a residential district just off the shortcut from Semen Road to Sheng Li Lu. We'd been getting on well and I'd been helping out at the café when I was capable. He offered to help me save on my hotel bill, which was running into hundreds of yuan that could be better spent on beer and kebabs.

It was a small house set in a little courtyard with a tall fig tree in the corner, surrounded by a wall ten feet high. It had been his father's house originally, but he had left and gone to live with his new wife on the other side of town. Tahir was proud of his accomplishments in DIY and home design, and was keen to show me the electric shower, the hot tub he'd built, and the heating system with its radiators and hot water. There were not many adobe houses around with a set-up like that. Tahir was practical and ingenious, always designing some new device or acquiring some new skill, and it was these strengths that had paved the road to his success in business. Looking about his house, I realised that even if you did have money in China, it was difficult to spend it. There was no doubt in my mind that this boy belonged in the west.

It was not entirely legal, because a foreigner staying as a guest in an ordinary citizen's home required registering at the local police station, but that would only give them the excuse to come a-calling, and Tahir, like most people, didn't need that kind of hassle. I loved the clandestine feel of it, being the only foreigner staying in a real Uighur home, and thus able to see how the Kashgaris really lived. I had my own bicycle to use whenever I wanted, and I loved pedalling the dusty back streets wearing my *shepka* (black cap), my Yengisar knife in its carved leather sheath, and thinking that I was a part of some greater scheme.

Tahir wanted to expand the Oasis but he didn't have the time or the energy to run the veranda bar as well as the restaurant, and so he asked Elizabeth, a New Zealander, and me to lend a hand. I jumped at the opportunity. It was just what I needed, and fitted in with the images I had of eccentric travellers abroad.

Running the veranda bar was a hectic number to say the least, but it was great fun. We opened at 6 p.m. and closed when the sun came up. Often I found myself just sleeping where I dropped, too tired to get back to Tahir's, and it wasn't long before I built myself a nest under the bar itself.

Tahir had agreed to give me cut-price beer and a share in the profits of beer and wine sales. Any other profits I made – from food, for example – were mine to keep. I started doing kebabs and selling hot chocolate cinnamon brandies, and brought in a happy-hour to entice the customers.

I had to rely on attracting a large number of drinkers, however, and that meant allowing the Pakistanis in – I simply couldn't afford to keep them out. In an attempt to keep the wide boys away, we hiked the prices a bit, but it didn't make much difference. It was no big deal, anyway: they were paying for the privilege of drinking in a bar that didn't close and the chance to hear the latest acid house from Europe.

We still had to cope with the usual problems of leching and skipping out without paying, though. Tahir told me that it was no use being soft with them: they had to know they couldn't get away with it, and that if they tried any funny business, they would have to face the consequences.

House Rule no.1 came into effect: pay and leave through the door in a civilised manner, or start messing about and go over the veranda. The threat was enough most times to keep blood off the pavements and ensure the books balanced.

One night, though, a group of seven or eight young men had come in, run up a bill of about three hundred yuan, then tried to do a runner when I had my back turned. But I had spotted them. I climbed through the window into the corridor and met them with a baseball bat as they came out. After herding them all back into the bar, I locked the door.

They claimed that they had left all their money in the hotel. I picked on the guy wearing the most expensive watch and told him to go back to Chinibagh to get the cash, leaving the watch as a guarantee. The others could wait with me for his return. If he didn't come back, I threatened to knock each of them senseless and toss them over the railings into the street below.

I sat on a table in front of them, swinging the bat for effect and watching the time. The twelve minutes that it took him seemed like a lifetime, and I believe I was more relieved than my captives when he showed up. If they'd have called my bluff, I don't know what would have happened.

The rest of our early-morning customers were hash-heads and smugglers. Thanks to donations and some shrewd bargaining, our tape collection had grown to include a lot of techno, house and DJ mixes from Goa. We could easily be seen from the road below, and it must have been a really strange sight for the locals: an odd collection of westerners dressed in weird clothes, gyrating all night long to inane drum beats and electric noise. (The effect of this music on the Pakistanis was even more remarkable. It seemed to take control of them, leaving them powerless to resist the beat, dancing and hollering in total abandon.)

As the days passed, I realised that the Germans were waiting for Thundernose to get them what they wanted, but they had arrived early and the harvest was late. There was other stuff floating around town, but it was usually old and dried out. A lot of the locals didn't know anything about storing hash, often just leaving it hanging up in a cloth bag in a shed.

The Germans got more and more impatient, asking anyone and everyone to find them something so they could start pressing and packing. All sorts of stuff started showing up but none of it was up to standard. Not wanting to throw it away, we got Reyhan the cook to bake it up into cookies.

Reyhan was as mad as they come and something of a sadist. She was pure Uighur and came originally from Wulja in the north of Xinjiang. She and Tahir had gone through a steamy affair which had been more about Reyhan's persistence than Tahir's desire. Even though the relationship had come to an impasse, Reyhan refused to believe that she was history. Paranoia and jealousy were her main driving forces and whenever she saw some tourist girl making eyes at Tahir, she would grab a machete from the kitchen and run the culprit out of the café, screaming and slashing the air. She'd return, laughing and whooping with excitement. Sometimes, just for the hell of it, she would come into the restaurant through the front door and walk up behind an unsuspecting customer at the bar, grab him or her by the neck and throw them to the floor, and then stand over them, laughing hysterically. Somehow they always saw the funny side of it and kept coming back to see what she'd do next.

Making hash cookies was a special pleasure for Reyhan. We would give her a bag of pollen weighing about a kilo and ask her to make, say, fifty cookies, expecting her to use a couple of hundred grams and leave the rest for another time. Later, we'd find Reyhan slumped in the kitchen totally out of it, laughing and giggling, with the empty hash bag lying on the ground. The cookies, stacked on a plate, were shiny dark-green things, almost pure hash with only a little sugar and flour added to bind it all together. They were foul, but nobody refused, and within minutes there'd be thirty adults acting like three-year-olds, falling about laughing with their eyes popping out of their heads.

*

Working at the veranda bar gave me the excuse and the opportunity to meet up with ShaSha whenever possible. I had my own keys and could go in and out as I liked.

As autumn rolled on the nights got colder, but I was still bedding down under the bar until one morning when ShaSha found me pale and nearly frozen under an old tablecloth. She had to shake me a dozen times before I finally emerged from my stupor. Supporting me with her shoulder under my arm, she took me into the storeroom and put me to bed under the warm covers that she had just left. I immediately fell into a long, deep, dreamless sleep that seemed to last for hours.

Eventually the darkness rose and I found myself being kissed on the cheek. Opening my eyes I saw ShaSha sitting on the edge of the bed, her blue eyes like an ocean imploring me to dive in. She had come to check on me, and told me that she had feared for my life. We held each other tightly and kissed, slowly at first, short pecks searching for the right response. Her lips were moist and succulent, inviting and eager. Our tongues met, hard like erections, fighting and probing. Two pairs of hands frantically searched for openings in clothes. My shirt was removed and warm fearless fingers ran over my nakedness like rainwater. Lips found my nipples and a tongue flicked them hard. My body throbbed with desire, straining for freedom.

ShaSha found my belt and undid it, looking straight into my eyes. As my shorts came down my sex sprang out, hard and aching to be touched. Hot hands gripped me and sent a shudder through my whole body, steaming hot blood was pumping through every vein at maximum pressure. I felt as if I was about to explode.

My lover, my lover, her long dark silky hair brushing over my groin, and her hot wet mouth taking me higher and higher and beyond. This was a heaven I'd never known before. Looking up into my eyes she communicated without the complication of words. Everything was being said perfectly. Using both hands, I gripped the neck of her shirt and ripped it from her body in one single action. Firm, pouting breasts pointed to me with dark, luscious nipples demanding my attention.

ShaSha's skin was a smooth and silky olive brown, firm and responsive to my touch. My tongue lashed its way down her stomach guided by the smell of sex. Nothing could stop me now. I had found that which had incited the act, and tasted its sweet fruit.

Swelling before my eyes, inviting my love, it was a potion, an elixir, an inflammable essence on the fires of lust. When we joined, we wrapped our bodies around each other in a hundred thousand ways. In a frenzy of drowning passion, we pushed and probed, searched and held tight, ripped and scratched, struggled and consumed.

Finally, as if struck by lightning, our bodies decided the time had come for release. As I felt the flood of a boiling orgasm envelope my sex I burst through it in a spasm of delirious and ecstatic pain, and it was as if we had split the atom. An hour had been dissolved into minutes. Lying back, exhausted, the sweat and product of our love still warm and sticky on our skins, we floated off into dreamland. I was in no doubt that what had passed between us was love. We had defined the act, and given ourselves up to the passion. No fear, no shame, no guilt.

Waking from the haze, it suddenly dawned on me that my head was lower than my feet. Glancing round, it looked like we had been hit by an earthquake. The little metal-framed single bed had broken loose from the headboard and crashed to the floor.

I got to my feet feeling weak. The blood raced back into my legs and I almost fainted. That was surely all the proof we needed to confirm our love, and it had been the best.

From that moment on ShaSha found a bed for me next to her in the storeroom, but with Reyhan, Elizabeth and ShaSha's daughter all sharing the same room, it was impossible for us to make love at night. That didn't matter, because when everybody else was getting up, I was going to bed; ShaSha would wait for me and every morning we'd express feelings that words could never convey.

We knew, however, that every footstep, every voice and every slam of a door could signal the approach of someone who might inform on us. Every moment was a stolen moment, but the fear of getting caught heightened the enjoyment. We wanted it again and again to be like the first time . . . and again and again we succeeded.

A Cultural Revelation

It seems as though people were looking at a rainbow in a drought year.

Emperor Hui of the State of Liang. The Spring and Autumn Period. Mencius

NANA was Sharapet's daughter from her marriage to Kang. She was a beautiful, bouncy ten-year-old, always laughing and dancing about the place and doing impersonations of her pop idols. We got on well, as she did with everyone she met.

As the weeks passed I tried to find out ShaSha's story. My Uighur was better, but there were still a lot of blank spaces, so she and I would spend hours trying to explain to each other who we were, going over the same thing time and again so as to be understood.

She had been born in her Aunt Aimahan's house in Kashgar between two very significant periods in Chinese history: the end to the Great Leap Forward and the beginning of the Great Economic Crisis. Although Beijing was far away – as far as London is from Moscow – the decisions made there had a serious effect all over Xinjiang.

While attempting to create an industrial base, Mao had neglected the agriculture sector and in 1959, thanks to a series of natural calamities and the setting-up of disorganised, chaotic communes which, through fear, had faked production figures, the country's grain production was at an all-time low. What resulted was the most serious famine to affect China in its entire history. It caused nearly twenty million deaths, and in Kashgar, as everywhere else, the people were struggling simply to survive, living each day hand to mouth.

ShaSha's mother worked to earn what little money she could to buy enough to eat, and had neither the time nor the means to raise a baby. When ShaSha was six months old, her parents separated, and the child was left with her grandmother on her father's side.

For the first five years of her life ShaSha was brought up in the coal-mining town of Kangsu, some fifty miles from Kashgar, high up in the mountains. She survived each day on a meal of maize mush or bean-flour pancakes. Luckily, the family had a friend who worked in the nearby pit canteen who managed to stash a little flour for them. In that way, once a week they could enjoy a special treat of *lamian*, noodles with hot peppers.

To add some iron to the diet, the women scoured the fields in springtime for the first shoots of lucerne that popped through the ground. Chopped up finely, this could be added to soups or used in dumplings. To fuel the fires, the kids were sent out to chase the horse-carts and collect the dung, shouting, '*Pok bar ma? –* Have you got any shit?' It was dried out in front of the house in the baking sun, and used in the clay tandoor ovens that are found in every back yard. In autumn they would go to the woods to collect leaves, climb trees, swim in the rivers and water channels and learn to play games like 'ride the donkey'. They chased horse-carts, grabbing on to the back and sliding along on their feet until their shoes were worn out.

By 1965 the Great Economic Crisis had passed and ShaSha had moved back to Kashgar to the family house in Cai Da Dui (Vegetable Production Brigade) in the south-west of the town behind what would later become the youth hostel. Life was slowly getting back some semblance of normality, but the carefree existence of a little girl playing hopscotch on the dusty lanes of Kashgar would soon be disrupted by an event that would last for ten years and affect those who endured it for the rest of their lives. Welcome to the Cultural Revolution of 1966.

According to most Kashgaris, the only good thing ever to come out of the Cultural Revolution was the construction of the escape tunnels which can be found under many of the older houses in town to this day. They were built for fear that the Red Guards would suddenly decide to drag everybody out and shoot them dead on the street. When the threat was over, the ever-practical Kashgaris converted the tunnels, cool in the summer, and below the frost in the winter, into cellars in which to store vegetables.

At fifteen, against all the protestations and advice of her teachers and grand-parents, Sharapet left school. She had excelled in sports and it was felt sure that she could become a teacher herself, if only she would enrol at the *shifan daxue* (teacher training college). But she was stubborn and wanted to go to the countryside to be with her friends following Chairman Mao's teachings of '*Shangshan, Xiaxiang* – up the mountains and into the countryside'. Mao had a high regard for the peasants, believing they could teach the city folk valuable lessons in life, not only about where their food came from but about how to live respectably.

Unlike the young people from the big cities on the eastern seaboard, Sharapet didn't have to go very far to find a commune; it was only a twenty-minute walk from her home. When she arrived there she found a large walled-in compound with a central administration block surrounded by residential units. The central area was used as a parade ground and a pitch for basketball and volleyball. There were no trees or flowers or grass to enhance the surroundings, just a big red flag flying on a tall pole in the middle of the yard.

There were over two hundred kids there, aged between fifteen and eighteen, and after a short induction course they became *zhi qing ren*, 'young knowledgeables'. During the week, four of the young activists shared a spacious but sparse room. Reveille was at six-thirty every morning, and after a brush of the teeth and a quick wipe of the face with a wet flannel, it was off for two hours of education on the thoughts of Chairman Mao from his infamous little red book. After a breakfast of rice porridge and a *mantou* or steamed bun, they went to the fields to help the peasants in their daily toil.

Sometimes this involved cultivating the land by hand, sowing seeds, pulling weeds or harvesting. It was hard work but the peasants, who were Uighur, did not pressurise the kids – in fact they protected them from any excessive demands. Lunch might be some bread and vegetables they had taken with them wrapped up in a scarf, or they might head back to the compound for noodles. Dinner was almost invariably rice and vegetables and was followed by another two hours of the little red book.

Discipline in the camp was not all that heavy and most weekends the young-sters were allowed to go home. They were not permitted to have relations with the opposite sex, or go running off whenever they felt like it, though. There were simple rules which were obeyed without question.

When she reached seventeen ShaSha's education in the countryside was over and it was time for her to get a job. The local government offered her a position in a coal-mine in Karamay, a famous coal-producing area in the far north of Xinjiang, but she refused to go, preferring to wait for something closer to home. It wasn't long before a job came up at the Kashgar Electric Company. This was more like it. She could even live at home with her grandparents.

The job had a three-year apprenticeship period, during which the candidate would learn the ins and outs of all the jobs at the company. The discipline there was not any more relaxed than that of the commune, and if anything it was worse. For example, it was company policy that relationships between the sexes were forbidden. The company was training a person to work, and this cost money. That employee was expected to remain with the company, and not go home to have babies.

Spreading her wings, Sharapet let nature dictate the rules. One night at a local dance, she was introduced to a young man known as Kang. He seemed good fun, and after a pleasant evening, she agreed to see him again.

The second time was different. Sharapet had never drunk much wine before, and knew nothing about its effects. Kang kept coming over, bringing glass after glass, and she started to enjoy it. It tasted sweet and warm, but she didn't know it was spiked with *baijiu*, the over-proof Chinese liquor. All of a sudden she had no idea who she was, never mind what she was doing.

Kang played the part of the great rescuer, unselfishly offering to take her home. The rest, as is the way of most tragedies, was almost inevitable. Although Sharapet had serious misgivings about the man who was the father of the child she carried, it was custom and circumstance that forced them together. Her family felt disgraced, and to save them from embarrassment it was decided that Sharapet should marry Kang. A letter was written to the chief cadre at the Electric Company explaining that Sharapet's grandparents were old, and that they wanted to see their granddaughter married before either one died. The cadre eventually relented, and agreed to the marriage, also allowing Sharapet to continue with her apprenticeship.

With the bride five months gone, the marriage itself was nothing more than a certificate and a stamp issued at the local registry office. There was no wedding, no party, no guests, no presents. There wasn't even a ring. As soon as the formalities were over, Sharapet rode back to the factory alone, stopping off to buy some sweets and a few bottles of beer to share with her workmates. Half an hour later she was back at work, learning how to calculate electricity consumption.

The marriage did not blossom. Rather, it ignited, and within a matter of days, it had burnt out the little hope there was of its success. Without love there is no reason; there is no empathy, no compulsion to conciliate and no cushion to insulate the heart from the rough road. The relationship was simply in a state of open hostility.

Kang had no interest in her and his ideas of fun had changed. He was more often than not to be found in the company of petty thieves and local thugs, getting drunk on *baijiu*. With an alcohol content of 90 per cent or more, even short-term abuse affects the mind, and very often makes the drinker violent. (From my own experience of drinking it and watching others who have become hooked on it, the best way I can describe it is to call it the alcoholic equivalent of heroin.)

Kang found himself in jail in Urumchi, 1,500km to the north, doing three years for aggravated burglary. When the baby was born Sharapet had felt duty-bound to take the child to visit its father, but doing so would have required two weeks off work to complete the journey, and that would mean that there was no job to go back to. Kang was released after thirteen months and came back in Kashgar, angry and resentful at Sharapet's apparent lack of concern for him. He snatched the baby and ran off to his family home in Hebei Province, some 3,500km away, giving no clue when or even if he would return.

Not surprisingly, Kang found life difficult with the young child, and soon reappeared on Sharapet's doorstep, insisting that they live together. To save face, Sharapet's grandmother urged her to do so for the sake of the child. Reluctantly, Sharapet agreed, and moved to a room in the Chinese housing scheme in the south side of Kashgar, where Kang felt safer and more at home. It didn't take him long to get back to his old habits, only this time he started bringing his work home with him.

The room they lived in was tiny, and contained little more than a raised platform with a cast-iron stove by the door. Newspapers had been plastered all over the walls and the tiny window to insulate against the severe cold of the winter. Water had to be carried over a hundred metres down a dark narrow alley, and the communal toilet was fifty metres in the opposite direction.

Kang's only income came from thieving, and he spent all of it on *baijiu*. Without her job, Sharapet would have had nothing to live on. Before long, Kang found himself back in jail, this time for gang fighting. The nine months that followed were for ShaSha an escape from fear, but when he got out it all started over again. His attacks on her and the child increased; many times she would cover the little girl with her body to shield her from the blows of a man who had lost all control. Her life was a nightmare.

All her relatives and friends knew of the ever-worsening situation and they advised her to get out, but she knew that if she even mentioned the word separation, Kang would go berserk. When news of the situation reached ShaSha's uncle, however, he threatened to go and find Kang and beat the living daylights out of him. Kang fled to Urumchi.

After a few months, thinking that the heat was off, he returned, and within a few days was back to his old tricks again. He snatched the child and went back to Hebei again. This time Sharapet decided to change her life. With the support of her family, she quit her job in the Electric Company and went to Urumchi. She had always been a talented singer and the numerous recommendations from her old teachers helped her to follow her dreams and join the Xinjiang Uighur Song and Dance Troupe.

There followed two years of real joy where she met new friends and was trained in traditional song, dance and theatre. It was not to last. Kang tracked her down eventually, forcing her to leave the Troupe and return to Kashgar to live with him once again in their old hovel.

One night in the winter of 1985 he arrived home late and started an argument, accusing Sharapet of infidelity. He was as drunk as he'd ever been, and totally out control. After taking numerous blows to the face, Sharapet decided to hit back with the only weapon she had: the threat of divorce.

Somewhere in Kang's mind, the lights went out. He went nuts. Grabbing a twelve-inch kitchen knife, he tried to stab Sharapet to death. In the two minutes that followed, to the accompaniment of one single scream of terror and the sound of puncturing flesh, blood splattered the walls and flowed like water from an overturned jug into the quilt steadily taking a life with it.

Suddenly realising what he had done, Kang fled in panic, leaving the body of his victim limp and contorted on the bed. Sharapet was slipping further and further down into the depths of eternal darkness. He had stabbed her ten times in the abdomen and thighs.

A neighbour saw the open door and the shape of Sharapet's body lying unconscious in a patch of light cast on her by a fading oil-lamp. A doctor was called immediately, and he managed to stem the flow of blood sufficiently to get her to hospital. Ten minutes more and she would have died. She had lost nearly six pints of blood and was in a critical condition for a week.

Kang had disappeared, not knowing whether his wife was dead or alive. He joined up with a few old partners and went on a spree of violent robberies. He was finally caught in 1986 and sentenced to seven years for malicious wounding. Sharapet was confined to bed for three months, not knowing if she would ever be able to walk properly again because of the damage to the tendons in the inner thigh.

As she finished telling her story, I was shocked and speechless. I had been prepared to hear a tale of hardship, but nothing like this. There I was, halfway around the world, having an affair with a woman who was married to a knife-wielding maniac. But there was no reason for me to put my tail between my legs and back off, I thought. None of this had been her fault. ShaSha had been unlucky, but she was still alive and now, most importantly, in a position to turn her life around. Nevertheless, all sorts of questions ran through my mind. Did knowing the truth about her past change my feelings? No. Was it going to affect what happened next? No. But what *was* going to happen next? I had no idea. I could feel something growing inside me, but I didn't know what. ShaSha was holding her arms out to me now. Would my conscience allow me to walk away? If anything, I was more determined to stand by her. But . . .

Can You Help Me?

Unfaith in aught is want of faith in all.
Alfred, Lord Tennyson (1809–92), *Merlin and Vivien*

IT was already November and Tahir was eager to shut up shop for the winter. The last bus had gone down KKH with its load of Pakistanis all wrapped up in anticipation of the excruciating cold of the pass, leaving Kashgar a town full of empty hotels and boarded-up stores. The only thing keeping the Oasis open was us, a group of ten strange individuals who refused to leave, and Thundernose was getting all the blame for it. 'The harvest is late this year, but I've got a bloke on a motorbike looking high and low, so it won't be long,' he kept saying.

The Germans were not happy. They were growing to hate the place, especially the youth hostel, and were drinking more and more and exhausting their savings. If something didn't happen soon, they wouldn't have enough cash to get to Japan to sell the bloody stuff.

I, on the other hand, was enjoying Kashgar more every day. ShaSha had given me a local name, which she thought was most applicable. I was no longer Rob, I was now Jumahun. It meant 'King of Friday', the Muslim sabbath and day of rest, and a reference to my 'every day's a holiday' attitude, which amused and bemused the locals no end.

With my new identity, I felt totally at ease with my surroundings and ventured out into town more and more, spending a lot of time down in the old bazaar opposite the Id Kah Mosque. Steps from the street led down into a cavernous world where a heaving mass of exotic Asian peoples jabbered in wild tongues. Pictures that I had seen of Kashgar and Yarkand taken a hundred years ago revealed the same faces in the same clothes, making the experience like a voyage through time.

Known locally as Audul Bazaar, it had been there since Marco Polo had come through Kashgar in 1272. Looking at it, I was sure that nothing much had changed, apart from the influx of plastic hairclips and other cheap junk.

The ice-cream vendors would have been the same, busy churning the milk by hand in copper urns chilled with ice from the glaciers of the Pamir. The hat bazaar would not have altered much either, with its stunning array of fur hats made from snow leopard, wolf, rabbit, wild dog and whatever else the trappers could snare. Embroidered skullcaps in a hundred different designs stacked and ready to wear had been in fashion forever, and the knife-makers selling all sizes of *pschak*, with beautifully ornate handles, followed a centuries-old tradition. The knives from Yengisar were especially sought after due to the high quality of steel used.

Wonderfully coloured hand-woven silk, known as *etlass*, draped high on lines, would have been unmissable. Apothecaries and hakims sold opium poppies, snakeskin powder, bat-wing and various dried penises, and dispensed the same potions that had cured the Venetian traveller on the other side of the range eight hundred years before.

Kebab smoke filled the air, mixed in with a whiff or two of hash and *mahouka*, and the wail of Arabic reed pipes (called *suona*) danced through the crowd like the Pied Piper, enticing and captivating. Open-fronted shops displayed woollen carpets, each hand-woven to a family design, unique and handed down through generations of gilem makers. Natural dyes producing vivid hues of burnt red ochre, cobalt blue and purpura crimson beckoned and invited inspection. Wandering up one alley and down another, pushing past people who had been there forever, I felt like I was immortal.

On the other side of the Id Kah *maidan* or square there was another fascinating area, where a dusty, potholed street led up through the jewellery quarter, the Zaarger Bazaar. Young boys and old men sat cross-legged in little booths, tapping, filing and blowing on charcoals, while they crafted exquisite gold and silver amulets, earrings and bracelets, while women with gold teeth glinting in the sunlight haggled for trinkets. Opposite, the incessant hammering of the chest-makers demanded my attention. Fathers and sons planishing copper and tinplate laboured from dawn until dusk to produce big shiny boxes fit for the treasure of Ali Baba himself.

At the top of the street the road forked to either side of an ornately decorated domed building. This part of town was known as Oustang Boey, and was renowned for a tea-shop with a beautifully carved second-floor balcony, strewn with vibrant potted plants of all colours. Old men with long beards perched on wooden beds slurping spiced tea and wolfing down steaming-hot mutton stew.

Turning the corner into the avenue of the cobblers, the smell of new leather took over. Black, polished riding boots hung high from shop shutters, whilst men adept in the art cut, stretched and sewed in murky alcoves. A cacophony of clanging and banging announced the beginning of the sheet-metal goods market. White-shirted men hammered cylinders, buckets and tin baths from clean shiny alloy.

A restaurant with a painted sign above the door depicting a rosy-cheeked lad making noodles tempted the passers-by with clouds of steam. The same lad, only in real life, stretched and banged the noodles he was making on a flour-dusted table, shouting, '*Laghmian, laghmian, kyla kyla. Yashshi bimisa, pul olmiymen.*' (Look, look, chilli noodles, chilli noodles. If it's not good, I don't want your money.)

Then, abruptly, the dream was shattered, and living history became modern China. A large avenue, flanked by square, characterless buildings with satellite dishes pinned to their cornices, carried the traffic of the interloper. Smelly green trucks bounced and rattled along with precarious loads swaying on the back, as big black cars with tinted windows cruised by like hungry sharks. This was Kizil Byrak ('red flag'), the south side, where the Han population of Kashgar lived in their cubist apartment blocks.

One of the few remaining statues of Chairman Mao left in China stood erect and menacing, looking out over a football field that had been used in the past as an execution ground for criminals. The feeling here was totally different and the only reason I ever went there was to change money in the bank, and buy hot green wild mountain chillis from the department store.

One Sunday ShaSha decided that it was time I went to see the famous Sunday Market. So we jumped on a horse-cart and sailed off round the back streets of Kashgar in convoy with what seemed like a thousand other carts. The closer we got, the tighter the people were packed together. People from every minority in the region bustled and pushed down a track heaving with horse-carts, bicycles and one-cylinder two-wheeled tractors with trailers.

The throng flowed over a bridge where animals drank and naked children splashed and shouted in the muddy water. Finally the market came into view with its bicycle parks overflowing with countless *Feng Huang* (phoenix), *Yong Jiu* (everlasting) and *Fei Ge* (flying pigeon) cycles. While the donkeys kicked and stamped and argued with each other, ee-awing and snorting in huge corrals, their carts were stacked up in their thousands, the shafts creating a forest of bare limbs all pointing to the sky.

We passed through the gates into the market proper, and found ourselves being swept along past mountains of fresh fruit – peaches, figs, apricots, pomegranates, apples, pears and melons, enough to feed a million. Sheets of freshly made caramel and chunks of crystal sugar the size of boulders lay glinting in the sun like diamonds. Hats and more hats, followed by cloth and more cloth. Piles of used shoes, piles of new shoes. Boots for every foot in the market. Cured and not so very cured hides stacked and stinking in the heat of the powerful sun. Proud men with faces more tanned than the leather strode by in knee-length coats of quilted black corduroy fastened around the waist by long scarves, their bony chests bare to the elements. Knives and daggers, swords and bayonets lay on rich red blankets.

There were pilau restaurants with legs of succulent mutton draped over cauldrons and hungry customers shovelling handfuls of greasy, hot rice into their eager, toothless mouths. Boiled sheep's stomach served with a vinegar-and-chilli sauce was a favourite among the poorer. Heaps of *samsas* (small mutton-and-onion pasties) lay beckoning near fiery ovens. *Mantas* (dumplings filled with minced mutton and yellow carrot) were dished out in cracked bowls and washed down with copious amounts of hot sweet tea. Liver kebabs, mutton kebabs, kofta kebabs, shish kebabs and nan bread, too hot to handle, came straight out from the tandoor. Whatever you had, you could sell it here. Whatever you wanted to buy, you could find it. People came to this market from all over the place, some taking days or even weeks to get there. For many it was a once-a-year trip, where they brought what they had, to get what they wanted. A family might sell a horse to get the money to buy a new cast-iron stove, and another might sell a sheep to buy a new axle for a cart. It was an example of trade in its purest form, unchanged for thousands of years.

Long-haired two-humped camels as high as buses stood tied to the far wall of the animal section. Small cows lay down chewing the cud while tethered to stakes in the ground. Fat-tailed sheep peculiar to the region were tied together in groups of four or eight while farmers peeled back their lips to look at the teeth to check their age. Hands and fingers flashed offers in a sign language, and old *hojas* spat in the palms of their hands and shook to make the deal. Donkeys stood in rows of hundreds, while young boys rode them back and forth, stabbing them with sharp sticks, and cursing them in a bid to make them go. Horses were paraded in front of the buyers. Barefoot boys, their shirts open to the waist, rode bareback, galloping the steeds as fast as they could up and down a dusty test track, and spinning them round at the top end in a balletic pirouette. A whip would crack and the horse would whinny, kicking up clouds of yellow dirt. Nobody went home clean from the Sunday Bazaar. A donkey could cost anything between twenty and three hundred yuan. A good horse might fetch three thousand, and a bad one nine hundred. But if you wanted a camel, the price was at least twelve thousand, a fortune by local standards, comparable with buying a top-of-the-range Merc.

Sunday Market was more than a market, more than a bazaar. It was an event crucial to the lives of thousands of people, and had been essential to the economy of the region since it was first inhabited. It had taken me three months to get there, but I was hooked. From then on I made the effort to go as often as I could, each time finding something new of interest.

*

The hash, when it arrived, was supposed to have come from a village somewhere between Sancha Kou and Aksu to the north of Kashgar, but I doubted if the Germans really cared. Their relief was visible, and they could now get to work pressing and packing and prepare to leave. The hash had been sent in muslin bags, ten kilos of olive-green sticky pollen, freshly shaken from the bush and moulded by hand into balls the size of grapefruit. It smelt beautiful, but smoking it in its current state was useless.

The THC (tetra-hydro cannabinol, the active constituent of marijuana) had not been activated or released and, without that, there was no getting stoned. Its pollen state also meant that it was extremely bulky, and thus difficult to conceal. To release the THC it was necessary to put it under pressure, to create an internal heat that broke down the walls which trapped the drug's potency. This process consequently reduced its volume and turned it black, making it look like the stuff everybody's familiar with.

The Germans all but disappeared from our late-night drinking sessions, preferring to use the hours of darkness to do their work. The pollen had an incredibly sweet and pungent odour that stank their room out, so it was best to be busy when there was less likelihood of the room girls barging in unannounced. Marius and Gerhard liked to press by foot. They would pack a bag with about half a kilo at a time and tie it tight. Then, while one of them sat down and turned the bag over and over and over again, the other would tread on it repeatedly, putting as much weight on it as he could.

Every so often the dope was packed tighter and and the bag retied. If the room was warm, about an hour of constant turning and pressing would cause the pollen to go really tacky and solid, sticking to the bag and behaving like putty. This was then turned out into a prepared tray of the size and thickness that was required which had been lined with a sheet of clingfilm. Another sheet was placed over the top, and it was then rolled out, using a bottle, until it was a flat, uniformly thick plaque of hash.

The Germans had each bought holdalls with removable bottoms made from stiff card that gave the bags their shape. These bases were covered in a plastic which, with care, could be taken off without damage, and the board removed. A new board was made with a compartment in the centre. Hash was pressed out into the shape and size of the compartment, heat-sealed using clingfilm and a lighter, wrapped in tape and inserted into the space. Another piece of card was glued over the top, and the whole thing put back into the plastic. Carefully resealing it, the whole thing was then slipped back into the holdall, virtually identical to the original and unlikely to be discovered by nosy customs bods. Or at least that was the idea. It was always said that if they were intent on catching you, it didn't matter where you put it.

The problem was that these boards could only take about 250g at most, so other hiding places had to be found. Marius, Gerhard, Don and Arno had been doing this for years, and were well rehearsed in the art of concealing dope. They had been busy for a long time buying books around town – in particular, nice books with hard covers made out of thick card. New books were much better than old ones, because it was easier to match up new materials than old stained ones. Back at the hotel these were painstakingly taken apart, using damp cottonwool and a scalpel. The card was removed and a new one was made, capable of stashing 100g or so.

Another efficient ploy was the Campbell's soup tin method. Many a traveller would at some time or another resort to eating canned foods so it was not unusual for customs officials to see bags containing cans of sardines or cooked ham and the like. The good thing about cans was that they could hold anything from 300g up to a kilo, and were relatively quick and easy to work on. The required tools were a fine-toothed file and superglue. The lip on one end of a can is actually a tongue-and-groove joint and when the lip is filed down evenly, it eventually releases the joint, and the top pops out. The contents could then either be eaten or thrown away, depending on taste, and a lump of hash put in its place, nicely sealed up in clingfilm. The top would then be glued back in place and sanded down to take away any residue and tell-tale marks. Nothing could be simpler.

By the end of November they were ready to go; Tokyo via Urumchi, Shanghai and the ferry to Osaka. Eduard, Orashi and Elizabeth had also made up their minds to do a trip and were still busy pressing and packing their gear.

I had to be making a move, too, and now that the pass was closed for the winter, I had no alternative but to cross China in order to leave. I was going to take some hash with me too. Unlike the Germans, I had no intention of going to Japan because I didn't have a contact there but I did have one address in Kowloon, given to me by a traveller whom I'd met six weeks earlier. He'd shown a lot of interest, and said that it would be no problem for him to sort out if I showed up. It might cost me half the profit but it also took away half the risk.

Because I was seeing so much of ShaSha in those final days, I'd asked Elizabeth to press me up half a kilo when she was doing her own. Cutting a slab off, I made two perfectly shaped insoles to fit inside my Reeboks, each containing 150g. I slipped them in and walked on them every day, moulding them to the shape of my feet, and at the same time trying to forget that they were there. With the rest I made a can of sardines, with eight 40g fishes inside. It was lighter than the original can, because fish are heavier than dope, but I figured no one would notice. The rest of the pollen I wrapped up to be dealt with later.

It was strange. I had come this far without ever really making the decision to do so. There was an inevitability to it. It was part and parcel of graduating as a real traveller. Did I know what I was getting myself into? I doubt it.

One day in the middle of all this activity, Tahir came and said that ShaSha wanted to speak to me. It was important, and she had asked him to be the translator, because she didn't want any mistakes to be made. It sounded a bit serious to me, and I wasn't all that keen. However, I agreed and went up to the storeroom with Tahir leading the way. ShaSha was sitting on one of the beds next to Reyhan the cook, looking all demure and innocent with her hands clasped together between her knees. I sat down opposite and felt my heart beating furiously. What the hell was this all about? Was she pregnant?

ShaSha started talking in *putong hua*, Mandarin. Her grandparents had sent her to a Chinese school rather than a local Uighur school, because without a good education in the Chinese language there was no chance of getting a decent job. Thanks to that, she was now more fluent in her second tongue than her first, and used *putong hua* whenever she had to explain something complicated. This was such an occasion.

'I have already told you a lot about my life,' she began, 'and you know that it has not been very easy. You say you love me, and I tell you that I love you . . . right? So . . . can you help me to escape all this?'

I sat motionless, jaw tightly clamped shut, eyes watching this young woman doing something she obviously found extremely difficult. She didn't expect an answer at that moment, and I nodded for her to continue.

'If you cannot, or if you do not want to, I think it would be better to stop our relationship now, before it becomes too painful for us to finish.'

Feeling as if I was running off onto a sheet of thin ice, I said, 'Are you saying that you want us to get married? So that you can get away from Kang and China?'

'Yes, that's what this is about. If you can help me like this, I will help you, and be a good wife to you always. If you don't want to then let us finish now before I love you too much.'

There was no way I could answer that question right there and then. I was in shock. My plans had already changed enormously, but this was a decision that could turn my life upside down. I'd run loads of different scenarios through my mind over the previous month, but had never come up with one like this. A lot of my ideas were also fine just as they were – dreams. This was reality, and it was biting hard.

'Let's slow down here a bit,' I said. 'This is a serious thing we're talking about. I can't just say yes. I'll have to think about it. I'm not saying no – in fact, I sort of like the idea. But you know I have to leave China before the end of December whatever happens, so . . . maybe I can use that time to make up my mind. The other thing is, if I come back and you're still married, what then? You'll have to get a divorce while I'm away.'

ShaSha agreed, saying that this would not be too much of a problem in light of what had happened, but the most important thing was for me to tell her that my intentions were good, and that I wasn't just pissing her about.

I didn't want to discuss it any more with Tahir and Reyhan there, and it showed. I wanted to talk with ShaSha alone. The conversation drifted off the subject a bit after that, but I couldn't help thinking about what this was going to do to me if I went ahead with it all. The few weeks I had left in Kashgar could be very important.

The Germans had left, Eduard and Orashi had gone, Cynthia was heading off soon with Elizabeth, and ShaSha had bought tickets for us both to go on the trip to Urumchi. She wanted us to spend as much time together as possible before I disappeared – forever, for all she knew.

The weather was cold in December, and we had to wrap up in down jackets, tall leather boots and rabbitskin hats. The bus was a Hungarian-made machine that cut the journey-time to the regional capital to just three days. When ShaSha had been an athlete in the provincial games twelve years earlier, it had taken nine days to get there, but of course there hadn't been a road then. The two-lane highway that now connected the major cities along this ancient trade route was 1,500km long, and skirted the desert for 1,000km before cutting through the Tian Shan mountains to Urumchi.

Although air transport had in recent years assumed some of the burden, the road was still the major supply route. Hundreds of trucks were busy day and night shifting goods up and down it like an army of ants. Unlike in Europe, where there are restrictions on the number of hours a driver can go without a break, truckers in China drove until they couldn't drive any more. Very often they simply fell asleep at the wheel, letting their trucks veer off the road or crash into one coming in the opposite direction. It was not uncommon to see the burnt-out remains of a recent head-on collision on a 15km stretch of straight road.

The scenery soon became a dramatic nothingness of grey shingle disappearing in waves as far as the eye could see. A caravanserai would appear from the middle of nowhere. They seemed to be perched on the very edge of the habitable world, the desert deciding whether they perished or not.

To the west, distant snow-capped peaks came briefly into view before vanishing into the grey. The winter sun, pale and watery, created a translucent, sepia-toned landscape that played tricks on the eye, where distance was indeterminable. No matter what geographical knowledge a traveller had prior to passing through this region, he or she could be in no doubt that they were on the edge of a huge wasteland, 327,000km square of dust and stones.

Regardless of the hardship, people continued to exist in the desert. Often, miles and miles from the last and next caravanserai, a donkey-cart would appear, laden with dried, twisted and gnarled tree stumps reclaimed from some prehistoric forest lost in the wilderness. The little load was two weeks' worth of labour, but the 40 yuan profit (the equivalent of £4) could provide a month of living. The locals I'd spoken to obviously had a love of and a longing for the desert, some referring to it as the 'old homeland' or 'end place', which was perhaps a distant memory of a time when rivers ran through it and communities thrived.

The first overnight stop was just before Aksu, the fourteenth-century Mongol capital and today a thriving oasis of over 340,000 people. Aksu (meaning 'white water' in Uighur because of the crystal-clear torrents that run through it from the 7,000m-high Kok Shaal Tau mountains on the border with Kirghizia) was an important city on the northern Silk Road, but had lost much of the medieval flavour that Kashgar retained.

The bus parked in a large compound and everyone was told to get off and book into a hotel that could easily have been mistaken for a prison. ShaSha and I went up to the reception and were immediately told that she would have to book in at another reception desk on the other side of the building because the hotel regulations stated that the sexes must be segregated. I couldn't complain at 40p a night, but draconian measures like that were ridiculous. It was 1989, for God's sake!

The hotel was a large rectangular affair, with cold, dimly lit stairways leading to bleak rooms with concrete floors and metal camp beds. It would have been difficult to find squatters wanting to move into a place like this back home. The toilets were way out across an unlit yard full of potholes and puddles. The squat slots were also unlit, and if you didn't have a torch there was a good chance you'd slip right through into the slurry below. Many refused to go in, choosing to do it in the privacy of the shadows outside, and thus turning the back yard into a minefield of squidgy turds.

The following morning at about six-thirty, with half an inch of solid ice on the inside of the bus, we set off again for another day of excitement in the middle of nowhere. No matter how intrepid or how hellbent you are to visit the most remote regions of the world, I believe there are only so many stones you can see before the journey becomes a grind. ShaSha and I occupied ourselves beneath a blanket that she had brought along to keep us warm. It was not unnoticed by our fellow passengers. I missed a lot of their angry remarks, though ShaSha heard them clearly, but refused to let it affect our enjoyment.

That night we stopped at an even worse hotel than the previous night's. Again it was single-sex accommodation, only this time in dormitories with broken windows and doors that didn't even close properly. The wind whistled in through the gaps, causing the dust to spiral like miniature tornadoes in the middle of the room.

The so-called restaurant decided to close as soon as we walked in, refusing to knock us up even the most simple hot dish or sell me a beer. It was at least -10ºC, and we were stuck miles from Korla, the nearest town, with nothing hot to eat or drink. In desperation I decided to try and hitch into town, but after an hour without success I gave up and went to bed, hoping that the night would pass quickly so we could have breakfast in the morning instead. I was out of luck. When we left at six-thirty everything was still closed, and we had to wait until nine before the bus stopped for a break.

The bus groaned into Urumchi at about seven the next night. I was looking forward to a good hotel with a hot shower, but that was easier said than done. The Xinjiang Fandian refused to give us a room, saying they were full, and the Bogda Shan Hotel wanted fifty dollars a night – out of the question, especially when I thought about the Semen which had charged me only three dollars a night. After a lot of hiking around we managed to get a double room in the Hong Shan Fandian. Everybody who books into a hotel in China must provide ID, whether it be a card or a passport. If ShaSha had handed over her ID, there would have been no way we could have stayed in the same room together, and more than likely the hotel receptionist would have called the police. I told them that ShaSha was my wife but that the police had lost her passport whilst processing her visa extension, but that we would get it back in the morning. The Chinese girl with whom I spoke looked at ShaSha's blue eyes and believed me immediately. Too good to be true: our first night in a hotel together.

Urumchi lies in the northern foothills of the middle section of the Tian Shan mountain range and is a comparatively new industrial city on the Lanzhou–Xinjiang railway line. It covers a massive 1,200km square and has a population of about one and a half million people, more than 50 per cent of whom are Han Chinese. It was formerly called Dihua, but in 1953 it was renamed Urumchi, which means 'fine pastureland' in Mongolian.

Urumchi may have been a fine pastureland once, but it is now a drab, dank, grey depressing sprawl. Built by communists for communists, the Kazaks, Uighur and Mongols who live there look out of place and indeed many of them feel out of place, but at least their presence keeps the city alive. Overshadowed by a dark hill scarred with exploitation, it is a place where life seems to have lost part of its meaning. All the streets look the same.

Most tourists pass straight through if they can, and the ones who do stay hardly venture much further than the hotel. I know that if it hadn't been for ShaSha, I would have done the same. Having a guide on hand who was fluent in Uighur and Chinese made a big difference.

On our second day in Urumchi we went to visit one of ShaSha's friends, Merhaba, who was half Kazak. She lived in a Chinese-style *hutong* (narrow alley) complex situated behind the Bank of China. She was twenty-seven and extremely pretty. She had a good job in the management department of a large shop down town which paid well enough for her to buy nice clothes and dye her hair auburn.

Merhaba was a lovely person, but I found it difficult to accept that the fashionable, suave woman I saw on the street with her friends was the same woman that lived in that hole. I could never have imagined that people could live in such conditions. The adobe houses in Kashgar were palaces in comparison. The first room was a six-foot-square box with a bed and a cast-iron stove. The other room was only marginally larger and had two chairs. It had no windows or water. The toilets, the usual communal slots, were quite a distance down the alley, where there was also a tap that supplied the water.

Despite the lack of space, Merhaba insisted that we stay in the tiny back room at her house so that we might avoid detection by inquisitive hotel staff. As it happened, it worked out well and we spent our days in the park taking photos and eating *jiaozi* dumplings in Hui minority restaurants or succulent kebabs in the markets. Urumchi kebabs were thinner cuts of mutton than those in Kashgar, with more chilli and cumin sprinkled on top. For the equivalent of a pound, you got twenty sticks of fresh barbecued mutton, and with fresh hot nan bread to soak up the juices. They were the most delicious things on earth.

When the girls were out shopping, I took the opportunity to pack up another 300g of hash in a fish tin, ready for my odyssey across Kithai. (That was the name the Uighur used when referring to the Chinese, and was the name used by the Turk tribes in ancient times for the region. It's probably where the word 'Cathay' comes from.)

Trying to buy a train ticket was near impossible, but thanks to ShaSha trudging up to the railway station at five-thirty one morning, I managed to get a 'hard-sleeper' ticket to Zhengzhou junction. That was two and a half days away, and it was then necessary to get off and buy another ticket for the last leg to Guangzhou. Seeing that this might cause me some difficulty, I asked ShaSha to write down on a piece of paper in Chinese, 'Please can I buy a hard-sleeper ticket to Guangzhou,' because there was no way I could say it.

After enjoying five days together like lovers, we said goodbye on a wintry morning in the middle of December. It was seven o'clock and couldn't have been colder. ShaSha had come on board the train to help me find my bunk. Looking into her eyes as they welled up with tears, I had to wonder if I would ever see her again. I knew that I wanted to, but who could say what might happen. So many of my initial plans were already out of the window. There was simply no telling.

As Chinese peasants pushed and shoved past us with their belongings tied to bamboo poles, clearing their throats and spitting out of the window, we kissed again and again. I stared deep into the sparkling sapphire blueness of her eyes and knew that I really did not want to go. My chest became tight and I was searching for air. I held her, never wanting the moment to die. 'I will come back. I'll do everything I can to come back. I promise.'

The whistle blew, and ShaSha had to go. Arms outstretched, our fingers slipping through each other's hands like rose petals, she was swallowed by the crowd. As the train pulled out, I struggled to get to the window to have one last glimpse, and there she was, standing firm amid a sea of confusion, waving a farewell that would be forever etched in my mind.

Absence

L'absence est à l'amour ce qu'est au feu le vent;
Il éteint le petit, il allume le grand.

Comte de Bussy-Rabutin (1618–93)

THE train gathered speed and I was on my way. It was the beginning of a new adventure, but this time the stakes were higher, much higher. I knew that it was a mistake to ponder doomsday scenarios, so I pushed all thoughts of what I was doing to the furthest recesses of my mind. From now on, as far as I was concerned, there was no dope.

Lying in my eyrie on the third bunk, I observed my fellow passengers with growing interest. Face flannels had been arranged on the racks, tea was brewing and the cards were out. Even though I had already been in China for four and a half months, up until this moment I'd had very little contact with the Han. Their incessant chatter reminded me of a tropical menagerie, a sound totally unrecognisable as the human tongue. There wasn't even one word that I could pluck out from the chorus that meant anything to me.

Every so often a loud, high-pitched, strangely nasal voice would erupt from a speaker less than three feet from my head, causing it to vibrate like a washing machine on spin. To add to the audio vandalism, an album of 1960s revolutionary love songs by a screeching soprano was put on for our entertainment. There was nothing else for it: I had to get drunk – either that or unscrew the speaker with my knife and cut the wires.

The train passed in and out of tunnels on its way through the mountains, and soon came out into the Turfan Depression, known as the furnace of Xinjiang, and at 154m below sea-level, the lowest point in China. Travelling slowly, we plodded on through a sea of dark grey stones. The land was barely distinguishable from the sky in the fading light of day. The city of Hami, a former capital of Genghis Khan, renowned for its melons and nowadays for being an oasis of multiple faiths, emerged on the horizon. A patchwork of Kazak, Uighur, Hui, Mongol and Han, Hami is famous for its diversity. Since 1981 when religious activities were revived, the city now has 270 mosques, three Protestant churches, one Catholic church and a number of Buddhist temples.

Xinjiang behind us, a thousand kilometres from Urumchi, the desert rolled on, breathtaking in its vastness. It seemed ridiculous to think that Beijing could have controlled the area so long ago from so far away.

The Qilian Mountains and the Qinghai plateau visible to the south were a welcome break in the monotony, and very soon the old locomotive chugged through Jiayuguan, the westernmost extremity of the Great Wall. Jiayuguan had always been an important military outpost and a supply centre for the Jade Road that flourished some thousand years before the Silk Road ever gained momentum. It carried tons upon tons of the much sought-after stone to the Qin Emperor from rich deposits near Hotan. It was not until the Ming Dynasty that this place was considered crucial to the defence of the north-west frontier. Emperor Hongwu built a fortress which controlled the Jiayu Pass and everything that went through it. In the pale light of dawn it looked a remote and desolate post, which, five hundred years ago, would have felt more than a little precarious on the lip of the Chinese empire.

Heading toward Lanzhou in the late afternoon we snaked into the Gansu corridor, in ancient times a natural passage from Xinjiang and Central Asia into the heart of China. Following the same route as the dreaded sandstorms that vent their wrath upon the region each year, we entered an eroded world of windblown canyons and crumbling mountainsides. Winds from Siberia move into the Jungar Desert Basin north of Urumchi, gaining momentum as they go. Channelled out into the open, they pick up dust and debris, whipping over Turfan, Hami, Mount Mazhong and down to Yinchuan. Compressed by the corridor, they gather force, speed and ammunition. Waves of sand anything from 300 to 700m high descend to wreak untold damage. It was said that one storm buried 120,000 head of cattle alive.

Lanzhou was an elongated affair in a narrow valley belonging to the Yellow River. There seemed to be one dirt track leading in and one dirt track leading out. Dirty grey factories pumped toxic-looking plumes of smoke in every colour of the rainbow into a thick brown cloud that hung over the city like a permanent fixture. My fellow passengers coughed and spluttered as they inhaled the pollution. The train, which was also puffing out white smoke which at night turned into a stream of cherry-red fireworks sparkling in the darkness, sped on, curving through long bends.

When we arrived in Zhengzhou I booked into a hotel and before long I was back at the railway station with ShaSha's note in hand to try and buy a ticket to Guangzhou. There were thirty-six ticket booths, all with destinations posted in Chinese above the windows, and in front of each were queues over thirty metres long. I had never seen anything like it, not even at a football match. I showed my piece of paper to a passing railway official and was pointed to the queue outside window 12. I waited.

Four and a half hours later I reached the window and presented my note. Wrong window. A small woman, probably with a headache, instructed me to go to window 19. Another queue of three hundred people or more stood there, motionless. Three hours later I got to the window only to be told that it was closed for today, but that I should come again tomorrow. The next day, I was there at five-thirty, just in time to join a queue of about two hundred people in front of window 19. Two and a half hours later, I was told that if I wanted a ticket for Guangzhou, I should go to window 27. By that time window 27 had about four hundred people in front of it, but still I joined up.

When I was within five yards of it, it closed. This bloody song and dance went on for another three days, until at last, with uncommon ease, I got a hard-seat ticket for the following day.

I was glad to leave Zhengzhou, I can tell you, but the closer I got to the border, the more I started to buzz. The moment was approaching quickly where I would have to decide if I was going to go through with it all or not. I started to become more and more wary of the people around me, especially an English-speaking Russian who had somehow found me on this, a train with over a thousand passengers. He was offering to help me in Guangzhou to find a hotel and some girls to have a bit of fun with. As I nodded and laughed along, I was already planning how to lose him.

This part of China was very different to the deserts of the north-west. Everything was green and lush, even in winter, and every spare inch of land was being cultivated with some crop or other. Little plots on the verges had rows of cabbage, and a plot no more than a foot wide and a yard long contained two rows of carrot. There was no waste ground at all. It was clear that people were feeding themselves every way they could, and I noticed that even the beggars working the tracks were fat.

Fifty-six hours sitting in the same position on a train is a killer, so when we finally pulled in at Guangzhou, I was more than delighted. Quickly losing the Russian in the push to get out, I headed for the ticket office. I didn't want to hang around any longer than necessary because of my visa. I was pleasantly surprised to be able to book a seat on the through-train to Hong Kong for the following morning.

That night I found a decent-looking restaurant. They brought all sorts of weird stuff to my table, and I ended up having to lead the waiter into the kitchen to point to the meat and vegetables I wanted to eat, and then go 'whoosh, whoosh' to indicate that I wanted it done in the wok. It worked, and I got what turned out to be one of the best Chinese meals I've ever had.

The morning I'd been dreading finally arrived, but I felt surprisingly calm and confident. As I left the hotel room I realised I had just passed the point of no return. This was it . . . this was really it. I was entering a twilight zone. I was throwing the dice, and one speck of dust on the baize could alter the course of my whole life. I was convinced that the line between success and failure lay only in my ability to remain cool, so I went to a bar and stiffened my courage with a cold beer.

I went through immigration at Guangzhou without really noticing it. Passengers were just herded through passport control and that was it, I was on the train. The through-train was a different world from the trains of the mainland, and was big, clean, air-conditioned and comfortable. There were no crowds, no hawkers, no sunflower seeds and no one had spat all over the floor. They even had a service trolley with Heineken and San Miguel, and by the time we got to the border I was well sedated.

Shenzhen was more like an airport than a train station. Stumbling around trying to work out where to go, I heard a voice shouting in English, 'Over here, sir. This way.' Shit, they've sussed me, I thought. But it was okay, it was just another post opening up for the rush. Damn it! I should have waited back a bit for more people to mix in with.

I got through passport control with a six-month visa stamped inside. It was reassuring in a way, but the biggest hurdle was yet to come. Nothing to declare, bag into the X-ray machine, I wondered if they would see my fish, but talked myself out of believing there was any chance of that. There was no way, simply no way. It all happened in seconds. I was suddenly through and free to get back on the train. It felt like a bit of an anticlimax because I had somehow expected the moment to last longer.

I spent the rest of the journey certain that there would be another check at Kowloon's Hung Hom terminus or that somebody was following me in an attempt to see who I was going to sell the stuff to. As I stepped off the train I glanced around carefully, trying not to look suspicious, but saw no one. But that didn't mean they weren't watching, did it?

Hong Kong was as vibrant as I'd imagined. As my taxi slipped through the back streets, I got the firm impression that this city was more Chinese than China itself. Everywhere I looked there were little shops with red lanterns outside them selling jade and restaurants with big golden dragons above the door. Even the writing looked more Chinese. (In Hong Kong, Taiwan and Singapore they use *fan ti zi*, the original complex form of a Chinese character, whereas on the mainland they use a simplified version.)

I was heading for Chunking Mansions in the Tsimshatsui area of Kowloon, to find a budget hotel recommended by Thundernose. Chunking was situated on Nathan Road, between the Imperial Hotel and the Holiday Inn, but could not be compared to either. The first two floors were a shopping arcade for cut-price clothes, bags, videos and watches, with a laundrette and loads of cheap Nepali fast-food restaurants. The upper floors, separated into five different blocks, were a mixture of Indian restaurants and inexpensive accommodation, all packed together with not an inch to spare.

Claustrophobic metal lifts went up and down constantly ferrying visitors from every country in the world to their matchbox-like rooms. The Chunking was a melting pot of global wretches, a centre for topless dancers, gangsters, pickpockets, junkies, prostitutes, down-and-outs and dope smugglers. Thanks to a twenty-four-hour shop in the basement, it never stopped. There was always a hangout, no matter what time of the day or night, to get a beer, something to eat and shoot the shit with a fellow drifter.

I found a room with Mr Fat on the ninth floor of D Block. With a TV, a fan and a communal shower, it was more than adequate. I immediately fell in love with Hong Kong. It was everything I'd expected an Asian city to be. I wandered around in sheer joy, watching the incessant hustle and bustle, people, cars, buses, boats rushing here, there and back again. Junks of all sizes crowded the harbour, and ferries hauled thousands of hectic humans across the waters, while huge grey warships cut an arrogant path through their midst.

The Cantonese language, with its clipped, hard consonants and elongated vowels, seemed to be more in keeping with the character of the people than the militaristic Mandarin. It gave the place its colour and music, its mystery and romance. A different smell wafted around each corner and attacked the senses. Roast pork, sweet and sour, and number 36 with fried rice hung in the air and invited you to dine in a city where food was more important than life itself. It was impossible not to feel hungry.

English-style pubs were everywhere: the Red Lion, the Sly Fox, Harry's Bar and the Australian Club. But before I went on a crawl I had business to attend to. I walked the length of Nathan Road until I found Mong Kok, an area of small businesses and residential blocks. The address I was looking for was in a block of seedy-looking flats with a broken-down lift. Triad graffiti covered the walls and I started to think that if this guy was a Triad, he might not see much point in paying for what I had to offer. He could just take it, and what could I do about that?

I knocked on a door at the end of a dark hallway, which was opened by an old lady clutching a fistful of majong tiles.

'Is Peter here? Peter Shu?' I asked.

The answer, in very fast Cantonese, went straight over my head. I tried again. The old lady, dressed in a black top, baggy black trousers and black cloth shoes, shouted to someone inside. A girl appeared wearing the standard issue metal-framed spectacles of the HK intelligentsia, and said to me in perfect English, 'I'm sorry but no one of that name lives in this house. You have made a mistake. I'm very sorry. Goodbye.'

The door closed gently but meant the same as if it had been slammed in my face. Weird, I thought. What do I do now?

There was no use hanging about in HK any longer, so I went to book a flight to Manila. 'I have a seat on a flight that's leaving tonight at 11.30. Can you make it?' I was asked.

'Sure I can make it,' I said, 'that'll do fine.'

I deposited half of the hooch in the left-luggage at the airport, and checked in. That would be my insurance, just in case things went funny somewhere along the line.

Manila Airport was teeming with new arrivals. They were mostly Filipinas coming home for Christmas, but I did spot the odd westerner snaking through the crowd. The woman at customs was so intent on going through my bag that I had to interrupt her and ask her about the meaning of the currency declaration form I'd been given. It was enough to break her concentration, and by the time she'd finished explaining what was necessary, quite a queue had built up behind me, and she waved me through without further inspection.

I had found a way of keeping myself together in these situations. While the alcohol numbed my senses, I concentrated on a burning flame in my middle eye, and like everything dissolved around me. Another day, another frontier.

The cheap hotels in Manila were all within walking distance of Mabini, the nightlife hub of the capital. My first impression of the place was that it was a town inhabited by gangsters, prostitutes, transvestites, sexual deviants, drug dealers, gold smugglers, addicts, freaks, corrupt policemen and a lot of poor people. With its sex shows, girlie bars, discos and cheap bars, Mabini was twenty-four-hour-a-day mayhem, a modern-day, twentieth-century version of Sodom and Gomorrah. It was the epitome of a society ravaged by religion, poverty and violence. But, no matter what conflict I felt personally, I couldn't help but be entertained by the place. Regardless of the inequalities, the ordinary people were hellbent on enjoying themselves, and if the tourists were paying, all the better. And the tourists did pay, whether they wanted to or not, and usually in more ways than they intended.

On my first night there, by pure chance, I ran into Marius at a small bar. He had a short, vocal timebomb in tow whom he adoringly called Chippy. She couldn't have been much more than seventeen, and had a ladder of razorblade-slash scars down the inside of her left arm. I learnt later that each scar represented a grief that she had experienced, and that cutting herself like that was supposed to bleed out the pain. She was not the only one either – hundreds of young Filipinas had the same scars, and they wore them like a badge of honour.

Marius was staying on the fourteenth floor of Boulevard Mansions, in a rather expensive suite, with Gerhard next door in another. They had obviously made good money in Japan and were now intent on enjoying it. Apparently they had had a big bust-up with Arno about money, and he was still stuck in Japan trying to unload. Don had gone home to Austria and Lucas had gone to Thailand on a honey safari.

Over the weeks that followed Marius introduced me to Manila. The city was a vicious, unsympathetic beast, where every winner is on the brink of losing. During Christmas and New Year the place exploded into inspired chaos. There were so many firecrackers going off and people being rushed away with burns, it looked more like a scene from *Apocalypse Now* than a street party. On a lethal mixture of alcohol and *shabou* (ice), crazed kids bombarded the jeepneys with fireworks, causing the passengers to bail out, screaming and running in fear of their lives. Billyboys strutted the pavements looking for rich Arabs with diamond-studded dicks, and drugged-up prostitutes laughed and taunted the passers-by. While whole families lay sleeping under corrugated iron sheets far below the towering hotels, a debauched whore threw bottles from the balcony, screaming, 'Fuck 'em, it's Christmas!'

It was good to leave Manila after all that, and the tropical island of Borocay was just the place to head for. A bamboo-timbered beach-house was the perfect spot to rest up and calculate the damage. Sharing a house with Gerhard was a mistake, though. In no time at all we were both hitting the booze at a frightening rate, and getting worse every day. If he went out to buy breakfast, he'd invariably scrap the idea of food and return with a bottle of rum and four cokes. I was becoming an alcoholic. How long could this go on?

After a month Marius and Gerhard returned to Manila, preferring table-dancing and sleaze to white sands and turquoise seas. I met up with Eduard, Orashi and Elizabeth who were staying on the other end of the island, and was introduced to the social side of Borocay. What with sailing around the island on nifty catamarans and going to raves and acid parties that lasted for days, it turned out to be just as hectic as Manila.

I found a new place to stay in the house of a Swiss guy who had moved there with his Filipina wife. He'd built his own bungalow in a huge garden full of coconut and mango trees on a hill in the centre of the island. Ricard was going up north for a month and was pleased to have someone to look after his place while he was away. It was just what I needed: total peace and quiet away from all the distractions with time to consider my future. Thanks to Marius and Gerhard trying to fix me up with every girl in town, I can't say that temptation didn't come my way.

I even tried to forget about Kashgar, but it was impossible. I had nothing else on my mind. I spoke about it to everyone I met. I thought about ShaSha every day and knew that I could not have a meaningful relationship with any other woman for as long as I lived. Her image was tattooed on my soul. It was a feeling new to me. It was not about lust or need or like or fancy. It was a oneness, a total absorption free from inhibition, a feeling of complete honesty and comfort. I made up my mind: I was going back to Kashgar to marry ShaSha come hell or high water.

I took the plane back to Hong Kong. In 1989, when you flew into HK, that is what you did, almost right into it, as if you were going to pull up on the high street. I was pleased to be back in a place where at least 10 per cent of the population knew what sanity meant. But I had things to do. I needed money, for one thing, and I also had to get rid of the rest of the fish. I'd sold the contents of the two shoes in the Philippines, and that had financed my stay there, but I was now nearly broke.

When Barclays Bank decided they were going to take two weeks to clear an International Money Order (issued by their own branch), the fish became top priority. But it was easier said than done. Surprising as it may seem, there are not that many people out there willing to purchase half a kilo of dope. Not for what it's worth, anyway. I was nearly on the streets. Mr Fat had given me a deadline, and if I couldn't pay by then, I would have to go.

Fortune intervened the day before I was due to be thrown out. A Serb freak called Stef told me about a film company who were looking for extras for a shoot that very night. I went along and got the job. I didn't have any difficulty assuming the role since all I had to do was sit at a bar in a pub and act like a customer. The film company supplied the beer and, after five hours of drinking, they paid us. I was impressed. This was the sort of job I could really put my back in to, or should

I say my liver. It was enough to keep me going, and I got another job the next night as a punter in a casino movie. A few days later my money came through, and that night I sold the fish to a topless dancer who was a regular at the twenty-four-hour shop. Things seemed to be going right at last.

Before I left I had one important task to complete. I wanted to buy ShaSha a ring to signify our betrothal. I discovered a little family-run jeweller's in the back streets of Kowloon, and found a gold ring set with seven opals which seemed to reflect the sun in the same shade of blue as ShaSha's eyes. It was perfect. There was nothing else like it in the shop. I knew that she would love it and know that I was serious, and that I really had come back for her.

The Return of Jumahun

Love is like any other luxury. You have no right to it unless you can afford it.
Anthony Trollope (1815–82)

HARD-SEAT for three days is hell, but I found a way of getting over that. Each night at about midnight, long after all the Chinese in the sleeper compartments had gone to bed, I would wander down and search out an empty bunk. Slipping in quietly, I could then manage about five hours' decent sleep, and as long as I was up early enough to miss the guards, it was fine.

Sleeper tickets were like gold dust and getting hold of one might take days, but hard-seat tickets were always available so it was much quicker to take what you could and then find a bunk once on the train.

My train only went as far as Turfan, and I decided I'd spend a bit of time looking around this ancient city. Unfortunately, the railway station at Turfan was actually nowhere near Turfan at all, and the settlement around it had virtually nothing to offer the weary traveller apart from a hoard of ruthless taxi-drivers who knew which side of their bread was buttered. There was no haggling at all, just a simple take it or leave it. Unless you decided to get back on the train or walk the 15km through the desert, you had no choice but share a taxi to Turfan.

The dusty, potholed track swerved down into the depression, 170m below sea-level. It was the beginning of April and the heat was already making itself known. Bouncing in a little covered pickup truck through a sea of ochre dust and gravel that had no beginning and no end, I tried to make polite conversation with a rather glamorous French couple who were both decked out in designer desert exploration gear. I felt like a tramp next to them, and most likely looked like one, which explained their tentative response. However, the Robert Redford lookalike couldn't help blurting out a catalogue of facts, which were intended to impress and make me think that he was some sort of an expert on the region. I knew that he wasn't, but said nothing.

Turfan appeared like the birth of an island rising from an ocean of desolation. I wondered why people had come here, of all places, to settle. What was the attraction? Until the eighth century Turfan had been a jewel in the Buddhist crown, but the spread of Islam from the west put paid to that. Muslim forces destroyed much evidence of the former culture and left modern historians with very little with which to decipher the mysteries of a once flourishing civilisation. It's one of the most important tourist destinations in Xinjiang nowadays, with the remains of many ancient cities and Buddhist grottoes within easy reach. It is a sizeable oasis, too, still relying for its survival on an intricate system of wells that tap into an underground flow of water from the mountains.

I was pleased to be back in the land of the Uighur. They looked familiar, and I could talk to them. I felt that I had something in common with them, and perhaps I did. A few cold beers under the trellised veranda in the Turfan Guest-house got me telling one old fellow about how I was going back to Kashgar to claim my bride. He was mightily impressed and called his friend over to tell him the news that this here *chetilik* (foreigner) was going to marry a Kashgari girl. It was all the excuse they needed to order up a bottle of sweet red Turfan wine, a plate of kebabs and nan to celebrate. The wine was more like a mixture of port and sherry but it slipped down well.

Dressed as if they were going out to dinner, Monsieur et Madame Redford appeared on the veranda. They passed by, shyly offering a polite *bonsoir*, but their confusion, especially on his face, was obvious. How was it that I was sitting there on such intimate terms with two old *hojas*?

The next day was spent walking around the remains of Karakhoja with the Redfords and four rather stolid Swedes who had turned up at the guest-house late the night before. My enjoyment had been somewhat bruised by having to pay sixty yuan for the pleasure; it had cost me only eighty-nine to come all the way from Guangzhou to Turfan. That night I booked a seat on the morning bus to Kashgar, and found out that the Swedes, the Redfords and a seventy-five-year-old woman originally from Sarajevo would be travelling with me.

The bus which drew up outside the gates that morning should have been retired and put in a museum years ago. None of us had ever seen anything like it, and even the Swedes made a joke about it. It was made of wood and looked ready to fall apart at any moment. Any windows that were not missing or broken were caked in a substance that resembled (and probably was) vomit. At least the driver was Uighur, which usually meant that we'd arrive sooner rather than later. Or so I thought.

Two hours after boarding we were still in the bus park waiting for a couple of passengers who never showed up. We were eight foreigners and four locals on a thirty-five-seater bus. Usually there weren't enough buses to meet the demand, but this was a local bus that stopped anywhere and everywhere and went nowhere fast. Viewed at twenty-five miles an hour, the desert looked bigger than before, simply endless. What must it be like to go by donkey to Kashgar? I had to marvel that there were people doing precisely that all the time who knew no different. They couldn't afford the bus and probably thought of it as some newfangled invention.

The old woman from Sarajevo loved the desert and constantly eulogised its bleak attraction like an art critic drooling over a painting. She had lived in Paris for fifty years, working as a designer for Chanel, and now spent her days travelling the wilder and remoter parts of the world. She was proud of having been to Laos, Cambodia and Vietnam, Alaska and Tierra del Fuego, and who could blame her.

I had been expecting a three-day journey, but as the bus seemed to be slowing down as we went, it became obvious that we'd be lucky to do it in four. It was nine in the evening when we finally rolled into Kashgar, but it was warm and still light. The town looked the same and I felt at home again. I booked in to room 505 in Chinibagh, and even though I was caked in dust I went straight down to the Oasis to find ShaSha.

As I walked over to the rank, one of the horse-taxi-drivers recognised me immediately, and called me over. 'Eh, Jumahun,' he said with a slap on the back. 'You have returned. How are you, my friend? It's good to see you.'

'Eh, Mehemet Ili, how are you, you old gangster? How's business?'

'Not so bad, my friend. You have come back for Sharapet, eh?'

'Sure, I've come back to marry her,' I replied almost boastfully.

'Excellent. We must have a party, kill sheep, eat, dance and get drunk, eh?'

'We'll do that, that's for sure, and you will definitely be invited.'

I jumped on his cart and we raced off to the Oasis. The first time I took a horse-cart, the driver tried to get ten kuai out of me. The second time it was five, and by the end of the week I was paying the same as the locals, two jiao. But now I didn't have to pay anything at all. Ah, it felt so good to be back.

Thankfully, the Oasis was open, and as I walked in one of the waitresses, a girl called Lanlan, started jumping up and down, shouting, 'Hey, it's Jumahun, it's Jumahun. Sharapet! Come quick, Jumahun has come back! Look!'

Thank God – at least that meant that she was there. ShaSha emerged from behind the bar, wiping her hands, and stood there smiling. We embraced and as our lips met I knew that she was my woman. The connection between us was electric. Everything fitted. We were perfectly tuned to the same station, and when we kissed the circuit flowed like a river through our bodies.

Drawing back and looking at each other for a moment, ShaSha said, 'I always knew that you would come back. It's good to see you, Jumahun.'

I produced the ring from my pocket and watched her as I placed it on her finger. 'So, shall we get married then?' I said as calmly as I could.

ShaSha grabbed me round the neck and kissed me again. 'Yes, yes, I'm ready,' she replied.

Once things had calmed down a bit, I gave her a pair of silver bangles that I'd bought in Kashgar earlier. They were old and quite unique with a Kirghiz design that I'd only ever seen once before. ShaSha loved them, saying they represented our two hearts coming together, and that it was a sign of good luck.

That night I gave her my jacket and a baseball hat to make her look like a foreigner and smuggled her into Chinibagh where we spent the night consummating our betrothal. Fearful of making too much noise and attracting the ever-vigilant management, we had to stifle our fervency like teenagers on the sofa, but the thought that we might be discovered heightened the excitement, and I felt like a cliff diver somersaulting into a sea of emotion that was waiting to swallow me complete, and I wanted it more than anything else in the world.

Early the next morning, after about an hour's sleep, ShaSha slipped out of the hotel, once again disguised as a foreigner. This was the last time we had to resort to those sort of tactics to be alone together, because within a few days a good friend forged us a cohabitation permit that was enough to keep the informers off our backs. This cloak-and-dagger stuff was a hassle, but I somehow enjoyed it. It was like messing around with the hash – I never once regarded it as criminal. It was just being naughty and a bit wilful. The authorities, of course, had different ideas.

Early one morning, about a week after I'd arrived back, I was woken from a beer-induced comatose state by a hell of a rumpus. Someone was banging on my door. Whoever it was didn't sound too polite, and I told them to clear off and leave me alone. The hammering continued until I was forced out of bed to open the door and see what they wanted. As I did so, a short scruffy little Uighur brandishing a pair of electric pliers tried to barge his way into my room. I wasn't having any of that, so I put the flat of my hand on his chest and shoved him back into the corridor. When he tried it again I slammed the door in his face. 'What the hell was all that about?' I wondered.

Silence fell, so I went back to bed and tried to sleep. Just as I slipped into that warm fluffy dream world, the banging started up again. This time I was really angry, and to prove the point, I picked up my newly acquired Yengisar knife, opened the door in one swift movement and said, 'What the fuck do you want, you bastard?', hoping that that would scare whoever it was away for good. It didn't.

This time it was the police, and they were coming in whether I liked it or not. It turned out that a quilt had been stolen and the manager was searching all the rooms. The scruffy little bloke I'd shoved out into the corridor turned out to be the manager. He was totally pissed off and accused me of attacking him. The police were not very happy either about the way I'd greeted them and ordered me down the station for questioning.

As they drove me away I waved to all the folks I knew as if I was campaigning for election. It didn't take long for everybody in the foreign community to know that I'd been dragged in by the cops. Speculation was rife, with most people sure that I'd been nicked for hash.

Once down at the station I was asked to write an apology to the manager and a piece criticising my own behaviour towards the police. Even though I felt that it should be the bloody manager writing the apology, I knew that it was pointless to argue, and did as I was asked. They fined me 100 FEC and told me to go back to Chinibagh and wait for the police to come and search my room. I wondered if they were joking. They were in effect giving me a ten-minute head start to stash my gear somewhere safe. So I did. I slipped it to Omar, my money-changer, and told him to keep hold of it. The police turned up half an hour later and, after lifting up the edge of the quilt and giving a quick peek behind the curtains, said thank you and left.

*

Getting the divorce papers had not been too difficult for ShaSha. She needed the hospital report detailing the injuries that she had suffered, which was more than ample evidence of a serious breakdown in the relationship, and then she had to post a notice in the local newspaper to let everyone know. If Kang had any objections, he could raise them there. Since he was being detained at 'the

Chairman's pleasure', however, that was not possible. Instead he wrote an angry letter stating that when he got out he wanted custody of his daughter Nana, and that it would be best if ShaSha understood that. He also made it clear that he knew ShaSha intended to marry a foreigner, and laughed at the prospect of her going abroad to live. There was no doubt about it: the man was pissed off and, according to both ShaSha and Tahir, he was bound to cause some sort of trouble when he returned.

I wasn't going to be scared off like that. I had already agreed to do what was right by Nana – there had never been any question about that. But ShaSha was casting doubt on the idea of the three of us living together without the shadow of Kang haunting us to our dying day.

Even though SahSha had her divorce papers, we needed a document that proved she was eligible to marry. It took three weeks of trekking from office to office and waiting in queues for the complicated bureaucracy to produce the goods. Even when the Uighur Bureau finally issued it, they told us it would have to be authorised by the Chinese Bureau, and that we'd have to take it over there for them to stamp it. When we showed up, we were told that they didn't do that sort of authorisation, and that we should go to the city administration bureau in the big building behind the Chairman Mao statue.

When we got there it was closed. The next day we were told that the man who dealt with authorisations was off sick. 'Come back tomorrow.' We went early and managed to catch a glimpse of the man, but were told by someone else that he was busy. The next day we finally got it. I wondered how on earth it was possible for ordinary people to take time off work to acquire important documents like this. I could only assume that most didn't bother.

We were now ready to undergo the rather daunting task of going to Beijing to post banns in the British Embassy. This wasn't going to be a holiday or a sightseeing trip. It was simply a necessity. We gave ourselves a week to prepare and set about purchasing the bus tickets.

The tourist season had been a little slow to get going that year due to the late opening of the Khunjerab, but by mid-May things were warming up nicely. Chinibagh dormitory was full of all sorts again, mostly hash-heads who spent their nights sitting around a campfire on the roof of the dorm passing *chilums* and telling stories about great dope purchases. The walls of the old library had been covered with graffiti supporting a free Tibet and the Dalai Lama. Dripping muslin bags of curds hung everywhere in an attempt to make cream cheese, and a group of Japanese freaks had built a Buddhist shrine and smoked dope as an offering to Shiva.

Hanu the mad Finn, whose reputation for incessant dope-smoking preceded him, was trying to recuperate from hepatitis B, which was enough to keep me well away from the place, but the others didn't seem to worry. Portuguese Qim, another long-term resident, barely came out in daylight, choosing to sleep off the effects of the night before in what were becoming dirtier and dirtier blankets.

The hotel management finally set about cleaning the walls and banned the use of hotel linen on the roof, threatening to kick offenders out, but it was too late to change old habits and the dorm continued its anarchic slide.

Seeing the town come back to life again made it difficult to tear myself away, but by the end of May we were on our way to Beijing, back on the bus and off through the desert again. My God, some people considered it a once-in-a-lifetime trip, and here was me on my third crossing. I enjoyed it, though, especially travelling with ShaSha. She introduced new aspects that I would have missed by myself.

The next evening we arrived in Urumchi, and went straight to Merhaba's house. The following day the three of us went to the station and Merhaba managed to get us tickets for nine-thirty that night. We picked up our bag and were away. The shiny black steam engine pulling the train had been built in 1935 and ran as smoothly and as efficiently as it did the day it was made, puffing plumes of white smoke up and over the carriages, as the bleak scenery of the Gobi flicked past frame by frame like a slide show.

Travelling as a pair made it impossible to find empty beds, so we just stayed on our hard-seats. We sat opposite each other and in that way were able to stretch our legs out as far as we could without disturbing our fellow passengers. Every time the train came to a stop, though, I got off to shake the cramp out of my muscles and buy beer.

Leaving the desert behind, the country came alive in all shades of green, with huge strips of land covered with lemon-coloured rapeseed stretching off into the far distance. We ate noodles and boiled eggs with hot pickled mustard tuber. ShaSha nibbled on sunflower seeds and I ate peanuts. We bought the famous roast chicken at Baoji Station and washed it down with gold-medal-winning Yantai beer. Somehow the time passed.

After seventy-two hours we pulled into Beijing Main Station. It was already dark and we had to look for a hotel. Expecting some sort of hassle, we had brought along the fake permit with the signature of the administrative officer of the Kashgar Aliens Registration Bureau and stamped with a red seal that our friend had made from a potato. It granted permission for us to travel together and share the same accommodation. It did the trick. We got a room with a king-size bed, armchairs, a fridge, a colour TV, carpets and a beautifully tiled bathroom with a hot shower, all for a staggering 140 FEC (£28). After travelling so far in such conditions, we figured we deserved it.

After a shower, we went out about eleven o'clock to grab something to eat in one of the many restaurants that lined the streets near the station. The place was deserted. The only cars we saw were big and black with tinted windows cruising the dimly lit boulevards like vultures searching for carrion. The restaurants were all nearly empty, which I considered sort of strange for a city like Beijing, but in my weariness thought little of it. The funny looks we were getting were nothing new either, so I ignored them too.

We lingered over our meal for nearly two hours during which I blanked out the fact that the restaurant was now empty and that the waitress was giving us the 'please piss off' look.

ShaSha and I had been so wrapped up in each other that we were completely oblivious not only to that night's strange atmosphere but also to the fact during the past month one of the most startling events of the twentieth century had unfolded. It just so happened to be the night of 4 June 1989, and we were in Beijing.

Tiananmen Square (which somewhat ironically means 'Gate of Heavenly Peace') is the largest public square in the world. In 1989, following the death of the radical Communist Party reformer, Hu Yaobang, and commemorating the seventieth anniversary of the 4 May Movement, thousands of demonstrators, led by a group of politically aware students, moved in to occupy the square and call for political reform and the resignation of the communist leaders. The Pro-democracy Movement, as it became known, gathered momentum, and in the weeks that followed more and more students and demonstrators from all over China joined in.

By the end of May there were hundreds of thousands of young people demanding the overthrow of the Communist Party. Three thousand of the students began a hunger strike which attracted the attention of the world's media. When numerous requests to end the demonstration were ignored and attempts to persuade the students to go home failed, Deng Xiaoping, the effective leader of the country and Chief of Staff for the PLA, sanctioned the use of force to evict them.

Prime Minister Li Peng then ordered the Red Army to take whatever steps necessary to clear the square of the threat to the nation's stability. In less than eight hours thousands of troops stormed into Tiananmen in tanks and trucks, and remorselessly massacred more than two thousand peaceful protesters.

Stepping out of the hotel the following morning, ShaSha and I, who knew nothing of this, were met by a strange sight, with soldiers everywhere. Trudging up Jiangguomenwai Avenue on our way to the embassy compound in Ritan Park, we were surprised to see officers of the People's Armed Police lining the roadside wearing combat hats and clutching automatic weapons. Trucks zoomed past with angry-looking troops scowling back at us. You didn't have to be a criminal to feel guilty of something in that atmosphere.

What the hell was going on? Whatever it was, it didn't matter – we had a mission to accomplish and we had to get on with it. The posting of banns was a very simple formality which only involved me filling out a short form and showing my passport. The banns would be posted in the embassy foyer for six weeks, and if no one cited any reason during that time as to why I should not be married, I would be issued with the papers permitting me to go ahead.

'Send them to me in Kashgar,' I said.

'Where's that?' replied the young vice-consul.

'It's in Xinjiang. You've never heard of it?' I asked incredulously.

'No, well, I've only just arrived in China, you see, and . . .'

As we left the beautifully tree-lined enclosure of the embassy, I had to wonder at the calibre of diplomat we were sending abroad these days. They ought to have at least some idea of the geography of the country in which they were posted.

We went straight back to the station and miraculously managed to get tickets for the train leaving for Urumchi that night at eleven o'clock. To kill time, and hoping to do a bit of sightseeing, we strolled down to Tiananmen. The whole square was cordoned off and armed police prevented passers-by taking photographs. Whatever was going on was pretty serious, that's for sure.

I was shattered before we even got on the train that night, and the prospect of another seventy-two hours' hard-seat was frightening. ShaSha looked wiped out as well, almost ready to drop. We decided to eat a good meal and neck a bottle of wine each in the hope that it would knock us out. It did. We must have slept solidly for eight hours in a sort of semi-sitting, sprawling position. I felt as if I'd spent the night in a shopping trolley and probably damaged my spine in the process. But we had to go on.

We stopped off in Urumchi for a day to try and recover but it wasn't nearly long enough. When we left at six the following morning, we were simply running on autopilot and alcohol. Three days later we rolled into Kashgar, beaten and broken. I was never so happy to arrive anywhere in all my life. It had been the most gruelling journey I'd ever done. We had covered the 9,000km to Beijing and back in fifteen days, and I was in no hurry to do that again.

Toy

> *Do not try to find out – we're forbidden to know – what end the gods have in store for me or for you.*
>
> Horace (65–8BC)

KASHGAR was a fighting town and reminded me sometimes of the Wild West you used to see in the movies. It had the same feel as you'd imagine an 1850s Midwest town might have. But the strange thing was that even though every man and boy carried a knife I never heard of anyone being stabbed. The fights I'd seen between locals all down in the bazaar all began with the two adversaries drawing their weapons and throwing them to the ground out of harm's way before plunging in with fists and feet. I considered that to be very honourable, and admired their presence of mind.

*

After nearly seven weeks, notification came that there was a registered letter waiting for me in the post office. I hopped on my Flying Pigeon and went down to collect it. The permission I needed had come from the embassy at last, and we could now go ahead and get married. Easier said than done, of course.

The very next day, ShaSha and I cycled down to the Chinese People's Government Office behind the Mao statue to inquire about the process and how best to go about it all. After the usual lengthy wait we were admitted to a dusty office where a podgy little woman listed the requirements in a bored tone. Every now and then she'd drift off in mid-sentence into a world of her own, coming back to reality a few minutes later where she'd left off. She was only able to work in one dimension at a time, which meant that any questions we had were ignored.

We left wondering how much more we knew. It wasn't a lot, but at least we had an idea of which way to go. The first thing to do was get a clean bill of health for both of us from the local hospital. That meant going down to the Gongren Yiyuan (Workers' Hospital) and having a blood test for AIDS, TB, polio, hepatitis and God knows what else. The results took a week to come back and we were then ready to move on to stage two.

That meant a visit to ShaSha's father's work unit's leader for verification that the divorce papers were genuine and that ShaSha was eligible to marry. The meeting took place in the barest little office just off Gulbagh Yol behind the Chinese market. Taking the advice of Sharif, her father, we went armed with a carton of Marlboro to grease the wheels. I was pleasantly relieved when, without any of the usual hedging and quibbling, the man signed the document as we waited.

Moving on to the Oustang Buey Paishou Suo, the registration office of the area where ShaSha was born, we had to make notification of our intention to marry. After being told to come back the following day, the secretary said that she couldn't complete the form because we didn't have a copy of ShaSha's birth certificate. The next day, with the requisite certificate in hand, she said she couldn't complete the form because we hadn't supplied the four photographs necessary for the records. The day after that, she said that she couldn't complete the form because we hadn't got permission from my government. Ha ha, we had! In fact, I had every document that I thought might be needed ready for her, and confidently placed the letter from the embassy on the table for her to inspect.

'It's not in Uighur. I can't read it,' she said.

'Okay, we'll get it translated.'

Off we went to see if we could find the schoolteacher whom ShaSha knew could do the job. Two days later, back in the office with the translation, the secretary said, 'There's no red stamp. Where is the red stamp? If there's no red stamp, it can't be a genuine document.'

'We don't have red stamps in Britain! The seal of the embassy is embossed into the paper! Please just hold it up to the light, and you'll be able to see it clearly,' I replied in desperation. If she was going to refuse to accept it, we would have to demand to see somebody with half an ounce of common sense to sort her out.

'Oh, yes, I can see it,' she said. 'Isn't that clever?'

I would dearly have liked to strangle her. I was braced for the next excuse but somehow, miraculously, it didn't come. She signed the document, and stamped it with a red stamp, as if to say, 'That's more like it.'

All this took us well over a week to accomplish, and I was starting to feel a bit wound up. Nevertheless, documents in hand, we rode off early one morning in search of the Kashgar Uighur Marriage Registration Office in an old part of town known as Chasir. It was a beautiful building, decorated in typical Uighur style with ornately carved verandas, colourful flowers everywhere and wood panelling lining each room. When we finally got in to see somebody, however, we were told that it was impossible for us to be married there because I was a foreigner and there was no record of me in their files. We were told to go and see a man called Erkinjan, who could be found in the Kashgar Chinese People's Government Offices behind the Mao statue.

Off we went. He wasn't in. Busy. Come back tomorrow. Eventually, we were told nothing could be done without permission from the Walimakum Kashgar Prefecture Special Administration. It was already too late to sort out anything that day, because if you didn't get there in the morning, you might as well forget it. It seemed 90 per cent of these office workers never got back from lunch, and if they did they were so drunk they slept all afternoon.

The next day we set out to track down this Walimakum place and found it hidden behind a department store on the main road from Id Kah down to the bus station. After waiting three hours, we were finally called in. Walking into a large musty-smelling office with tall windows, a man told ShaSha in Uighur that my presence would not be necessary and that I could wait outside. 'Bloody cheek,' I thought. 'What the hell is all this about?'

I waited outside for nearly an hour, and at one point thought about going in to see what was happening. Not wanting to get anybody's back up at this crucial stage of the game, I decided to hang on a bit longer, and continued to pace about in the carpark like a nervous father waiting for a baby to arrive.

When ShaSha at long last emerged from the building, she was close to tears. It turned out that she had been interviewed by two old *hojas* who had done all they could to dissuade her from going ahead with the marriage.

They had begun by saying, 'How can you be sure that he hasn't got a wife already or maybe a whole string of wives dotted all over the world? These foreigners are not like us. They come from a decadent world and have no morals. You must listen to us because we know about these foreigners, we have read books. He will cheat on you, use you only for your body. It is well known that they take pretty young women like you and force them into prostitution or sell them to Arabs. It is true, we do not lie. You will be crying long before you arrive at his home. Do you know this man's family? Maybe he is a criminal on the run. How do you know? You must remember, you come from a Muslim family and your religion, your customs and habits are different. Do you know if he is circumcised? You will find it very difficult to live with a man who is unclean, believe us. Think about what you are doing, because if and when you have a problem, don't come back here asking us to sort out the divorce.'

During this diatribe, ShaSha had remained silent, waiting patiently for the moment when she could speak. Eventually, she said, 'But I believe in him, and he believes in me, and that is everything.' The old men took their time but eventually, with one final warning, they took out a big red wooden seal and stamped the document that permitted us to proceed with the marriage.

That night back at the Oasis, we were visited by Erkinjan from the Kashgar Chinese People's Government Office. He knew that if he showed up there he was in for a freebie, because he was now the only person left who stood in the way of us achieving our goal. We both greeted him at the door, and while ShaSha laid a plate of kebabs in front of him, I popped down the road to get a bottle of *baijiu*. (Very few foreigners attempted to drink the extra-strong alcohol, so Tahir never kept it in stock.) Another carton of Marlboro on the table and he had no reason to complain.

We had arranged to see Erkinjan in his office bright and early the next morning, but when we got there he had not turned up. We assumed that he must still be suffering from the effects of the *baijiu* of the night before. Okay, then, we'd have to come back the following day.

Another bottle of *baijiu* and a carton of cigarettes were included to make sure, and off we went. Apparently it was better if he assumed that I didn't know about the wine and smokes, so I was advised to wait outside while ShaSha went into the office. Ten minutes later I was called in and Erkinjan set about issuing the papers we had struggled so hard to get.

From a tall wooden cupboard he took out two red cards, the size of birthday cards, with Marriage Certificate written both in English and Chinese, and the Chinese symbol known as *shuang xi*, 'double happiness', on the front in gold print. Underneath that, in Chinese and in English gold capital letters, was written, 'PRINTED BY THE MINISTRY OF CIVIL AFFAIRS OF THE PEOPLE'S REPUBLIC OF CHINA.' Folding them in half, he proceeded to glue into place a photo of ShaSha and a photo of me into one and then the other. Then, using a quill-nibbed pen and a bottle of ink, he wrote our names in Uighur using Arabic script. I was asked to put a red ink thumbprint over my name and ShaSha did the same over hers. The photos were given an indentation stamp with an antique-looking machine, and the whole thing was then stamped with a red seal with a big red star in the centre. And that was it. In that somewhat disappointingly unceremonial fashion at 11.34 a.m. on 19 August 1989, Erkinjan pronounced us man and wife.

It had taken four months, twelve documents, twelve photographs, three cartons of Marlboro, three bottles of *baijiu*, one traffic offence ticket for riding two up on a bike and nine thousand kilometres to achieve, but it was worth it. We now possessed that all-important document, which in Uighur was known as the *toy khet* (marriage licence).

That night we slept on the floor of the Oasis doing guard duty for Tahir again. We had had a few bottles of Turfan red wine and spent the evening planning our wedding party. Traditionally, weddings around Kashgar were colourful, ritualistic affairs in accordance with age-old customs. The day of the wedding would begin with the women gathering at the bride's house and the men at the groom's. While the men were busy eating, drinking and singing, the bride was prepared for the marriage by her maids, who would most likely be her aunts or older sisters. She was bathed and dressed in clean clothes and a veil was placed over her head. Then the mother would start on a wailing session of distress at the loss of her daughter. Very soon, all the women would be weeping.

This would go on until early evening when the groom would appear with his best friends on horseback with a gift of a dead sheep draped over his saddle. The bride was rolled up in a carpet and slung over the back of his horse. The groom then galloped off to his house while the women jumped on awaiting carts and followed.

The carpet was carried into the main room by two men, and each holding an end. They banged the rug on the floor three times and in one swift movement let the bride unroll from her parcel. The bride and groom would then join hands and be brought before Allah for recognition by a local *mullah* and be pronounced man and wife.

That night the marriage would be consummated upon clean sheets which were inspected in the morning by the groom's womenfolk. If it should be that there was no blood, a nan bread with a hole punched in it was nailed to the front door of the house for all to see that the bride had not been a virgin. Occasionally, where doubt existed, the bride would be supplied with a fresh chicken liver, which she inserted into her vagina beforehand, thus keeping the bread and the honour of the family intact.

We were not going to go through all that, because my home was over four and a half thousand miles away, and it was anyway a bit late for any of that clean sheets and chicken-liver rigmarole. Instead, we decided to hire a small family-run Huisu restaurant which we had discovered by accident a couple of months before. They did brilliant *jiaozi* – the steamed meat-filled dumplings that we both loved – and were very friendly and clean. With its cobbled floor, bare walls, wooden benches and plastic tablecloths, the little place was nothing to look at, but none of that mattered. I thought it was perfect.

We booked it for the 28th and set about drawing up a guest list. ShaSha's father would be our guest of honour; then Nana, Tahir, Reyhan and Akkuz, ShaSha's younger sister; Rushengul and Titigul, two old school friends; Adiljan the assistant manager from the hotel; and Tudahun, the teacher and an authority on local history. Elizabeth, who had just arrived back in town; Narvazkhan from the Pakistani restaurant in the hotel yard; Raja, a self-professed *muhajidin* and killer of Russians; Pijiu Brother, my Hunza Tajik drinking buddy; and Sawud and Mehemet Ili, the taxi-drivers. There were also several people I'd never seen before, and altogether there were about twenty-five of us.

When the day arrived, ShaSha dressed herself in a beautiful white lace dress that came down to the ground. She looked radiant, simply gorgeous. I was proud and without doubt the happiest man in the world that day.

We all jumped on to a couple of horse-carts and made our way through the streets with the jangle of the horse bells to accompany us. It was a typical Kashgar summer's day: cobalt-blue sky, hot with a trickle of wind filtering through the poplar trees. There was not enough room for everybody, so Adil and Raja brought up the rear on their bicycles, waving and shouting, 'Good luck to Jumahun and Sharapet. May you live forever and sire twenty sons.'

No. 1 Production Brigade (north park)

An shen li ming – One's life has the whereabouts and one's spirit has its entrustment.

Chinese saying

APART from running the veranda bar I had also started a horse-trekking business, hiring all the horses I needed from Mehemet Ili and then taking out groups of tourists across the high plains for an experience they would never forget. Working behind the bar made it easy to spread the word that I was leading treks, but the best advertisement was to gallop to and fro in front of the Oasis on my black stallion and let the customers see for themselves what fun could be had. I charged 100rmb for a whole day, with the freedom to gallop as fast as you like thrown in for free, and the riverside picnic outing, with kebabs and cold beer, for 130rmb, all inclusive.

I had devised an extraordinarily scenic route which on more than one occasion caused people to shed tears of joy. They loved it. Our picnics were like a dream, where time seemed to stand still. As we lay back on tufts of Siberian fescue, listening to the horses munching, four or five small boys might appear, shepherding their flock exactly as boys had done for the last two thousand years.

Once the tourists found out I was married to ShaSha, they immediately assumed that I was a local expert, and started coming to me for all sorts of advice and assistance.

'Where can I buy a nice carpet?'

'Where can I buy gold?'

'Could you help me buy a pair of riding boots at a good price?'

'Would you mind changing some money for me, please? I'm a bit wary of these black-market types.'

'Can you purchase two bus tickets to Turfan for us, please?'

The list of requests went on and on, and of course I could help them. If I couldn't, I soon found out how to.

ShaSha and I weren't able to make any immediate plans to leave Kashgar and go back to Britain because our next task was to apply for ShaSha's passport, and no doubt that would take a while. We were not too concerned because we were enjoying life where we were, and there was still the question of Nana's future to work out. But there was a good chance that we could make a move some time in the spring of 1990.

So, with the knowledge that we would be staying through the winter, we had to find ourselves somewhere to live, because the Oasis and the Friendship Hotel would be closed, and we didn't want to stay in a hotel. Tahir was all in favour of us buying a big house between us and sharing it. But we decided the most sensible thing for us to do would be rent a place, and in that way give ourselves the freedom to pack up and move on when we felt like it. Enlisting the help of everybody we knew, we started the search. We looked at several places around the town but none of them really appealed to me.

Time was moving on, but I was comforted by the knowledge that if the worst came to the worst we could always spend the winter in the Kashgar Guest-house. Then one day ShaSha's sister Akkuz came by with the news that my mother-in-law had found a place that might be suitable for us to rent in the Chamalvagh ('north park') area about ten minutes out of town by bicycle.

We went to take a look. The road had become a thick powder, six inches deep, and as our bikes surged through the drifts, we kicked up plumes of ochre-coloured dust that settled on our clothes like icing-sugar on a cake. We crossed a little bridge and climbed a steep hill with a baker's shop on the brow. Three dogs, disturbed from their siesta, leapt from a ditch, barking and trying to nip the tyres of our bikes, but gave up when I stopped to pick up a stone.

On our left were freshly cut corn fields surrounded by trees with silver leaves and birds darting through the branches, and there was the smell of approaching autumn in the air. Turning off the country track, we rode down a lane between high mud-brick walls and when we reached a little country mosque, we turned again, down an alley so narrow that we could touch both sides at the same time.

The alley had four compounds on either side. Stopping outside a blue double door with mulberry trees on either side, ShaSha said, 'This is it. Looks not bad, eh?'

ShaSha had been given the key by her sister so that we could go in and have a good look around without being hassled. The keys unlocked a massive bronze padlock that we clicked open like a pair of kids about to enter a secret garden. Pushing the doors wide apart, we wheeled our bikes into a huge compound. In the left-hand corner there was a whitewashed flat-roofed bungalow with a set of reddish-brown double doors in the centre. The yard was nothing but packed earth, with not a blade of grass to be seen.

We opened the doors into a room with what ShaSha called a *supa* taking up three-quarters of it. (A *supa* is a raised section of a room, used as an eating or sleeping area.) To the right a door led to a large bare room with two windows, and a door to the left led to another room containing a *supa*. There was brick flooring throughout, and a hole in the back wall of each room where you could attach the metal chimney-pipe of a cast-iron stove.

Painted in olive green to the dado line and white to the ceiling, the place looked clean and bright. It had electricity (one bulb hanging on a flex in every room) and water, by way of a tap in the yard. Basic, yes, but beautiful and brand new, and the whole thing faced south which was exactly what I wanted. We both agreed that it was perfect for us, and that it had loads of potential. I especially liked the big yard, and my imagination swept me away to a time somewhere in the future where I had a horse, some chickens, a couple of sheep and a garden full of flowers. Could it be done?

We'd been given the address of the landlord and, after locking up, went straight round to see him. He lived in an exact replica of the house we had just seen, only his must have been at least ten years old. The front of the bungalow was shaded from the sun by a grape-covered trellis with dark, ruby-coloured fruit hanging temptingly within reach. A path led to a garden crowded with heavily laden fruit trees and flowers that bloomed in a multitude of different shades. If he had told me it was called Eden, I'd have believed him.

He introduced himself as Apturyim and went on to explain that he had built both places with the help of his three sons. He had no daughters, a fact he seemed very proud of. He also wanted me to know that he was a man of means, that he had made his own fortune from the scrap-metal business, and that he was a good Muslim, respected in the area.

In light of our position, I acted with reverence and did my best to boost his ego, biding my time for the chance to ask, 'How much do you want for a year's rent, paid in advance?' I knew this was bound to sound attractive and would be very difficult to refuse. When the time finally arrived and I asked, I watched his face struggle for composure, trying his best not to look as if he was going to take advantage of me, and waited for some astronomical figure to be plucked from the air and thrown at my feet.

'Six hundred rmb,' he said at last. All of a sudden, I was the one struggling for composure. That was the equivalent of a hundred dollars! Had he misunderstood my question? Was that what he wanted for a month or a whole year? 'Yes, yes, for a year,' he replied when I asked.

I struggled to work out how much a week that was in pounds. Damn it – £1.40! 'Okay,' I said, and then in a surge of generosity, asked, 'You want it in dollars?' Of course he did, and I paid him on the spot.

The next week, ShaSha and I were busy moving stuff that she had stored in her grandmother's house up to Chamalvagh. I had friends on the lookout for old carpets, and was lucky to find some real beauties with the traditional Xinjiang *otchuk anna* (seeded pomegranate) designs in rich natural blues and reds, which immediately added warmth and character to our new house.

We went to Sunday Market and bought a stove. It got me a funny look. No wonder – it would've made a pretty odd souvenir, that's for sure. I picked up a cart-load of firewood on the way home and ordered a ton of coal. It was another world now. Kashgar had opened its doors and I was now part of it.

As soon as we laid the first *gilem* (carpet) on the *supa*, ShaSha and I moved in, but because Chamalvagh was twice the distance from Nana's school as the Oasis we let her stay on there for as long as the café was open so that it would be easier for her in the mornings.

I bought more carpets for the walls and potted plants to add some colour to the yard. I bought forty-five rose bushes and stuck them in the ground, urging them every day to grow tall. I bought a ewe and two lambs, and penned them in behind a wall of mud bricks. I bought fodder from the horse-cart boys and sometimes kept my rented stallion overnight on a bed of maize stalks next to the sheep. Standing on the roof, I could see the mountains on the horizon shimmering in a purple haze, defining the westernmost boundary of the Middle Kingdom, on the other side of which lay Kirghizia.

My new neighbours also spent a lot of time on their roofs, many of them sleeping there on hand-woven rugs during the heat of the hot summer nights. In the autumn they used the space to dry grass, tomatoes, apricots and chillis, creating a tapestry of colour on the skyline.

I got to know people all over, and they accepted me because they could see that I lived like they did. Aunt Aimahan came round and built a mud tandoor oven with her bare hands for us in the yard. It proved to be one of the most useful appliances we ever had, saving us on fuel and allowing the house to stay cool in the heat of the day.

ShaSha's mother came round, bringing Akkuz with her daughter Ramilah and half-sister Gularem. It wasn't long before it became a regular thing to have the house packed with women, all sitting cross-legged on the *supa*, chattering away in sing-song tones, gossiping and making *jiaozi*. I liked being a part of such an animated gathering. When my mother-in-law felt like a break from all the chat, she'd tip me a wink and we'd both pop outside for a spliff, as if it was the most natural thing in the world to do. And, in Kashgar, it was.

Finally, in late August, business at the Oasis started picking up. Travellers were coming in from all directions and from all walks of life. As a guide, I was coming into contact with all sorts – Belgian bankers, Dutch diamond dealers, the owner of a Maltese shipping company, and Gigi, a French photographer who was compiling a book on the last great horsemen of the world. There were journalists from *Time* and the *Far Eastern Economic Review* with too many questions, doing their best to convince us they were just taking a break. There were falcon smugglers, gold smugglers and dope smugglers galore – even more than the year before.

Eduard and Orashi showed up, then Peter and Cynthia, installing themselves in the same rooms at Chinibagh as the last time. But the old consul had become a depressing place that autumn. The Chinese authorities had decided to demolish the original admin building and build a new hotel with all mod cons to please foreign visitors. Which foreign visitors they were thinking of, I don't know, because most people liked the squalor of the old barracks – that was part of the magic. In fact, it was *all* of the magic.

By knocking it down, they were destroying the place's character and attraction, so there was no reason actually to stay there any more. It was as if the Chinese wanted to erase the memory of British colonialist ambitions, regardless of the historical value. Thankfully, they decided to leave the old residential block as it was, but for how long nobody knew. Cynthia did her best to preserve the memory of the admin block by painting it in watercolours from various different angles, just before the bulldozer came one bright sunny morning and reduced it into splinters, dust and rubble.

*

As Elizabeth, Eduard and Orashi loaded up with the dope they had stashed from the year before and split the scene, another gang of old hands hit town. From India came two Germans by the name of Frederick Peter and Krossi whom I had met in the Philippines. Long Dutch Derrick was in town, and a few weeks later Don arrived back from Austria with Wally and two more Germans, Rolla and Willy, in tow. Then two young English gold smugglers, Sim and Duke, arrived. Nobody knew how they had come to hear about Kashgar, but they were nevertheless accepted into the crowd like comrades to a revolution. Everybody wanted one thing and one thing only: to buy good quality, unadulterated hash in sizeable quantities to take to Japan or Europe. All eyes were on Thundernose as usual, waiting for him to come up with the goods.

The demolition of Chinibagh and the subsequent construction works had been too much for Thundernose, so he and Cynthia had found a new place to stay halfway down Dust Bazaar on the way to Id Kah. It was the Norbish, a local-style Uighur-run establishment which had previously been closed to foreigners. It wasn't long before the others followed suit and the owner, a shrewd operator named Amin Haji, had never had it so good.

Norbish had about twenty rooms on two floors around a central courtyard with a carved wooden veranda. The rooms were basic but the place had charm and character, accentuated by a manic-depressive room-boy called Mahmoud.

By the end of October Tahir could see no point in keeping the Oasis open any longer, as apart from the smugdrugglers, as they had become known, there weren't any other foreigners left. Li Jiangping's Hole in the Wall then took over as the number-one drinking spot.

The steady weekly rise in the price of tomatoes went hand in hand with the approach of winter. Melons were available all year round because they were stored in clamps but many other essentials like aubergines, courgettes and fresh coriander had already disappeared from the market stalls, and soon we were left with just cabbages, potatoes, carrots and dried capsicums.

The boys were getting restless again, just waiting, waiting, waiting. Then it happened. The dope arrived and everybody was flat out night and day, pressing it up. Most people were intending to move one or two kilos using the easier methods of concealment like shoes, books, cans and false-bottomed bags, but Don and Wally decided to up the stakes this time and had cooked up a much more ambitious scheme.

Go is a game that originated in China some three thousand years ago, and is today the national game of Japan. It is a game for two, played with black and white flatish, rounded stones usually on a solid wood board about eighteen inches square and about two inches thick. The board is squared off by nineteen vertical and nineteen horizontal lines, the object being to capture your opponent's stones and take control of the largest portion of the board. With the number of mathematical possibilities being 10 to the power of 720, it is a far more complicated game than chess.

Neither Don nor Wally was able to play *go*, but that didn't stop them wanting to send a few boards home. These would be boards with a difference, however. They planned to make five in all, each one capable of holding four kilos of the black stuff. They bought everything they needed in the bazaar and the department stores around Kashgar. With pieces of wood in all sizes, plus glue, clamps and saws all over the place, their room looked more like a furniture factory. Wally had been pressing using a jumbo-sized mortar and pestle so as to put more pressure on the pollen and speed up the process.

The job had been going really well, but the onset of some very cold weather caused problems to develop. It was taking longer and longer to press the hash up because they couldn't keep it warm enough. Another shopping spree was needed to buy electric cooker rings with which to heat up the dope. They bought six in all. When the lads weren't pressing, they kept the rings on to keep the room warm, causing Haji's electricity bill to go through the roof.

When the job was done, they wrapped up each board in the most professional manner with printed game instructions, a 'Made in China' guarantee and a receipt from a department store. They then hauled them all down to the post office and sent them to various European destinations. I agreed to take the mortar and pestle, the saws, the clamps, the heaters, Stanley knives, rolls of unused clingfilm, tape, pots of glue and tubes of Uhu up to my house. Maybe I could find a use for it all one day.

By mid-December nearly everybody had what they needed and they were all starting to leave in ones and twos, each following his own agenda. By Christmas only Thundernose and Cynthia were left, so we invited them round for ShaSha's first Christmas dinner. I felt almost like a missionary, but by the time we'd got through a pile of roast chicken, potatoes, peas, carrots and gravy, two cases of beer and six bottles of Turfan red, I was feeling more like a bacchanal.

News from London

Oh for a lodge in some wild wilderness,
Some boundless contiguity of shade,
Where rumour of oppression and deceit,
Of unsuccessful or successful war,
Will never reach me more.

William Cowper (1731–1800)

WHEN Peter and Cynthia finally departed for Hong Kong, I thought that I was the only *chetilik* left, but much to my surprise I discovered two Australians and a Greek hanging about town. I could see no reason why ordinary travellers would to want to endure the bitter cold of a Kashgar winter, and so I immediately assumed that they too must be smugdrugglers.

I never found out what the Aussies were up to, but the Greek, who actually lived in London, did his best to make me believe that he was some sort of antiques expert tracking down a rare piece of pre-Islamic art. Kashgar was the sort of town where everybody wanted to feel part of the intrigue, and it was always much better just to wait for them to give themselves away. By mid-January, though, even the Greek had decided to leave us all to the freezing wind and ice.

Twenty centimetres of snow fell in three days and then the temperature plummeted to -27°C at night, and afterwards only ever rose to about -8°C in the day. We managed to keep our house warm by stoking the cast-iron stove up until the whole thing glowed a bright cherry-red in the dark, and gave off so much heat that we could sit around in our underwear.

Outside, it was a different story. I needed boots, a padded *chapan* and a rabbitskin hat, but that wasn't enough to stop my beard turning into a solid block of ice in the short time that it took me to ride home from town of an evening. The water tap in the yard had long since frozen up, and we were having to carry water from a deep well quite some distance down the alley by the mosque. We used three buckets a day, which cost us the equivalent of three pence a month, or one penny per thousand gallons.

Our electricity bill came to £1 a month, and other weekly household expenditures were fruit and veg at 50p a week, yogurt at 12p per litre, three dozen eggs for £1 and 3kg of mutton for £2.70. Government-run shops sold meat and vegetables for half the price of the free market, but the quality was so poor you saved nothing by buying there. But the government depots did supply rice, flour, oil and vinegar at a discount price as long as you produced a *hukou* or resident's book. In that way, even the poorest families were able to acquire the basics. ShaSha was allowed to buy 25kg of flour for 9rmb (90p), 1kg of rice for 1.80rmb, a litre of oil for 2rmb, and five litres of vinegar for 3rmb. Each month on a specified day, both of us would go down to the depot. It was always a hive of activity, with queues of men, women and donkey-carts, everybody and everything covered in a fine coating of white flour. After filling our sacks, I draped them over my bike and slowly walked the mile and a half back home.

The ton of coal that I'd bought back in the autumn had come from Beicheng, a small mining town near Aksu that was renowned for hard coal. It had cost 150 yuan (£15), and was enough to see us through the winter. The cart-load of firewood had cost 15 yuan, but that disappeared fast and I would have to buy three of those before March was out.

After Thundernose left, even Li Jiangping's place closed down, so with nothing much to do of an afternoon I embarked on a Kashgar seedy-bar survey. Every afternoon I'd go out to find somewhere new to while away the hours and study the locals at play.

After visiting nearly thirty different bars, I chose five that soon became regular haunts. One of them was the Huiru Café, a rather sleek-looking joint down by the Yahwagh helter-skelter store. I called it Lanlan's after the girl who worked there. She'd also worked at the Oasis in the summer. It wasn't long before she got involved with the boss's son, but he turned out to be a right bastard and Lanlan's face was often bruised. Somehow she remained happy, though, and always found a new excuse to explain the marks away.

On the other side of Kashgar near the Chinese market was a classic seedy joint called the Red House Café. When you went in straight off the street it took about five minutes for your eyes to adjust to the dingy light that was supplied by two red bulbs in the ceiling. Apart from a couple of stools near the bar, the rest of the place was partitioned off into six cubicles, all with dirty red-velvet curtains for extra privacy. Every so often a little shriek or a giggle escaped from a recess and heads turned with knowing smiles and the odd nudge. Skinny young Chinese girls brazenly offered themselves for the price of a drink. Or had I misunderstood? I don't think so. After my second visit they realised that I wasn't interested. All I wanted to do was to drink a beer or two by the fire, write down my observations and savour the atmosphere.

On Semen Road was Fang Ping's place. As far as bars in Kashgar were concerned, this was quite a decent joint, but it too had the ever-popular dim lights and cubicles which the Kashgaris loved but which made me feel like I was on a train. A good fire was always stoked up, and ShaSha's schoolfriend Tutigul worked there, which meant cut-price beer. The clientèle varied greatly from black-marketeers and thieves to customs officers on leave from Pireli, film actors from Urumchi and an impotent Uighur police chief who desperately wanted a translation of the instructions to a so-called aphrodisiac that he had bought from a Pakistani in the autumn.

*

By late February, the winter started being overtaken by an early spring. Temperatures, although still well below freezing at night, were reaching an incredible 18°C during the day. Clear blue skies were only ever interrupted by the white of the doves gliding through the air. The Kashgar air was so clean that at night the stars didn't twinkle, they just hung there in a huge sky.

ShaSha and I were getting to know each other more every day, finding out our likes and dislikes, developing routines and quirky habits. Patience was needed sometimes but the power of our love steamrollered us through the odd difficult patch. We spent the long nights around the fire, smoking, drinking wine and talking, searching for each other's soul. We danced naked, I painted her picture on the wall and we made love in the glow of the stove.

Longer, warmer days saw the two of us playing badminton in the garden and taking long walks in the countryside behind our house. At the top end of the alley the road turned into a track which then cut through a field and passed the *mazar* where ShaSha's grandparents were buried. From there you could either turn back into the tree-lined lanes or meander down the hill, through a birch coppice and on to the banks of the river.

The spring seemed to activate my farming blood. I watched the locals prepare the land and felt a strong desire to join them. The simple agriculture which they practised attracted me much more than the mechanised, intensive disassociated version I had grown up with. These people ate the crops they grew. The sheep they kept were fed with scraps and treated like pets, and the stalks from the corn fuelled the fires that baked the bread made from the corn they had sown on the land fertilised by the manure from their own toilet. It was a direct relationship between man and earth, and seemed such an idyllic existence that I seriously considered looking for an acre or two of land to rent.

In the meantime, and to satisfy at least part of my yearning, I contented myself with the garden, every day tilling, planting seeds and planning a spectacular display of colour for the summer. I scratched out the design of our favourite carpet in the dust, marking where different flowers would bloom in the appropriate colours to match. I planted sunflowers, morning glory, nasturtiums and chrysanthemums. I put in a row of squash and six rows of maize and still hadn't covered the plot. I was engrossed with the task in hand, and it was as if I were cultivating nature's expression of our love.

Li Jiangping's opened up again, and I could happily quit my marathon bar-crawl and install myself back by the window in one of my favourite places. There were no other foreigners in town apart from Pasha Khan, a Gilgiti with a Tartar mother, and his friend Malik, a psychotic Pakistani with suicidal tendencies. Both had missed the last bus through the pass in the autumn and, not having enough money to go home via Hong Kong, remained shacked up in the Norbish all winter.

Unlike the Brits who had lived in Kashgar at the turn of the century, I had the luxury of a shortwave radio with which to keep in touch with events back home. I became almost nostalgic listening to *Just a Minute, Desert Island Discs*, Alistair Cooke's *Letter from America* and the football on a Saturday. However, one night in the third week of March while listening to the news at about two o'clock in the morning, half asleep and the worse for wear, I was immediately sobered up by a report that stated there had been a Muslim separatist uprising in the village of Aktu, 10km south of Kashgar. Although rather sketchy, the report went on to explain that members of the East Turkestan Separatist Movement had killed a number of Chinese soldiers at a small barracks and had taken a number of government officials hostage in an office building. Beijing had immediately sent a large number of troops from the provincial capital Urumchi to deal with the unrest.

What the hell was going on? How did the BBC know about it when I didn't? Who was in Kashgar supplying them with information? Was I going to come under suspicion of spying? Yes, more than likely. With these thoughts running riot through my head, I woke ShaSha and told her the news. She too wanted to know how London could find out about an event that none of the locals had heard of. I asked her what she knew about this secret army of freedom fighters and was shocked to hear that they were a real and significant threat to Chinese rule.

The history of Islamic separatism in Xinjiang had been long and at times as bloody as any revolution the world over, with uprising after uprising, all of which had either been crushed or had fallen apart as a result of in-fighting. After a hundred and fifty years in the hands of a succession of chaotic regimes, Chairman Mao moved in. He proceeded to dish out the same treatment to the Turkic minorities as he would do to the Tibetans. Any dissent would be paid back a hundred times. His two main tactics were to destroy the religious base and to dilute the population with the forced migration of hundreds of thousands of Han into the region. Mosques were torn down and communist apartment blocks went up in their place to house the immigrants. He would claim that before the so-called liberation, the Xinjiang people had been illiterate and had lived like animals. Communism had brought schools with books and pens and had helped raise the living standards of ordinary people. What he didn't say was that the books were full of lies, propaganda and disinformation, aimed at preventing the Uighur from learning the truth about their own past. Chinese schools were funded by the government, whereas Uighur schools had to make do with donations from local groups. Uighur children had no hope of securing a decent job if they were unable to speak, read and write *putong hua*. But going to a Chinese school meant forsaking their own culture.

Chinese-run factories were permitted to produce over-proof *baijiu* which was sold cheaply and aimed at the Uighur youth. (It is well known that even today Xinjiang *baijiu* is much stronger than that found anywhere else in China.) The wealth of Xinjiang was exploited and drained from the province with only a minuscule percentage of the profits finding its way back. Communes were set up around the cities for the incoming Chinese, while the Uighur were sent to reclaim the desert. Religious persecution and the destruction of hundreds of mosques sent Islam underground and with it the ashes of the Independent East Turkestan Republican movement.

The Red Army also cleansed the region of any remaining Soviet influence. Russian propaganda continued to flood in, however, by way of radio broadcasts and illegal literature. As far as rebellion and revolt were concerned, though, Xinjiang entered the quietest period it had enjoyed for over a hundred years – though that may well have a lot to do with communist suppression of the facts and not be a reflection of actual events.

For many years no one knew what had happened to the separatist movement. Some even believed it had been wiped out completely. But suddenly without warning in the spring of 1980 it raised its head and announced its return, and Kashgar was the scene of a serious uprising that resulted in the deaths of thousands of Han Chinese at the hands of ordinary citizens.

ShaSha remembered it well. At about eight o'clock one evening she had been riding her bicycle up the avenue on her way home from work at the Electric Company when she saw several gangs of Uighur youths with sticks and knives chasing panic-stricken Chinese men and women, beating them until they lay wounded and bleeding by the roadside. Because of her Chinese-style work clothes, she was mistaken for a Kithai and nearly dragged to the ground by a group of angry men. It was only when she spoke to them in Uighur that they realised she was one of them and let her go. An Uighur woman who had been watching ran out and pulled her quickly into her house to safety. Inside, ShaSha found twenty or so Chinese cowering in a small room, each one scared to death. The woman lent ShaSha an *etlass* dress and a headscarf so that she could make her way home with less chance of being beaten up.

As she pedalled as fast as she could, gangs of wild-eyed Uighurs roamed the streets unopposed, looking to kill anybody who looked remotely Chinese. Chants of 'Go home, Kithai!', 'Get out of Turkestan!' and 'Free East Turkestan!' could be heard echoing from different corners of town. As the word got round, more and more youths joined in, until there were so many out on the rampage that even the local police dared not venture out. The government offices behind Mao's statue were bombed and stones were hurled through the windows of other Chinese buildings all over town.

Kashgar was in the hands of the mob until the early hours, when suddenly everybody disappeared. As dawn broke there was no one to be seen on the streets of the city. It was as if they all knew that retribution was on its way. The incident had been reported immediately to Beijing, and ten hours later a platoon of crack troops was flown in from the capital. With the assistance of local police informers, they set about restoring order and rooting out the ring-leaders. Hundreds of arrests followed, but those who had instigated the revolt had already fled across the border to the USSR. A curfew was imposed and everybody was ordered to stay at home for a week.

Estimates vary as to how many people were killed, but it was certainly a far more serious incident than the Chinese media ever let on. Most people said that hundreds of bodies were carried away, some even estimating thousands. Whatever, it was a very different story to the sixteen or so casualties that Beijing admitted to.

*

The next morning ShaSha and I went off in different directions to try and find out what was going on. She went to her mother's house but nobody there had heard anything. I went down the bazaar to talk with the cart-drivers and the money-changers and got only vague looks and shrugged shoulders in response. If anybody did know, they were keeping very quiet about it. I rode every street that day looking for signs of unrest but all I found was that I was being tailed by two not so very undercover local police.

At first I couldn't be sure, but then I started to see the same two faces everywhere I went. While cycling a particularly busy bike lane I suddenly pulled off to one side to see who was following and what they would do about the unexpected change of direction. I propped the bike up and sat down on the verge to watch. Two pairs of sunglasses appeared in the crowd and when they saw me they started to brake. Then one decided against it and quickly ushered his mate on. I watched them continue to the next junction where they stopped and pulled over for a chat, all the time looking back in my direction. I crossed the road and rode as fast as I could back where I had just come from. Again, for no apparent reason, I pulled over and sat down on the verge, partly hidden by a tree trunk. Two minutes later my new friends were there again, panicking because I'd vanished. Suddenly they both spotted me, and it was then that I waved, and said, '*Ni hao* – hello.' At this, they turned their heads quickly in unison the other way, colliding with each other and almost causing a mid-lane pile-up. I was now certain they were police – any ordinary Chinese would have instinctively replied, '*Ni hao.*' Laughing, I walked my bike over the road and pedalled off at full pelt back the other way, and went through the same manoeuvre all over again. It was getting farcical, and I started to worry that they might just arrest me for taking the piss.

I decided that it would be best if I tried to lose them as quickly as possible, and the best place to do that was in the old bazaar. I knew it like the back of my hand and it was always so crowded that it was easy to get swallowed up and disappear in no time. If I could get three minutes on them I could park the bike and leg it to Li Jiangping's and sit it out there for the afternoon. My plan worked, and as I sat by the window staring out onto the street thinking about the bizarre position I suddenly found myself in, I saw the first sign that something really was going on.

A shrill voice, forced through a megaphone, could be heard coming steadily up the street, and it didn't need a genius to work out that this was a warning of some sort. Li Jiangping scuttled out to watch the approaching trucks, ten in all, each fully loaded with young soldiers standing to attention in the back. The lead truck was announcing a curfew, and anybody found on the streets between eleven o'clock that night and seven in the morning would be arrested. Li Jiangping didn't know what was going on exactly, but if there was a curfew then things were pretty bad. She was visibly worried, well aware of what could happen to a Chinese particularly in this part of town if the Uighur resorted to street violence to make their point. She apologised and said that she had to close up right away because there was no way she would be seen out after dark. I raced back home to tell ShaSha the news, and hoped that she might be able to tell me some of her own.

All she could do was confirm what I had heard on the radio and nothing more. That night I tuned in to the BBC for more news. They said fighting was continuing but that there were as yet no figures on any casualties. I had been everywhere that day and not seen one foreigner, so where was this information coming from? It was no wonder I was being followed all over town.

The next morning I was back out on the streets, asking my friends what was going on, but people were nervous and still knew very little. It was all a mixture of gossip and speculation which took a lot of filtering to find the truth. Army trucks draped with red banners and loaded with troops continued to flow through Kashgar, heading south. Jet fighters which looked like the Russian MiGs I'd seen in books as a kid appeared in the sky, zooming deliberately low over the city in twos and threes, making sure everybody knew they were there.

The same two cops (whom I'd christened Wang Dang and Doodle) were back on my tail, and I gave them a similar runaround as the day before, wondering if they were enjoying it as much as me. That afternoon, however, as I sat in Li Jiangping's, two Chinese, both with tinted spectacles and black leather jackets, walked in and immediately approached me, saying they were police. I'd never seen either of them in the PSB office before, and wondered which department they were from. I was almost certain that they were going to tell me to get out of town, and was trying to think of what to say as an excuse why I shouldn't. They tried their best to make it look as though they had found me by chance, but I knew that that wasn't possible.

'Passport, pulease,' said the one with three days' bumfluff on his chin. 'Whata you do 'ere? Tourist?'

'No, not really. I'm living here with my wife who is a Chinese subject.'

They knew very well who I was, and then went on to say, 'You can stay 'ere because you mally. That is our law, but it is betta if when you 'ere, you don't go talking to too many people because that is against law. Yes?'

'Sure, sure, sure, no problem. I understand perfectly.'

'Okay, *zaijian.*'

Before I had time to say '*zaijian*' back, they'd gone. Wow! My first official warning. But what a result, though – they were allowing me to stay after all.

Casualty figures started to be reported on the radio after about four or five days, and indicated that the Chinese were having a tough time. This news had obviously also been heard in the bazaar. There was a confidence in the air, and stallholders and hawkers were taking a far more belligerent attitude towards their Chinese customers than usual, and using the slightest of reasons as an excuse to tell them to go back to where they had come from.

As the days went by, a new type of aeroplane appeared in the skies, a much more modern machine that was a lot bigger and flew much higher than the little tin buckets I'd seen in the first few days.

One morning we were awakened by a cacophony of roaring and beating that shook the house to its foundations. I ran out, only to come face to face with a gigantic helicopter gunship hovering very close to our garden. Had they come to get me or what? I stared at it, and it seemed to stare right back at me as if we were two boxers in a ring waiting for the bell to sound. After a couple of minutes that had felt like an hour, the thing rose and arched out a path low into the valley, beating the air until it seemed to ripple all around. This became a regular occurrence every morning, and it appeared that the Chinese were using a nearby field as a temporary base.

It gradually became possible to piece together a vague picture of what was going on in the countryside. Apparently the rebels had originally planned to initiate twelve separate synchronised revolts in and around the Kashgar area which involved the storming of government buildings. What they had planned to do after that wasn't clear. To give themselves an element of surprise in attack, and a means of getaway that could negotiate a variety of terrain, the rebels chose to travel on horseback. Horses were also easy to maintain, and much easier to come by than motor vehicles.

During the winter of 1989–90 they set about buying the horses they needed in the various markets throughout the region, sometimes purchasing twenty or thirty animals at once. Such demand created a shortage which resulted in the prices shooting up and it became necessary to force the sale of a number of beasts from reluctant owners.

On one occasion in the village of Blaqsu, near Aktu, it seemed that a certain militia buyer had tried his best to convince one dealer that he would playing a noble part in the impending *jihad* or holy war against the insufferable Kithai. This had been overheard by a lay official who reported the matter to his superiors, but they had all but ignored the warning until a week later when another report came in. It appeared that one particular horse dealer had no intention of selling and no desire to support any holy war, refusing point-blank to part with his favourite stallion. The buyer, desperate to complete the shopping list on time, told him that if he didn't want to sell it was tough because he was going to take it anyway, and rode off with the horse.

Realising that there was something unusual going on, the local police sent four officers and an Uighur translator over in a jeep to check out the buyer in question. Unable to explain the unusual amount of animals corralled there, the young rebel panicked. He knew that he could not allow the Chinese to go back and report what they had seen, so he decided to kill them on the spot. Killing an Uighur brother was out of the question, however, and the translator's life was spared. He was allowed to go, swearing to keep his mouth shut.

When the other members of the cell found out what had happened, they knew it was only a matter of hours before they would all be exposed, so they decided to take the initiative and go through with their part of the mission one day ahead of the other groups.

The hostage situation at the government building in Aktu had not lasted twenty-four hours before the rebels realised the hopelessness of it. The Chinese were sending in troops by the truck-load and it was clear that very soon the place would be completely surrounded. If they were going to get out alive, they had to make a run for it under cover of darkness. That night they slipped out through the back, walked their horses quietly for about a mile and then bolted for the mountains. When the Chinese realised what had happened in the morning they gave chase, but upon reaching the foothills they had to abandon their trucks and proceed on foot.

News spread to the other rebel groups, who decided to abandon plan A and join the others in the mountains to fight a guerrilla offensive on the approaching Chinese infantry. Sweeping out from hidden positions they descended on the young PLA troops at full gallop, wielding swords and yelling, 'Death to the Chinese!' and 'Long live the Republic of East Turkestan!'

This scenario had not been mentioned in the training manuals of the Red Army, and the soldiers were simply not able to deal with a horde of extremely pissed-off Uighurs on horseback. The rebels cut and sliced their way through the ranks, decapitating and dismembering as they went. The Chinese turned tail, running in disarray in all directions.

The number of jet fighters patrolling the skies increased, and I started to see low-loaders laden with tanks parked up on the roadside on the way to Yengisar. Wang Dang and Doodle persisted in what had become for me a boring game of cat and mouse, and apart from the curfew life seemed to go on as normal. Then, one Sunday while perched in Li Jiangping's, I saw a westerner sitting next to a Japanese guy going past on a donkey-cart with their rucksacks piled up between them. That was strange. I knew that Kashgar would have to be a closed city by now, what with the uprising and everything, so how had these two got through?

Within half an hour I found out. The westerner walked into Li Jiangping's just like a regular, ordered a beer and sat down opposite me. Unmistakably German, he was short and in his late thirties, with the archetypal Weimar Berlin face made familiar by the paintings of Georg Grosz. Predatory piggy eyes with a bulbous snout punctuated by burst bloodvessels gazed at me in anticipation. I nodded and said hello. Little did I know that I had just initiated the most ill-fated of meetings.

'Hi, I'm Werner,' he said, and then asked me in accentless English if I were Rob, the same Rob who knew Fred and Krossi. I nodded and replied that I did indeed know of these people, whereupon he said, 'They told me that maybe you could help me out and find a piece of dope.'

Sipping my beer, I considered his request. He seemed genuine but I refused to say too much. I explained that it was a difficult time of year to find anything tidy, but agreed to see what I could do. He said he was in no hurry, willing to wait as long as it took.

In Urumchi he had heard that Kashgar was closed because of some unrest, and that they were refusing to sell foreigners bus and air tickets. He had then gone to Turfan, and been sold a ticket to Kashgar without any problem. He had moved into the Norbish and turned out to be a passionate beer drinker and a man after my own heart. We got on well from the start and met in the bar every day for a session of shooting the shit and quaffing ale.

When the weather was really warm we sat out on the pavement and watched the convoys of trucks go by carrying frightened and bedraggled youths gripping the metal rails with whitened knuckles. 'Was that a bullet?' Werner said one day out of the blue. Looking over my shoulder as a dark speck whistled past, I replied, 'No, mate, that was a bird.' After a few beers we'd start singing, 'Oh, what a lovely war,' and as the gunships clattered overhead we'd hoist our glasses and shout, '*Vive la révolution!*' We had no idea of the extent of the fighting. For all we knew, Kashgar could be overthrown and fall into rebel hands any day.

A month had gone by and the Chinese air force was conducting a twenty-four-hour-a-day surveillance of the mountain region trying to discover the location of the various rebel strongholds. As time went by, the separatists used up their hidden caches of food and ammunition until eventually the day came when they had no choice but to make a break for it. When they did, the Chinese mowed them down mercilessly. The Chinese radio was officially claiming that there had been twenty-eight deaths so far, but other sources said the figure was much higher. I heard that the rebels lost nine hundred men and that the Chinese had lost double that. That could hardly be described as a minor incident, which was what the Chinese media wanted us all to believe.

Twice Times Triplicate Squared

It has, I believe, been often remarked, that a hen is only an egg's way of making another egg.

Samuel Butler (1835–1902)

A MONTH had passed and the uprising had been quelled, but the authorities were still on the lookout for suspected rebels, and were conducting raids on the villages where they believed them to be hiding out. Werner was still in town, boozing and sleeping and doing nothing to secure the dope he needed. Eventually, without too much trouble, I managed to find a kilo of reasonably good stuff from the Pakistanis, and put Werner on to it.

With that, I thought I'd done my part, and that he would soon be gone. But he came to me and explained that it was very difficult to press and pack the dope in the hotel room, and that he was more than willing to pay me to do the job for him. He had picked up the hash for about two hundred dollars, and could well afford to dish out another hundred or so for me to plaque it up and wrap it. Expecting to make about four thousand dollars when he sold it back home in Germany, or double that in Japan, it was a small investment for a little peace of mind. A hundred dollars to me, of course, was nearly a month's living expenses, and certainly not to be sniffed at. And, anyway, it was money for old rope. I had all the gear necessary to do the job and I figured it would take me no longer than three or four hours to press it, roll it out, cut it to the required shape, wrap it and slip it into the shoes that Werner had brought specifically for the purpose.

When it was done, Werner spent a week walking about in his shoes, trying to get used to the feel of them and gain confidence. It was no good hobbling about because that would only draw attention. I had heard about a guy called Fat Moti who had stumbled through customs in Karachi barely able to lift one foot in front of the other. When customs officials pulled him over, they discovered he had about two kilos of gold packed into each boot. Moti had been too greedy and paid the price for it.

*

With Werner gone, ShaSha and I started thinking about applying for her passport. It turned out to entail another tour of government offices which by that time we both knew only too well. The first call was to the grandly named Kashgar (People's Republic of China) Bureau of Exit-Entry Administration of the Ministry of Public Security in a big building overlooking the boating lake. The woman there told us that ShaSha required a health certificate from the hospital, a notarised certificate from the local police station to prove that she had not been convicted of any crime or that she was under surveillance as a suspected member of an illegal organisation, a letter of recommendation from her work unit (or that of her father), a copy of her birth certificate and a letter explaining the reason for her application with a photocopy of our marriage certificate and eight photographs. To our amazement, we managed to amass what was needed in the space of a week and made the application for which we were charged three hundred yuan. It was an extraordinary sum of money, the equivalent of a month's wages to many people in Kashgar.

The woman informed us that we would be notified when the passport was ready – in about forty days' time – and that it would be necessary for us to go to Urumchi to pick it up. No problem; we had to go that way, anyway, and could simply pick it up on our way to Beijing to get ShaSha's UK visa.

Our plan was to apply for a tourist visa to start with, just to go home for a few months to see my parents, and then come back to Kashgar to deal with our affairs. In that way ShaSha could get an idea of life in Britain and decide if she liked it or not. We arranged for Nana to stay with Auntie Aimahan while we were away, where we were sure that she would be happy and well looked after. Time was running out for me, too: my visa had nearly a year's worth of extensions on it already, and money was disappearing fast. But Tahir had reopened the Oasis and I was getting plenty of work from all angles; there was always someone looking for a smoke and plenty of people eager to go horse-trekking.

The notification arrived at the end of May and ShaSha and I were back on the bus that I'd sworn never to take again, the three-day Hungarian express to Urumchi. But, even though I had bad memories of it, the journey never failed to amaze me. The desert always looked different and there was always the chance of an adventure. This time in Urumchi, we stayed with ShaSha's Aunt Amangul and cousins Ahmed and Emet in their apartment. The building, which belonged to the flour factory they worked at, was pure communist architecture at its very worst: drab and unfriendly with cold, dark corridors that smelt of wet concrete and dog piss. But this was more than made up for by the greeting we got from the family. We were looked upon as special guests, treated with the utmost kindness and generosity. I felt accepted immediately, and got on well with my new relations.

It took three minutes and one signature to get hold of that most prized of Chinese possessions, a document that allowed the bearer to leave the country: thirty-two pink pages bound by a brown cover with the communist emblem on the front, and valid for five years.

Within a day we were on the train again, doing seventy-two hours hard-seat to Beijing. By that time we'd logged up so many hours travelling that we took it all with a pinch of salt. There was nothing to it, as long as you were prepared. We had a good tin mug and plenty of top-quality noodles, because the stuff they sold in the stations tasted like cardboard.

When we arrived in Beijing it was hot, sticky and crowded. There were still a good number of police about but nothing like the year before, which made for a much more relaxed atmosphere. Looking for somewhere a bit more peaceful, we booked into the Qing Hua Hotel near the Beijing Language Institute. Compared to the centre of town, it was a giveaway at fifty yuan a night and at least comparable to a British three-star hotel. The fact that it took nearly an hour to get there from the station was made up for by the presence of a decent bar scene and loads of foreign students in party mood.

The day after we arrived, ShaSha and I went straight to the British embassy. I was confident that we would be dealt with quickly and efficiently by professional civil servants in a way that it would put the Chinese bureaucrats to shame. I was expecting to wait a week at most for ShaSha's visa to be processed, and that within ten days we would be on our way to London. We were both excited at the prospect and had started to plan what presents we could take home for my parents. I also had loads of plans and ideas for us when we got there. We were going to have a good time, that was for sure.

The Visa Section was not what I'd expected. It was rather cramped and far too small for the queues of Chinese applying for visas. Taking an application form for a British tourist visa, we sat down and filled in the details. A sign above the counter informed us that in the event of a visa being denied, all charges were non-refundable. The fee for a tourist visa was 360 yuan, and for a settlement visa 1,830 yuan. It was a good job that we weren't applying for settlement then, because we didn't have enough to pay for that and our tickets. I still had an international money order for two thousand pounds, but I was afraid that it would take forever to change in Beijing and preferred to deal with it in Hong Kong. Handing in the application form, I asked politely how long it was going to take. A miserable-looking man with a beard, corduroy trousers and a jacket with leather patches on the elbows looked up and said, 'You will be notified by post of a date when you will both be required to attend an interview here in the visa section.'

'I see,' I replied, actually seeing nothing at all. 'And how long will it take for the notification to come through?'

'We're very busy as you can see, so I should say in about six weeks.'

I ran what he was telling me through my brain again, and exclaimed, 'Six weeks! Are you sure it can't be done any quicker than that?'

'No, sir, that's the quickest.'

My head was thumping as I considered what effect this had on all our plans. There was no way we could stay in Beijing for six weeks because not only would we be broke but my own visa would expire. Looking at the man, whose nameplate revealed him to be Mr D.G. Morris, I said, 'Have you any idea how long it took us to get here?'

'No, I haven't,' he replied curtly.

'Nine days, it took, and what you're telling us now is that we should go back to where we came from, which will take another nine days, wait for your notification, and then take another nine days to come back for an interview. Right? Do you think that's reasonable? I can't afford to stay in Beijing for six weeks, and I don't see why I should be expected to do so. Do you provide accommodation? Or maybe we could bed down here – it's no worse than the train, is it?' He tried to say something, but I was in full flow. 'Do all visa applicants from Xinjiang have to travel 12,000km to get a visa? Or perhaps by the time they've spent all their money on tickets back and forth across the continent and then lost their jobs through absenteeism, they're too broke to go anywhere anyway?'

'Sir, I should like to –'

'Please don't give me some excuse. I'd like to speak to your superior.'

The look on Mr Morris's face told me he couldn't have given a shit where the hell we'd come from, and he was getting just as annoyed as I was. 'I happen to be the chief officer in this section,' he snapped, 'and I am quite capable of dealing with whatever problems you have.'

'Okay,' I said, trying to keep calm. 'I want to make an official request that unusual circumstances be taken into consideration, thus making it possible for you to grant my wife and I an interview on a date that is both convenient and manageable so that we are not forced to endure unnecessary hardship or be subjected to unreasonable expense. If it is within your power to grant us an interview within the next week, we should be extremely grateful.'

'Okay,' he said, 'you can have the interview this afternoon at one-thirty. Is that all right?'

I got the impression he was taking the piss but I replied, 'Yes, that would be wonderful. Thank you kindly.'

Half past one came and as soon as we entered the building Mr Morris appeared and said that he would be talking to ShaSha first, so would I mind waiting.

'But who's going to translate?' I asked. 'You'll need me to –'

'No, we won't, Mr Davies, we have our own translators, thank you.'

Watching her being led away was like seeing her being sent to the gallows. What was going to happen to her in there? Half an hour passed, and I was just lighting up my fifth cigarette when she emerged from a long, narrow room lined with tall windows, looking calm but worn out.

'If you will,' said Morris, sweeping his hand in the direction of the door.

As I entered the room and sat down on one of those moulded plastic chairs with metal pipe legs and a springy back that you see in waiting-rooms all over Britain, I felt quietly confident, not for one moment thinking that there could be anything that could hinder our progress. Mr Morris sat opposite me with a big blue folder open wide in front of him. Shuffling a bundle of papers he went on to ask me a number of introductory questions. Where was I born? Where was I schooled? How many O-levels did I have? Had I been to college? And then to the first obstacle: Where did I work?

'Well, I help my brother-in-law in his restaurant in Kashgar,' I said.

Mr Morris looked up. 'Sorry, where was that?'

'Kashgar,' I replied.

'You mean you haven't got a job in Britain?'

'No. I left Britain two years ago, and met my wife-to-be on my way overland to Australia.'

'What do you do for money, Mr Davies?' he asked.

'Savings, and I earn my keep,' I replied.

'How did you meet your wife?'

'I met her in her brother's restaurant where she was the manageress.'

'In a restaurant?' said Mr Morris as if I'd said 'topless bar'. 'Do you speak Chinese?'

'No, I don't.'

'Does your wife speak English?'

'No, she doesn't,' I replied, knowing full well he'd just interviewed her.

'Then pray tell me how you manage to communicate with each other?' He looked as though he thought he'd won the game with that one.

Leaving just enough space for effect, I said, 'We speak Uighur.'

He looked at me with his head tilted to one side like a dog, and asked, 'What's that, then?'

If he doesn't even know what Uighur is, I thought, how the hell can he be qualified to deal with us? Patiently, I gave him a full explanation about Xinjiang, and I could tell that it was all news to him. He must have dropped geography in his first year.

He took down a few notes, let out a 'umph', and then continued with, 'Were you perhaps offered some incentive to marry your wife?'

I saw what he was getting at. 'No,' I replied in a rather indignant tone.

'Why does your wife want a tourist visa?' This was the next stage, and I could tell it was the nitty-gritty, because he was using a more official tone. I told him that we just wanted to go and visit my folks and then come back to sort out our affairs. Moreover, it was cheaper and hopefully a lot less hassle than a settlement visa.

'So your wife doesn't want to settle in Britain?'

'She hasn't decided on that yet,' I answered.

'Does her daughter want to go to Britain?'

'Possibly, but not in the immediate future because she is still at school and at a crucial stage.'

Mr Morris stopped and looked at me, and after a pause, said, 'I put it to you that if your wife is issued with a tourist visa, she has every intention of staying in Britain and will try to do so without the knowledge of the authorities.'

What the hell was he talking about? I was certain the bastard was looking for any excuse, no matter how small, to stop us. 'No, no, no! She's coming back! We are coming back! She has her daughter to think of.'

'Pshaw,' he blew. 'It's not unusual for Chinese women to run out on their children. And if that's not the case, they wait until they have melted into British society and then invite their children, their brothers, sisters, mothers, fathers and grandparents over to visit, who also suddenly and conveniently disappear from view. I think we have covered almost everything now, Mr Davies. Thank you. Would you mind waiting outside, please?'

'How did it go with you, Shash?' I asked as soon as I saw her sitting there.

'I don't think I was very good. Too many questions I didn't know the answer to, like, your grandmother's name and your parents' address. We never talked about these things, and anyway I cannot remember these Welsh names, they're very difficult – all that "llech" and "ach" and "wlch".'

I couldn't believe it. What did my grandmother's name have to do with our marriage? If you didn't know the answer, was the visa denied? But even though we'd been given a hard time, I could still see no reason for them to not grant ShaSha's visa. I was a British subject making the application together with my wife, and that surely had to count for something.

As these thoughts ran through my exhausted brain, Mr Morris appeared, and called us over to the glass-faced counter. He held ShaSha's passport in his hands, and I thought, 'Yes! There's the visa.'

'Ms Sharif, I regret to inform you that your application for a British tourist visa has been rejected. If you do not accept this decision, you can appeal to the Immigration Appeals Office at this address here in Hayes in Middlesex.'

Anger was not the word for the feeling that was pulsing through my veins at that moment. I was stunned and in no doubt that he'd made that decision purely on a personal level, just because I'd lost my temper with him that morning. How dare he allow his personal feelings to influence his judgement? He was supposed to be a professional. If this guy was a postman and he took a dislike to you, he'd be the sort to not put your letters through the door. How was this possible, and in our bloody embassy to boot? If it had been the Chinese, I could've accepted it – it would've been what I'd expected, even.

As I stared at him, hating him with all my heart, I understood that it was no accident that he was now standing behind the glass telling us this.

'Could we please be given a reason for your decision?' I managed.

'I am afraid I am not at liberty to reveal details of the decision-making process, but I can tell you that after discussing certain aspects that came to light during the interview, we have come to the conclusion that the marriage is not sound.' With that he closed the blue file, and pushed ShaSha's passport over the counter.

'What do you mean, "not sound"?' I retorted, raising my voice to such a level that all the other applicants turned to see what was going on. 'Where the hell is the proof to say a thing like that?'

Mr Morris looked tired, but no more than I felt, and he continued: 'There is also some doubt as to your wife's intentions, you see, because her passport indicates that it is her intention to settle in the United Kingdom, and yet she is here today applying for a tourist visa, denying that she intends to settle.'

I had no idea what he was talking about. 'What and where is this indication, please?'

He picked up the passport, opened it and pointed to a slip of paper stapled to the seventh page. It was all in Chinese so I asked ShaSha to translate it for me. Sure enough, it said that she intended to settle. Why had no one pointed this out to me sooner? Even ShaSha had not seen it.

Morris went on: 'There is also the question surrounding custody of your wife's daughter. It has to be made clear one way or the other. Do you wish to adopt or will you relinquish custody to the natural father? Either way, the child must be taken care of legally.'

I felt drained. I knew then that no amount of arguing was going to change his mind. We were nothing, squashed like a pair of insects underfoot.

We left the building in silence, crestfallen and weary. What to do next, indeed? I did my best to reassure ShaSha that everything was gong to be okay, but it looked as though I might have to go back home without her, and I didn't want to do that. I believed strongly that once a man and woman were married no outside force should be able to part them. How could I be expected to go home without my wife? Why should some bastard in an office have the power to dictate whether we stayed together or not? If I was going to stay with ShaSha in China, however, there was no getting away from the fact that I had to go to Hong Kong to get a new visa. I could set the appeal in motion from there by telephone, enlisting the assistance of the family lawyer.

Since ShaSha couldn't leave now, there was no need for her to undergo the agonies of a further train trip, so she agreed to head back to Urumchi and wait for me there. I jumped on a hard-seat to Guangzhou, promising to see her before the week was out. At forty hours, it was a relatively short journey and, to my amazement, I was in and out of Hong Kong within two days with both money and visa. Back in Guangzhou, though, I decided I'd probably go insane if I had to endure the 108-hour hard-seat to Urumchi by myself, so I took a flight instead, and left that very morning on the eleven o'clock plane. Five hours later I was in Urumchi, stupefied by modern technology and so happy I'd eliminated the hardship of China Railways that I could have cried.

Careful with That Axe

An xia hu lu fu qi piao – Hardly has one gourd been pushed under the water when another bobs up.

Chinese saying

THE three weeks we'd been away felt more like three months, and I was happy to be back. My garden had erupted into a psychedelic jungle that barely allowed us to reach the front door, as climbers and vines stretched their tentacles up, over and around the path. The sunflowers, already chest-high, fluttered their huge green leaves as if in welcome.

Summer was always a joy in Kashgar – a tapestry of vivid colours with the smell of ripening corn and fruit wafting through the air, intoxicating and inviting. The tourist season was in full flow and I was soon leading groups of trekkers into the countryside for a taste of paradise again. Thundernose and Cynthia were the first of the heads to arrive back in town, but it didn't take long before a whole hoard of Asia freaks drifted in, all looking for a piece and the peace to smoke it in. And, more often than not, it was to me that they came to help them in their quest.

Dicky Mint and Nicola were old friends from home who had popped over to see me and ShaSha while they toured Asia. Dick and I had picked potatoes together in South Wales, harvested grapes together in the South of France, and worked side by side on a giant concrete mixer in a factory in our home town. We'd organised huge raves on the banks of the river before the concept of rave was ever known, and we'd plucked the odd salmon from cold pools on dark nights only a hundred yards from the gamekeeper.

As soon as they arrived, we embarked upon a four-month-long reunion bash. As we talked, Dick told me that my name was being banded about as far down the highway as Rawalpindi as a man who could assist in the procurement of combustible substances. I should have taken that as a warning but I was too busy making the same mistake that most people operating on the edge of the law make: I was basking in my own notoriety. But Kashgar was a fairly liberal town, and I'd never heard of anyone here being busted properly. There had been a rumour about some guy being stopped for dope at the airport – all he'd got was a 1,000 FEC fine and been refused a visa extension.

*

Cycling past Li Jiangping's one afternoon, ShaSha and I suddenly heard a girl shouting our names. As we pulled over to see what the fuss was about, Marie, a

French friend of ours who was studying the Chinese language in Beijing, came running up the pavement towards us, waving her arms and obviously in some distress.

'What's the matter?' I asked, thinking that she was maybe suffering from heatstroke or that she'd lost her passport.

'It's Kang!' she gasped. 'He's out of jail and back in Kashgar looking for you and ShaSha!'

Oh fuck, I thought, that's all we need. 'How do you know?' I asked, trying to remain calm. 'Have you seen him?'

'Yes, yes. I was at Tahir's house yesterday evening looking at some of his carpets when Kang and a huge monster friend of his from jail broke the door down and burst in. He demanded to know where you were but Tahir refused to tell him. Then the big one grabbed him and Kang hit him in the mouth, threatening to kill him if he didn't tell. I tried to get him off but he punched me in the face and knocked me down. They realised then that I was a foreigner and sort of backed off a bit.'

I looked at ShaSha as Marie told her the same thing in Chinese, and I was relieved to see that she showed no sign of any panic at all. I envied ShaSha's ability to remain ice cool in the hottest of situations, and wondered how she managed it. 'What the fuck do we do now then?' I said.

'He doesn't know where you live, or what Rob looks like,' said Marie trying to help.

'Okay. We keep away from all the places he knows, like Tahir's, Aimahan's, ShaSha's mother's, and her father's place. We also keep away from home because if he does find it, it's too isolated, too far from the cops and there's nobody near by to raise the alarm if he attacks us. I think the best place is the storeroom of the veranda bar. We can lock ourselves in there pretty securely, and there's always loads of people about. How's that sound?'

Everybody agreed and the three of us went back to the house to throw a few overnight things into a bag. Just as we were about to leave, though, there was a bang on the door and I was terrified it was Kang and his henchman.

'Hey, Rob, it's me – Tahir,' said a voice.

Thank God for that. I undid the padlock and opened the doors. Tahir walked in with a bag from which he withdrew an axe.

'Here,' he said. 'You're going to need this.'

I looked at the chopper, and then at Tahir. 'Are you serious?'

'Sure, I'm serious. Kang is a bad bastard and capable of anything. You've seen the scars on ShaSha, right? And he's very angry that she's run off with you.'

'Oh, that's sweet. Don't tell me that trying to stab her to death was a sign of his love. He's got no fucking right to be angry. Shit, ShaSha's the one who should be angry.'

'You're still going to need this, no matter who's angry. I bought two this morning, one for you and one for me, and got them sharpened in the bazaar.'

'And what the fuck happens if I split his head open with the bloody thing?'

'It won't matter. The police will be glad he's out of their way at last. They won't do anything to you.'

I wasn't so sure about that, but I agreed that it wouldn't be such a bad thing to have on me just in case. Even if it only frightened him and his goon a bit, it might give me the extra time needed to make a run for it.

When I showed ShaSha the small axe with its blade all honed up and glinting in the sun, she conceded that it might well be useful and that she felt more secure knowing I was armed.

After Tahir left, we discussed whether it was prudent to go to the police and inform them of the situation. I wasn't keen but ShaSha thought that it might be for the best. Everyone seemed to be quite calm about the whole thing, just talking matter-of-factly about axing some guy without fear of any repercussions. This was Kashgar, after all, and it did seem to fit in with everything else that went on there.

Early the next morning after a night in the storeroom, ShaSha and I went down to the PSB to let them know that Kang was back and on the prowl. The Chinese officer, whom I knew from when I'd been arrested for supposedly attacking the manager of Chinibagh, seemed nonplussed by the whole thing, and told me that they already knew that Kang was in town.

'What happens if I accidentally kill him if he breaks into my house or attacks me in a bar?'

'Don't worry about it – you just protect yourself,' he said as if rather bored with it all.

'You mean I won't be prosecuted if I kill him?' I asked, not really believing what I was saying.

'No.' By this time he'd had enough, and without another word he left the room.

'That's it, then, Shash – a licence to kill, just like 007,' I joked as we left the building, looking at the bag containing the hatchet strapped to the front of my bike.

I had never met Kang or even seen a photograph of him, but I had no problem recognising him when he walked into Li Jiangping's that afternoon. He was unmistakably Chinese but unusually tall and with thick glasses and his arms were a mess of crudely done jail tattoos which only added to the ugliness of his general appearance. The guy was an out-and-out criminal and wanted everyone to know it. The sixteen-stone tough whom he had in tow was straight out of a Jackie Chan movie and looked as if he could take a punch like it was a mosquito bite. It would need more than a little chopper to knock him down, that was for sure.

Kang clearly didn't know who I was, but I knew that he was asking Li Jiangping if I had been there that day. She told him that she didn't know exactly who I was, because all foreigners looked the same. Of the three other foreigners there, only Thundernose knew what was going on, and that's the way we kept it. Kang left and I blew a sigh of relief.

'Just knock his glasses off,' was Peter's friendly advice when they left. 'Without those milk bottles, he won't be able to see a thing.'

It was inevitable that I was going to have to come face to face with this thug some time or another, but not knowing when or where it was going to happen really bugged me.

A week passed and I was starting to hope that he might just have faded away, when he walked into the Oasis and sat down. He'd come on his own – a sign of a more moderate approach, perhaps? I was doing my stint behind the bar at the time, and watched as he called Tahir over for a word. After a few minutes Tahir came back and he and I went down to the kitchen to talk. With ShaSha present, he explained that Kang had assured him that he had not come for trouble. He only wanted to speak with ShaSha about Nana's future. Since he was her father, it was the only right thing to do, but I was not going to allow her to be alone with him. If he wanted to speak to ShaSha, he would have to speak to me too.

We went back upstairs and walked over to the table where Kang sat waiting. Without any pleasantries we took our places opposite. I took off my knife and placed it on the table in front of me, partly as a sign of goodwill but more to let him know that I had it. After a rather stand-offish greeting I was introduced and we shook hands. I tried to make it as firm as possible, as if it wasn't costing me any effort at all, suggesting that I was incredibly strong and that such a solid grip came naturally. Who the fuck was I kidding?

ShaSha and Kang spoke in *putong hua*, so I was at a loss as to what they said. For a long time afterwards, I believed that it was a straightforward discussion about custody but, as I sat there oblivious, Kang was telling ShaSha that it wouldn't cost him very much to have me murdered and that if she didn't agree to hand over Nana, that's exactly what he would do.

I was totally against the idea of handing over the little girl, but even in my ignorance I could see that it might be the only way we could agree to find a peaceable solution. ShaSha loved Nana but sometimes she saw Kang's eyes looking back at her which caused her to recoil in fear as the memories of that bloody night came alive again. She knew that she had to find a way to get Kang out of her life forever, and it seemed like the only way to do that was to let him have Nana and thus eliminate his reason to visit her. Tahir believed that by refusing we would simply be asking for trouble. We would have Kang casting a shadow upon our lives for as long as we lived, making not only ShaSha's and my life hell, but Nana's too. We would be defeating the object of holding on to her.

The most important opinion of all, of course, was Nana's. We sat her down and explained as best we could what was going on, and then asked if she would like to go away with her father. Nana, although not jumping for joy, was surprisingly agreeable to the idea. She said that she was happy to be with him and that over the last few days when Kang had taken her to the park, to the cinema and to the boating lake they had had a really good time. At least he had taken the time to start building a little trust, but three pleasant afternoons were hardly the basis of an enduring relationship. Not in my mind, anyway.

In the end, it was a family decision, and the family made that decision, for better or worse. Nana went off to live with her father and his family in a small village in Hebei Province. It was a sad day for all of us when she left. She had always been a centre of attention and a really fun kid. She had called me Jumahun Dada, and accepted me as her father ever since the marriage, and we had got on well. At least now I could get rid of the axe and the immense pressure that went with carrying it every day.

*

In late August Werner rolled back into town with a sidekick called Dieter glued to his side. Dieter wore small, black-rimmed, insanely ugly spectacles that made his eyes look like piss-holes in the snow, and said 'eh' in the voice of a dalek all the time. But, like Werner, he loved to drink, so together with me and Dicky we made a hell of a team. Li Jiangping was raking it in.

Werner and friend had done a tour of China before coming to Kashgar, and they gave us a brilliant report on Hainan island: good weather, unspoilt beaches and loads of cheap, fresh seafood. It sounded like the way Ko Pha N'gan and Ko Samui had been a decade ago, before they got fucked up by developers and package tourists. I'd heard enough, and made up my mind that we were not going to spend another frozen winter in Kashgar. I'd take ShaSha to Hainan for the honeymoon we'd never had.

By November only the diehards were left, waiting once more for the harvest to roll in. Dicky and Nicola had gone to Hong Kong, hoping to find some work and make enough money to get home. Sim and Duke appeared with Wally and Willy close behind, and this time they had brought their girlfriends along to keep the bed warm. Thundernose arrived back and the party was nearly complete. Then Dicky showed up again, this time Nicola-less. He explained that she'd easily found a job in HK working in a bar but that it had been impossible for him. Somehow he'd calculated that it was cheaper to stay in Kashgar than HK and had returned. It was a great excuse to sit in Li Jiangping's Hole in the Wall again, shoot the shit with the team and spend crazy nights zooming around Kashgar on Timothy Leary's bike.

*

In the late autumn of that year I had been introduced to a man who was a friend of a friend from Kizilsu, a settlement on the edge of the Taklamakan. His name was Batur, and he stood tall with a thick bushy moustache and eyes that burnt like coal. Batur was all Turk, and I could easily imagine him on horseback wielding his *yataghan* in defence of his nation. He was a farmer with a small-holding and a part-time job moving earth for a nearby commune. There was no pot of gold at the end of his rainbow, but like most Uighur he had a quality of life that made us in the western world look like poor neighbours in comparison. He had fresh milk and curds every morning, organic vegetables, mutton from his own sheep, nuts and fruit from his own orchard, fresh clean water, blue skies, a donkey-cart to go places and a pace of life that allowed him to savour it all. VCRs, colour televisions, aluminium wheels for the car, Paul Smith shirts and the internet were totally meaningless and useless accoutrements for him.

On our first meeting in the Oasis, Batur had offered me a lump of pollen about the size of a matchbox, which I took gratefully out of interest, moulding it and pressing it in my hands as we continued with our conversation. In less than two minutes it was black and sticky, giving off a pungent perfume that conjured up the vision of a luxuriant plantation, full of ganga with the sap crystallising and shining on the leaves. I put a light to a thin string of it that I'd rolled out like Plasticine, and rubbed the ash between my fingers. It had all burnt at the same speed and temperature, leaving a smooth, consistent powder which told me that it was as clean as clean could be. This was the stuff everybody had been searching for. There was no need for any machinery to knock this beauty in to shape – it was simply top quality.

Batur said that he had about three kilos of it stashed away, but could probably find a lot more of the same if I needed it. I knew that it would be easy to pass that sort of gear on, and arranged for my new business acquaintance to come round my house and drop it off. Thundernose over the years had fixed his price at two hundred dollars a kilo. I suspected that he was probably paying about fifty dollars a kilo, which was quite a common around Kashgar, but when Batur asked me for the equivalent of twenty-five dollars a kilo, I had a completely new insight into what was going on. Furthermore, I felt that I was hardly committing any crime when the stuff was more or less being given away.

Dicky had been sleeping off the exertion of an alcoholic nightmare in which he had been ravaged by a warrior Uighur lesbian in pink knickers, but was woken by a waft of the most piquant-smelling dope in the world. Sitting bolt upright, he found me trying to weigh it out, with lumps of pollen the size of sugar bags strewn all over the floor.

Back in Britain, buying our poxy little eighth of an ounce every Friday night for twelve quid, we had always dreamt of a time when we could be surrounded by the stuff, and now that dream had nearly come true. There were 877.5 eighths sitting there, with a street value in Britain of £10,530, all of which I had paid about forty quid for. It was enough to take your breath away.

Two kilos of that consignment went to Werner and Dieter, and the rest I kept for personal use. It was such a pleasant smoke, I simply refused to sell it. Batur thought his numbers had come up, and within a few weeks was round at the house again with another three kilos, only this time it wasn't half as good, and I told him I didn't want it. He thought for a moment and said, 'I can't take it back now because it's too dangerous. Coming to Kashgar is no problem because there are no checks, but going back is a nightmare. You take the stuff and I won't charge you for it. Next time I'll come with good stuff. Okay?'

My God, I thought, it couldn't get any cheaper than that, could it? Anyway, I had no option but to agree, and promised to see him soon.

I quickly pressed up a kilo and stashed it under the floor of the kitchen where it would be well preserved. The rest I buried in a hole in the garden, postponing the decision of what to do with it until later. Before ten days had passed, Batur was back with another find, and this time it was even worse than before. All of his crowd smoked it in the pollen state with their *mahouka*, never bothering to press it up, and he really couldn't tell the difference between good and bad dope, even after I had shown him. Again he left it at my house, but I couldn't go on stashing dope in holes all over the garden, and knew that I had to get rid of it one way or the other.

I decided to sink it in the river, and so, bright and early one morning, I took a bag filled with stones and the bundles of unwanted contra to the banks of the Tooman River at the back of our house. I threw it in, expecting it to disappear immediately. No such luck. The bloody thing floated off down in the fast-flowing current, around a bend and out of sight. I ran along the bank, hoping that it would get caught up in some branches, but the bag continued on towards Kashgar.

All of a sudden, I spotted two men bathing further on downstream, and knew that I had to do something or else the dope was going to sail right into them. There was no time to strip off, so I jumped into the swirling waters and struggled to catch up with the bag of hash. I was swimming as fast as I'd ever swum in my life, and just managed to grab hold of it about fifty metres or so in front of the naked men. They had been so busy comparing genitalia that they were completely oblivious to my antics. I quickly stabbed a hole in the plastic to let the air out and the water in. It sank, and for good measure I dived under and found a stone to keep it there.

Honeymooning

The appetite grows by eating.
François Rabelais (?1494–1553)

AFTER the crowd had split, ShaSha and I decided we needed a break and set off for Hainan. Getting there was the most gruelling trip we'd ever undertaken. Three days' bus to Urumchi, four days' hard-seat to Guangzhou, and then 36 hours' 'hard boat' to Sanya. But it was worth it. The island, situated at the southernmost limit of the Middle Kingdom, was China's largest, and enjoyed an all-year-round tropical climate with an average temperature of 25ºC. It was covered in luxuriant tropical forests, rice paddies, orchards and coconut plantations. The sea that washed its shores was bountiful and was harvested by thousands of fishermen who balanced precariously on wooden junks that bobbed in and out of view as the waves crested and fell. Pristine white beaches lapped by the crystal blue waters of the South China Sea were almost deserted in the winter of 1990. Tourism was something that had not really arrived, but the odd building-site indicated that it was fast approaching.

We found a neat little hotel called the Holiday Inn in Dadong Hai. It was a ten-minute cycle-taxi ride from the port and just a two-minute walk from one of the best beaches in the world. After seeing the room, I made it clear that we intended to stay for at least three months. So, for the equivalent of two pounds a night, we had a spacious room with a cooking area out back, a shower, a fan, mosquito nets and a covered veranda looking out over the ornamental garden of the inner courtyard of the single-storey complex. There was a restaurant selling platefuls of fresh crab and a bar that sold cold beers for as long as you wanted to drink.

The place was far from full but the guests seemed to fall into just two categories, smokers and drinkers. A group of six German freaks, three guys and three girls, had already been there for at least a month, and intended to stay on for another two. They spent their days passing joints, lying on the beach and having sex. Joe, a sixty-five-year-old ex-US merchant navy boiler engineer, was doing his second spell at the hotel, but because of his excessive drinking and habit of cursing the Chinese for trying to poison him, it looked as though he might get thrown out at any moment. Gripping a small pink plastic microphone, he would stagger from his room, zigzag across the lawn and proceed to give a discourse on the faults and crimes of the Chinese as a whole.

Next to our room were two Danish hash smugglers, one of whom we'd met in Guangzhou on the way. They'd got their gear in Canton and brought it down to Hainan to pack. They had bought hundreds of bars of Bee and Honey Sandalwood soap, which they'd emptied out of its packaging, and were busy replacing the soap with hand-moulded pieces of hash they'd heat-sealed in clingfilm. The post office must have thought they were really clean guys when they posted it all back to Copenhagen.

A week after we arrived, Wally and his girlfriend showed up and took the room next to us. Already Hainan was beginning to feel like a home from home. You couldn't go anywhere without meeting smugdrugglers – they were all over the place. The town of Dadong Hai lay ten minutes' walk up the beach from where we stayed, but was little more than a collection of seafood restaurants and bars. There was a brothel trying to make out that it was a massage parlour, and a zoo which housed fewer animals than the restaurant. A new hotel had been built in typical Chinese kitsch style, which catered to the tastes of rich Cantonese tourists. They walked down to the water's edge fully dressed in suits and shoes or high-heels and took photos of each other all from the same spot. One or two of the braver ones even went as far as to splash their hands in the sea before springing back from the approaching waves, all embarrassed and giggling.

Foreign students from universities all over China spent their winter breaks at Dadong Hai, and the bars were packed every night with revellers from all over the world partying into the early hours. Christmas, New Year and Chinese New Year were good excuses for us to go over the top, and the mornings after the beach would be littered with human driftwood, groaning like washed-up sea lions.

ShaSha and I spent those three months simply having the best time either of us had ever had in our whole lives. We ate lobster, crab and langoustine. We sat in beachside cafés and sipped cool cocktails. We swam and made love in the sea and on the beach under the full moon. We ran naked for miles along empty beaches, laughing like the first man and woman on earth. We were in love and anyone who was close by could feel it rippling through the air like electricity. We were radiant. We climbed mountains and went to see the minority villages of the Miao and Li peoples. We took boat trips up and down the coast and went to a Muslim enclave as guests and were taken to their mosque to pray. It was a special time, a time that cultivated a harvest of memories that would become even more precious in the years to come.

However, the news from back home regarding ShaSha's visa appeal was not good. I telephoned my parents to see what was going on. They told me that the appeal had been turned down but that it was in the process of being sent to an Independent Appellate Authority: we had to wait for the announcement about when and where a hearing would take place. I accepted that to be the way it was, and I questioned no further.

As far as I was concerned at that stage, there was nothing to do but to await the outcome of the appeal. We decided to head back to Kashgar, but first I had to go to HK again for another visa. Seeing as there was only the innocuous 'UK ENTRY CLEARANCE APPLIED FOR AT B E BEIJING' in her passport, I thought it might be worth a try taking ShaSha over with me. But, of course, the very fact that it said 'APPLIED FOR' indicated that the visa had been denied, otherwise it would have been stamped there on the page instead. Without that, we might well have been able to enter HK together, but one look at it was enough for the Chinese Exit/Entry of Aliens Department to turn her back on the spot. We parted, actually wondering if we would ever see each other again.

In conversation with my mother over a dreadful telephone line from a phone box in Kowloon, I managed to work out that she had received a letter that had been sent to my solicitor by our MP who had contacted the Migration and Visa Correspondence Unit at the Foreign and Commonwealth Office in London, and she had already sent me a copy of it to my address in Kashgar. Before any more could be explained, we were cut off and I failed on countless further attempts to get through. The next day I was on my way to Guangzhou with my new three-month visa, wondering what could be waiting for us when we arrived home.

I was not to know at the time, but the letter would never arrive. I actually found out some time later, while researching this very book, that the reply explained that 'following the interview at the Embassy in Peking on 4 June 1990 the Entry Clearance Officer (ECO) was not satisfied that ShaSha was genuinely seeking entry to the United Kingdom for the period of the visit stated by her'. In arriving at his decision after a deferment period, 'the FCO noted that although Mrs Sharif said that she wished to visit the United Kingdom for a maximum of two months, she had obtained an exit permit for settlement. Mrs Sharif was a Musilm from Kashgar, the scene of recent civic disorder between the Chinese and ethnic Muslim minority' – and she was unemployed. I was supposed to have refused an extension of stay in Kashgar and had no sure plans for the future. In light of these facts, the ECO could not be satisfied that ShaSha was a genuine visitor. The appeal had been heard with only the ECO's statement as evidence and they had upheld the decision. Well of course they would.

The appeal had now been sent to an independent authority specially set up to deal with disputes and we should wait for a date. To finish off, he suggested that we reapply but this time go for the Settlement Visa. In his words, 'As apparently the marriage is accepted as genuine, it would seem likely that such a visa would be granted.'

Had I known this, and how easy it was to resolve the problem, we would never have gone back to Kashgar that spring.

A Subtle Hint

Shang tian wu lu, ru di wu men – Neither road up to heaven nor door into the earth.

Chinese saying

WHEN we got back to Kashgar I realised, having seen so much more of China, how different Xinjiang was to most of it. There were minorities everywhere who strove to retain their own identity, but they could be looked upon as being related to the Han (if they'll excuse me saying so) whereas the Uighur, Kazak, Kirghiz and Tajik were races apart, both culturally and ideologically. I could never feel the same sense of belonging with the Chinese as I felt with the Uighur. I felt a kinship with them. I understood how they felt. Had not Wales been occupied and subdued by a more powerful neighbour? Hadn't we too turned to a religion of our own to ease the suffering? Hadn't our language and history come under threat from an unfair and prejudiced education system? Did we not suffer the same jibes when we went to London as the Uighur did when they went to Beijing?

Maybe one of the reasons why I kept on seeing people that I felt I recognised or who at least looked familiar was that my ancestors and those of the Uighur were one and the same. The earliest archaeological traces of the Celts had been found in the region of the Upper Danube dating from about the thirteenth century BC. It is believed that from there branches spread to northern Italy, Galicia and Celtiberia in Spain, Gaul, Ireland and Wales in the west and Galatia in Asia Minor in the east. But where did they come from? And where else did they roam?

In the last hundred years at various sites in and around the Tarim Basin area, Chinese archaeologists have discovered the well-preserved remains of a people that colonised the region some three thousand years ago. The mummies, as they were somewhat misleadingly called, were taken and stashed away in the museum in Urumchi, where they lay forgotten and ignored. It was only by chance in 1987 that they were seen by Victor H. Mair, professor of Chinese studies at the University of Pennsylvania, who realised that he was looking at the faces of Europeans, Caucasians, and not those of Chinese or Mongoloid origin as he would have expected. The mummies stood over six foot tall, with round eyes, high noses and long fair hair. They had been buried with hats, boots, leggings and colourful clothes that bore a strong resemblance to the plaid found on British/Celtic mummies predating 500BC. The existence of these mummies not only refutes Chinese claims that their culture evolved in isolation, but proves beyond doubt that East Turkestan developed for thousands of years quite separately from China, thus nullifying Chinese excuses for the present-day occupation.

*

I had for some time been wanting to go to Hotan on a carpet-buying expedition in order to beef up my collection in readiness for the coming tourist season, but had always been prevented from doing so by some crisis or other. This time I took my chance and went down on my own for a little adventure. It was only ten hours and 500km away, so not really that big a deal. But since Hotan was a bit of a backwater compared to Kashgar, it would be a change, a little like stepping back fifty years or so.

Passing through Yengisar, Yarkand and Khargilik I felt the time-machine working its magic, but I was forced back down to earth with a bump when the bus was held up for four hours in the middle of the desert while the Red Army exploded some device that shook the ground and the bus as if there had been an earthquake. Thanks to the delay, we rolled into a dark and deserted Hotan at midnight.

Throughout history, Hotan had been a rich and populous city, famous for its jade, gold and skins. In modern times, it had been discovered by W.H. Johnson, leader of the British India Survey Team, in 1865. He was the first westerner to visit the city since Marco Polo, and found it to be ruled by an ill-tempered eighty-year-old. He also found that the Muslim population had only recently risen up against their Chinese overlords, leaving the region as a whole in a rather unstable state.

I noticed that Hotan people were quite different from Kashgaris. Many wore tall black lambswool hats, and the women wore black yashmaks with an opening for the eyes that reminded me more of those worn in Iran than the brown drapes of the Kashgari women. There were fewer Kirghiz and Tajik, hardly any Pakistanis and only one or two western tourists.

I spent most of my time sitting with the carpet dealers in their shops, drinking tea and going through their stock discussing the various designs and where they came from. Some mornings I went through the back streets, knocking on doors and asking if anyone had old carpets to sell. '*Asalaam Aleikum, yahshimusiz? Quorna gilem bar ma?*' I had seen the Pathans at it in Kashgar and knew it was the best way to get a good deal. It was also a great way to see how people lived. I got invited into their houses and drank tea and ate the thick noodles that Hotan was renowned for. By the end of a week I had bought four carpets and made preparations to take them home.

I continued my search in Kashgar, steadily amassing a little collection which I hoped I could sell to the tourists that summer. When it came to selling, I had a tried and practised routine that worked at least six times out of ten. I watched and waited until the Oasis was fairly full, then I'd grab a couple of my rugs from upstairs and walk into the café with them on my back, claiming to have just bought them. I would unfold one, and ShaSha would come over and remark upon its beauty. More often than not, someone would take an interest and start asking how much, where from, and so on. I always said they were from people's houses because it was more attractive, and usually related a little tale about how I'd found them, and what sort of people I had bought them from. Sometimes it would be a *mullah* with one leg, sometimes the family of a famous ethnic dancer, and sometimes a victim of Chinese oppression who had been in jail for twenty-five years. The tourists found that they could deal with me more easily than with the sharks down in the bazaar, who, for the most part, were their own worst enemies, being too greedy and having an annoying take-it-or-leave-it attitude.

It was already early June. My garden was bursting into life but the plants needed so much water that it took two hours morning and night to keep them alive. It was hard work and I would tip buckets of cold refreshing water over myself to keep cool as I schlepped back and forth between the blooms.

Tourists were pouring into town, and it looked as if it was going to be a good year. Thundernose was back with Cynthia, talking about doing two trips so as to be able to put a bit away for a time when they might be too old to go gallivanting all over Asia druggling smugs. Tight on their heels were Werner and Dieter, who had plans to go east this time and spend their profits in Australia. Thundernose already had a stash left over from the year before which had lain buried throughout the winter in a hole in my garden, and we took the best part of a morning digging a hole the size of a Land Rover trying to find the damn thing.

He only needed a kilo of it and paid me to press it up as he waited. My technique was pretty slick by that time and, with production-line efficiency, I could take a kilo from pollen to plaque within an hour.

The Germans had been pleased with what I'd done the year before, and came to me again to help them find a piece. I hadn't seen Batur for over six months, however, so in order to get things moving I decided to go and pay him a visit. Kizilsu, the settlement where he lived, was closed to foreigners, though – there wasn't even a permit to apply for. That meant that I needed to melt and blend in with the locals. My mission, albeit of my own creation, seemed to be in keeping with the clandestine reputation of the place. Wearing the same clothes and carrying a small black plastic holdall, like the government cadres did, I became one with the crowd.

After having used up about three gallons of diesel ticking over for three hours, our thirty-five-seater charabanc finally set off with twenty more passengers than it was officially intended for and a depleted top speed of fifty kilometres an hour. Within minutes, I knew that this was going to be the most memorable bus ride that I'd ever taken. I was sat in front of a dirty, small but extremely active child who knelt on his seat staring and spitting small sunflower seeds all over me.

Across the aisle, just behind the man with a goat, sat a woman with a screaming baby. All attempts to quieten the child caused it to scream even louder until it reached a pitch similar to a band-saw when it hits a knot in a piece of oak. The bawling finally ceased when baby, in triumphant joy, shot a pellet of caked turd at the goat followed by a spray of foul smelling, yellow scour which ran down the woman's leg and onto the floor. Two chickens which had been clucking away aimiably at the back of the bus, suddenly decided that they wanted to fly. One went one way, the other another. Everybody joined in trying to catch then. Screaming women, squawking hens, and feathers everywhere.

If that wasn't enough, the small child in front figured that it was a good idea to be sick out of the window. Big splats of vomit came hurtling in through the broken window next to me, and into my face.

After turning off the main highway to Yarkand, we very soon ran out of paved road. The bus continued, lurching and jolting from side to side as we dropped into potholes and gullies that got deeper and more painful the further we went. A man sitting behind me asked where I was going, which was the last thing I wanted, but I managed to slip out a quick throaty answer that seemed to satisfy him. For five minutes at least. It soon emerged that 90 per cent of the passengers were either related to one another, or were neighbours. They wanted to know where I was from and who I was going to see in their village. Quickly, I became a distant relative coming with some family news from Urumchi. They pressed me to find out who, and when I mentioned Batur's name, three men immediately claimed to be his brother. It was no problem – it didn't mean that they were related at all. Everybody knew where his house was and promised to tell the driver when we got there. I thanked them all, and apologised for my limited Uighur, explaining that we only spoke Chinese in our house because my brothers thought that it was the modern thing to do. My fellow passengers laughed, and agreed that that was the way of things in the north. It looked as if I had bluffed my way through the crisis, but I then heard a voice questioning my accent, asking how it could be that I sounded like a Kashgari when I was supposed to come from Urumchi. That could be answered away with any amount of replies so I brushed it aside. Thinking about it afterwards, though, it was actually a compliment.

I was glad to get off the bus in the end because what had started as *Twenty Questions* had developed into *Mastermind* and my bluffs were running out. I stood alone in a cloud of dust left behind by the bus and tried to get my bearings. It was a long dusty track lined with poplars and behind them high mud-brick walls that protected homes, gardens and orchards from nosy passers-by. I approached the only door in sight and knocked on it with three firm strikes. It was opened by a boy of about twelve who, to my relief, didn't bat an eye.

'Good day to you,' I said. 'Is this the house of Batur?'

'Yes, yes. Come in.' The boy called out and very soon Batur emerged from the house.

It was not what I'd expected at all. It was a three-storey mansion with carved arches and beautifully painted balcony rails all overlooking the biggest compound I'd seen. Behind the house the orchard ran down to a river where cows could be seen drinking. Beyond the river, flat pasture disappeared uninterrupted into the distance. After the family introduction, tea and noodles, Batur showed me round his estate. He had apples, pears, peaches, apricots, plums, pomegranates and figs. He had a grape trellis loaded with voluptuous black fruit. He had walnuts and almonds. There were cows, sheep, donkeys and chickens; rice, melons, wheat and all the vegetable crops found in the market grew near by. Then, on a plot of land a couple of minutes' stroll from the house, there was a field of marijuana, standing eight-foot high, rustling in the breeze and giving off that wonderful pungent smell of good weed.

'Can't smoke this. This is for rope,' Batur said, leading me through the thick jungle of stems. He stopped and introduced another plant with a sweep of his hand, saying, 'Now, this is a smoking plant. We always keep them out of sight in the middle of the plantation. That way nobody steals them. The inspectors don't know the difference, and probably don't care anyway. These smokers are all female and grow well together with the others. I think they enjoy the company.'

As night approached, Batur's wife Minerva lit the oil-lamps and we sat around on a fairly new carpet on the *supa*. The aroma of boiling mutton wafted around us, teasing our senses and giving us an appetite for a huge rustic meal. I had never seen anyone eat quite so much as Batur did and still manage to look so slim, but I guess he worked all the fat off during the day in the fields. After supper we talked late into the night about farming, the difference in stock numbers, sheep and wool production, the influence of the weather and mechanisation. Even though we came from two vastly different cultures, we had found common ground.

The next morning I was up early to help fetch water from the river with the kids before sitting down to a breakfast of fresh curds and hot bread with the family on a rug under the trees in the garden. It was such an idyllic setting and Batur and his family led a life of such contentment that I could have stayed there forever. What did we know in the west any more about quality of life? Somewhere along the line we had taken the wrong turning. We had travelled as far as we were going to go down the road of civilisation.

Within a week of my return, Batur showed up at our house and, luckily, had some quite nice stuff which took no time at all to press up. As soon as I was done, I took it down to Li Jiangping's in my black bag and let Werner take it from there to his room. They were pleased and paid me in dollars, FEC and rmb. By mid-July they were gone but I expected to see them again before the year was out, and had even taken an advance order to reserve a nice lump of the harvest of '91 for them.

Some time around the end of August I was in Fat Mamma's Grease Pit showing Jimmy the Jock how to cut out the soles of his shoes when I was tapped on the shoulder by the PSB officer who normally gave me my visa extension. 'Sorry to bother you,' he said, 'but would you mind coming over the road to the Semen Hotel for a moment? We'd like a word with you.'

'Not at all,' I replied casually. 'How can I be of assistance?'

'Oh, it's nothing much. We just want to check your passport.'

I believed him. I was so sure that no one knew what I was up to that I actually believed him. Not one flicker of doubt.

I walked with him round the back of the reception building and into a visitors' lounge where another PSB officer immediately stood up and came forward to shake my hand. 'Sit down, sit down,' he said in a way that put me at ease. 'We've been asked to check up on you, because those in higher places are wondering why it is that you and your wife are still here. Is there a reason for your staying here so long?'

I went on to explain the problems that ShaSha and I had encountered with the British embassy and the fact that they had refused her a visa and we were now waiting for an appeal to be heard. Heads nodded and pens jotted down a few notes.

When I'd finished, they both seemed satisfied, and said, 'Well, that's all. Thank you for your help. We'll let you get back to what you were doing.'

I rejoined Jimmy and thought no more of it until later, when I was back home reclining on the cushions on the *supa* having a smoke. As I reran the interview through my head I came across something that, even though I couldn't put my finger on it, gave me a shiver and caused my heart to miss half a beat. What was it that the PSB man had said? Maybe it was in his tone, something sinister, something pointed, something that put me right on edge. Just for that moment, at least.

The next morning I had almost forgotten about it. In hindsight, I missed every sign that could have warned me that my time was up. I knew that I was getting known among the travelling community because people were coming miles just to see me. In the spring, while travelling through Lijiang, I had come across my name in a restaurant visitors' book where some bright spark had told the world that they could buy dope from me. Really, it was only a matter of time before some law-and-order freak saw it and handed it over to the police. But I was securely in the belief that I was invulnerable. I believed that the fact that I was under the spotlight in Kashgar was protection in itself. I mean, I wouldn't dare . . . would I?

My visa ran out on 5 September so I popped down to see my usual PSB man. It was only my second extension that year and shouldn't have been a problem. But for no apparent reason other than the rather weak excuse of 'changes in the law', my normally accommodating policeman only granted me a three-week extension. That was crazy. What sort of bullshit was this?

'But we're not ready to go yet,' I told him. 'We'll need more than three weeks to arrange our house and store the furniture. It then takes us two weeks to cross the country, so how the hell am I supposed to work with this?'

He wouldn't give in but he did say that if I was still in town in three weeks, I should come back to him and he would see what he could do. I had no other choice but to accept, but I was angry as hell. I was sure this was his way of telling me that he wanted a backhander. The bastard already got plenty from me as it was, what with cartons of Marlboro and bottles of *baijiu* when he came to the café. Eventually I came up with the idea of inviting him to my birthday party, hoping that that would soften him up sufficiently to give me another three months on the 25th.

After discussing the situation with ShaSha, we decided that it wasn't such a bad idea to leave early for a change, and that we could go first to Beijing to see what was happening with the visa. If there was no joy, as I pessimistically expected, we'd resort to plan B, which was to sail from Qingdao to Guangzhou, nip over to Hong Kong for my new visa, and then go to Hainan for the winter. It had been our intention all along to look for a place in Dadong Hai to rent and open up as a restaurant. That way, we figured, we could make some money and enjoy the sun at the same time.

Then Marius arrived. I hadn't seen him since the Philippines, and even though I suspected he'd had a hand in stealing my Nikon, I was still sort of glad to see him. He was like that. He could kill your mother and still invite you for a drink afterwards with a smile on his face. He had a new friend with him this time called Sver whom he'd met in Goa. Marius told me that after I had left Manila, he had been set up by his Filipino neighbours and arrested for having under-age sex. He claimed to have spent six months in jail in Manila, which he said was one hell of a joint, full of murderers and psychos, but that with enough money you could get your pet whore in for the night. He'd apparently got off in the end, and was as incorrigible as ever.

He had a new plan. He wanted to step up the pace of business so that we could all make some serious money for a change. He wanted to do three or four years of hard work to make enough money never to have to do it again. He had kindly fitted me into his scheme as a cross-country courier. All I had to do was take the hash, in 10kg consignments, say, down to Guangzhou where it would be picked up by a relay team of smugglers who would take it to Japan via Taiwan.

Marius suspected that the route from China was no longer practicable because the Japanese were getting just as heavy with boat passengers as they were with air travellers. China was known to be a heroin-producing country and a distribution centre for much of the smack from the Golden Triangle. Marius believed that no one would suspect a thing if the stuff was coming in from Taiwan. He asked me to help him find three or four kilos to start with, but I had to tell him that September was the worst time of year for it, and that I was being forced to leave soon so it was doubtful that I could get him anything. But, as usual, I said I'd have a go.

Within a week I got a message from one of my black-market mates to go and collect two kilos from a man waiting for me in the Red House Café. This was as risky as could be and not at all the way I liked to handle things, but there was something dragging me down that road which I was powerless to resist. As it happened, all went well, and I arranged to pass it on to Marius that night at my birthday party in Fat Mamma's.

There were only about twenty of us in all, mostly my Kashgar pals, the police and a few foreigners I'd got to know. The dope was lying under the table, and Marius, Sver and the PSB officer were sitting on either side of it, oblivious to its presence, drinking and laughing like the best of friends. It was so outrageous I had to laugh. I couldn't help but notice, however, that every time Marius or I went to the toilets, the PSB officer followed. Very strange indeed. What was it that he thought we might be doing there?

But it was all forgotten once the *baijiu* came out, and we started toasting everybody and everything, getting more drunk by the minute. The PSB man started to look scared, probably fearing that he was going to forget his own name, and it wasn't long before he was making his excuses to leave. 'Oh, dear, do you have to go so soon. The party's just getting going. Do stay for another one at least,' I pleaded. Thankfully he was having none of it and rather unsteadily disappeared into the night. As soon as he was gone, I gave Marius a sample to play with. To my disappointment, he wasn't impressed. This time I had no intention of taking another swim in the river or digging holes in the garden. I wanted to get rid of it, so the next morning it went back where it had come from.

A few days later I went for another visa extension, and again the PSB officer refused to give me the three months I wanted. He did, however, agree to give me one month, which I had to accept graciously. It was all right – we were near enough ready to go, anyway. I promised Marius I'd look into the situation in Urumchi. I was fairly certain that with my knowledge I could find a supplier who could meet his needs. Whether I would become a part of his operation was still not decided. My main priority was to get ShaSha's visa, and if we succeeded, we were gone.

Just in case we did end up in Hainan again, I threw a few hundred grams of Jumahun Al in my bag, barely concealed and wrapped only in a plastic bag. There was enough to smoke and to sell so as to help pay the hotel bill like the year before. But if we were to leave the country, it was no big deal just to shuck it. I wasn't going to include ShaSha in any cross-border antics, especially when it could be such as important crossing for us both. ShaSha and I left Kashgar on 3 October and got into Urumchi three days later. It was gone eight when we arrived, and too late to go bothering the relations, so we decided to stay in the Xinjiang Hotel, a five-storey example of Chinese architecture, lesson 1. Built in a semi-circle and facing the railway station, it was a favourite haunt of Pakistanis and budget travellers alike. The rooms were clean, and there was a cheap restaurant and a decent bar serving cold Xinjiang beer late into the night. The hotel was always busy, the foyer packed with guests and black-marketeers, hustling to change money, locate train tickets, sell rubies and find girls – 'nice girls', ' good girls', 'religious girls' and 'no-problem girls'.

We were more than relieved to get a room and get under the shower for half an hour to wash the dust and road-weariness from our bodies. Squeaky clean, we made love again and again with such passionate and frantic desire that we found ourselves in every corner of the room. Travelling always seemed to have that effect on us – something to do with being cooped up for days at a time with no way of releasing all that emotion, I guess.

The next morning we dumped our bags in left-luggage, booked out and went to look for ShaSha's cousin. As fortune would have it, he was not to be found, and after a day of wandering around the markets of the city, we returned to the hotel and booked in for another night. As ShaSha made us both a cup of tea, I went to retrieve our bags, but the woman behind the counter refused to give them to me, saying that it was my wife who signed them in, therefore it must be my wife who signed them out. Rules, rules, rules. God, I hated people like that. Bloody pedants. I stormed back to our room and asked ShaSha to go and sort it out. When she returned I made us a snack, using some tomatoes I'd brought from my garden in Kashgar.

A View from a Window

Times go by turns, and chances change by course,
From foul to fair, from better hap to worse.

Robert Southwell (1561–95)

BANG, bang, bang. 'Must be the hotel staff – I wonder what they want,' I said to ShaSha, getting up from the bed and reaching for the door handle. As soon as I touched it, the door seemed to open by itself. My fingers were ripped from the handle and the door was flung wide open. Suddenly I was face to face with a wall of people, like the front line of a rugby side, pushing me back into the room. It wasn't the maid, that was for sure. In an instant the room was full of light, and I realised that one of the gatecrashers was filming me with a huge video camera perched on his shoulder like some futuristic vulture.

I was told firmly to sit down on the bed. I tried to find ShaSha, but they had surrounded me, cutting off my view. They didn't have to tell me who they were – I knew. The moment that had always lurked at the back of my mind, like a cloaked figure down an unlit street, suddenly stepped out in front of me.

My heart racing, I quickly scanned the crowd. There were three Chinese and three Uighur men dressed in green trousers and black leather jackets – instantly recognisable as the PSB's attempt at plain clothes. There was a cameraman and his lighting lackey, two female Uighur officers in uniform, and two male Chinese officers in uniform. Cramming the doorway, seven or eight hotel staff craned their necks to get a glimpse of the action, and jangled keys to prove they had the right to be there.

A voice in Chinese suddenly cut through the hubbub and spoke to me. I understood nothing, but I knew what was being said. A translator chipped in, and using fairly good accented English, said, 'My name is Arsilan, I am a translator.

This is Officer Sun and we are from the Xinjiang PSB. Acting on information received, we believe you can assist us in our inquiries. Please give us you passport.'

'Certainly,' I said, and then thinking that it was best to try and act as cool as possible, added, 'Would anyone like a cup of tea? I was just making one.'

'No,' came the reply. 'But you can have one if you want.'

'ShaSha, you want one?' I managed to get a glimpse of her. She was sitting on the other bed, legs crossed, looking unbelievably relaxed.

'No, thanks,' came the answer from behind the wall of bodies that had closed in again.

I weaved my way through the crowd and poured my tea, went back to the bed, sat down and lit a cigarette. Suddenly I caught Sun's eyes on my leg. It had started to tremble, and it was as much as I could do to keep it under control. 'What a bloody giveaway,' I thought.

Sun was a short man of about fifty. His eyes shone with eagerness, his hair was black and he looked fit and quite capable of handling himself if things got ugly. Arsilan was a tall Uighur in his late twenties with big hangdog eyes, a nervous twitch and not an ounce of venom in him.

'What is your name and nationality?'

I answered in what I thought was a calm, controlled manner, but I heard it as if I was speaking with a bucket on my head and my voice was far from steady.

'What are you doing here in Xinjiang?'

'I'm just on my way to Beijing with my wife to get her a visa.'

'Is this your wife? Do you have your marriage papers? How long have you been married? Where did you meet? Where do you live? Do you have any children? What is your business? How do you make your money? Are these your bags? Are these your wife's bags? Please take each item out of the bag, one at a time, and show them to the officer.'

I glanced out of the window at the grey city around us, looking as if it had been built in honour of George Orwell's *Nineteen Eighty-Four*. Mechanical people surveyed by the policemen in pill boxes were getting on and off slow-moving electric buses, that sailed through the dirty slush of last night's snow storm in no hurry to get anywhere. The buildings bristled with satellite dishes and the mountains were dotted with domed observatories picking up our every breath.

This was it. The moment had arrived. There were two big lumps of dope in my bag. If I could get out of this, it would be a miracle. As I began to remove the various items of clothing, the video camera came closer to watch my every move. Each one brought me closer and closer to my stash. I was doing my best to delay the inevitable, and thought about trying to hide it inside a shirt, but in the end when there was only the dope and a pair of socks left, I had no choice but to hand it over.

'What is this?'

'It's *neshe* – hashish,' I replied.

'What is it for?'

'It's for me to smoke. It's for my own personal use.'

The Uighur officer butted in. 'There's a lot of hash there. You can smoke all that on your own?'

'Yeah, sure, why not? It's got to last me three months. What's there – four hundred grams? That's not even four grams a day – two or three joints at most.'

'Excuse me, what is a joint?' asked the translator. I told him. He told Sun. Sun said something to him, and he asked me, 'Where did you get this hashish?'

'From Kashgar, in front of the Id Kah mosque, from some guy.'

'What was his name?'

I thought quickly. The most common name in Kashgar was Mehemet Ali, so I said it.

'Maybe you can also give us a description of this Mehemet Ali.'

'Black hair, moustache, dark eyes, between forty and fifty years old,' I said, describing half the adult population of the town.

'Do you think you can write a statement, detailing the circumstances of how you purchased this hash, and how you came to be here in Urumchi, and your intended destination?'

'Sure, no problem, just give me a pen,' I answered, thinking that the way out of this had suddenly presented itself to me. I knew this territory from the time when I'd shoved the Chinibagh hotel manager and got hauled in. It was simply a matter of writing down some sort of story and saying that you were stupid, mistaken and very, very sorry. A self-criticism would sort this out without a doubt. A fine to cover their expenses, and that would be it.

As I began to write, the two female officers started to escort ShaSha out of the room.

'Hey, wait a minute! Where are you taking my wife?' I demanded.

'Don't worry, Mister Robert, it's only for a few questions.'

ShaSha and I exchanged glances, and there was a knowledge between us. The fact that she was still quite calm encouraged me greatly but I suddenly thought that maybe they would treat her differently. I was a foreigner, and they couldn't very well torture me, but they could do whatever the fuck they wanted to one of their own, couldn't they?

She turned back in the doorway: 'See you later.'

But before I had time to reply, she was whisked away.

By now the video had stopped filming and it was getting dark outside. I wanted to get the whole thing sorted out as fast as I could so that I could go for a beer, but it was taking forever. Arsilan was reading my statement to Sun, who was listening in a way that made it clear that he didn't believe a word of it. However, it didn't take long, and when he was done, he said, 'I think we will be needing something a little bit more detailed than this. But that will have to wait until tomorrow. I must now inform you that while we are investigating this matter, under Chinese law you are to be put under observation. That means that officers of the Xinjiang PSB must be present with you at all times. You and your wife will for tonight be moved to different rooms. Sort out your belongings and get ready to leave.'

'Observation' didn't sound too bad, and he only said it would be for tonight. No sweat. They hadn't even body-searched me, hadn't even looked in the pocket of my waistcoat where I still had my stash box with about five or six grams in it. They hadn't checked my shoes. If I'd have stuck it all there, they wouldn't have found anything.

I got my bag together and was escorted out of Room 731, down the corridor, into the service stairwell and down two floors. I ended up in room 525, a rather nice suite with separate bath, lounge and bedroom. Three of the police immediately installed themselves around the TV and switched it on.

'Who's paying for this?' I ventured, in Uighur.

'You are,' said the local officer whom I now knew as Abliz.

The bedroom into which I was shown was a very comfortable twin, with a view overlooking the back of the hotel.

'You will sleep here tonight. In half an hour we are going out for food. Are you hungry?'

'Not really. More thirsty than anything. Can I get something to drink, like a beer?'

'We'll see, okay?'

At six-thirty that night I was escorted by six officers of the Xinjiang PSB out of the room to the lift. They had used their radios to co-ordinate with the women who were watching over ShaSha to meet there. It felt already like days since I had seen her, and I was overjoyed to be able to stand next to her and touch her hand. We all bundled into the lift and went down to the foyer. Here we were instructed to approach the reception desk and inform them of our new room numbers. I whispered to ShaSha, 'Remember, you know nothing. It's nothing to do with you. You didn't know, right?'

As we left the building, I saw ShaSha's cousin coming in through the door. He immediately spotted me and came over. Suddenly noticing the cops flanking me, he asked what was up. Before he could reach me he was rudely pushed aside and told in no uncertain terms to get back. I just managed to say over my shoulder that there was a bit of a problem, but then we were gone.

Outside, ShaSha was taken off in one direction, while I was led over to a waiting jeep. Six men in one of those was not easy, but we only drove round the corner and stopped outside a little restaurant. I was directed into a cubicle where I was left to sit alone. The police took a small banquet table in the centre of the room from where they could watch me, and then told a waiter to come and take my order.

'Fried beef and onion, rice and a beer, please,' I said, feeling as if I was pushing my luck. But in less than two minutes I'd got my beer, lit up and started drinking. Before the food arrived, I'd had another two beers and the cops had been over to tell me to cool it a bit. I was beginning to think they were going to put a stop to it, but as I ordered more and more bottles, they ignored me and got on with their own session. By the time they came and told me it was time to go, I was moderately pissed and confident I could at least get a good night's sleep.

Back in the room, I mentioned that the hotel bar was still open and suggested we could have a drink there, but this didn't go down as well as I'd hoped. Abliz looked at me and without a trace of humour said, 'I wouldn't joke – this is a lot more serious than you think.'

That left me pondering, but as I still had to get rid of my stash, I said good night and went to the bedroom. I expected one of them to follow me but they were more interested in the TV and sat down to watch. Quickly, I took out the blim and ate it. I opened the window, checked for any suspicious sorts wandering about and threw the stash box as far as I could into the bushes below. Good night and sweet dreams.

The next morning, before I knew it, they'd been out and bought some *you tiao* (deep-fried pastry) and *bao zhi* (steamed stuffed buns) for our breakfast. I loved *bao zhi* and scoffed them down in no time with gallons of black tea that I made from my own supply. It was time to go again, and down in the foyer we met up with ShaSha. I paid the hotel bill which, instead of my usual 25 yuan, had gone up to 240 yuan. The bastards were going to break me at this rate.

In the back of the jeep I put my arm around ShaSha and did my best to comfort her. I wanted to ask her what had happened but instead decided to keep quiet. Belting through Urumchi as fast as we could go, we soon arrived at a Chinese hotel situated up a back street. After a lot of messing about at the reception desk in typical Chinese chaotic fashion, we entered the lift and took about twenty minutes to climb the four floors to the most expensive room in the hotel. Another suite, it had a lounge with a TV, a table and three armchairs and, behind a curtain, three single beds.

ShaSha and I were told to sit on the beds while the PSB came and went and shouted into walkie-talkies, argued with each other, shouted out through the window and smoked. We lay down on opposite beds and stared at each other. I shook my head, blinked my eyes slowly and blew a kiss. I've no idea if the message I intended was received. She turned, lay on her back and closed her eyes.

When we woke up, the police were saying that ShaSha was leaving. The previous night she'd been told to remove her earrings, rings and bracelets and put them in her bag. She now gave me the little bag, urging me to take care of it for her. We then had only just enough time to grab each other's hand and say, 'Don't worry, it'll be all right. I'll see you later.' And she was gone.

There was something about it all that really started to worry me. 'Where are you taking her to? What's the reason for all this?' I asked almost pleadingly. But no one said a word. Without really thinking about it, I found myself at the window, waiting for her to emerge with the escort, and suddenly ShaSha was there, but there was no PSB, no police with her. She was on her own, walking free. I couldn't work it out. What was going on? I watched her turn left out of the hotel, walk up the road and disappear. I played what had happened back through my mind again and again. Maybe there was something that I had missed. But what? This image would haunt me and puzzle me for longer than I could ever have imagined.

*

My friendly captors now began their investigation in earnest. They rearranged the lounge area, bringing in another desk and half a dozen chairs. They placed five chairs behind the desk and table, and one in front. I knew which one was meant for me, and when they were ready, I sat down.

Sun began. 'Acting on information received, we suspect you, Mr Davies, of involvement in serious crimes against the People's Republic of China. We can only advise you that co-operation is the best policy. If you are honest with us, we can help you. Please tell us again how you purchased the hashish. By that we mean from whom, where, how much and how many times.'

I retold my story about Mehemet Ali, wondering what information they had received. If someone had grassed me up, it could only be that slippery bastard Karim who used to drink in Li Jiangping's from time to time. I'd never trusted him, but what damage could he do? He knew nothing of what I'd been up to, and the only people who did know were all long gone.

'Did you ever sell any hashish to other foreigners?'

'No way.'

'So how did you manage to survive all these years living in Kashgar? Where did you get your money from?'

'I've told you – my savings.'

'Tell us about the other foreigners you met in your brother-in-law's café. Were they selling hashish or smoking it?'

'There were loads of people. I don't know who they all were, or what they were doing. I just sold 'em beer.'

'What were their names? How long did they stay in Kashgar? Were there any people like you living there doing business?'

And so it went on. Three hours of the same questions, over and over again, and every so often they'd add a new one to the list. I watched them play at being dumb, then the good-guy bad-guy stunt. Then angry and then really pally. The questioning switched from one to the other, each one coming from a different angle, probing and scratching away at my defences. As it went on, I got the impression they didn't know anything and were just fishing. I even stopped feeling concerned. I was quite confident that it was some charade they were going through just to scare me into giving them all my money before they kicked me out of the country. I didn't want to get booted out if I could help it, but it wouldn't be the end of the world if I did.

Thundernose had deliberated upon this possibility many a time, and had always said, 'They never jail foreigners in China. They don't want us in their jails.' To me, that made a lot of sense. They'd always done their damnedest to keep western eyes away from anything sensitive, so they were surely not suddenly going to throw one of us inside to gain first-hand experience, were they?

When the interrogation was over, they put their congenial-host hats back on and suggested we go out for a spot of lunch. 'Good idea,' I thought. I was starving and needed a drink. Immediately next door to the hotel was a large, ostentatious Cantonese restaurant called the Guangzhou Rose Garden. Arsilan, Sun, Li, Hua and I stepped inside through the pagoda-style porch with its red lanterns and into a throng of midday diners. Li was the driver of the jeep, a gangly, bespectacled youth with inch-long fluff on his acne-scarred face. Hua, at least in his own mind, was a special investigator. He wore expensive suits, had a bleeper, a nice Japanese watch and boffin glasses. In his mid-twenties and originally from Beijing, he wanted everyone to know he was no Xinjiang boy but educated and culturally aware.

We grabbed a table for six with a revolving server in the middle. Arsilan told me that Hua often came here and knew what was good. If I didn't mind, he would order for all of us.

When the food started to arrive on the table, I was amazed. This was like nothing I'd ever seen before. It was a large shoulder of mutton laid on a nan bread which had been roasted in an oven with its gravy. There were the usual selection of vegetable dishes and Guangzhou-style fried rice with prawns. It was brilliant, a meal I'd never forget.

After lunch, we trooped down the street to a small kiosk to stock up on cigarettes. I'd had three beers with the meal but they still allowed me another three to take back to the hotel. Back in the room, Hua advised me to have a go at rewriting my statement. I thought about it and decided it was a good opportunity to sit down and write out all this bullshit I'd been spinning and rearrange it into a more credible story. Moreover, by writing it down, I might remember it better or even fool myself into believing that it was the truth. I retired to the bedroom with a bundle of paper, a pen, my beer and my cigarettes. While I scrawled, ruminating over the events of the last couple of years, I realised that if I actually wrote the truth it would indeed look a bit naughty, so I stuck with the Mehemet Ali plot and nothing more.

That night we all went out again to eat, this time in the jeep. I enjoyed tearing around Urumchi in this little four-wheel drive over the icy snow which had begun falling that afternoon. The weather had changed dramatically in the twenty-four hours since I'd been nabbed. Winter had really arrived and it was getting very cold and windy. The restaurant that evening was a traditional Uighur establishment just off the main carpet bazaar. We ate *jiaozi* dumplings filled with mutton, onion and carrot, seasoned with black pepper, with *lamian* meat sauce poured over them. It was just what we needed on a freezing-cold Urumchi night.

Li had been to get his computer-game console and disks. The poor boy was obviously bored just sitting around the hotel smoking and drinking tea and needed something to pass the time with. He wasn't the only one; I was already sick of playing patience and could barely eke out the five bottles of beer they allowed me until I was tired enough to sleep without effort. Li set up a game called *Tanka* (Tank). I had a few goes but got bored with it. Li and Hua continued, though, laughing, jumping and squealing like little kids as their computer-generated weapon blew holes in a wall. How could I take these guys seriously? They were hardly behaving like the evil communist inquisitors I'd heard about.

The next morning, just before question time, a message arrived at the door. ShaSha was in a 'house of detention' and she had written a note asking me for clothes because she was feeling cold. So she wasn't free after all. I prepared a parcel with T-shirts, a scarf and my wool-lined leather coat, and before they took it all away I managed to slip a brief note into the pocket lining that said, 'My spirit, please don't worry. Everything will be all right. See you later. Love you.' Whether she would get it or not was another matter. My thoughts leapt through a thousand different versions of where they might be holding her. I asked Arsilan about the detention house but his description gave nothing away. I had to be optimistic, though, and in the end found it impossible to believe that it could be anything more than a cheap hotel.

After the third day, I was starting to get a bit edgy. I felt I should maybe broach the subject of a lawyer or, perhaps better, a little greasing of the palm. But it was not easy. I needed to get Sun on his own, so that there would be no witnesses, but they were always in a group. I would also need Arsilan to translate. Not an ideal situation at all, but it had to be worth a go.

That night in the restaurant, while Hua was paying the bill, Arsilan came over to my cubicle for a chat. Here was my chance.

'Hey, Arsilan. Don't you think that this would be better sorted out with a bit of co-operation? You know, we could help each other out a bit, and everybody could just go off happily on their own way. Do you know what I mean?'

'Yes, I can agree with that,' he said. Did he know what I was hinting at? It was hard to tell.

I continued. 'Yeah, things in Urumchi are getting expensive these days. It'd be nice to go out and buy stuff without having to worry about it, wouldn't it?' Fuck! I shouldn't have said it like that. Too blunt.

'I'm happy that you are thinking about co-operating with us,' he replied. 'It's a good idea, and better in the end for you.'

What the hell is he on about, I wondered. Maybe he's just ignoring me. I'll ask him straight out if I can pay a fine and go then. That was probably a better tactic and less likely to be misunderstood, too.

Suddenly it was too late. Hua was back and we were leaving.

That evening, as we sat about watching TV, Hua came over to me and said, 'It's best we talk about the money now, I think.'

I looked up. What did he mean?

'I've been paying your food bill every day out of my expenses, and I need to be reimbursed, otherwise I am out of pocket. I have worked out that you spend 150 yuan a day on food. Will you sign here to permit me to take 500 yuan from your money?'

Was that his way of asking for a bribe? I didn't think so. 'No,' I said, 'there is no way in hell that I have eaten 500 yuans' worth of food. I know how much it costs. Check it again.'

The bastard was trying to rip me off. I couldn't believe it. I thought he'd come for a bribe and instead he was trying to screw me for thirty quid. Half an hour later he was back, saying that he'd mixed up Li's receipts with his own, and that the actual sum I owed was 210 yuan. That was more like it, and since we were eating good food in neat restaurants, I was quite happy to pay.

The situation was crazy, though; it was like being on a gastronomic tour of the city. In Urumchi you could find specialities from all over China and every day we ate a different dish. One day it'd be beef noodles from Gansu, then the next 'dog no bark' dumplings from Tianjin. Then there was Xian's famous mutton pancakes, Shanxi's hand-cut noodles, Sichuan's fried hot-pepper dumplings, Shanghai's spring rolls and various dishes from the pots of Mongolian restaurants. I was seeing Urumchi through different eyes now, and hoped that I would soon be able to show ShaSha what I'd discovered.

The days went by in much the same fashion: breakfast from the street, interrogation, lunch in some restaurant, an afternoon of TV, cards and *Tanka*. Another restaurant in the evening, and then back for beer and more cards and *Tanka*. When I asked how long this was going to go on, all Arsilan would say was that he hoped it wouldn't be too long. It was weird: they didn't seem to be interested in me any more. Had my story convinced them?

On the sixth day, while I was playing *Tanka*, the phone rang. Hua answered it and listened for about two minutes without saying a word. After a nervous '*Hao le, hao le* – okay, okay', he slammed the phone down and ran about the room shouting orders at Li. He ripped the computer game out of my hands, unplugged it and switched off the TV. Then Arsilan came over and said, 'Three policemen from the Shanghai PSB have just arrived in Urumchi. They are coming here now. They believe you can help them and want to speak to you. We will try to help you if we can. For the moment, would you please go to the other room and write a statement about everything you have told us.'

Now what? How am I supposed to be able to help the Shanghai PSB? My mind started doing somersaults trying to find a link and something to work on in preparation, but there was nothing. What the fuck was going on?

When they arrived I was in the bedroom behind the curtain, feeling the tingle of blood shooting through my veins. I could hear all the hellos and introductions on the other side and felt like some prize pig the neighbouring farmers had come over to see. Without warning, the curtain was drawn back, and I turned to face the pack. They advanced, their beady little eyes homing in on their prey, teeth bared with fake smiles.

Arsilan piped up nervously, and introduced them to me. 'This is Officer Huang, Officer Qu and Officer Zhu of the Shanghai PSB,' he said. 'They say they are looking forward to speaking with you.'

I stood up and shook each one by the hand saying, '*Ni hao.*'

Huang, clearly the leader, was a short, fifty-five-year-old Ronnie Corbett lookalike in a black leather bomber jacket. 'I hope you will co-operate with us in the same way that you have done with the Xinjiang PSB,' he said.

'Sure,' I replied, thinking that it wouldn't be too much of a problem to spin out the same yarn over again.

Huang eyed me and, with a knowing smirk, turned away. Instant dislike. I already hated him. As false as I'd ever seen. I knew he was going to be trouble.

Soft-Sleeper to Shanghai

Ye chang meng duo – A long night brings many dreams.
Chinese saying

IT was too late that day for them to begin questioning me, so after half an hour of small-talk they left. Although I couldn't understand what was being said, I got the impression my Xinjiang friends were not at ease.

Arsilan spotted me watching, and came over. 'Shanghai people no good, always come here with big nose,' he said out of the blue. Then he turned and walked away.

We didn't see any more of the visitors until the next morning, just after eight, and once pleasantries and cigarettes had been passed around, they were ready to knuckle down. The Xinjiang cops all left the room, and I was told to sit down on my chair. Huang took control of the proceedings, introducing himself and the other two once again. Qu was quite burly, about twenty-five, with metal-framed glasses, a square head with thick hair and a soft, shingly-sounding voice. Zhu, who had been brought along to act as translator, looked no more than eighteen, and had curly hair on top of a squint face. At least his smile looked genuine, which was more than I could say about the other two. Huang was Karl Malden and Qu was Michael Douglas, and it was *The Streets of Urumchi*, a Chairman Mao Production.

'We have read carefully the statements that you have written. We think that you are not co-operating with the police as much as you are trying to make out. From information received, you have been apprehended on suspicion of dealing on more than one occasion in large amounts of hashish. What we would like to know is how you can explain this.'

Good question. How could I explain it?

'Well, it must be a mistake,' I ventured. 'Maybe I'm being mixed up with someone else.'

Huang looked at me long and hard, and then grinned. 'We wouldn't come all the way from Shanghai if we thought it was a mistake. You can start your story again from the beginning, but this time don't forget to include the occasions when you sold hashish to other foreigners.'

I began to tell the same story again, but Huang interrupted me, and said, 'I want to show you something. This is a statement written by a person who says that you sold him hashish. Take a look and tell me how you explain it.'

He handed me the sheet of paper. It was written in English, but I couldn't concentrate and could read nothing of its content. Instead I searched for a name, a signature, but there was nothing to indicate who had written it. Who could have done that? Was it a trick? I was sure that nobody I had sold to would write something like that. Shit, didn't we have a code of conduct between us? My brain started to feel heavy. I'd believed it was all coming to an end, but here I was now facing another inquisition.

Damn it, they must have pulled somebody in – but who? Must have been Jimmy. He was last to leave. But, hell, that was only 250g – they can't do much to me for that, surely. Suppose I was to own up to that – what would they do? They don't jail foreigners in China, just give them a fine and a kick in the arse. Well, fuck 'em, I'm not going to say anything.

'Maybe he's named me in order to protect someone else,' I said hopefully.

Drawing a bundle of photographs from a folder on the desk, Huang handed them to me and asked if I recognised anybody. I took my time and studied each one, using the time to think out my options. There must have been twenty-odd photos there, all of various traveller types sitting around tables in bars and restaurants. I was dreading the thought of coming across someone I knew. How would I react? Would it be a giveaway? I didn't know any of these people, though, not until the very last picture, when a face popped out at me that looked quite familiar. Was that Gerhard dressed up as a chef? I didn't know the people with him or recognise the location, but it sure as hell looked like him.

'No, I don't know any of these people.'

'Well, some of them know you,' Huang said cheerfully.

'Lots of people know me. If you work in a restaurant, it's hardly surprising, is it?'

'How many times did you buy hashish from Mehemet Ali?'

'Only once.'

'Who did you buy it from before?'

'I forget. Somebody else outside the Id Kah.'

'What was his name? What did he look like?'

'I don't know, I never asked him his name. Ali Mahmoud, perhaps, I dunno. He looked a lot like Mehemet Ali, funnily enough, though.'

'Did many of the foreigners smoke hashish?'

'Not really. It was usually the Pakistanis who smoked. '

'Did you smoke it in England?'

'Yes.'

'So you brought your habit with you to our China. Are you an addict?'

'What are you talking about? There's no such thing as a hash addict. It's not heroin or opium, you know.'

'How do you know? You inject the hashish in the same way.'

This was getting bloody silly. What was the angle behind that question? Maybe he doesn't know what hash is, I wondered. Surely not. But, then again, it wouldn't surprise me.

'You have been named as the principal source of illegal drugs and the master-mind behind an international smuggling ring. This is a serious crime against the people of China. Let me warn you that without your full co-operation, things will get very serious. You want to co-operate with us, don't you?'

'Sure.'

'But it doesn't look as if you're trying very hard. Where were you taking the drugs that were found in your possession?'

'To Hainan, for my own use.'

'We think that you intended to take the drugs out of the country.'

'Well, that's bollocks. You can't prove where I was going, and if I was going to take it out I would have packed it up and hidden it. It wouldn't just be lying in a plastic bag in the bottom of my hold-all, would it?'

'You know how to hide drugs in order to take them out of the country, then?'

'I can guess.'

'Did you sell your drugs to any Chinese people?'

'No. I don't know any Chinese people.'

'And how exactly was your wife involved in your activities?'

'My wife was not involved. She knows nothing.'

'Nothing about what?'

'She doesn't know that I bought hash.'

'Can you tell us which foreigners were in Kashgar in July this year?'

'There were hundreds of people passing through. I can't remember all of them.' That was it, then. It was Jimmy they were on about, because Werner and his mate had gone by that time.

Suddenly, Huang got up and said that that was enough for now. Thank God for that, I thought. It was as if they were galloping around me on horseback like Red Indians, getting closer and closer each time they went past. Damn it, how long could this go on for? Twenty-four hours was all the time they had back home, and here I am on the eighth day, dropping myself in the shit every time I open my mouth. I should have a lawyer. But they hadn't arrested me. The threat of it was there, but if I started on about rights and lawyers they'd probably assume that I had something to hide. I had to play the whole thing down, and just go along with them as if it was no big deal. Anyway, they don't jail foreigners, so it's no problem. As long as I deny selling and don't shop anybody, there's bugger all they can do. What I'd sold Jimmy only came to about sixty quid. What the hell was that in the world of crime? It was hardly the bloody Mafia, was it? It was inconceivable that anything worse than a fine could come of it, and the quicker it was over, the quicker I could see ShaSha again. What a bloody mess I'd got her into.

Half an hour later Qu took control and began to ask personal details from a questionnaire. It started off quite routinely with my name, age, date of birth, address, schooling, profession and employment record. This I could understand, but when he went on to enquire about my parents in the same way, even wanting to know their political persuasion and my mother's maiden name, I failed to see the relevance. Bewilderment turned to anger when he continued asking the same questions about my grandparents.

After lunch, Huang led the charge. 'It would be better if you realised the seriousness of your situation as soon as possible. Maybe you'd like to tell us of your involvement in international drug trafficking.'

'What involvement? I have done no such thing.'

'This statement here says different.'

'Then it's a load of shite.'

It really didn't make a lot of sense all of a sudden. Jimmy didn't know anything. Who could've told on me?

They went on in the same vein for another three hours. I tried to play it all down, thinking that admitting to a few minor infractions was a good tactic, but as time went by I knew it was a mistake. But what was going to come of it, anyway? A kick in the arse, that's all.

'I never sold dope,' I protested. 'I had plenty. I just gave it away. It's no big deal.'

'How many times did you just give drugs away?'

'I don't know. It's hard to say.'

Why did I say that? To them, it's still trafficking. Just because you give it away doesn't make it legal. I was off down the slide now. I'd trapped myself and they were so happy They loved me and I even started to like them.

'Would you be willing to come to Shanghai with us to assist us in our investigation? It would be good for you to do so.'

What the fuck were they up to now? Maybe this was the kick in the arse. Maybe that was it, then; they just wanted me to admit to something and that was it. And, anyway, if I was truly in the shit, they wouldn't bother to ask me if I wanted to go, would they?

'What about my wife? Where is she?'

'Your wife is here in Urumchi. She can wait for you.'

'How long will I have to go to Shanghai for? I mean, can I come back here afterwards?'

'If you continue to co-operate, I'm sure we can settle this very quickly.'

I was asked to write another statement that evening. It was easier to write them now because I had started making copies and could refer back to see what I had written before.

The next day was 17 October. I'd been cooped up with the *Gong An* under so-called observation for ten days now. Apart from 400g and a confession that I'd once laid a piece on someone, they still had nothing on me. What were they going to do?

Before I left, the Xinjiang cops came in with a very official-looking document with red stamps and big Chinese characters all over it. 'What's this?' I asked, fearing some sort of trick.

'Oh, it's a document that says that you agreed to undergo observation for ten days and volunteer information of your own free will.'

'Why have you waited until now?' I asked. 'Why didn't you give it to me in the beginning?'

'Oh . . . we forgot.'

Forgot my arse, I thought. Suppose I'd refused to sign the bloody thing in the first place. What would have happened? Would they have had the power to 'observe' me and interrogate me? I went ahead and signed. Then there was another document, an 'I agree to be handed over to the Shanghai PSB and volunteer to go to Shanghai to assist them with their investigations' document. Feeling that I didn't have much choice in the matter, I signed. Next they showed me the ticket they had bought for me with my own money. It was the most expensive train ticket money could buy in China. A first-class soft-sleeper ticket at tourist rate, and paid for in FEC, for God's sake. For another hundred I could have flown.

Later that morning, Arsilan took me aside and told me in a very conspiratorial tone that it would be better to leave the bulk of my money in Urumchi when I went to Shanghai, because the Shanghai PSB would more than likely confiscate it for good. We agreed that the best course of action would be to transfer it to ShaSha. I wrote a note of transaction in duplicate which Arsilan and I both signed. I kept the copy. I agreed to hand over to Sharapet the equivalent of about three thousand US dollars in a mixture of HK dollars, FEC, rmb and US dollars. I held on to two thousand HK dollars which Arsilan said I would need in Shanghai.

The other problem was our jewellery. Again, Arsilan told me that the Shanghai police might confiscate it and not give it back. I eventually decided to stash a bundle of ShaSha's silver rings and bangles in a bag of clothes that I was leaving behind with Arsilan for her, and to take the wedding rings with me. I was sure that no one would take them away.

As we finished sorting out everything, Arsilan turned to me and said, 'It's a shame you didn't tell us what you told them. We may have been able to hold on to you and sort out something better for you.'

Bright and early the next day, I paid for the hotel and left for the station in a jeep convoy. Whisked through the hoards of milling peasants and into the first-class waiting-room, we waited only for about half an hour before the express to Shanghai was called. I said my goodbyes to the Xinjiang PSB and to Urumchi, a city I had grown to love for its bleak, hard exterior and its wonderful restaurants.

*

So here I was on the train to Shanghai, a seventy-two-hour slog through the heart of China. The dragon's mouth was open and I was about to be swallowed whole. The dragon wouldn't chew; it would take its time and use all its gastric juices to digest this foreign devil.

Once on board in the rather lush soft-sleeper section, they gave me first choice of bed and I'd taken the top bunk on the left. That meant they wouldn't have to disturb me in the mornings, and I could sleep in. It was a comfortable arrangement, with crisp clean sheets on wide comfy beds, curtains, mirrors, carpet and a door that could be closed for complete privacy.

As the train crept on through a land already in winter hibernation, I felt the distance grow between me and ShaSha. We had rarely been so far apart, but in the past I had been sure that we were going to see each other again. This time I didn't know, and as the train wormed its way deeper and deeper into the vast central provinces, I was less certain. China felt a lot bigger than it had done before and a lot heavier somehow – like diving, where the deeper you go, the more pressure there is.

I talked English to young Zhu in the hope that I could make a friend of him and perhaps get a hint of what the hell was going on, but he was either thick as shit or had been trained really well in the art of deception. They did do their best to keep me at ease, though, agreeing to buy me beer and cigarettes, and during the course of a day I managed to get quite well oiled. We bought food from the platform vendors in the day and headed for the dining-car in the evening. The cops had made it known who they were and what they were doing, and this had the desired effect on the train staff who treated us with deference and gave us the best food and service I've ever seen on a train anywhere. It was a good example of communist China, a land where everyone is equal and some are more equal than others.

When they were awake, I tried to sleep. When they were asleep, I was awake. But I was never left on my own. Young Zhu kept me company at night while I drank beer and read *The Journeyer* by Gary Jennings which had been a birthday present from our friend Petra. My God, was I glad of such a book now. I dived into its story and wrapped it about myself as insulation from reality.

The only time things got a bit weird was when I went to the toilet. Two came with me, and while one stood in the corridor keeping other passengers away, the other kept the door open with his foot and watched. I hated it and stared back defiantly to make him turn away.

On the last day, at about eleven in the morning, with the train travelling much faster, hurtling through the Henan countryside as the pale sun dissolved the edge of the horizon, I rolled out of bed to find Huang staring at me.

'I think you must have been a very badly behaved child,' he said with all the authority of a psychotherapist.

'And how exactly do you come to that conclusion?'

'You always sleep late in the mornings, and this is a sign.'

A sign? Badly behaved child? Total nonsense, I thought, and ignored him. How dare he invade the warm and safe memory of my childhood.

As night fell, the train rattled over the Nanjing Bridge, and we were almost in Shanghai. Time had gone so fast, just when I'd wanted it to slow down for once.

'Excuse us, but we are going to have to put these handcuffs on you now. It's the law, you see.'

PART TWO

In the Belly of the Dragon

Room and Bored

'Will you walk into my parlour?' said a spider to a fly:
''Tis the prettiest little parlour that you ever did spy.'

Mary Howitt (1799–1888)

I LOVED railway stations, and even at this time Shanghai Central was of no less interest to me. In the confusion of activity, handcuffed by three very nervous policemen with walkie-talkies blaring unintelligible messages into the night air, I strained to look around and check the place out, almost forgetting the tightness of the manacles. Passengers were scuttling towards the exit with huge bundles of belongings, shouting and yelling at each other, while frenzied wives and mothers screamed at those inside to squeeze suitcases and big bags out through the windows.

Eight policemen formed a wedge around me and cut a path through the oncoming crowd as we headed in the opposite direction. A coat was thrown over the cuffs but it was obvious that I was under arrest. One thrust my bag into my hands while the others nervously checked up and down the platform and shouted into their radios. Two burly guys in white shirts flanked me. They were sweaty and looked more like truck drivers than police officers, and were doing their best to let me know they were in charge, guiding me with firmly applied squeezes just above the elbow and jabbering a different sort of Chinese to the one I was used to. The sole uniformed officer had a half-smoked cigarette clinging to his bottom lip and one trouser-leg rolled up and looked as if he was going on a day-trip to the beach.

After crossing three platforms, we found ourselves in front of a large wooden gate that a railway official hurriedly opened for us. Waiting in a small parking lot were three white Toyota Land Cruisers with *Gong An* written in big blue letters down the side. I was quickly bustled into the back of the second one and told to sit in the middle.

After some discussion two officers jumped in on either side of me and then another two in the front. The one on my left said hello and tried to start a conversation in English but I was less than interested, preferring to watch what was going on. Suddenly the radio belched into life, spilling out static and staccato bursts of nonsensical singsong. Another car drew up alongside us and before I knew it we were belting through the back streets in convoy with the *woah woah woah* of the sirens wailing and flailing like knives cutting their way through Shanghai's murky midnight atmosphere.

'Hang on a minute,' I thought. 'This is a bit over the top. They're treating me like some bloody mass-murderer. Is there really any need for all this fuss?'

From my position in the middle I could see out through the front window as the Toyota was slung into corners and frightened pedestrians fled to safety. As we slalomed through the traffic, cars emerging from side streets were forced to brake, while cyclists veered off the road. The driver seemed to get more and more charged up with every narrow escape, and drove faster and faster. 'Been watching too many movies,' I whispered to myself as he and the others puffed away on their smokes.

'Can I have one?' I asked, using the other sentence I knew in Chinese.

'No,' came the reply.

'Where are we going?'

'Some place nice.'

'Is it another hotel like in Urumchi?'

'Yes, that's right, like a hotel.'

Convinced that they were not taking me to jail, I decided that they were just using me as an excuse to have a thrash around the streets like the American cops they saw on TV.

Although my view was restricted, this was unmistakably Shanghai; known in the west at the turn of the century as an 'adventurer's paradise', it was a city where anything and everything was available to those who looked for life with spice, and where excess was easily affordable. Shanghai attracted every sort of human driftwood: writers, poets, businessmen interested in making a fast buck, sex tourists, drug addicts and criminals from all walks of life turned up to experience the best the east had to offer. It was said that there were ten thousand whores in Shanghai, and that that is why today you can still see Chinese men with straight noses and brown hair in the streets.

I had seen plenty of photographs of Shanghai and I knew what to look out for, but on this trip all I remember seeing were dozens of half-built high-rise blocks with bamboo scaffolding wrapped around them.

After about twenty minutes the convoy slowed down and turned into a large gateway with stone pillars and big red wooden doors. Accelerating swiftly up a gravel driveway flanked by a two-storey Chinese-style building with a sloped tiled roof and a balcony, I realised that we had arrived.

Another gateway appeared in the headlights on the right, where a large group of people were waiting and milling about. As soon as we pulled up, the doors were flung open and three unbelievably bright lights were switched on, blinding me and forcing me to bow my head. Dragged out of the vehicle by the cuffs, I was immediately surrounded by all these people as they bawled into their bloody radios, and at least three guys with video cameras tried to get a shot of my face. I did my best to turn away but someone grabbed me by the back of the neck with a thumb and a forefinger embedded into my flesh and then used his other hand to wrench my arms down. It was the first time in thirteen days that anyone had got heavy with me and I realised that the weather had changed.

Bustled through the covered gateway into what looked like a courtyard and into a small room on the right of a large iron gate, I immediately noticed a wooden chair bolted to the floor with a restraining bar across the front of it. It looked like the electric chair out of a Cagney movie, and the surrounding decor wasn't far off either. Facing the chair was a high desk on a podium behind which sat an officer in uniform looking on in apparent disgust. The crowd in the doorway was blocked by a guy in plain clothes who was shouting and screaming in guttural tones and pushing the people back with his hands. It was chaos.

'What a bloody performance,' I thought as I looked around in disbelief. Then, all of a sudden, I just felt very small.

When Huang, Qu and little Zhu, the translator, pushed their way in I was sort of pleased to see them but they acted as if I was a total stranger and an enemy. The serious-looking cop on the podium ordered my cuffs to be taken off and that I strip. It was explained that I was being booked into the Shanghai Number 1 Detention House. 'Doesn't sound too bad,' I told myself. 'I mean, a house isn't like prison, is it?'

With the video camera filming my every move down to my long johns, I asked them if they wanted to see my arse, but Zhu told me it wasn't necessary. Any of my clothes that had any metal in them like buttons or zips were taken away, as were my belt and shoelaces. I was left wearing a T-shirt and my underwear.

Next to go was my watch, a jade pendant and my rings, including our wedding rings. All this, plus the two thousand HK dollars I'd had in the back pocket of my jeans and the note of transaction, were placed in a brown envelope with a list of contents. A copy of it was given to me, but I didn't have any pockets to put it in. They handed back my boots, and asked me my name, address and age, which I dutifully answered.

'From now on and at all times you will be known as number 392. You will address others by number or rank only. Time to go,' said the officer on the podium.

'Can I have my cigarettes?' I asked.

'No smoking!'

'What! No, no, no, I gotta have my smokes,' I exclaimed. 'It's too serious without them. Go on – just give us a couple for tonight.'

'Nobody smokes. It is against the rules.'

'But it's fucking torture, man!'

I was guided out of the door by a guard who looked as if his face had once been set alight and then put out with a shovel.

It was a long building with a high ceiling that reminded me of some kind of Dickensian workhouse. With its dank atmosphere, dim lights casting impenetrable shadows and the echoes of metal doors slamming and bolts being shot, I felt as if I had truly ventured through a rip in time.

I was led up a staircase to the next floor. On either side, I could see a line of hefty, well-built timber doors and little windows with iron bars. As I climbed the stairs, I could just make out the shape of countless bodies lying on the floor of what I realised were cells. Where was I exactly? This was no hotel, that was for sure. It didn't even look as if it belonged on the face of the earth.

The second floor was laid out in the same way, and as we walked down the corridor I could see the numbers painted above the doors on the left: 21, 22, 23, 24, 25. The door in front of me was wider than most, with a spy-hole in the top, a little closed hatch below it and a huge bolt running across the middle, on the end of which was the biggest padlock I'd ever seen, as big as a bag of sugar with a key the size of a wrench. They unlocked it to reveal a scene that I could never have imagined.

'They've sure as hell fucked up here. This can't be right,' I thought. The bodies on the floor, wrapped in an array of blankets and quilts, all sat up to greet me.

They stared in disbelief as I, a *yang gui zi* ('foreign devil'), entered their world. The looks on their faces questioned my presence in the same way that I questioned my own. 'What the hell am I doing here?'

As the guard barked at one of the occupants and a space was made for me next to the last one by the door. I sat down and the door was slammed shut. Looking around, all that I could think was that it was a cock-up. They'd made a mistake. It had been too late to bother with a hotel. It must be like that, because they surely don't expect me to stay here, do they? Maybe they'll move me tomorrow.

There were four Chinese sitting there, their backs against the wall. In the far right-hand corner was a raised section with a tiled wall around it, with a bath and a sit-down toilet behind it. One of them crawled over and, putting his arm around me, said, 'I am your friend, I speak a little English.'

I removed his arm. 'Get the fuck off me!' I snapped. I'm not having any of that shit, I thought. Best get this straight right from the start. 'What did the guard say?' I asked abruptly.

'He say come back give you blanket ve'y soon,' he replied peevishly.

When the blanket was tossed in five minutes later, I cringed at the sight of it. It had obviously been well used, and even felt warm, but what was I to do? I was feeling bloody cold. Ignoring the Chinese, I lay down. I was actually more tired than I knew, and I just wanted to close my eyes and erase the sight in front of me. Perhaps by morning it would all have gone away.

*

At six o'clock my roommates were up and busy stacking their bedclothes in one neat pile under the barred window adjacent to the door. I just wanted to go back to sleep.

Some time later I was woken by the creep from the night before and told that the guard was coming back to take me out. I'd missed breakfast but that was not what was worrying me most. God, I needed a cigarette. I ground my teeth, clenched my fists and watched as my leg started quivering. I'd kill for a smoke.

Suddenly the observation hatch opened and the guard called my number. As I stood up the door was opened and I was ushered out. They're going to take me to the hotel now, I thought. Feeling a bit better, I did my best to get a look in at the other rooms, but the windows were too high up and full of little round faces all staring out at me. At the bottom of the stairs we turned left under a covered walkway into a building of identical little rooms on either side of a narrow corridor. We entered room 19. One electric bulb hung from a long flex in the ceiling, and there was a wooden chair bolted to the floor with the restraining bar hanging down and a desk behind which sat Qu. He looked totally different – a terrible twin, maybe – in full winter uniform, with its high-buttoned collar stiffly done right up to the chin and piped epaulets, and not a trace of emotion. Beside him sat a stranger, but it was he who stood up first and offered his hand. He introduced himself and informed me that he was going to be the translator. To intensify the atmosphere, Huang walked in wearing his black leather jacket and his pet scowl, carrying a huge blue file.

They gave me my cigarettes and told me I could buy more if I wanted, but that I would only be allowed to smoke them in the interview room. I was already lighting up the second one when Qu, speaking in a voice that he had obviously kept in a box for the occasion, said that I was being officially arrested under some act or other of the Chinese law.

'What was that?' I asked, having difficulty taking it all in.

'The Banning of Narcotics Act, promulgated 30 December 1990.' He went on, blue cigarette smoke filling the air, illuminated by the sunlight that searched its way in through the cracked and stained window. 'Under suspicion of dealing in a banned substance, and also possession of the same substance, the Shanghai Public Security Bureau will detain you until their investigations are complete. It is our duty to inform you that a crime of this sort carries the death penalty. In order to gain leniency, we advise you to co-operate fully with the officers dealing with your case and any other representative of the government who may seek your assistance. Do you understand what you have just been told?'

'Yeah,' I managed, my mouth open catching flies, and already going for my fourth smoke. I felt as if I'd been hit in the chest with a sledgehammer. I could feel my heartbeat booming inside of my head. I've slipped into the Twilight Zone, I thought.

'Would you please sign your name here, and place a thumbprint over it.' A sheet of paper with a heap of Chinese characters on it was pushed over to me with a pen and a small round container with a red-ink sponge inside.

'Wait a minute. What is it?'

'It is a document that says that you are fully aware of the fact that you have been arrested.'

I signed and, as I did, asked, 'Excuse me, but do you think you could tell me where my wife is?'

Huang looked up at me quickly and scowled. Then, baring the yellowest set of long irregular incisors this side of the grave, said, 'We don't know. Isn't she in Xinjiang?'

'Yeah, but where in Xinjiang?'

After a second, he turned and said almost convincingly, 'We will try and find out for you.'

And that was that. The cigarettes were taken back and I was escorted back to cell 25 and my new friends. I was suddenly struck by the immensity of it all. They had no intention of moving me to a hotel. I was going nowhere, not for a long time . . . at least not for a couple of weeks, anyway.

The room began to close in on me. I needed to think, I needed to walk, but there was nowhere to walk to. I could, if the others were sitting down, find five steps in a straight line, but it wasn't enough. I felt my mind turning in on itself, searching for a place big enough to find the answers to my questions and close out the impact of my immediate surroundings. The light at the end of the tunnel was disappearing fast, and I had to reconsider my situation. What was I going to say to these people? How was I going to hold my story together so as not to screw myself or ShaSha or anybody else?

I found inane things to do to pass the time. I rolled up bits of paper and threw them at the spyhole and I sailed a plastic bowl in the bath. Water was rationed. It was only on in the morning and the evening for one hour, so in order to wash during the day we used the bath as a water tank.

We had very few words of common language between us, because the creep,

Jiang, could only speak a few sentences. Like that, I was left with my eyes as the only tool to recognise friend or foe. Without the extra complication of having to decipher fanciful stories, lies and bragging, I found that I could make a fairly good assessment. As hours turned into days, I studied my 'comrades in detention' and tried to work them out, their characters and their backgrounds. I found out later that once a person had been arrested, he was automatically expelled from the Party and thereafter not allowed to be known as a comrade any more. Instead we were all *tong fan*, which meant 'together prisoner person'.

The man on my left was known as Lao Gu, or Old Gu, *lao* being a term of respect used by the young. I'd guess he was about fifty-five. He'd worked as a controller on the docks in Shanghai and was accused of accepting a bribe of seven thousand pounds. I was fairly disquieted to hear that this was his thirteenth month in detention, though he seemed to accept it as normal.

The guy on my right was a young man of about twenty called Zhou. I was led to believe that he had assisted his father in dumping a large quantity of toxic waste in a river. He was, however, shackled with medium-weight leg-irons, which Jiang claimed was because he'd had a fight in his previous cell, and the irons were a safety measure. It would be a while before I'd suss that this was bullshit.

Jiang was tall and in his late twenties. He wore cracked glasses and was covered in bumfluff. All day every day he did things with bits of paper. He eventually revealed to me that he was trying to find a way to devise his own program so as to be able to write Chinese on the computer. He was writing the common strokes of certain Chinese characters on little cards that he'd made by sticking pages of magazines together with rice glue. He made that by keeping rice from breakfast and putting it into a sock, which was then left to soak in water for an hour. Then he tied it tightly and kneaded the whole thing, sock and all, until a thick paste began to seep out through the cloth. The resulting gunge was as effective as any wallpaper glue on the market, and he stuck sheets and sheets of paper together to make card. The final product was left under a weight and, when dry, folded in half and cut using a thick thread taken from the quilt.

Rice glue turned out to be the most useful tool we had to help us pass the time, stretching the ingenuity and essential for the making of playing cards, binders, work boards, book covers and pen stems to hold the quills that were made from old toothpaste tubes. Since we were only allowed to have a nib pen and ink from the guards if we were writing a confession, the home-made version became a prized possession. As I watched Jiang play with his cards and Mr Gu sew his bedding and a bag which he hoped to use when he was released with a needle that he had fashioned from a pork bone, I realised that I had to find a way to kill the time.

I started writing, especially late at night, and to do that I had to pinch ink from the bottle every time it came and dilute it with a little water. Because paper wasn't allowed either, I'd write the night away on the pages of old magazines, practising *go* moves or anything that came into my head. I would listen to the ships sounding their horns as they sailed up the Huang Pu River, and imagined the places they had come from and the exotic destinations they were bound for. Their freedom emphasised my confinement, increasing the pressure and the self-recrimination.

Monkey Masks

There was things which he stretched, but mainly he told the truth.

Mark Twain (1835–1910), *The Adventures of Huckleberry Finn*

THE police had left me alone for four days, and when the call came on the morning of 25 October, I was so happy if only just to get out of that bloody cell and down to the interrogation room for a smoke. I also thought there might be a chance that they were going to ask me to pay up and let me go. My high spirits didn't last for long.

Huang and Qu and the translator were waiting for me in room 14. It was exactly the same set-up as before, including the cloud of blue smoke. The only difference now was that an angle-poise lamp had been placed on the desk, bent up and back, and facing me. It was like a black-and-white Fu Man Chu movie from the 1940s. They had to be taking the piss.

The door was open and a procession of people came up the corridor and peered in, talking loudly and laughing. It felt like a bloody circus. Then I noticed an unopened carton of two hundred Peony on the table. The translator, who had decided to call himself Alan (probably after Delon), broke into it and passed me a packet. I lit up and Huang began.

'I want first to advise you of the importance of co-operation,' he said. 'It is only by your full co-operation that you can receive leniency. You are suspected of serious crimes against the People's Republic of China, and if, after trial in the People's Court, you are found guilty, you will be punished in accordance with Chinese law. Do you understand?'

'Yes.'

'The people of China have suffered at the hands of imperialist drug barons like you before and have not forgotten. The Opium Wars are still fresh in our memories and we will not let this desecration happen again. The sooner you confess your crimes against the people of China the better it will be for you.'

'Hang on a minute – you're talking about the Opium Wars? That was a hundred and fifty years ago. It's nothing to do with me, is it?' I said in disbelief. 'Fucking nutters,' I thought to myself.

'Do you feel it necessary to call the British consul now?'

I didn't want to involve the consul yet, as I imagined it might damage ShaSha's visa application. Moreover, the way he'd asked implied that it wasn't something they approved of, and I didn't want to go making any more enemies than I had done already, by being linked to the bloody Opium Wars. 'No,' I said. 'I don't think that's necessary just now. How about seeing a lawyer, though?' I asked. I knew immediately from the look on Huang's face that he didn't want to hear it.

'According to Chinese law you will be allowed to see a lawyer after, if and when you are indicted. When we have completed our investigations we will send our findings to the Procuratorate. If they should decide to indict you, you may then seek the help of a lawyer.'

It was becoming a decidedly dodgy situation. And what the hell was a Procuratorate?

Qu continued: 'You have had time to think over your position and we now give you the opportunity to make any changes you feel may be necessary to the statement you made on 16 October in Urumchi. You are advised again that full co-operation is the only way to gain leniency.'

'Well,' I ventured, 'I think I've covered the most of it already . . . there's not really much more that I can add.'

The looks on their faces told me they were not convinced. 'We believe that there are some omissions, and some mistakes on your part,' said Huang.

'No, I don't think so.'

Every day for the following week we played cat and mouse, and I was beginning to think they might have swallowed it all. Then one day Huang said, 'Have you ever met two German nationals by the name of Hauser and Schmidt?'

Oh no! How the fuck did Werner and Dieter get sussed? I couldn't believe they could have been nicked because they had left months before, back in July. And what about Thundernose? Had they caught him too?

'I'm not familiar with those names. They sound like surnames, and I only ever know people by nicknames or their Christian names,' I said, fairly truthfully.

'We have signed statements from these two Germans confirming that it was you who sold them hashish. They have since made other statements which reveal that they dealt with you on numerous previous occasions. Maybe you'd like to hear what they say?'

Huang was loving it, and could barely stop himself sniggering.

'Go on, then,' I said.

He began with Dieter's first statement, dated 7 August, and read out the bits he liked. Then he read Werner's, dated 9 August. Both named me as the source of all the hash they had been caught with. The later statements he handed over to me to check for authenticity, and while I tried to read what was written there, he read from a Chinese version, which Alan translated.

I had to think, and think quickly. I had been accused of the whole deal plus all the pressing as well as the previous deal we'd done in the autumn of 1990. Everything pointed to me, without a single mention of anybody else's involvement. 'Bastards!' I thought. It looked pretty certain to me that Werner and his mate had been caught getting on the boat to Japan, and it was fairly sure that they were still in the detention house. But where? Was Thundernose banged up too? If he was, how come his name hadn't been mentioned? Quickly, I deduced that this was probably because he wouldn't have opened his bloody mouth as fast as the Krauts.

'Do you wish to make another statement?'

What to do? They had me for the dope in my possession and were threatening to jail me for that alone. If it went to court they had two witnesses to testify against me and say that I was their dealer. Who were the judges going to listen to – me or the two Germans? If I tried to claim innocence and they then found me guilty, they would undoubtedly come down hard. But the thought of what might happen if I confessed scared me. It would mean I had nothing to hold on to. Decision time.

I spoke in English. Alan translated and Qu wrote it all down in Chinese. When I was finished the whole thing was read back to me. It didn't sound at all like what I'd said.

'Is that correct?' Huang asked.

'No, it's nothing like what I said.' They'd missed all the little details I thought were crucial and twisted it all around to suit themselves.

We went through it all again, sentence by sentence. And then we did it again, until my brains were cooking and there was only one cigarette left in the packet.

Eventually I agreed that it was somewhere near and I was then asked to write at the bottom of each page, 'I have read the above, and it is correct.' I then had to sign my name and give it a red thumbprint.

'Hey, Alan,' I said, 'how long am I going to be here?'

'Oh, about two months. Until the investigations are complete.'

Two months was a long time, but not that bad. I checked the date and started my countdown. With most of my optimism still intact, I made myself believe that when the two months were up, they would fine me and give me a deportation order. Things could still work out all right. If they didn't allow me back into China to get ShaSha, I'd have to try and get a fake passport in Hong Kong.

*

Lunch that day was cold cabbage and rice, the same as it was every day except Sundays when they gave us broad beans and rice. The Chinese occasionally got some fatty pork, but because I didn't eat pork out of respect for ShaSha's Muslim faith, they gave me a fried egg instead, which was invariably cold and sometimes green. Breakfast was rice with fermented bean curd or tofu delivered at seven o'clock in metal containers shaped like binocular cases handed in through the observation hatch two at a time with a pair of disposable chopsticks stuck in the rice. We had less than five minutes to finish the meal before the guard came back for the containers, so everybody emptied their food out into another bowl so as to be able to eat at a more leisurely pace and at a time that suited you better. Lunch arrived at eleven, and supper, usually fried egg and rice, at four-thirty in the afternoon. That meant a hell of a long time until the next meal, so most people, or those who could afford it at least, ate a bowl of instant noodles at nine in the evening when the last hot-water ration was handed in. As the days went by, my cellmates' noodle-eating annoyed me more and more. It was like a competition to see who could make the most noise, slurping, sucking, belching and snivelling.

We got hot water three times a day. It was just hot enough to make tea and noodles but you had to be quick. Sometimes it was possible to get the *lao dong*, the worker who was responsible for the dispensing of food and water, to give us a little bit extra, enough to have a good strip-down wash, but it was a rare deal and for the most part those who were hygiene-conscious had to make do with a cold wash. The workers were usually short-term prisoners with sentences of just two or three years who had decided that it was a better idea to stay where they were rather than go to Tilan Qiao, the Shanghai city jail. It sounded a fearsome place, a destination that struck terror into the hearts of everyone.

Apart from interrogation and a haircut, we were never let out of the cell. There was rumoured to be a small exercise yard at the back somewhere, but nobody had ever seen it. Exercise was a matter of waiting your turn in the cell to pace up and down for a couple of hours a day.

If anyone had the misfortune to be ill, a guard in a white coat who made out he was a doctor came round and got you to stick your arm out through the hatch so he could take your pulse. Conditions were nearly always diagnosed as being normal for one's age, and treated with *Niu huang jie du pian*, which if translated comes out as 'cow bezoar detoxicating tablets'. The dictionary reveals bezoar to be 'a stony concretion found in the stomachs of goats, antelopes, llamas, chamois, etc., formerly esteemed an antidote to all poisons'. These little yellow pills made you belch and your breath stink, the very same as a goat, and caused the almost inedible food to taste as if they'd poured diesel over it.

For the first month I was hauled out of the cell three times a week for questioning and asked to go over my story time and time again. 'From the beginning, please . . .' I could sense that the police were not entirely satisfied with my version of events because I was leaving too much out. I was deliberately vague and evasive. They wanted names, but I was always mixing them up and I never mentioned anybody's surname. I even included people who didn't exist, and did my best to make it damn difficult to identify anyone clearly. I was also still hoping that word of this fiasco had filtered down through the grapevine, and that the people I knew were staying the fuck away from China. At that time I still believed there was a code of honour between smugglers and dealers. That romantic little notion was soon to evaporate. I was waking up to the real world, a world where looking after number one was the only thing that mattered.

It was clear that things had changed and that the government wanted to stamp out the growing trend of foreign hash dealers operating in China. They'd brought in a new law at the end of 1990, because previously there was nothing in the books on how to deal with hash. It had been purely discretional, with the police just trying to scare people into coughing up as much as money as they could as fines. I was among the first to go down under this Banning of Narcotics Act, and was to be made an example of for propaganda purposes. I still believed that after I'd served that purpose they would fine me and let me go.

Jiang had told me that there had been a British guy in cell 25 a few months back who had been able to smoke every day in the cell. Jiang was getting the odd smoke himself in from the *lao dong*, which we'd share in the dead of night. That was until he told me he didn't have any. The smell woke me up at four in the morning and I caught him finishing off a whole one on his own. The argument that followed put paid to both our nocturnal nicotine hits and from then on I had to rely on interrogation for a smoke.

Towards the end of November I was asked again if I wanted to see the consul and this time I decided it was necessary. I was still getting deeper and deeper into shit. Jim Short, the vice-consul in Shanghai, turned up and we met in a Portakabin outside the main compound. Jim, his translator, eight policemen and their translator sat on big comfy red armchairs while I sat in front of them all in the middle of the room on a very hard wooden chair. No worries – I was getting used to it and just happy to be able to devour my five cigarettes in the allotted measly half-hour visiting time. The massive turn-out of top-brass officials indicated that they were very serious. I couldn't believe that my little bit of hash could have created such a stir but by turning out in force like that in front of my consul gave the impression that I was public enemy number one.

I had been instructed that I was not permitted to discuss my case or say anything defamatory about the police, the detention house or the government. That left me with hardly anything to talk about, and what was the point of the visit if I couldn't speak about the case? It was nevertheless nice to speak to someone in English for a change. Jim asked me how I was and what the conditions were like, but what could I say? I told him that it wasn't very good, but I also knew that complaining wasn't going to change anything or make things better for me.

I learned from him that the other Brit had been sentenced to four years, and had already begun serving it at Tilan Qiao, confirming what I'd heard. It was not good news at all and showed they were ready to jail foreigners after all. I'd assumed that he must have been carrying heroin to receive such a stiff sentence, but now I found out that it was actually just over seven kilos of hash. This was definitely a blow, but I still managed to cushion it by telling myself that his crime was more serious. He'd been caught smuggling and with much more than I had. Like that, there was no way they could give me four years. I continued with my two-month countdown, positive that I would be away.

Jim also mentioned that the papers in Hong Kong and back home had got hold of the story and were trying to get information from the consul about me. He assured me that it was against the policy of the British consulate to divulge such details. I wondered what was being said, and how it was being taken at home. Surely now everybody would know that I had been busted and would stay well clear.

Before time was up, he also managed to tell me that there was another Briton in the detention house, a guy called Webster from the north of England, who was also in for a hash crime. I wondered who he could be. Had I met him somewhere? Or was he the guy I'd heard about in the summer? But what the hell had happened to Thundernose? Was he or was he not in the same building?

Back in the cell, I contemplated the poster on the wall which Jiang managed to translate to me as saying, 'Confess your crime to gain leniency, inform upon those you know or suspect of criminal acts even if and especially so if they are members of your family, like your father, mother, brother or sister, in order to gain leniency.' What a sick bloody country, I thought.

Every night the detention house echoed with the screams of those who were being tortured and those who had confessed and knew they were heading for the 'small peanut', the name they used for the bullet. The rattle of shackles up and down the stairs as prisoners were taken out for night-time interrogation was in itself a warning that if you didn't confess it could be you next. It was hard enough to get to sleep as it was with the lights full on, but with that nightly horror show it was almost impossible.

I stayed awake as long as I could, scribbling away and learning a little Chinese so as to be able to ask for things and not feel so totally shut off from my surroundings. As I lay there in the dead of night, I relived every second I'd spent with ShaSha. It was almost mystical the way in which I could summon such vivid recollections in the smallest detail, replaying my favourite moments again and

ABOVE: Id Kah Main Square
© Tom Broadbent

RIGHT: In the name of God
© Tom Broadbent

BELOW: The Sunday Market
© Tom Broadbent

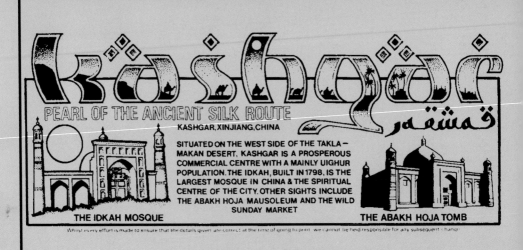

kashqar

PEARL OF THE ANCIENT SILK ROUTE

KASHGAR, XINJIANG, CHINA

SITUATED ON THE WEST SIDE OF THE TAKLA-MAKAN DESERT, KASHGAR IS A PROSPEROUS COMMERCIAL CENTRE WITH A MAINLY UIGHUR POPULATION. THE IDKAH, BUILT IN 1798, IS THE LARGEST MOSQUE IN CHINA & THE SPIRITUAL CENTRE OF THE CITY. OTHER SIGHTS INCLUDE THE ABAKH HOJA MAUSOLEUM AND THE WILD SUNDAY MARKET

THE IDKAH MOSQUE

THE ABAKH HOJA TOMB

Whilst every effort is made to ensure that the details given are correct at the time of going to print, we cannot be held responsible for any subsequent change

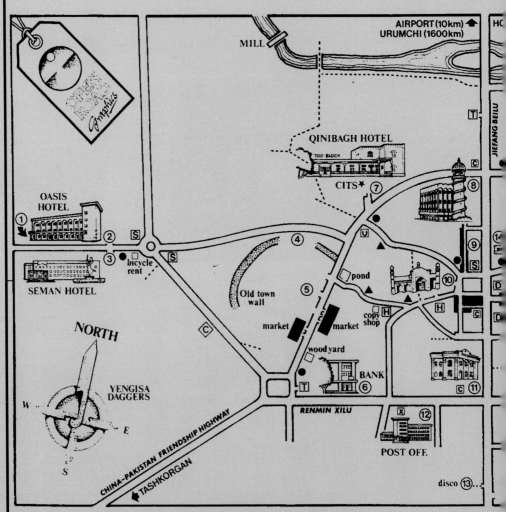

Map of Kashgar
© John Calanan

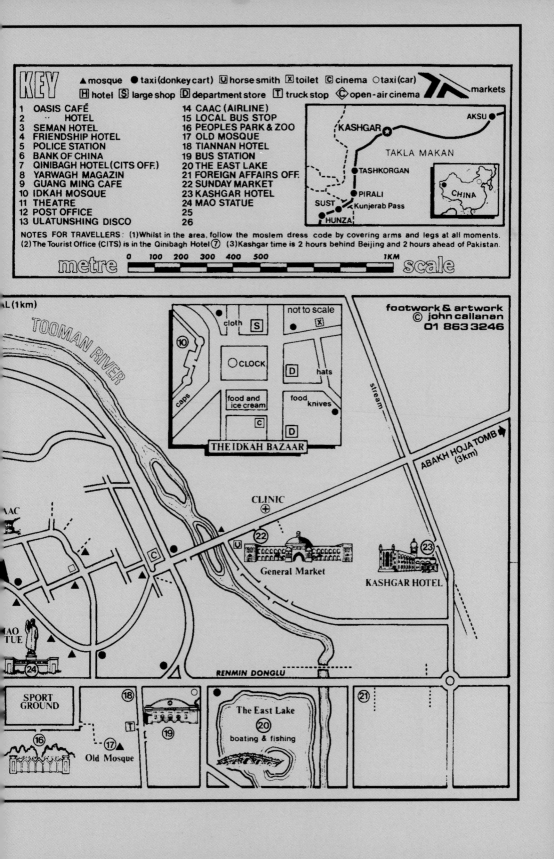

KEY

▲ mosque ● taxi (donkey cart) U horse smith X toilet C cinema O taxi (car) ↗↗ markets

H hotel S large shop D department store T truck stop C open-air cinema

1 OASIS CAFÉ
2 ·· HOTEL
3 SEMAN HOTEL
4 FRIENDSHIP HOTEL
5 POLICE STATION
6 BANK OF CHINA
7 QINIBAGH HOTEL (CITS OFF.)
8 YARWAGH MAGAZIN
9 GUANG MING CAFE
10 IDKAH MOSQUE
11 THEATRE
12 POST OFFICE
13 ULATUNSHING DISCO
14 CAAC (AIRLINE)
15 LOCAL BUS STOP
16 PEOPLES PARK & ZOO
17 OLD MOSQUE
18 TIANNAN HOTEL
19 BUS STATION
20 THE EAST LAKE
21 FOREIGN AFFAIRS OFF.
22 SUNDAY MARKET
23 KASHGAR HOTEL
24 MAO STATUE
25
26

AKSU

KASHGAR

TAKLA MAKAN

TASHKORGAN

PIRALI

SUST Kunjerab Pass

HUNZA

CHINA

NOTES FOR TRAVELLERS: (1) Whilst in the area, follow the moslem dress code by covering arms and legs at all moments.
(2) The Tourist Office (CITS) is in the Qinibagh Hotel ⑦ (3) Kashgar time is 2 hours behind Beijing and 2 hours ahead of Pakistan.

metre   0 100 200 300 400 500   1KM **scale**

AL (1km)

TOOMAN RIVER

footwork & artwork
© john callanan
01 863 3246

cloth S not to scale X

10

CLOCK

caps

D hats

food and ice cream

food knives

C

D

THE IDKAH BAZAAR

stream

ABAKH HOJA TOMB
(3km)

CLINIC

AAC

U 22

General Market

23

KASHGAR HOTEL

MAO TUE

24

RENMIN DONGLU

SPORT GROUND

18

T

19

16

17 Old Mosque

The East Lake
20
boating & fishing

21

TOP: The old Administration building in Chinibagh
© Tom Broadbent

MIDDLE: The destruction of the Administration building in Chinibagh
© Tom Broadbent

ABOVE: No sign of Timothy's here
© Tom Broadbent

ABOVE: Oasis Café, a study in oils
© Robert H. Davies

RIGHT: Chamalvagh ('north park'),
an oil painting (from memory)
© Robert H. Davies

BELOW: Li Jiangping and daughter
© Dicky Mint

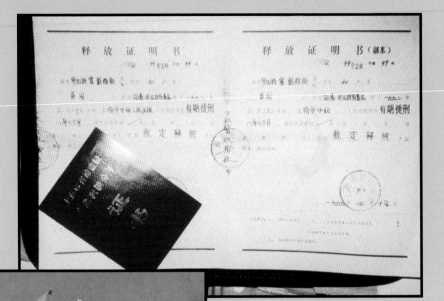

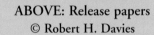

ABOVE: Release papers
© Robert H. Davies

LEFT: The Reformers on stage
© Robert H. Davies

BELOW: Reform Activist
Certificate
© Robert H. Davies

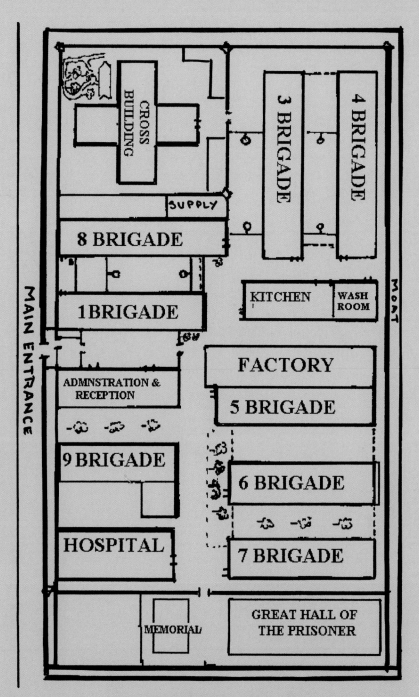

Map of Shanghai Tilan Qiao Prison
© Robert H. Davies

The Kiss
© Robert H. Davies

again. The time we spent on the roof of the hotel celebrating the moon festival, walking our dog Kaiser by the river, throwing water over each other on hot summer days in the garden and cycling down dusty tree-lined lanes holding hands and shouting, 'I love you!' at the top of our voices.

During the day the whole place was rocked by the incessant jabbing of jackhammers knocking down the building next door. This, together with the ever-increasing cold, really punished the nerves and led to more bouts of depression and self-reproach. The shadows that I watched crawl across the wall every day, marking time, grew into the image of a hunched and weeping figure lost in turmoil and heading for purgatory. It was as close to hell as a man can get without dying. The description in *A Portrait of the Artist as a Young Man* by James Joyce where a small bird moves a mountain, a grain of sand at a time, summed up perfectly the experience of enduring those hours, day in, day out. 'At the end of all those billions and trillions of years, eternity would have scarcely begun.'

I would spend as long as possible balancing on a small ledge at the window, looking down into the courtyard, waiting to see people leaving or simply the guards going about their business in freedom. I watched the cranes operate on a distant construction site, swearing that if they let me go right then and there, I would work on that site for nothing for four years rather than spend one more minute in that cell.

I soon realised that we in cell 25 were actually quite privileged. We were, after all, only five to a cell. Nearly all the other rooms contained fourteen or more people, and in the rooms downstairs where they were holding criminals who had already been sentenced and were awaiting prison allocation there were up to twenty-five or more per room. It was said that no one went for a piss at night in these cells because they wouldn't be able to get their sleeping spot back afterwards. For so-called troublesome detainees, there was a special cell on the ground floor. It was said to be a metre high and a little bit less than that deep and wide. It had no light and most times the troublemaker would be squeezed inside, handcuffed and wearing a 'monkey mask'. This was a tight-fitting leather mask that covered the whole head and was laced up from behind. It had only a very small hole through which to breath, and that meant that the subject had to remain completely calm in order to receive sufficient oxygen. If he got excited he would simply pass out.

With fewer interrogation outings I was getting less nicotine, so every time I felt my craving reach the point where I could bear it no more, I'd climb up onto the window-ledge and shout down the corridor, '*Bao gao, guan li yuan!* – Report to the controller!' until eventually someone would come to my assistance and I'd request to speak with the chief warder. Every time he'd take me to his office for a chat and offer me a smoke. Once a week was as much as I could push it, but it made a difference.

At the beginning of December I was called out for more questioning. They tried to make out that they had new information and that I was not telling them the whole truth. They were right, of course, but there was only one thing worrying me, and that was the kilo that I had stashed under the floor of the house. I'd come to the conclusion that if it was found during a police search or by the landlord doing some renovation, they'd nail ShaSha for it. Also, I figured that if I did own up to it, after all that time, they would surely think that I had divulged everything at last.

They'd been trying to get me to implicate ShaSha at every opportunity, once making out that they had a photograph of her smoking hash.

'How do you know it's hash?' I'd asked.

'It's the way she's holding it,' said Huang.

'Pshaw!' I replied, disbelievingly.

After making my final statement, throwing in the kilo under the floor for good measure, they asked me to go back to the cell and write it all down in my own words. It amounted to twenty-four pages. To confess to a crime is probably one of the most difficult things to do, but when I did finally spit it all out, it was one hell of a relief. Rolling into December, I started having interviews with the Shanghai Municipal People's Procuratorate's acting procurator, Chen Rongqing. I had to recount the whole story again and again and again. But I had become used to it all by then, and just concentrated on the cigarettes. However intimidating this guy was in his light-green uniform with red epaulets and his sneering grin, he did permit me to write a letter to my parents and to ShaSha, whom he promised to locate for me. During the two months of interrogation, I had been prevented from contacting my family in any way. Without the help of the consul, no one would even have known where I was. But that was nothing compared to the Chinese – they weren't allowed to write to anyone at all the whole time they were in detention. People simply disappeared from their workplaces or off the street and that was that. A family might – but only might – find out the whereabouts of a loved one after an extensive search and endless visits to police stations.

The letter to my mother and father was a nightmare to write. It was full of clichés and truisms. How could I explain what I had done? I tried to assure them that it was not their fault, that it was only my own recklessness that had got me into it all. I was fine, and in good health and spirits. Of course, I was ever mindful of the fact that it would be read by the police and therefore I censored myself no end. I had to wonder sometimes who I was trying to impress, the police or my parents. I dreaded the moment they would open it and learn from my own hand that I had come to such a miserable end.

Time dragged by, but I was thankful that Alan the translator had taken an interest in me and was willing to help in whatever way he could. I had expressed an interest in studying Mandarin, *putong hua*, and he had gone out to a foreign bookshop in Shanghai and bought me some study books and a little dictionary. I was damned if I was going to waste the opportunity to really accomplish something during all those long hours, and immediately immersed myself with the study of Chinese characters. I spent nearly every waking minute writing the complicated ideograms out over and over again for up to fourteen or fifteen hours a day. I had become increasingly lucid, I was alert, thinking more clearly than I had done for years, and found that I could actually make myself remember things. After all, I had nothing to cloud my vision – no alcohol or hash and very few cigarettes. I felt that I could accomplish anything I turned my hand to. There was no mountain I couldn't climb, figuratively speaking at least. In actual fact it was simply an escape mechanism, but it was in this way that I soon managed to write a letter to ShaSha, wherever she was, using Chinese. It was a simple letter but it conveyed the message of concern, everlasting love and steadfastness, and I included in it a poem I'd found in one of my study books. It was by Li Shangyin (810–861), a famous poet of the Tang Dynasty, and was written for his wife. At the time he wrote it, Li was in Sichuan while his wife stayed at home somewhere in the north.

A Poem-letter to My Wife, Written on a Rainy Night

You ask me when I'll be back,
but the date of my return has not yet been fixed.
The night rains in the Daba Mountains
are filling the pools with cool autumn waters.
When will we sit together at our western window
and trim the wicks of our wedding candles,
While talking about this
rainy night in the Daba Mountains.

It said it all so succinctly, and as soon as I read it I knew that it had been sent to me especially. It was a message that I knew ShaSha would understand more than any amount of my own ramblings. I addressed it to her father's house and hoped that he could get it to her, if indeed he knew where she was. I tried to reassure myself that she would be at home, but the vision I had of her leaving the hotel in Urumchi on her own that day still haunted me. There was something not right about it.

Many times I wanted to tell the police that I was already a reformed criminal. I'd had enough. The detention house was worse than any prison I'd ever heard of. They had never even portrayed a place like this in the movies, and it was punishment enough as it was. I swore that if they let me go, I would never do anything illegal again.

By late December my leg joints had started to swell up, and I was putting on weight fast. Without cigarettes, food tasted good. Even cold egg and cabbage had its attractions. They gave me a lot of bread because they thought that foreigners didn't eat rice, but I swapped it for loads of starchy rice and stuffed my face every day. My knees couldn't take the extra weight, though, and I had stopped pacing and stayed sitting down on my bed roll sixteen hours a day studying.

I had heard that the Germans were going to court somewhere around 14 December, but in a consul visit just before Christmas I found out that their case had been withdrawn. Surely that was good news. But the consul was non-committal. It was as though he knew something but wasn't prepared to tell me what. He did give me news of my family, however, and mentioned that the Hong Kong press had done a good job on me, labelling me a 'drugs baron'. I had to laugh. Since when did Pablo Escobar spend three days on the bloody bus to Urumchi, travel third-class or sell a kilo of hash for $200?

As I returned from seeing the consul one day, I caught a glimpse of myself in a large mirror that hung on the wall. My hair and beard had gone completely grey. My eyes were ringed and sullen and my stomach bulged out over my trousers. What the hell had happened to me in those few months? The weather was freezing cold as well, and I had been issued with an old blue padded jacket and trousers which gave me a definite gulag look.

For Christmas, I was told that I could purchase extra food, anything I liked within reason. This was great news, though apparently I had been able to buy things all the time, only no one had told me. I ordered a kilo of black tea, two kilos of garlic, six bottles of chilli sauce, twenty packets of mustard tuber pickle or *zha cai*, two kilos of dried beef, five packets of Lacovo (a chocolate drink powder), a kilo of peanut nougat sweets, ten kilos of apples and ten kilos of tangerines. To my surprise it was accepted, and within a couple of days it all arrived in the cell. I was suddenly a big banana in our room, but more importantly I could pay back Lao Gu for his months of generosity. Without him, life would have been a lot worse. The rest of them had turned into the most miserable bunch of bastards I'd ever encountered. I was fast learning about the Chinese mind and their attitude toward foreigners. Behind all that smiling and 'we are friends' crap, they hated us. Resentment and jealousy coursed through their veins like a virus. This was only the introductory lesson, though; the degree course would come later.

One evening, I got a tap message through the wall from cell 24. I'd figured for a while that there was a foreigner next door but I could never catch sight of him. I could barely hear through the walls as they were so thick, but I always imagined that I could hear English being spoken. (The detention house had been built in the 1930s to hold political prisoners and suspected spies. Each cell was originally intended for one prisoner only, to be held in total isolation, hence the thickness of the walls. Apparently they had been given a bed and a desk in those days, a far cry to the way the place was run now.)

The message that came through that night was in a code that substituted letters by numbers. It took an eternity to transmit and decipher, but I eventually found out that it was Werner next door. He was not optimistic of our chances of release, saying that he had been re-indicted. 'How's that possible?' I thought – and why the fuck had it taken him nearly three months to contact me? He also said that he knew of Jiang, and that he was KGB – which meant that he was a grass, in detention-house lingo. 'Look at his fingers – it's black ink on his thumbs.'

Of course, if he had been writing statements about his case while on his trips out of the cell, there would be red ink there, like everybody else. That also explained the cigarettes and the extra hard-boiled eggs that he got regularly. Bastard.

It was also at this time that I realised that Thundernose had somehow got away. If he was here, I for sure would have found out by now. What had happened? I wondered. It was Christmas, and my countdown had already reached its target. In my heart I knew that I wasn't going anywhere, but I continued to manufacture probable dates for my release, always believing that they would never keep me in for long. If I did get a sentence, it would only be about eighteen months maximum, and with good behaviour I could be out in half of that. Moreover, if they took into account the period I'd already served, I could be out and about in just over six months. I could handle that. I could use the time to learn Chinese. From then on, I made every effort to make as much progress as possible.

In the cell we managed to put old scores behind us and settle down to a

Christmas celebration with a midnight feast, all singing carols sitting cross-legged in a circle in the middle of the room. I was surprised to find that many carols were popular with the Chinese although not necessarily for their religious connotations. They particularly liked *Silent Night* and *Jingle Bells*, which sounded like *Jinger Bears* when the Chinese sang it.

The two *xun dao* or interrogation unit leaders managed the detention house in two halves; each controlled his own half independently from the other, and we were apparently lucky to have the one we did. According to general consensus, the other one was a right bastard. I cannot disagree since Xun Dao Jiang did go out and buy a Christmas cake for me, invited me to his office on Christmas Day for a chat and a smoke and allowed us to watch the little black-and-white TV for the day. From then on we got it every Friday from nine in the morning to seven-thirty at night. I appreciated the effort that had been made, and even wished him a Merry Christmas.

After New Year, which had been marked all over Shanghai by the most deafening firecrackers I'd ever heard, I was once again taken out for questioning regularly, first by the police to go over my story again, then by the procurator, and later by the translator who wanted my assistance to enable him to understand hash culture. Or so he said. I was asked about how it was smoked, why indeed it was smoked, what the effects were, why we pressed it, where it was grown, who smoked it and how much they were willing to pay for it. It was as if someone somewhere didn't know shit and was too embarrassed to come right out and ask.

Just before Chinese New Year, Jiang was moved to another cell. He tried to make out that he was going home, but the tap service managed to track him down to cell 12. You just had to watch and see where the boiled eggs went. His replacement, who arrived a few days later, was a guy called Sun, an architect from somewhere out in Jiangsu, the province directly north of Shanghai. He too was in for bribery, this time involving 90,000rmb or roughly £9,000 at that time. Considering he was an architect, this guy was extremely dumb. He would ask me things like 'Is there rice in Xinjiang?' or 'Are there any discotheques in Xinjiang?'. Best of all was 'Are there any Hami melons in Xinjiang?.

'Hami is in bloody Xinjiang, for God's sake!' I told him.

When I used the toilet, Sun would stand in front of me, peering in, up and around my bum, as if expecting some strange new western method of having a crap. Or maybe he thought gold bars would pop out. I couldn't handle this performance every day, and told him never to do it again. From then on he sat down, but he could never resist a glance or two as I pulled my pants up.

On Saturday, 1 February 1992, two days before Chinese New Year, I was taken downstairs, but instead of going to the interrogation rooms or the visiting cabin, I was taken out and around the back of the building to the right, to an extension on the main building. Inside it was all carpeted red with a stage at the far end with a big courtroom-type bench on top. It was not a big room – you could only maybe get twenty people in there seated at a push – but it was arranged so that there was a wooden chair with restraining bar positioned in front of the stage, with a row of armchairs against the far wall.

Behind the bench sat Chen Rongqing, his assistant and a new translator. In the armchairs were Huang, Qu and Alan. As I was marched to my seat, a horde of other men in green came in and milled about behind me. I got the impression that they'd never done this before and that there was no one prepared to take control. Not to worry: when it came to the nitty-gritty they knew how to kick you in the balls, so it didn't matter. I was being indicted.

Chen Rongqing read from his script in Chinese while his quite eloquent translator read the English version.

After a lot of introductory waffle, he read: 'The following has been proved through examination: in June and July of 1991, defendant Robert H. Davies sold 2,500g of hashish for US$500 to German nationals Werner S and Dieter H (handled in a separate case) in Kashi City, Xinjiang Uygur [*sic*] Autonomous Region and processed the hashish into chunks at the request of the buyers before concluding the transaction.

'On 7 October 1991, defendant Robert H. Davies checked into Room 731 of Xinjiang Hotel in Urumchi, Xinjiang Uygur Autonomous Region, carrying with him over 400g of hashish, which was discovered and seized on the spot by public security officers. Following the occurrence of this case, PSB officers also found and seized more than 1,100g of hashish which the defendant hid at his residence.

'The above-mentioned facts are clear and have been proved true by confessions of co-defendants S and H, seized narcotics and the *Criminal Scientific and Technological Test Report* of the Ministry of Public Security of the People's Republic of China. These evidences are reliable and full, and the defendant has made a confession to the same effect.

'To sum up, the Branch of the Shanghai Municipal People's Procuratorate affirms the following: defendant Robert H. Davies, in defiance of the law of China, trafficked in and illegally carried and hid hashish in relatively large quantities. His acts have constituted the crime of traffic in narcotics and the crime of illegal possession of narcotics respectively, which should be punished according to Article 171 of the Criminal Law of the People's Republic of China and Clause Two of Article Two and Article Three of the Resolution on Banning of Narcotics passed by the Standing Committee of the National People's Congress of the People's Republic of China.

'For the serious enforcement of China's law and for the maintenance of social security and order, the branch of the Shanghai Municipal People's Procuratorate hereby institutes, according to Article 100 of the Criminal Procedure Law of the People's Republic of China, a public prosecution against Robert H. Davies.'

The Most Frightening Man

Though you can believe what you choose, you must believe what you ought.
Cardinal Newman (1801–90)

I LISTENED to the indictment being read out with my heart pounding in my chest. I had finished interrogation more than four weeks before, and it had been long enough for me to distance myself from what had happened. Even though it had been my decision to confess, I felt as if I had been cheated somehow, because it all sounded completely different now. They had taken from me that which I had not been willing to part with. How had they managed that? I had done more than enough to co-operate, but they had turned and twisted it all, and left out the things I thought were important.

There were consolations, however. The police had not caught anybody else as a result of my confession, and they still didn't know the identity of Batur because even though I had stuck to the true sequence of events I substituted Batur for another. I had created a name for him, one I wouldn't forget: 'The Mullah', a mysterious and infrequent visitor from the desert whom I'd meet in bus stops, on street corners and on benches in the park. He dropped by my house in the dead of night. I had no idea where he came from. How could I? He never told me. Wherever it was, it was off limits to foreigners, anyway. Even better, no one could ever disprove my description of this man because no one else had ever seen him. Thank God Batur at least was safe.

But where was ShaSha? I had not heard one word. Did that mean she was not at liberty to reply or simply that she had not received my letter? I couldn't see what reason they could have to lock her up, but this was China. The hours and hours of sifting through every particle of information, trying to read hidden meanings into anything and everything the police or procurator said, produced every scenario imaginable, though none I could have faith in for more than a few hours. I forced myself into believing that she would be all right, that we would be all right.

The prosecutor asked me if I thought the indictment was accurate. I agreed that it was what I had confessed to but I was not very happy with all that talk about processing. What exactly were they trying to say? I maintained that I had only changed the shape of the hash. I had done nothing to alter the composition or the potency of it. Processing implied that I had had some sort of factory going. How could they prove that? The prosecutor brushed my protest aside, claiming that I couldn't be charged with it because processing wasn't a crime. Why put it in the bloody indictment then?

Most of the green bods then left the room, and I was alone with the prosecutor and the British vice-consul and a short bald little man in his fifties, who was supposed to be a translator. I was then informed that I could hire a lawyer. It was 7 February, four months since ShaSha and I had been rudely interrupted in Room 731 of the Xinjiang Hotel. Four months of constant coercion, threats and manipulation. Wasn't it a bit late for a lawyer? Hadn't the damage already been done? Nevertheless, I still felt that I needed somebody to help me. I could take the court-appointed lawyer if I wanted, but I didn't think much of the idea of a free lawyer – I mean, what incentive did he have? The consul then handed me a list of about fourteen lawyers and their law firms, each one with some innocuous comment written below like:

Yun Cui Dong, Shanghai No.1 Law Firm
Respected in legal circles.
Zhang Min, Shanghai No.2 Law Firm
Relatively cheap, speaks English.

Yang Chen Zhou, Shanghai No.3 Law Firm.

Expensive but well known.

I asked the consul why that last bloke was well known. The answer I received was 'because he's expensive'. That was the limit of his assistance. All he was prepared to say was that Webster had hired one guy, sacked him for incompetence and hired another called Ma Yu Min, who was also known by his English name, Philip Ma. He spoke English and was a dean of the Shanghai Law School. He belonged to the Shanghai No.8 Law Firm. He was also reassuringly expensive at US$70 per hour, which I assumed was an indication that he was competent. Not really knowing what I was doing, I plumped for Philip Ma.

Twelve days later on Wednesday the 19th, Mr Ma and his assistant rolled up at the detention house to see me. On first sight he reminded me of a doctor, a man of about sixty-five or seventy, balding and wearing half-frame spectacles on the end of his nose. The assistant was a young woman in her early thirties, dressed in a business suit and smelling provocatively of expensive perfume. They both spoke good English and were extremely polite.

After brief introductions, Mr Ma said, 'Do you know when you are going to court?'

'No.'

'Oh! Nobody's told you then?'

'No.'

'How strange. It's 3 March.'

'But that's only two weeks away. Will we have enough time to prepare?'

'Oh, I think so. But first we must agree terms and draw up a contract. Can you guarantee payment? Who will actually be paying the bill?'

'I'll arrange it with the consul,' I replied, getting the feeling that I was just about to be ripped off.

He pulled a contract written in Chinese from his briefcase, and began to read it out aloud in English. I'd never heard a lawyer's contract before and wondered if they were all the same. The first part identified the lawyer, his firm and that it was with him that the contract was being made to act as defence for Criminal 29, who was due to be tried on a drug-trafficking offence. The second part was the agreement on the cost per hour of US$70 not including any expenses, and for prompt payment. The third part stated that the lawyer could not be held accountable if the defence proved unsuccessful, that the defendant must at all times tell the truth to the lawyer, and that if it were proved that the defendant had been telling lies then the contract would be terminated. The fourth part stated that this was a legal document.

'I've only just received your material from the prosecutor and as yet I am not acquainted with your case. I will go back to the office now and read up on it. I'll see you next week when we will go through it all in detail.'

That was it. I hadn't even had time for four smokes. The bastard had come, made sure he could get his money, got me to sign an escape clause for when he ballsed it up, then made his excuses and buggered off without one word of advice.

On the afternoon of Tuesday the 25th, I had my first proper meeting with him. That was not what I expected either. He showed me a law book in English translation which stated that the maximum sentence for each charge was seven years.

'But that's fourteen years,' I said in horror.

'Oh, they won't give you that. You confessed and even told them the whereabouts of that one kilo in your house. You assisted the police in their investigation. Did anyone get arrested due to your statement?'

'I doubt it. Most of the people I know are probably in Jamaica by now.'

'That's a shame. You see, your German friends will undoubtedly get leniency for turning you in. You should remember that they never thought to protect you or your wife, so why do you continue to protect them and their friends when it could gain you leniency?'

At that moment I wondered if this guy was actually on my side or not. Was he a police spy or something?

'Since you have confessed to the crime of trafficking in drugs, you cannot plead innocence,' he went on. 'You will have to plead guilty. What we can do is plead for leniency, on the grounds that you co-operated with the authorities in their investigations and of your own free will, and confessed to your crime. Do you have any idea of how long you might go to jail for?'

'To be honest with you, no. I mean, this other English man got four years, which was pretty stiff, so I guess it will be a lot less than that, right? Especially if you can help me.'

'You think maybe two, two and a half, perhaps?' he said, almost reading my mind. This wasn't exactly what I wanted to hear. He continued, 'Do you know that the Germans were in court today? I was there as an observer, to hear the accusations they made against you.'

'What happened?'

'I learnt some things that might help you, but we will go into that later. I want to hear your side of things.' He then asked me to relate my story as it had happened, just like the police and the prosecutor had done before.

This meeting lasted for just over an hour, which didn't seem long enough to me, but he promised to come back the next day. We had gone on to discuss the effects of hash and its prevalence in Xinjiang. When I told him that it was everywhere, with grass growing in the hotel gardens and on the side of the road, he said, 'It's best that you don't mention that in court. The judges might take it the wrong way.'

'But it's a valid point. It proves that the use of hash is accepted there. It's part of the culture – everybody smokes. Even if they don't, they don't care if someone else does.'

'Ah, but you see, that is like saying there are two laws in China. The judges will not want to hear that.'

What the fuck's he talking about, I thought. The judges don't want to hear that? Surely judges were supposed to be impartial, prepared to listen to all mitigating circumstances and evaluate their relevance.

Two days later, on Thursday, 27 February, four days before the trial, Ma came again. We went through the story once more and discussed the amount of profit I had made in comparison to the profit the Germans could expect to make. I had told the police that I didn't know where the Germans were going. I simply never asked these questions, so I told the lawyer that I could only guess that if indeed they were going to sell the hash in another country, in Japan, for example, they could easily make US$10,000 per kilo, which was a 5,000 per cent profit. My profit was only 200 per cent, but they had a greater risk. Theirs was international crime. I didn't cross borders.

Ma then pointed out that I had to prove that I had never received any part of any profit that the Germans had gained from previous trips, and that I was not expecting any from this one, because I didn't know where they were going or what their intentions were. We also had to prove that I had never sold hash to any Chinese, and that apart from the purchase, the only people involved in my business were foreigners. It was important that we prove I had never encouraged any Chinese nationals to break the law, or done them any harm by the sale of drugs.

The next point concerned the amount. 'The Englishman' who had been given four years for trying to take seven kilos onto the boat to Japan had been described in his indictment as having 'a small amount of hashish'. How was it that in my indictment I was charged with trafficking, carrying and hiding hashish 'in relatively large quantities'? If you added up all the amounts referred to in the indictment, it still came to only four kilos, just over half the Englishman's 'small amount'. Ma asserted that the court must make a clear definition of what constituted a small, relatively large and a large amount. He continued: 'Do you believe that the hashish you possessed was a particularly potent example – stronger maybe than other hashish?'

'No. Hell, no – if anything it was less powerful. It wasn't like that Pakistani stuff that's all mixed up with oil and alcohol. That's why everybody liked Kashgar hash – it was clean and tasted really good. It was a nicer high.'

'Might not the potency of the drug then affect the amount? For example, if the content of active drug in a kilo of hash is 50 per cent, then you only have five hundred grams of the actual drug, and so on. If you had a kilo of sugar with one gram of heroin in it, does it mean that you have a kilo of heroin? There is no mention in the indictment of drug content. The court should make clear what it is that you have been found with. Tell me, is there any difference in strength between the leaf marijuana and hashish?'

'It's hard to say. Sometimes there is and other times there isn't. It depends on what it is and where it comes from. Dutch home-grown under lights can blow you right out, but I doubt that's the case in Xinjiang.'

At this point the meeting came to a close. Ma and his assistant promised to see me again on Monday, the day before the trial, when we would go through the trial process and he would advise me on what to say. He seemed to have found plenty of weaknesses in the case against me, and I was feeling a bit better.

On Saturday the 29th I had a surprise call-out. As I walked down the stairs to the interrogation block I thought it must be my lawyer, but when I entered the room it was Chen Rongqing, the prosecutor, sitting there grinning as usual. That bastard always made out he was my best friend, while at the same time turning a knife in my chest.

'I just wanted to clear a few things up before the trial,' he said. 'Could you go through your story once again, from the beginning.'

I set off down the road again, telling it all just as I had done countless times before. I didn't have to think about it any more, it just came out in a torrent.

Watching Chen as the translator fed it all back to him, I got the feeling he was hardly listening. Suddenly he raised his hand and bid me to stop. 'Tell me,' he said, 'did the Germans tell you where they were going?'

'No. I assumed they were going home.'

'Did they tell you they were going home the time before?'

'No. They told me when they got back.'

'Did they tell you that it was their intention to sell the hashish?'

'No, and I never asked. I assumed that they were just saving money, because hash is very expensive in Europe.'

'I believe that you are not telling me the truth. You knew where they were going, and you knew that they intended to sell the hashish. In your own best interests, I suggest that you co-operate with me on this. It is I who suggest to the judges that you receive leniency, but I can only do so if you co-operate with me. Do you understand my meaning?'

'I suppose I do,' I replied, thinking to myself that it was awfully coincidental that he should come here the day after I had spoken to the lawyer about it. I left, wondering what the consequences would be if I pissed him off, and at this stage how important it was, anyway.

That afternoon I was called out again. Must be the lawyer this time or perhaps the consul, I thought. It was neither. Instead, it was the most frightening man I'd ever seen in my life. As the door opened, I peered through a cloud of cigarette smoke and saw three figures behind the desk. The one in the middle was lit from behind by the dirty window. He sat back from the desk, his hands on his thighs, aloof, as if he didn't want to know the other two. He wore a grey Mao suit, buttoned tightly round his throat, which added to his severe countenance. His glasses were slightly tinted, leaving me to guess the direction of his coal-like eyes which no doubt at that moment saw straight through me.

The man was introduced as my judge. He was about forty, slightly balding and with a voice that sounded like a concrete block being cut with an electric grinder. He reminded me of a serial killer, which I suppose he was in a way. On his left was a cute little girl in the shortest mini-skirt I'd seen in a while, and on his right was a clerk. A translator arrived late and sat back against the wall to my right. He had decided to call himself Peter.

Tell your story from the beginning, we advise you to co-operate with the court and the prosecutor, it will be in your best interests so as to gain leniency blah blah blah. I had my smoke and was very soon back in the cell with the Gollums, as I had christened my roommates after the character in *The Lord of the Rings*.

Monday came around fast enough, and I was nervously pacing the cell when my number was called. There were so many questions I needed answering, but I kept forgetting them as fast as I thought them up. Down in the interrogation room, my lawyer and Li Yi Jun, the assistant, greeted me with a packet of Winston. That made a nice change. After the initial pleasantries, Ma lost no time in telling me that he had acquired the *Criminal Scientific and Technological Test Report*. He went on to say that it was all rather vague, in his opinion, and that this could be a very important oversight in the prosecution's case. 'The test result states that the content of tetra-hydro-cannabinol in the hashish seized is from 7.16 per cent to 10.18 per cent. Now, according to the Ministry of Justice, a substance must have a THC content of 10 per cent before it can be called hashish and classified as illegal. Anything under that figure cannot be called a banned substance. This result states that the hashish seized was from 7.16 per cent to 10.18 per cent, so how much was between 7.16 per cent and 10 per cent, and how much was between 10 per cent and 10.18 per cent? Do you understand what I'm saying?' said Ma looking rather pleased with himself.

'Yes, I see. So the answer to that will affect the amount of banned substance I actually dealt with, right? If I only had two hundred grams that was over 10 per cent, what then?'

'Well, this is what we have to find out. Another thing that puzzles me is the way they refer to the hashish. Do you know what an "ester" is?'

'Ester? Isn't it like the cream of something, or the essence? I don't know, you tell me.'

He didn't tell me. Not then, anyway. Almost as soon as he'd mentioned it, I'd forgotten about it, and we were already on to another subject. He gave me a rundown of what I could expect to happen at the trial, who would speak first and say what. I was advised to prepare something to say to the judges when it was my turn to speak, something about my foolishness, my sorrow and deep regret over having caused so much harm to the people of China by breaking their law. 'Remember, too, it's probably best if you don't mention the fact that there is hashish everywhere in Kashgar.'

This advice didn't fit at all. I hadn't done harm to any Chinese people. No one in China was dying because I'd sold two Germans a bit of hash. Nevertheless, I knew that I was going to have to grovel a bit, because that was the Chinese way.

After the visit I got straight down to knocking out a statement for the court. If they were going to give me the chance to speak, I would have to use it wisely. The consul had told me in his last visit that there might be quite a few foreign journalists present at my trial, because the case was being covered eagerly by all the Hong Kong papers, especially the *South China Morning Post*, and the *Daily Mail* back home. There was surely a way for me to let the world know my real situation here without the Chinese picking up on it.

Trial and Error

When walking into a still valley, one would feel glad to hear the sound of footsteps.

Chinese saying

USING my money, the translator Alan had been out and bought me a jacket, black trousers, a shirt and a pair of shoes. They obviously didn't want me to show up in public looking the dishevelled mess that I and the rest of the detainees had become in that hell-hole.

The detention house was more than enough to drive a man insane, and the harder they came in, the harder they fell. Heavies, gangsters, murderers and the like all broke eventually, and if they refused to confess they were simply kept there without charge or trial until they did. The latest arrival to our room had been in for three years and he'd just done a deal with the prosecutor and now they were close to sending him to trial. He had no other way to get out. They would keep him there indefinitely otherwise, so his best chance was to get a sentence – at least then he would know how long he had. His crime? Selling fake gas canisters.

So there I was in the minibus with eight Chinese guys, all of us handcuffed, two of them with leg-irons, whizzing through the streets of Shanghai again. We were accompanied by three young guards whose only job was to take defendants to and from court.

At eight o'clock in the morning Shanghai was already fully awake, the streets teeming with activity. It had been nearly four and a half months since I'd seen real life and, despite the circumstances, I was overjoyed to be able to witness ordinary people going about their daily tasks in shops, markets, restaurants, barber shops, on bicycles, in cars, or simply walking down the street. This was what it was all about: the noise, the pollution, the hustle and bustle, senses alive with smells of food, petrol, cigarettes. 'I can smell a pineapple somewhere, and vinegar. That's oil frying in a pan, those are peanuts, that's a burning clutch,' and a million other reminders of a life of freedom.

Half an hour later we had arrived at the court-house, a five-storey newly constructed building with a flight of steps leading up to the front doors. That entrance was not for us: we were whisked in through the main gate and around the back to a covered carpark where we were all ordered out. As we sauntered across to a door at the side, I noticed that we only had one guard with us, as the other two had gone on ahead. For a split second it crossed my mind that if we all did a runner, one of us just might make it. But it probably wouldn't be me. A foreigner had no place to hide. Obvious routes out of the country would be blanketed and I'd stand no chance.

We entered a short corridor with an glass-fronted office at the end and two rows of holding cells leading off to the right. We were told to line up, and as we did so one of the Chinese said something out of turn. He was punched in the head, thrown to the floor and kicked a few times. Quite an effective method of achieving immediate obedience. We were each shown to a cell and pushed in, the open barred door slammed shut behind. At the rear there was a concrete bench, but if you stood in the middle and stretched out your arms, you could touch the corners diagonally. Outside each cell, high up on the wall opposite, was a remote-control camera watching every move I made. I wondered why they were necessary, when all of a sudden the guards came down the alleyway to the cell next to mine. They had a long stick with which they could easily reach the back of the cell, and proceeded to beat the young prisoner in there until he screamed and begged them to stop. He'd apparently being trying to scratch his name on the wall along with all the others that had been put there in the vain hope of immortality before they were condemned to death.

The place smelt new, but you had to wonder how many of the frightened souls who had passed through there were still alive. In that cell, I probably felt as low as I could ever imagine. It was indeed the pits of existence. There was no lower.

At about eight-thirty Prosecutor Chen Rongqing came by, grinning and acting as if I were his long-lost buddy again. I hated his falseness, and he knew it. I knew that he hated me, and he knew that I knew, but still we persisted with the game. He reminded me of the benefits of co-operation, and left me sixty Marlboro as a gesture of goodwill. Waiting in that most miserable of cells lasted an eternity. I wanted to go back to my room at the detention house and be with the Gollums again.

When the time came at last for me to go up, I felt like I was on amphetamines. I was, I think, verging on panic, and folded the pages of my mind into ever smaller pieces, trying to concentrate on what was about to happen. I was taken out of the cell, out of the holding area, across the carpark and through a door that revealed a flight of stairs enclosed in iron bars. We climbed at least four flights and entered a corridor through a fire door.

There were a lot of people hanging about waiting for me, but I didn't look at any of them. My cuffs were taken off and two guards took me into the courtroom. Looking to the left, I could see rows upon rows of people sitting down behind a metal barrier. I wondered if ShaSha was there. No time to think.

It was a large room with tall windows on the far side that looked out on to a half-built tower block. I was taken to the middle of the room and told to sit down. The guards sat beside me, their caps pulled tightly down so that the peaks almost touched their noses. Six feet in front of me there was a pulpit-like thing on a podium and enclosed on three sides. I guessed that it was meant for me. On my right was the lawyer's bench, on my left the prosecutor's. In the middle was a long bench on a podium with the red-and-gold emblem showing the Heavenly Gate and the five stars of the Central Committee of the Communist Party of China hanging high up on the wall behind it. On the ceiling were six TV cameras all facing the public. This was as heavy as you could get.

From stage right my lawyer and his assistant entered the room and took their places. The prosecutor, his assistant and the translator Peter took their seats on my left. Suddenly there was a loud voice shouting something from the door on the right, and everyone stood up. My guards lifted me to my feet, and I watched as four men in navy-blue judge's uniforms with red epaulets and peaked caps trooped into the room, mounted the podium and stood stiffly behind the bench. They all turned in unison, saluted the emblem, turned back to face the court and sat down. The one on the far left now stood and revealed himself to be a clerk called Chen Jie. He proceeded to introduce the others one by one: 'Chief Judge Yuan Hanjian, Judge Shen Weijia, Acting Judge Zhou Zhiguo.' They saluted the public, took off their caps and placed them on the bench in front of them. The clerk went on to explain that the assembled judges had been invested with the power to try and pass judgment according to the Criminal Procedural Law of the People's Republic of China upon those brought before them who have a public prosecution against them.

Continuing, he said, 'Prosecution counsel, do you have any objection to the presiding judges?'

'No. No objection.'

'Defence counsel, do you have any objection to the presiding judges?'

'No. No objection.'

'Bei guoren Lobota Haw Dai wis, do you have any objections?' That was how they pronounced my name, and I hated it. 'Bei guoren' meant 'the accused', and was always spat out of the mouth with distaste and hate, as if it was some germ-laden pus.

'No,' I said, wondering what would have happened if I'd said yes.

Checking out the guys, I spotted that the judge who had visited me in the detention house was not the chief judge but the acting judge, Zhou Zhiguo, and it was he who then rose and spoke: '1992, third month, third day, I, Zhou Zhiguo, representing the Chinese People's Republic People's Court, declare open a public prosecution of Lobota Haw Dai wis, criminal 29, case number 282 from the Shanghai Municipal People's Procuratorate to the Shanghai Municipal Intermediate People's Court.'

Everyone sat down. I was pushed down by the two robotic guards, and a warning was given to the public about the illegal use of tape-recorders. Chen Rongqing was then asked to read the indictment, and I immediately noticed that he was using his stage voice, which was an octave higher and full of over-pronunciation and inflection. The show had commenced.

Then it was my turn. I was summoned to the box by Zhou Zhiguo and asked a lot of questions about who I was, how old I was, where I came from, occupation, schooling, political affiliation and all sorts of facts about my marriage to ShaSha, our house in Kashgar, right down to what I was doing the day the Xinjiang PSB gatecrashed my room on 7 October 1991.

'Did you confess to the crimes described in the prosecution's case against you of your own free will?'

'Yes, I did.'

'How do you now plead?'

'Guilty.'

He then asked me to relate my story from the beginning, and off I went again, relating a tale which by this time I knew by heart. When I had finished I took the bit of paper from my pocket on which I had prepared the statement to the court and read: 'I came to China as a wide-eyed traveller in August 1988 to see for myself the wonders of this fabled land. Due to my own weaknesses and naïveté, and the influence of western popular culture, I became involved in the smoking and trafficking of hashish. The ease with which a foreigner could obtain hashish and the relaxed attitude of the local population in Kashgar led me to believe falsely that hashish was accepted and indeed permitted. Since my arrest I have learnt about the law and realise now the harm that I have done to the people of China, and sincerely regret the trouble I have caused in this wonderful country which has always shown me such welcome and respect. I hope the court will accept my apology, and permit me to express my sorrow and regret in a positive way as a free man.'

As I was reading, I realised that I had jumped the gun. Ma was looking at me and shaking his head. There was another slot later in the proceedings set aside for the accused's obsequious pleas for leniency. I watched the judges as my words were translated to them, and they looked back at me as if I had just broken wind. That's it, I thought, I've really fucked it up now.

I was told to sit down. It was once again the turn of the prosecutor. He read from a piece of paper, and went on to lambast me, accusing me of being a foreign drug addict, a result of western capitalism's weakness and hypocrisy, bringing to the sacred land dirty habits to harm exploit and scar the honourable, hard-working people of China in the same way as the unscrupulous British sea captains of the 1850s.

I looked at my lawyer and wondered what I was paying him for. We'd been here half an hour and he hadn't said a single word yet. Surely this tirade of the prosecutor's was objectionable. Suddenly it stopped and my lawyer started talking, again reading from a piece of paper. I waited for a great list of mitigating circumstances to be presented, and maybe a few procedural errors by the police, but he only carried on about how I'd confessed of my own free will and had done my best to co-operate with the authorities. Eventually, though, he brought up the points about the classification of quantities, and the vagueness of the test results. I expected the prosecutor to answer these questions but he said nothing. Without warning, I was told to get in the box again. The chief judge wanted to question me.

'Did you know that you were breaking the law when you sold hashish to the two Germans?'

'No, I did not. The law had only come into operation the year before.'

'Then why did you hide the drug under the floor of your house?'

'Because it is a good way to keep it fresh, that's all.'

'Why did you conduct your transactions with the Germans in a secret language?'

'I'm sorry, Honourable Judge, but I think you must be referring to a mistake that was made during interrogation in the translation of one of my answers. I was gesticulating. I used my hands to describe a chaotic situation when we were all quite drunk and so I couldn't remember who had named the price.'

'So you used your hands to conduct the deal?'

'No, like I just told you, it was a mistake in the translation.'

Why the fuck wasn't my lawyer helping me out here? It's been the same crap like this all along, I thought. This was an issue that had already taken a day to resolve before, and I had been assured that it and other mistakes of theirs had been erased from the records. It was now clear that they hadn't. That meant that the judges had been given everything, mistakes and all.

'Did you know the Germans were going to Japan?'

'No. I was not aware of that.'

Suddenly the prosecutor rose to his feet and voiced an objection, which somehow now gave him the chance to question me.

'Did you not inform me, not less than a week ago, that you "had an idea that they might be going to sell the drugs abroad, because they had bought more than the time before"? It is a good idea to co-operate with all branches of the justice system, Mr Dai wis. You do want leniency, don't you?'

I hadn't said that, and there was that bloody threat again. Not even subtle. But the seed had been planted the week previously, and it was either agree with him or risk suffering his wrath.

'I might have assumed that they could do something like that,' I conceded.

'Thank you,' said Chen Rongqing with a grin.

There was a little bit more reading from pieces of paper and then I was given chance to make my statement to the court. Since I had prematurely shot my load at the first opportunity, I wasn't sure what to say. Without the use of any notes, I simply said that I was sincerely sorry and that if given the chance I would do all I could to deter other young people from committing crime in China. It was the truth. I wanted to tell everybody to stay the hell away from the place. The days of Happy People Productions had ended.

The trial was over. I felt stunned but relieved. I felt as if I had been a part of something but had been left out. It had been a theatre, a play, and I had been the only one on the stage without lines. I didn't have a clue what had happened in there.

My guards hauled me out of the courtroom as fast as they could and I had barely enough time to scan the public benches to see if anyone I knew was there. Just as I shot through the door, I spotted two women sitting together, one taller than the other, Chinese in appearance, the other wearing sunglasses, sitting in the chair as if she didn't want to be seen. My first thought was that one of them was ShaSha. As I hurtled down the stairs, my feet hardly touching the ground, I wondered why and how and if I had been mistaken. This would be yet another vision that would perplex me for a long time.

As soon as I was locked up in the holding cell again, a telephone rang and shortly afterwards I was heading back to where I'd just come from. I was whisked through the now empty court and into an anteroom where the vice-consul was waiting to speak to me. My God, a chance for a cigarette and to express my emotions to a sympathetic ear. I babbled on about how happy I was that it was over. I mentioned that I wasn't sure exactly what the hell had gone on in there and asked Jim how he thought it went. His answer was as noncommittal as ever.

The general consensus of opinion back in the detention house was that the longer you waited for the verdict to come through, the better. Apparently it meant that the case was not clear-cut, and that the collegiate of judges were taking time to assess every aspect before passing judgment. I don't know whether this was any consolation or not during the interminable three weeks that I waited to be told what I hoped would be good news.

On 23 March I was taken downstairs and for the first time in nine months met up again with Werner and Dieter, who, during our separation, had become 'the Two Germans'. There was another man there, too, whom I immediately recognised as the person I'd thought was Gerhard in the photo. As we waited for two Chinese lads to be fitted in medium-weight leg-irons, he introduced himself. This was Webster, the other Briton I'd heard about. He must have been about fifty, I guessed, just under medium height with long straggly ginger hair. He seemed just like any other veteran traveller and hash-head, but then I sensed something else, something sinister, and my heart pumped an extra beat. It was his eyes: they seemed to lack that sparkle of human compassion, and were suspicious, darting all over the place.

On the bus to the court he explained how he'd been busted with over seven kilos. He had the same lawyer as me and said he figured he wouldn't get much more than about four years. The rest of us tended to agree with this line of thinking, hopefully assuming that we would get even less – at most two and a half, and if the Chinese were really serious about putting us inside, we'd be out after a third or at most half of the sentence.

The Germans sat opposite me, and while Werner was more or less his old self, Dieter was sullen and brooding. I never for one minute looked upon them as the cause of our predicament, simply being glad to see old friends again and have the chance to swap a few experiences with guys who were on the same wavelength. It became clear after five or ten minutes that these feelings were not reciprocated. I felt that there was a reluctance, especially on Dieter's part, to accept that I held no grievance. It would become evident as time passed that he had the same inability when faced with any American or Briton to accept that they did not hold him accountable for the atrocities of the Second World War. He himself could not forgive his father's or his own failings, so how was it possible for others to do so? This could only mean they were fawning and being obsequious, which was a terrible defect in a human, and made them worthy only of scorn. Dieter scorned the world.

'Where's Thundernose Vern?' I asked.

'He slipped through. He was first in the queue. We were ten places behind. They fucking knew we were packed. They knew!'

At the court they put us in cells as far apart from one another as they could. We waited and smoked, thinking about how differently we would act once we were out of there. My hopes were high. I had confidence that within at least a year I would once again be reunited with ShaSha and be back in Kashgar.

At ten-thirty the guards came and took the four of us up to the court. We were made to wait in a little room just before the entrance. For some reason they called me first. I entered a hushed courtroom. The public gallery was full. I was instructed to stand in the box and waited for the last of the judges to enter and be seated. The same performers were on the stage in the same positions as last time, and without further ado the chief judge began to read: '1992, third month, twenty-third day, Criminal Verdict of Shanghai Intermediate People's Court. Criminal number 29.'

After a short introduction as to who I was, there followed a long statement in Chinese outlining the case against me, mentioning how much money I had made from processing and selling the three kilos of hash to the Germans and what the THC content of it was. It ended with: 'After defendant Lobota Haw Dai wis was arrested, not only did he confess his crime of trafficking in narcotics, but also his crime of illegally possessing 400g of hashish and a further one kilo at his home in Kashgar. Therefore he should be given a lenient punishment. The verdict is as follows.'

The judge read it out in Chinese and I listened like a man waiting for his lottery numbers to come up. Was that an eight he said there? It sounded like one. Maybe he said eighteen months just like I'd thought in the first place. Well, that's not too bad at all. I waited for the translator to confirm it.

He began: '1. Defendant Lobota Haw Dai wis, committing the crime of trafficking in narcotics, should be sentenced to eight years' imprisonment; committing the crime of illegally possessing narcotics, be sentenced to one year's imprisonment. The actual sentence will be eight and a half years' imprisonment.

'2. Inflicting 10,000rmb of fines on defendant Lobota Haw Dai wis.

'3. Confiscating all the illicit money gained from the drug trafficking and the seized narcotics.

'If the defendant does not accept this verdict, you can hand over your appeal and its duplicate to Shanghai Intermediate People's Court and appeal to Shanghai High People's Court within ten days from the second day after you receive this verdict.'

My mind collapsed like a house of cards. What the fuck did he say? No, that must have been a mistake. The translator must have screwed it up again. Shit, there's no way they can be serious. It's just not possible. God, I couldn't even bring myself to say it. It had to be a cock-up.

Before I knew it, I was back in the holding cell, calling out for a cigarette. I felt as if I'd been hit by a bus. Suddenly, though, I could sense an incredible anger rising from the pit of my stomach.

Within fifteen minutes, Webster came in through the door, looking like a scalded cat. 'How much did you get?' I shouted.

'Fifteen fucking years,' he replied, as the guards dragged him around the corner and out of sight.

'How many people did you kill?'

Silence.

Ten or fifteen minutes later, Dieter appeared. He was grey, and his mouth hung open so far it was almost dragging his chin to the floor. I had never seen such a picture of shock, and the sight of him shocked me. Werner followed.

'How much, Wern?' I asked.

'Eight.'

What! I got more than them? 'Fuck it, we didn't kill anybody, did we?'

In no time the place was full of guards and judges and prosecutors. They wanted to see us now. Have a look at the foreign devils, the big noses who had come to desecrate the sacred Middle Kingdom with their dirty habits. You could see the joy, the satisfaction, in their little black squinty eyes. This was more than law and order – this was revenge for pinching Hong Kong and a hundred and fifty years of shame.

'Sign your name here, you agree sentence, you understand sentence.'

'Yeah, but I want to appeal.'

And Let No Man Suggest Otherwise

If you prick us, do we not bleed? If you tickle us, do we not laugh?
If you poison us, do we not die? And if you wrong us, shall we not revenge?

William Shakespeare, *The Merchant of Venice*, III, i

THE trip back to the detention house was a different affair from earlier in the day. I was exhausted but I could still feel the deep emotions of disbelief, shock and outrage boiling up inside me. By the time I got back to the cell I was nearly frantic. The *xun dao*, concerned that we might not be able to cope with such a shock, called me into his office to gauge my mental state. It was almost as if he'd known in advance that we foreigners were going to be stung, though he admitted to me that he never thought that I would get eight and a half years. He was, of course, also worried that any attempted suicide would affect his end-of-year bonus.

Without delay, I started drafting my appeal. With the beady-eyed drooling Gollums looking on as I lay on the floor with my bits of paper and my home-made pen trying to compose something that would save my skin, it suddenly dawned on me that the conditions in which I was being forced to ponder my future were totally unreasonable. The bastards wouldn't even give me a table, a pen, a decent bit of paper and a little peace and quiet to do it in.

I envisaged that a good appeal could at least halve the years that had been shovelled on me. I believed that justice would prevail, and that what had happened in the Intermediate Court was simply a mistake. I eventually wrote seven and a half pages of what I believed then to be a sound argument against a terribly harsh sentence.

I listed seven points that showed my confession and my willingness to co-operate had not received the leniency they deserved; I elaborated on the degree of actual criminal intent on my part as opposed to the Germans' and their motive to gain vast profits; the fact that the Englishman dealt with in a previous case had only been sentenced to four years for an amount close to double that involved in my case; the fact that I did not rely on the proceeds of drug sales to live; that since the Germans had bought more than one consignment the prosecution's test results did not indicate that they were the results of tests done to the actual hash that I had sold and were anyway too vague to establish the true amount of actual drug that had been transacted; the fact that there had not been one witness available for cross-examination by my defence; and finally that as a foreigner in Xinjiang it was very difficult to determine what law, if any, concerned hashish. I went on to explain that it was grown everywhere, smoked everywhere and was a socially acceptable habit. Why I was the only one to be arrested for it? How was it that in nearly four years there I had never heard of a single person being taken to court for such an offence? It looked as though there were two laws operating in China, or maybe even three: one law for Xinjiang, one law for Shanghai, and one law for foreigners.

Philip Ma turned up on the 27th to get his money and get me to sign another contract for what they called 'the Second Trial', the last opportunity for me to challenge the verdict.

When he showed up again on 31 March, he agreed that I should pursue my arguments, but he also continued to talk to me about the ester stuff which he had mentioned before. I still couldn't figure out what he was on about. It sounded a bit like I'd been set up but I assumed that in a case like mine, which was directly in the spotlight, they would all be on their best behaviour. With the amount of press interest, especially foreign press, they would hardly try to fuck me over, would they?

However, if what Ma had told me was right, the prosecutor had indicted me in connection with a substance that was actually ten times stronger than hash, and yet in the English translation it was still called hash. How could this be? Ma informed me that he was going to make an additional study of materials in the file kept by the Shanghai Higher People's Court and also make an academic study on *dama* (hashish) and *dama zhi*, the substance he believed was a chemically prepared cannabis ten times the strength of the ordinary stuff. I still didn't get it. How could there be a mistake? The way I figured it, *dama* was grass and *dama zhi* was hash. When they referred to it in court, it was called hashish, so where was the problem?

I didn't see him again for two weeks, but I was visited by a new prosecutor, Zheng Luming, and his henchwoman, acting-prosecutor Wang Kangmei. She was a severe character who looked as if she beat her kids, her husband and anybody else who crossed her path. He, in contrast, was shy and nervous, embarrassed even. They came to grill me about my reasons for appealing, which I felt was none of their business, because it would give them time to prepare counter-arguments. But there was always that implied threat.

Philip Ma turned up and told me that the trial was going to be in two days' time, on 17 April. So nice of them to keep me informed, I thought. We went through the whole thing again, and he explained how the second trial would be played out. He described how this time he was going to challenge the prosecutor directly about this ester stuff, and ask him to define the difference in meaning between *dama* and *dama zhi*. I tried to ask him what he was talking about, but he wouldn't give me a clear answer. He remained evasive, almost as if he didn't really know himself, or that he didn't want me to know. His questions gave me the impression that he didn't have a clue what hash was, or what any other drug was for that matter. I had assumed that a lawyer would know these things, the same way that I had assumed that the police would, but it was becoming clear that these Chinese had no idea. To them it was simply drugs, *dupin*, whether it was heroin, opium, coke, grass or hash.

My confusion and apprehension grew. I felt that I was drowning in a sea of incompetence. The people who were meant to be helping me were ignorant and scared and only really interested in helping themselves. The law was a system of loopholes that worked only in the prosecution's favour.

Two days later I was back on the minibus to the court-house. It was the same building and same routine as before, only this time it was a different courtroom, smaller than the Intermediate Court but no less imposing. The place was once again packed with what I assumed were reporters from all over the world. My consul had informed me that I had received extensive press coverage after the first trial with headlines in the *South China Morning Post* reading, 'FRIENDS DISPUTE CHINA'S "GODFATHER" TAG FOR WELSH DRUG DEALER' and 'SHANGHAI POLICE TIE BRITON TO DRUG RING'. What the fuck was going on? Talk about getting things out of proportion. These bastards in the press were playing right into the hands of the Chinese and doing me no favours at all.

The chief judge that day was a woman called Zhou Jie. Her male cohorts and the clerk were introduced. The translator was Peter again. I couldn't get over how young they all were. Surely they should have been a bit older with more experience.

After all the usual introductions we proceeded in much the same fashion as before. The judge outlined the case and how I had been sentenced to eight and a half years by the Shanghai Intermediate Court but had had the audacity and disrespect to appeal against it (at least that was how it sounded to me). I had no doubt that they were not happy by my non-acceptance of what they deemed to be a lenient sentence. I was then called upon to relate my story and then inform the judges of my reasons for appeal. I expected that each point would be dealt with in turn but this was not to be the case. When I asked questions like 'Where is the dividing line between "small amount" and "relatively large amount"?' and 'Why is it that neither my lawyer nor I are allowed to cross-examine witnesses?', I was ignored. Nobody said a word. When I asked how it had been possible that an Englishman with over seven kilos concealed about his person, discovered boarding a boat for Japan, only got four years, I was told bluntly: 'There is no comparison of previous cases in Chinese law.'

'If that is so,' I responded in disbelief, 'how do you have justice? Like that, a man who steals six eggs can end up serving a longer sentence than a man who steals a thousand eggs. Is there no such thing as correlation or a "leading case" in China?'

That was too much for Peter. He had no idea what I was on about and asked me to say it all again in a simpler way so that he could understand what I was talking about. I wanted to hit my head against a wall and strangle the bloody moron. Eventually I got it through to him.

'Each case is decided on its own characteristics, and there can be no comparison with other cases,' was the reply.

When I had finished explaining my arguments, the judge started to question me. 'You claim that you have co-operated fully with the police,' she said, 'but according to the statements in your file you were first apprehended on 7 October 1991 but did not start telling the truth until 21 October. How do you explain that?'

'I was not arrested until 21 October.'

'How is it that your final statement, in which you disclose the whereabouts of the drugs hidden under the floor of your house, was not made until 18 December?'

'That was the length of the investigation and I needed time to remember everything.'

I knew that I had not got away with that one, and if it continued in this way I had more chance of getting a few more years added on.

'You claim to have supplied names, and yet none of them has so far been confirmed. Why do you think that is?'

'I don't think it is for me to question police methods, but possibly these people slipped through the net and have left the country. They would not have waited around to be caught, would they?'

Nothing was working. Their faces revealed the contempt they felt for me and the fact that they thought that I was lying.

Since I had complained about the lack of actual evidence, they brought into the room a bundle of hash and asked me to identify it as being the hash which I had sold to the Germans. There must have been about three hundred grams wrapped up in plastic tape in the shape of a shoe insole. How was I supposed to be able to say what it was? After I explained that I was unable to actually see it, the judge ordered the policeman who was holding it as if it was radioactive device to open it. Once done, I was asked again.

'Since there is so much hash that looks pretty much the same as any other hash, it is very difficult for me to say if this is really what I sold to the two Germans,' I explained. 'All I can say in truth is that it's the same colour.'

I couldn't imagine what that exercise was supposed to prove.

Next up was my lawyer. Ma's first tactic was to question the prosecutor about the definition of small, relatively large and large amounts of hash. This was again met with silence. It was as if they only had to answer the questions they wanted to. Ones they didn't like could be ignored. He asked about the percentage of THC content required by law to classify it as a banned substance, and that if it was indeed 10 per cent then a large portion of the seized drug, according to test results, fell below that level, thus rendering it legal. How much, though, was not known, which in turn brought the claim that I had sold 'a relatively large amount' into question. This was once again met with silence. As I watched, I had the same feeling that I'd had in the first trial. It was a big game, a play being acted out by some amateur dramatic society who had done all their rehearsing behind closed doors and not told me which play it was. They all knew what was going on – they even knew the outcome before we'd even set foot in the courtroom. They knew how pointless and futile it was for me to persist in trying to prove that I was not the 'drug kingpin' they needed me to be.

Philip Ma went on to question the prosecutor about the substance *dama zhi*, asking how it might differ when compared to *dama*. He argued that it was impossible to claim they were one and the same, and demonstrated this by holding up cards with the three characters written on them, presenting two on their own and then the three together. I watched him dubiously, still wondering what the hell he was talking about, and it looked as if the judges were equally baffled. Then, when he too realised that they weren't listening, he stopped talking and sat down.

I now had one final chance to plead for leniency and rattled off another declaration of sorrow and repentance. I swore to mend my ways and never again commit such a heinous and pernicious crime on Chinese soil ever again. I then went on to clear up one point that had been niggling me for many months, namely the inference by the police and prosecutors that I had only married ShaSha in order to conduct this alleged 'worldwide drug-trafficking operation'. I wanted the record put straight and finished my plea by saying: 'I came to Kashgar and fell in love with my wife. I want it noted that love was the only reason we married. Let no man suggest otherwise.'

As soon as I said the word 'love', all the months of extreme pressure and anguish came to a head. I was nearly in tears, and only just managed to hold myself together. I was not happy. Everything had gone as wrong as it could, but I still managed to cling to the hope that I would get a bit knocked off. Surely they wouldn't go through all this for nothing. Surely it would look good for them if they showed a little compassion.

Back in the detention house I waited for the verdict, each day that passed adding to my hope and confidence that there would be a good result from all this. After six months I knew how to pass time in that little space and I continued to study the Chinese language with a real passion. I had memorised two thousand characters and practised them by writing letters to ShaSha. The only problem was I couldn't send them to her. I had persisted in trying to get permission but was refused every time. They wouldn't even tell me where she was, every excuse in the book being given, and I was now quite sure that the letter Chen Rongqing had allowed me to send way back in January had probably never left Shanghai. I had waited for a word that ShaSha was out there and that everything was okay with her, but had heard nothing. I resigned myself to the fact that as long as I was in the detention house, I would never know where she was or receive a letter from her.

Between trials, a new guy named Cheng came into the room. He was well educated and could speak English fluently. I was immediately suspicious of him, sure that he was another KGB. But, thinking about it, I realised that it didn't matter if he was. I had already confessed and been tried. Still, it was not a very comfortable feeling.

After listening to his stories, though, I soon relaxed and realised that he was a mine of information. We very quickly struck up a friendship, and spent the days teaching each other Chinese and English. Cheng helped me a great deal. At least he gave me the right answers. The other Gollums would never say that they didn't know anything but would just tell you the first thing that came to mind.

Cheng had worked for the China Travel Service in Hong Kong but was suspected of misuse of funds. This was a joke as far as he was concerned, since he had used the funds to attract more business and in turn make larger profits for the company. The police in Shanghai, thinking that he might not want to leave Hong Kong to face these charges, put his mother in the detention house in order to entice him back. It worked. He told me that he had been born in 1954, so when the Cultural Revolution began in 1966, he was twelve and the perfect age to join the Red Guards. He grew up with Mao's teachings firmly implanted in his brain. He had studied them inside out and could recite off by heart great chunks of Mao's doctrines. He had believed in it, and loved the Communist Party more than his parents or his brother and sister. Since being arrested and interrogated, however, things had changed. He felt let down, deceived even. It had taken just one seed of doubt in his mind for the whole façade of communism in China to crumble. Cheng could see clearly for the first time in his life, and questioned how he could not have seen through all the bullshit before. This was a perfect example of how Mao had targeted the youth and manipulated them in their formative years, engendering a blind love that was rewarded by the freedom to express immature frustrations against those who oppressed them.

Eventually, twenty-five days after the trial, on the morning of 13 May, I got the call. Downstairs were Werner and Dieter, also ready and waiting, I assumed, to get their verdict. But, no, they hadn't even had their appeal trial yet. They'd been waiting fifty days since the last verdict.

On the bus we tried to work out why they had been left to wait while I had gone through in record time. We even mulled over the possibility that they might still deport us. There was always that hope in the back of my mind. Surely they didn't want foreign devils seeing what went on in Chinese jails.

Back in the bowels of the court, I was forced to wait in the holding cell while the two Germans made their appeal. Just before twelve-thirty, they both returned. Werner was quite confident but Dieter was looking as dispirited as usual. At one-thirty I thought my time had come, but instead they called the two Germans out once again. I thought that they must be having an extra session to clarify some point or other, so when they returned ten minutes later saying that they'd just got the verdict and their appeal had been kicked out, I was stunned with disbelief. How the hell could it be? They'd only just had the trial. It was impossible that the Chinese could have drawn up the final verdict with the translation in an hour. The only possible answer was that the bastards had written it all out beforehand – before the Germans had even arrived in the courtroom, because there was no way a Shanghainese was going to miss his lunch to type out documents that could wait at our expense.

Even though the Germans' appeals had failed, right up until the very moment the judge read out the final judgment I somehow kept hoping that I would get a result. Again the courtroom was packed. There were people standing at the back and in the doorways. But there was no messing about; I was hauled in, put on the stand and the judge immediately began to read. The first half was all the same old stuff as the first verdict, but then she said: 'In his appeal, Lobota Haw Dai wis admitted his crime of trafficking in and illegally possessing narcotics. However, he argued that he trafficked in narcotics to "help" other people; and that after he was arrested, he could confess all his criminal facts and tell other people's criminal activities. Thus he asked for lenient punishment. The examination shows that Lobota Haw Dai wis not only illegally sold narcotics but also gained several thousand renminbi from dealing. His subjective intention to gain profit from dealing is clear. And the information provided by the appellant after his arrest was not confirmed. As for the fact that the appellant could confess all his criminal facts, leniency has already been taken into consideration in the first trial. Thus the court rejects Lobota Haw Dai wis's demand for leniency in his appeal.

'The court affirms the original verdict ruled that Lobota Haw Dai wis committed the crime of trafficking in and illegally possessing narcotics. The facts are clear, the evidences are reliable and full, the conviction is accurate, the sentence is appropriate and the trial procedure is legal. The ruling is as follows:

'1. Rejecting Lobota Haw Dai wis's appeal

'2. Maintaining the criminal verdict (Criminal No. 29, 1992) issued by Shanghai Intermediate People's Court.

'This is the final ruling.'

There's Always Hope

He that lives in hope, danceth without music.

George Herbert (1593–1633)

I WAS led through to another courtroom to speak with Philip Ma. My feelings about the man at that time were not good. I had gone over the whole thing again and again, and now suspected my so-called lawyer of having chartered his course with me very carefully, tempting me on and on to continue with the appeal when he knew full well that I was being fixed up and used and that my chance of getting a result was nil. He had practised law for over forty years and was not only familiar with the court's methods but was friendly with the judges themselves. He did not want me to know the whole score because they didn't want me to blow it all open in the court.

But before I had a chance to dwell on all that, he once again set about raising my spirits. The first thing he said to me was: 'Robert, don't forget, there's always hope.'

'Is there? Would you mind telling me exactly where this hope is?'

He explained that even though this verdict has been deemed 'final', I could still make a petition to the Supreme Court in Beijing. Ma was more confident than I'd ever seen him, in fact. He began to speak to me slowly and clearly, pulling out from his briefcase copies of all my court papers in Chinese and English, including the one I'd just got.

'Look at your indictment,' he said. 'In Chinese it says *dama zhi*, in English it says hashish. Your Intermediate Court verdict says *dama zhi* in Chinese, and hashish in English. Now look at you appeal verdict: it says hashish in English, and *dama* in Chinese. They've dropped the *zhi*! If you look up a Chinese-English dictionary for the meaning of *dama*, it says "hemp, marijuana or cannabis". If you look up an English-Chinese dictionary for the meaning of hashish, it says that it is a narcotic made from a mix of stalk and leaf from the Indian hemp plant. It does not say *dama zhi*. There is no such word in the Chinese dictionary. You cannot find it!'

(I should explain that there are fifty-four *zhi*s in the common-usage Chinese dictionary. Twelve are neutral tone, nine are rising tone, ten are rising/falling tone, and twenty-three are falling tone. The *zhi* which had been used is a rising/falling tone *zhi* meaning 'ester'.)

Ma continued, 'If they had been attempting to accuse you of trafficking in hash oil, they might have used this *zhi*.' He pointed to a neutral tone *zhi*, which looked almost identical to the untrained eye, but which meant 'fat' or 'grease'. In Chinese this makes them as different as 'aardvark' is from 'zymurgy' is in English. '*Dama zhi* (rising/falling) according to the academic study I have made is a cannabis derivative made by a series of very complicated chemical processes. It is at least ten times stronger than *dama*. *Dama* is not either of these two substances, and yet they have maintained your sentence for crimes involving the trafficking of *dama*. You were sentenced for crimes involving trafficking *dama zhi* (rising/falling). They have changed the drug but not the sentence accordingly. You responded in both courts to the English "hashish", while all the time they were referring to *dama zhi*. If they had translated that correctly, and said "esterised cannabis", would you have pleaded guilty?'

'Well, of course not!' I answered in disbelief, trying to take in the magnitude of what he had just explained. Suddenly all the pieces fell into place. Now I realised what he'd been getting at all along. All his strange questions now made sense. He'd also been checking me out to see if I knew what this super-drug was. 'Why the hell didn't you tell me before?'

'I wasn't sure the last time I saw you. It was only when I completed my study when I went to Hong Kong and when they made this mistake of dropping the *zhi* that I became certain.'

I wasn't so sure. Wasn't it more likely that Ma had been got at by the powers-that-be, and that securing the conviction was more important than justice? Maybe his conscience had prompted him to disclose these facts to cover himself if and when I discovered the discrepancy myself. If I'd had that information before the trial, I would have had a real and solid argument for an appeal. If I had brought it out into the open, all the foreign press would have understood that there had been a serious irregularity in the first trial. Instead, the lawyer babbled on in Chinese about some point of contention, which after it had been badly translated into English meant nothing to anyone. The first trial was now clearly a mis-trial, because I had been deceived in the courtroom by the prosecutor and the translator. Those bastards had had the nerve to stitch me up with some bloody super-drug that the lawyer couldn't even find in the dictionary directly under the glare of reporters' flashlights from all over the world. There was a bigger machine at work here, I could feel it, but it would take some time yet before all the pieces really fell into place. For the moment I contented myself with the fact that I had a case against the Shanghai courts with evidence that they themselves had given me in black and white. *Dama zhi*: now you see it, now you don't.

I tried to explain all this to the Germans on the minibus on the way back to the detention house but quickly saw that it was all over their heads. They weren't paying me any attention. They were still coming to terms with the next 2,650 days that they might have to spend in jail. I gave up and turned to look out of the window. This might be one of the last opportunities for a long time to see life going on in the streets. I watched people repairing bikes, selling fish, buying fruit, smoking, girls in mini-skirts on bicycles zipping past in the traffic, the smells, the action. I loved Shanghai. I loved China.

Back in Gollumville I heard that the two Germans had been put in the same cell together. Why couldn't they stick the other Brit in with me, then? I could do with a bit of company. My prayer was soon answered, but within a very short space of time I regretted ever wishing for such a thing.

At first, having a fellow traveller to swap yarns with and share the experience we were both going through was great. Webster and I poured out to each other all the months of frustration with the food, the cells, the Chinese prisoners, the guards, the police, the lawyer, the prosecutor, the judge and of course the bloody sentences. What a relief to be able to express yourself in your own language, to get it all off your chest without fear of retribution. You couldn't trust the lawyer, and you certainly didn't want to piss him off; you couldn't talk to the consul freely since every word was being recorded to use against you; you couldn't tell the other prisoners what you thought, because they were all spies, just waiting for an opportunity to ingratiate themselves with the police or prosecutors and win that bloody boiled egg; you couldn't write to anybody, and even if you could, they'd censor it and use it against you. With all this pent-up emotion now exploding to the surface, we had a job getting a word in edgeways.

But, as the days passed by, things cooled off and I started to look again instead of listening. My instincts came back and, as the saying goes, 'actions speak louder than words'. I noticed things were not right.

Webster told me that he was from a working-class background in a rough part of Manchester. He had not had a very good schooling since he'd not bothered to go very often. He was more often than not to be found with lads older than himself out shoplifting or breaking into houses. I didn't have a problem with that – after all, we were on the same side of the fence now. He had split to Asia some years before and had found his true calling doing the infamous 'milk runs' from Hong Kong. He had not been satisfied with just one or two trips to keep him on the road and wanted more and more. He had gone at it full time, doing as many runs as he could before he was forced to take a rest from sheer exhaustion. He would do a few months' R&R in Thailand or the Philippines, then go back on the trail again, taking technology and gold to Korea and Japan. He made piles of money but always blew it on drugs of different sorts.

He boasted about how he had educated himself in Asia, reading books and travelling. He claimed that he was a poet and that he was a yoga instructor, albeit a fake one, only using it as an excuse to get into women's pants. He broached the subject of heroin, hoping I'd pick up on it and confess to being a fellow junkie, but I wasn't. I had never even seen one gram of the stuff, so I said nothing. He had let me into his secret, however, and this changed my attitude towards him immediately. Every day I watched him, as I had watched the Chinese, looking for the body language that would confirm my suspicions. When he noticed that a coolness had slipped between us, he started to tell me about all the fights he'd been in in the rooms before he'd joined me. Was this supposed to frighten me into being his friend? I was able to imagine the sort of pressure he must have been under in the other rooms, though. They were packed to overflowing, with fifteen or sixteen men in each room. Specially assigned room-monitors ruled. They were the law. They controlled everything that went on in the room – who cleaned the toilet, who wiped the floor, who got the meat when the food came through the door. Under that sort of pressure, it was easy to snap.

On the surface, our relationship continued in good humour and Webster was the soul of the party. One day, as we sat around in our shorts in the warmer May temperatures, however, Webster teased himself up to an erection. In disbelief and embarrassment, our Chinese roommates laughed nervously, giggling like little girls with their hands over their mouths. It's well known that the Chinese, for the most part, have little willies, and even if they had big ones they were certainly not used to seeing another man's erection. Webster urged them to have a feel. He whipped his tool out and showed it to them in all its glory. Maybe because they felt intimidated, two of the Chinese, Hong and Song, started to fondled and stroke Webster's member.

I suddenly realised that I had been laughing, just as excited as the others, but all of a sudden I'd stopped. I was sitting with my mouth open in disbelief at what I was witnessing. It wasn't funny any more. I wanted out of there. I did the next best thing and picked up my Chinese study book and started to read. That was it for me. But what could I do? We were trapped together.

Webster had been sentenced to fifteen years for much the same crime as the Englishman who'd got four. He was devastated. He turned out to be younger than I'd guessed, but it still meant that if he served his entire sentence he'd be nearly sixty when he got out.

I had calmed down a lot since the appeal verdict and had tried to rationalise the situation as best I could. I believed that the Chinese were well aware of what they had done, and that they had done it deliberately so as to kill two birds with one stone. With the worldwide broadcast of severe sentences for handling drugs, they would scare away all the foreigners who thought they could use China as a base and still leave themselves the legal means whereby later, when the whole thing had cooled down, they could cut the sentences and let us go without having to put us inside their jails and be witness to what no other westerners had seen in over fifty years. I believed that it had to be like that, and, since the British consulate was undoubtedly in full knowledge of the situation (after all, they had attended the trials in person with their own translators), they must have understood what had happened. I was sure that the British would not stand for any funny business and would be ready to step in and save me if it all went wrong. I explained all this to Webster, and he agreed that it was a possibility. If it wasn't, it sure as hell eased the blow and gave us a bit more hope.

Because we had that hope, we could afford to speculate what it might be like if we did wind up in Tilan Qiao, otherwise known as Shanghai No.1 Jail or the City Jail. Webster, who prided himself on having been inside before, seemed to be looking forward to it. 'Yeah, there's bound to be loads of Filipinos and Koreans there,' he told me. 'Maybe a few Thais. Bound to be a fucking rough place. Have to go in there and make a point straight away. No good letting them bastards get the upper hand. Tell ya, find the hardest cunt and get stuck in. Don't matter if you get smacked up – all the other fuckers will be scared off after, know what I mean? And you'll earn a bit of respect. Bound to be a good black market in there, too. Can probably get a hold of anything – dope, booze, even the odd whore, maybe.'

'Yeah, I hear it's like that in Manila. A friend of mine was locked up there for a month or two and got his favourite Mabini girl in every other night.'

'Ah, there's no doubt we'll have a good crack there.'

Fuck me, were we ever wrong.

When Philip Ma did eventually turn up, all he wanted was his money. I'd already paid him US$1,000 for the first trial for what he claimed was fourteen hours' work. This time, at the reduced rate of $60 an hour plus expenses, he was claiming twenty-two and a half hours and $150 for his trip to Hong Kong. This amounted to $1,500 exactly.

Before he rushed out through the door, I did manage to squeeze a bit more information out of him. 'The Englishman had a "small amount", even though he was found with over seven kilos strapped to his body. He was said to have had *dama* by the court, but marijuana in the English language press. If you had had the same substance he had, your amount would have been less than small. In that way, how could they increase your sentences so as to satisfy the Ministry of Public Security in Beijing? You see, they came out and called for stiffer sentences for foreign drug criminals than that handed down to the Englishman. After you had already been sentenced for *dama zhi*, they changed it to *dama*, the same as the Englishman. The legality of the whole trial is in question. In the last paragraph of your verdict, they claim that the facts are clear. Are they clear to you? They are certainly not clear to me. You could also petition the Supreme Court on other points, but they matter not in the shadow of this. For example, the court said that the information you provided was not confirmed. Is that your fault? Surely it is the job of the police to confirm information. If they don't go out and look for it, how is it that your word is cast in doubt?'

I listened as hard as I'd ever listened in my life, taking notes and trying to remember all that he was saying. The bastards had really fucked me over, that was clear. I had believed in justice and believed that it was the duty of the court to seek out the truth and uphold the defendant's right to it. Who had taught me such nonsense? Instead, they had entered into a conspiracy with the prosecutor to use us to satisfy the demands of the government.

I was as mad as hell now. Back in the cell, I told Webster, 'There's no way they're going to keep us in jail for long. Not with a case like we've got against them. According to British law, it would have been kicked out. We'd already be free men. They conceded that we didn't have bloody *dama zhi*, so therefore we were not guilty of the original charge. Not guilty!'

'That's ripe, innit, you're not guilty of what we accused you of, it was something else, but you can still keep the fucking sentence,' spat Webster.

On 2 June 1992, nearly eight months after my apprehension in Urumchi, we were told to get our stuff together and prepare to leave. I felt a mixture of emotions. It was so good to think that I was getting out of that bottomless pit of torment, but I didn't know what was in store next. Downstairs, we met up with Werner and Dieter. There was a Dutch prisoner with them. He did not look like your usual traveller type at all but more of a businessman as he stood there gripping a briefcase tightly. In his late forties, with short light-brown hair, a moustache and bright blue eyes, he stood a good six foot tall and looked as if he'd been an athlete once. He introduced himself as Larry. He said he was from Amsterdam originally but had lived in the States all his life. He too had just got fifteen years courtesy of the People's Court for transporting hash. He had a huge list of grievances, and they poured out one after another. No one was listening.

I was more concerned about the return of my personal belongings. Everything was there except the receipt for the transfer of my cash to ShaSha. I was sure I had put it in with all the rest of my stuff, and I certainly didn't have it on me now. I decided that it was no big deal, and that ShaSha had probably already had the money given her.

It was a beautiful morning. The sun was already high and reaching into the cool, crisp shadows. The *xun dao* and some of the guards we had got to know were there to see us off, waving and shouting the Chinese equivalent of good luck.

As we all drove out of Diyi Kanshou Suo (No.1 Detention Centre), I can't tell you the relief I felt. It was overwhelming to think that I would never have to experience that lowest pit of human subsistence again. But that feeling of elation was short-lived. As soon as we turned the corner a sense of foreboding immediately took over. Suppose everything failed and I had to spend the next seven and a half years in jail? This would be my last chance to see these wonderful, chaotic and lively streets at close quarters. I made the most of every second, and stuffed my memory with the sights and smells of old Shanghai.

The bus drove out on to the Bund, known as the *Waitan* in Chinese. It was the famous waterfront lined with the beautiful buildings of the old British and French settlements. The far end was dominated by the enormous bulk of the Shanghai Mansions Hotel. I watched huge container ships negotiate the river, bypassing full-sailed junks tacking back and forth on the river. I saw crowds of pedestrians walking in every direction, lovers having their photos taken and the odd foreigner asking the way. What would they say if they knew that this screaming, wailing minibus with its darkened windows contained five foreigners heading for the biggest prison in Asia to serve a total of forty-six and a half years with Shanghai's most dangerous and screwed-up cons? Their holiday would probably be over in ten days – how could they possibly identify with us? We had stepped beyond the normal existence of man and were heading for the Black Hole of China, the deepest corner in the belly of the dragon itself.

Crossing the bridge, Larry pointed out the Peace Hotel: 'See that room on the top floor with the balcony, that's where they busted me. Great view up there, and real cheap. There was nearly nine kilos in the ceiling.'

Within five minutes the bus turned in through a huge iron door that slid open with a noise like thunder. Through another smaller door, we came to a halt in a long, dark courtyard surrounded by tall five-storey brick buildings that were blackened by pollution, almost for effect. This was Tilan Qiao.

Ten Don'ts

Like a wandering fish swimming in the bottom of a cauldron,
occasionally it has to breathe for a short moment.

Zang Gang, *The Later Chronicles of the Han Dynasty*

THE Huang Pu River glides slowly through China's largest city, and on the north shore of the eastern bend lies Tilan Qiao, a bustling commercial district of Shanghai. It is also the name by which the majority of residents call the Shanghai No.1 Jail, which is situated in the centre of this area at 147 Changyang Lu. Not only is it a very large prison, it is also the administrative centre for all the Reform-through-Labour and Reform-through-Education camps found within the region.

Apart from Tilan Qiao, which means 'Carry-a-basket bridge', there are numerous other large-capacity jails within easy reach of the city. The majority of these prisons' inmates come from Shanghai, but some are immigrants from the surrounding provinces. According to the Ministry of Justice, there are over seven hundred prisons in China housing 1.4 million prisoners, but, as with all official figures in China, it is unwise to believe that it's quite as simple as that. Amnesty International estimated the real Chinese prison population to be 20 million. That works out at sixteen or seventeen prisoners in every thousand inhabitants. The Shanghai authorities claimed in 1992 that the whole prison population of its administrative region was in excess of ten thousand. Independent estimates suggest that since Tilan Qiao can accommodate nearly ten thousand prisoners on its own, the real figure is more than likely to be between twenty and twenty-five thousand prisoners. This does not include the five thousand or more prisoners who are sent by train out of the province each year to the gulags in Heilongjiang, Qinghai and Xinjiang. Nor does it include the thousands of prisoners serving the three-year 're-education' sentences that are administered by the local police without the need of a court judgment, or the hundreds of people languishing in detention houses from anything from six months (the legal time limit by which a detainee should go from being arrested to indictment to trial) to up to four years or more without trial. It does not include the suspects snatched from the streets and put under indefinite *shou rong ju liu* (house arrest), *shou rong shen cha* (detained for investigation) or *ge li shen cha* (isolated for investigation).

The authorities can be very accommodating and are able to house any suspect in any place they consider most useful or confusing to those trying to find out their whereabouts. Suspects may be held in detention houses, labour camps, re-education farms, main prisons, local police stations, railway stations, airports or even hotels, as I was.

Tilan Qiao lies like an enormous cold black stone in the middle of the boiling wok of daily human existence. There is no buffer, no moat, no kind of no-man's-land between the city and its walls that rise tall and grey, draped with electric wire and patrolled by squaddies of the Red Army. Shops do their business in the shadows of the walls, hotels and apartment blocks tower above them, often seeming to bend over to take a look inside. For the most part, the people on the outside ignore the jail's presence and go about their daily affairs without the slightest thought as to its existence or those who tread the mill deep within the bowls of the monster. It sits there like an eclipse robbing the streets of sunlight, a nightmare thrust to the back of people's minds. Anyone who does spare a thought thinks of it with either hatred because of crimes committed against them, or with sorrow because of loved ones lost to the machinery of communist justice.

Tilan Qiao was built in 1903 by the British and was intended mainly for the local population. The foreigners who lived in the international settlements were as often as not beyond the reach of the law since money or connections would soon pluck you from its grasp if you did stray. At that time it was known as Shanghai East Prison and was said to be the largest jail in Asia. Cells ran down the centre of the buildings, forty-five on either side. Apart from the ground floor, each six-foot-by-eight-foot cell with its open iron-bar frontage looked out on to a narrow walkway through the safety railings and down to the ground.

Across from these was another large five-storey building in the shape of a cross. This evil-looking edifice housed the most serious offenders and those sentenced to death. The Cross Building, as it soon became known, contained the infamous *fengbo ting* (disturbance booth) which was a cell the size of one man in a crouch, with no windows and a limited supply of air. It was meant for prisoners who had become violently out of control. The building also contained the *shinei xingchang* (indoor execution field), a hanging room complete with trapdoor and pit.

Only a few years after it was completed, the *Dong Fang Zazhi* (*Eastern Magazine*) wrote an article condemning the place. The translation read: 'On inspection, it is a jail that maltreats and abuses its inmates. The ordinary people are talking. There have been many executions in the last few years, and the Chinese people are not unaware that this is a dangerous course, and should be avoided at all costs.'

Tilan Qiao symbolised the feeling that as long as foreigners remained on Chinese soil the native people had no rights in their own country. There is no doubt that the place was used by the colonialists to clear the streets of anti-imperialist trouble-makers and business competitors. The prison itself was run on the tightest of budgets but that didn't prevent unscrupulous guards siphoning off what they could. Conditions were appalling, but where in the world at that time were they any better? The British themselves wouldn't have been seen dead in the place. Instead, they brought in Indian Sikhs to guard the prisoners. With their beards, red turbans and khaki uniforms, they became a dreaded sight around Shanghai, instilling fear and loathing in the people.

The foreign devils and their Indian henchmen gone, the place continued to operate as a jail and remained full. All that changed were the criminals and the crimes they were charged with. As well as the common thieves and murderers, the next eighty years would see all the jails of China filling up with political prisoners, spies and other so-called enemies of the state. Maltreatment and executions would continue and, in later years, increase. The Chinese had copied the 'big noses' they had hated so much, only this time they were persecuting their own.

Getting out of the bus with my bag in hand, I immediately noticed the Chinese prisoners in their summer uniform of white short-sleeved open-necked shirts and light-grey trousers, both trimmed with the blue piping that was the symbol of the Shanghai *laogai* (reform-through-labour) prisoner. In comparison to the average Chinese on the outside, they actually looked quite smart. They stopped what they were doing and stared at us unabashed. It was no doubt strange enough for them to see the odd foreigner on the streets of Shanghai, but to find five of them in the inner sanctum of the reform-through-labour HQ was unheard of.

Opposite the administration building I got my first view of a cell block lurking behind a high wall. It was black, dirty and simply massive, with all its windows covered by black shutters. The admissions room was full of Chinese, maybe twenty-five or so fresh from the detention house, all having their photos and prints taken. Compared to the guys in uniform, everybody looked like death warmed up, like refugees or asylum-seekers from some war-ravaged republic with our unshaven faces, hollow cheeks, sunken eyes, waxen complexions, and all dressed in various wrinkled and discoloured shirts that were ripped and full of holes, standing around like dumb animals in a market. The others looked so clean and healthy, I was envious.

After about five minutes, an old guy with white hair weaved his way through the crowd. In perfect English he introduced himself: 'Hello, my name is Joseph King. I am here to help you and be your interpreter. This way, please.'

Unbelievable. The man spoke as if he'd just come out of Cambridge. He was in his late fifties and looked fit, alert and well nourished. We shuffled forward, following this messiah into another room where it was quiet and we could sit down. He brought forms for us to fill in: name, age, address, nationality, crime, sentence, date of arrest and date of release. Writing down my release date brought it home to me: 21 April 2000. I had not once calculated it; instead, I'd shoved it to the back of my mind, classified it as irrelevant because I was going home soon, very soon, once we had cleared all this mess up. But hell, like this, if I didn't get out, I'd miss my fortieth birthday and the millennium party.

Once we'd completed the form, we went back into the chaos to have our pictures taken. It was the biggest camera I'd ever seen. The assistant held aloft two massive flashlights and I waited to be cooked. *Whoosh*. I limped blindly back to the others and joined the queue to have my fingerprints taken.

Joseph King then asked us if we had any medical problems. As it happened, I did have something that had been bothering me for a couple of months. I had discovered that my left breast had a hard lump in it which in turn made my nipple extremely sore. I would have disregarded it if it hadn't been for the fact that Webster had one too. We had asked the doctor in the detention house what they were, but all he'd done was ask me my age and then say, 'Oh it's normal for your age.' Webster's had been leaking fluid from the nipple so when he asked the quack about it and got the same reply, we thought it a bit strange. He was nearly fifteen years older than me, so how the hell could it be an age thing? We speculated that it was a reaction to secretly administered truth drugs that had been put in with our food.

Joseph King took me to the other side of the room to consult with a woman there. It was hard to tell if she was a doctor or a nurse. She was about four-foot-ten high and bound almost head to foot in white cotton, hat and mask included. She had a quick feel, wrote something down and that was it.

I was then called over to a scruffy little bloke in a creased uniform behind a table. I gave him the form and he filled out a card with a lot of red Chinese writing on it. He eventually handed it to me with a plastic cover and a safety pin. This was my identity card. I was now Prisoner 13498.

When all was done, another prison officer appeared and informed us that we were now being taken to the brigade that was to be our home for the duration of our stay. Told to leave our bags where they were, we toddled off in line with the officer and Joseph King through another huge steel sliding door. We were at last truly on the inside. We walked straight on down a concrete roadway flanked by high buildings and turned left past the entrance.

'That's One Brigade,' said Joseph, 'and that building on the right is the kitchen, and here's Eight Brigade. To your left again,' he pointed, 'are Three and Four Brigade.'

Between One and Eight there was a fenced-in basketball court. Straight on between Eight and Three was another, this time unfenced. One confusing feature I noticed was that Eight Brigade was in fact marked Two Brigade, but who was I to complain? The officer guided us into Eight and stopped in front of a kiosk where another officer was sat inside. I could just see down the length of the building with cell upon cell to the right and forty or fifty prisoners sitting around tables playing cards and watching TV.

'Upstairs,' said Joseph King. 'By the way, I'm also known as Jin Feng. I am the son of a Christian pastor and went to school at St John's in Shanghai. I graduated in English from Fudan University, and I now teach English here in the prison.'

'What did you do?' I asked.

'I was a hooligan,' he replied in a matter-of-fact sort of way.

'You don't look much like a hooligan to me.'

Up we went one floor and then another.

'Here we are, Three Middle Brigade,' said Jin Feng jubilantly. There was a big blackboard facing us and an office to the right. Inside I could see a huge tank full of all sorts of exotic-looking fish.

'Is that the restaurant?' someone asked in an attempt to be funny.

Suddenly, through the iron gate that separated the little foyer from a long narrow gallery lined with cells, bounded a tall, clean-shaven young man wearing gold-rimmed spectacles and a business shirt and trousers, his arms outstretched. Must be from the consulate, I thought.

'Hello and welcome. My name's Mark, and this is Three Middle Division of Eight Brigade.' So this was the infamous Englishman.

'Where are the rest of the foreigners?' asked a voice.

'There aren't any. This is it. We are the only foreigners here. There are three Pakistanis dotted around the place, but we're it as far as westerners are concerned. We are the only foreigners in prison in all of China, in fact,' Mark answered almost proudly.

'But where are the Filipinos and Thais, the Russians and Koreans?' I ventured.

'Nope, got none of them. Oh, wait a minute, there is one Korean over in One with a Pakistani. But that's it, no other foreigners.'

This is crazy, I thought. We can't be the only foreigners to have committed crimes in China. Why the fuck are we being locked up when all the rest are obviously just getting kicked out?

'Excuse me,' intervened Jin Feng, 'but you can talk and get to know each other later. The captain would like to speak to you now around the corner.'

Captain? Anyway, we followed Jin Feng and went round to the other side of the building.

'That's where everybody lives, and this is where the Chinese work all day. This is the electrical repair unit of the prison. They fix televisions, fridges, video recorders and umbrellas here. They also mend clothes and shoes – when they feel like it.'

We sat round a table on narrow benches near a pile of cannibalised TV sets that conveniently blocked the view to the work area, and waited.

'When the captain arrives, please all stand up,' said Jin Feng.

After about five minutes, a little fellow appeared wearing a cap that looked too big for him, a khaki summer uniform shirt and green trousers. He was quite good-looking compared to many I'd seen, and somewhere between forty and forty-five years old.

'Stand for the captain,' Jin Feng shouted.

By the time we had thought about it, and half got off our arses, he was telling us to sit down again. With Jin Feng translating, the little man began: 'I am Captain Yu. I am also known as Yu Zhong. I am the head of *San Zhong Dui*, Three Middle Brigade. I will be in charge of you as long as you stay in this jail. Welcome to Tilan Qiao. I sincerely hope that we can all get along together well, and that you will all co-operate with us here.

'I know that you all come from far away and that your families miss you very much. It is my hope that you will all work hard and go home at the earliest possible date. I am a good man, and if you are good I will be good. But I must warn you that there are rules and regulations here that must be obeyed. You will be rewarded for good behaviour and punished for bad. You are here to serve your sentence for the crimes you committed according to Chinese law. This is your punishment. It is now in your hands to reform yourselves.

'You may be interested to know that this prison was built by the British, your ancestors maybe, so you cannot really blame us for the surroundings,' he laughed, obviously finding that particular aspect extremely funny. 'It is an old prison, but our methods are modern, and we are working hard to keep up to date. Our former leader Chairman Mao Zedong made great changes to the prison system. He saw jail not as a place simply to pass time away, but a place that mirrors society. It is a place of education, a factory or a farm, where prisoners work to help the society they have damaged by their criminal acts. Through hard work they can reform themselves. There is no man who cannot be reformed. Labour becomes the reformer's only road, the method by which he can express his true repentance and help repay his debt to society. The most important aim of this prison is to work in a humanitarian way to reform criminals, to help them see the errors of their ways through education and allotted time for introspection. By teaching them morals, we help them to be cultured and responsible and ultimately law-abiding citizens and useful members of society.

'Seeing as you are foreigners, we do not expect you to join the others in reform labour. You will have what we call lenient conditions, in effect intellectual status. You will have time to embark on self-study plans of your choice in the same way as Mark is doing at present.

'For your own safety, I should warn you that many of the Chinese prisoners in this brigade are here for violent crimes. I therefore do not want to see any of you talking to or consorting with them in any way. I repeat, this is for your own safety.

'I hope that you will all work hard to reform. We want you to return to your families as soon as possible. Jin Feng and another monitor will be able to tell you more about the everyday operation of the prison. You will all soon receive an English translation of the rules and regulations which we expect you to study. If you have any questions, you can come and report to me in my office at the end of the corridor. That's all for now. I will speak to you all again.'

'Stand for the captain,' said Jin Feng, as Captain Yu got up and took his leave. Again it was only Mark who actually made it to his feet. The rest of us seemed to have a reluctance to stand.

'Well, what the hell was that all about? Reform, introspection, labour, debt to society, useful member?' I asked.

'I got a useful member here,' said Webster, gripping his groin.

'He says he's a good man. Let's call him Benny from now on, right?' piped up Werner.

'Doesn't *yu* mean "fish" in Chinese? Could call him Benny "the fish" Goodman seeing as he's also got that dirty great tank in his room.'

The banter continued as we tried to forget whatever it was we'd just been told. It was all so alien and frightening in its delivery that it made us more confused than ever. What the hell were we supposed to do here?

Returning to the other side, we walked into Eight Brigade. Jin Feng then introduced us to a tall, chubby Chinese prisoner in his late thirties whose right index finger was missing. It turned out he was the *shiwu fan* (general affairs prisoner) known in the Shanghai dialect as 'nummer 1' – number 1. This guy was the leader of the inmates in Three Middle Brigade. He was like a manager, the link between the officers and the prisoners. If the officers wanted anything, they dealt only with this guy. It was his duty to sort out the everyday running of the brigade. The captain wanted nothing to do with mundane issues such as work details, supply of food, bedding, arranging the emptying of shit buckets and so on.

It was also up to the number 1 to keep the place under control, and he in turn had his own assistants, a little clique of right-hand men. There was the workshop foreman, for want of a better description, the prisoner in charge of supply, the propaganda and art prisoner, the secretary and the political education liaison prisoner. In addition to these 'capos' who sat at a table apart from the rest when they weren't working, the brigade was split into five sub-groups, each of which had a leader who was generally known as *xiao zhou zhang* (small-table captain). These lesser capos kept control of these smaller units using any method they thought appropriate.

After that little insight into the running of the landing, we were shown to our cells. Unlike the Chinese who were shacked up two and sometimes three to a cell, we got one six-by-eight-foot cubicle all to ourselves. It came with a wooden pallet, a *matong* (shit bucket) and two cotton quilts. The cell was completely closed on three sides with an iron-bar door in the front. We were told that it would be open from five-thirty in the morning, reveille, until eight-thirty at night, when all prisoners were locked up. During the day we were free to come out and sit at our desks and keep ourselves busy with self-study. Five-thirty seemed like an awfully early time of the day to be woken up, but at least we didn't have to go and join in with the slave labour next door.

As we listened to the introduction, a little fellow with a bald head and glasses appeared, also with his right index finger missing, and slipped our names and numbers into a slot on the front of the cell. This was Zhou Wanjia.

Originally there had been forty-five cells on a landing, but in recent years cells one and two had been knocked together to produce what was now used as the captain's office. A cage with an iron gate had been bolted in place to divide the office from the prisoners' area. In this way the inmates could be allowed out of their individual cells while effectively being locked in. Cells three, four, five and six had had their doors covered with zinc and were used as storerooms. Cell seven was the number 1's office and command centre. Cell eight was his storeroom and cells nine and ten had been set aside to provide us with storage space for our luggage, food and books. Number 1's boudoir was cell eleven, which he shared with his favourite arse-licker, a slight, wiry figure called Shen Ji. Next was Mark's cell, then came Werner in cell thirteen, then Larry, Dieter, Webster and finally me. Next door to me was Zhou Wanjia and Jin Feng.

Pasted on the back wall of each cell was a large notice in Chinese entitled *shi wu shi* (ten don'ts.) After translation they read:

Don't sit down in the cell when a captain tours.
Don't eat food in the cell.
Don't spit in the cell.
Don't piss or shit on the floor.
Don't sleep or lie down in the cell unless authorised.
Don't keep the cell untidy.
Don't leave the cell until told to do so.
Don't enter the cell until told to do so.
Don't keep dangerous implements in the cell.
Don't hide contraband in the cell.

This was about as much as I could bear for one day. I was having difficulty taking all this information in. I wanted to make up my bed and sleep, but that wasn't allowed. I wanted to dream of Kashgar, of Hainan, of anywhere but this fucking place. I could feel the pressure building already. It wasn't as simple as just locking you up and leaving you to serve your sentence. No, they wanted to invade your brain and fuck about with your thinking.

The so-called desks were in a sort of corral or sheep-pen which we had to climb into every time we wanted to use them. Mark explained that years before there had been these huge cut-outs in the floor so that the guards could see from the bottom to the top of the building, but these had been filled in and covered with a wooden floor. The corral was the original safety rail.

Before I knew it, it was lunchtime, and a couple of Chinese prisoners were sent off to find something for us all to sit on. They came back with wooden benches, three feet long and about five inches wide. We were expected to sit on these things from five-thirty in the morning until eight-thirty at night studying, but I couldn't see how that was possible. I'd been on the damn thing for half an hour listening to Mark describe the way of things in Tilan Qiao and was already saddle sore.

The six of us sat in a row, nearly touching each other, like sardines in a tin. How we were going to spend eight years like that? My only consolation was that I had a window in front of me. I could see the brigade opposite, the kitchen and a piece of blue sky, the size of a crisp packet. I could watch the officers going to get their meals and prisoners pushing carts laden with food containers, which, after nearly nine months in detention, was bloody exciting.

'We eat all our meals here,' Mark explained. 'They have a canteen over there above the kitchen, but it's only for the officers, and not that many of them use it either. They tend to take along bowls, fill them up and take them back to their units. You'll be getting different food from the Chinese. Theirs comes all together on big trays and is dished out for them by other prisoners. In that way they can control who gets the biggest portions of meat. You'll see in a minute that ours come in individual metal containers with lids to keep them warm and free from interference. Foreigners' food is cooked separately from the rest, in a different kitchen actually. It's what they call "small wok" as opposed to "large wok", which the Chinese get. I've been getting really good food here. You'll be surprised, but of course it couldn't be worse than the detention house, could it? Breakfast is rice soup, or porridge as they like to call it, with some pickled vegetable. Sometimes it's turnip or gherkin, and there's garlic, carrot and beetroot. You can also get a *mantou* a bit later when they bring them round. Lunch is usually at about ten-thirty. The prisoners are served first, and that allows the officers to have their lunch later at a more civilised hour. Dinner is at four-thirty, which makes rather a long night of it, but you can buy packet noodles and eat them if you're hungry.'

The food did arrive eventually and it was excellent. The container had a tray inside which contained beef-and-onion stew and underneath there was a large portion of hot rice. This helped me feel a lot better because as long as I could eat properly, I felt I could cope with anything. Our food was cooked by a Muslim in a separate kitchen set aside for all the Muslim prisoners, and we had the opportunity to choose between Muslim, vegetarian or even a vegan diet. Mark was a staunch vegan and Larry and Webster were vegetarians. I choose to eat a Muslim meat diet. It suited me fine because I had not eaten pork for over three years out of respect to ShaSha and her family, but it was not so good for the Germans. They were craving pork, and wanted to eat the same food as the Chinese, but it was simply not permitted.

After lunch, the introduction continued. 'Every month, if you have money that is, you will be able to purchase items from what they call the *da zhang* or account list. There's all sorts of goodies on it, like apples, oranges, chocolate, pickled vegetables, peanut butter, jam, preserved tofu and toiletries. Here's an old one so you can see for yourself. It's translated from the Chinese list by Zhou Wanjia, he's in charge of that for us. He's not such a bad guy but a bit sensitive at times. He's in for beating his wife up. Apparently he locked her up in a room and went in every so often and kicked the shit out of her. You wouldn't think so to look at him, would you? He got seven years.'

Mark handed me the list. It was an interesting selection of items, but we were going to have to ask the Goodman if we could get some black tea and coffee. It was at this point that I first came into contact with the prison bureaucracy. I went to Benny's office and knocked the door. I waited to hear a sort of 'Come in' sound. Mistake. He shot out and called Zhou Wanjia, who told me I must never do what I had just done. In future I must first ask permission from either him or the number 1 to make a report to the captain. Once this was granted, I could leave the brigade area and enter the captain's area. I must never cross the red line painted on the floor without permission. I then had to stand on another red line painted in front of the captain's office and say, '*Baogou duizhang* – Report to Captain,' and wait until he called me in. That didn't seem so difficult apart from having to ask permission from a Chinese prisoner. Anyway, I did all this in the required manner and found myself standing on the report line for nearly ten minutes. I could see the captain inside chatting and smoking with his pals, deliberately ignoring me. This strained my patience a bit but I stood my ground stoically until I was eventually called in.

After I explained our requests with the help of Zhou Wanjia's translation, Benny simply said, 'Write a report about it.' This seemed ridiculous, but I was assured by Mark that this was how things were done. You couldn't get anything without writing a report. Reports were the bedrock of life here. Nothing could or would happen without a report.

Later that day another officer appeared on the scene. He was a young guy in his twenties with glasses and a square head who introduced himself as Jin Mouling. He was from the Education Department, the *Guanjiao Ke*, and he explained straight away that our very existence in Tilan Qiao was under his control. He welcomed us and expressed the hope that we would all work hard so that we could gain the earliest possible release. He informed us that we could write two letters per month to family members only, and that we were required to write their names and addresses down on a form. All incoming and outgoing letters would be translated and checked for material that might be damaging to our reform.

The Germans were told that they had to write in English because the authorities had not yet found a German translator. This pissed them off no end. Dieter was fuming, and told Captain Jin that he was unable to write in English and it was in any case a violation of his human rights to be forced to write in a language other than his own. He threatened to complain to his consul. The captain was somewhat taken aback but did say that he would discuss it at a higher level and let the Germans know soon.

We were not allowed to write about our cases or make defamatory remarks about the prison. Nor could we write about prison secrets, such as the names and numbers of the guards, prison population numbers or the positioning of the buildings. We were forbidden to say anything that might cause offence or slander the government of the People's Republic of China. We were told that it was only permissible to write the truth. It didn't leave us much to say.

For some reason I had taken an instant dislike to Jin Mouling. I was not alone. He seemed to have the same effect on everybody he came in contact with, including his fellow officers.

After breakfast on the second day, I immediately got down to writing my letters. I'd been able to send just two during the previous nine months. I knew that the one to my parents had actually arrived but was uncertain about the other. This time I hoped things would be different. I sent my two letters off, one to ShaSha and one to my parents, telling them of the change in circumstances. With a mind to not upsetting the authorities and giving them the excuse to refuse to post them, I censored myself so much that when I reread the letters they were so bland and uninteresting I felt like ripping them up. I told ShaSha I wanted her to come to Shanghai and find a place to live so that she could visit me every month. I promised to do everything in my power to look after her, but in order for me to do so it was best that she be near me. I assumed that she had the three thousand dollars to be going on with, and that this would cover her expenses getting here. I said that I believed with her help I could hope to be released sooner, and that it would be no time until we would be back together again.

Many of the guys in detention had come on in false machismo and claimed that they were going to divorce their wives because it would be unfair to them to live without a husband for such a long period. I knew that they were only saying this in the expectation of the dreaded 'Dear John' letter, but I had no intention of throwing away our love and the marriage that we had struggled so hard for without a damn good fight. It was far too precious to relinquish.

I was not the only one to assume that since we were a small group of foreigners from the same hemisphere in the same circumstances and with the same grievance against the Chinese, we might form a close-knit group where we all worked together towards one goal, namely justice and a clarification of the substance that we were all put inside for having. But it didn't take long to find out that it was never going to be like that. Within days, the splits became obvious and differences in opinion cropped up regularly.

Mark insisted that he was innocent and that he had been duped. He denied all knowledge of the nature of the drug found wrapped about his person, saying that he thought it was a herbal remedy for back pain. He refused to discuss his case with the rest of us, even refusing to show us his indictment, which would have been enormously helpful to the rest of us in our fight. He knew that we'd all used his name as an example in our trials, and was afraid that if we continued to complain, his sentence might be increased to match ours. He had been in Tilan Qiao for nearly eight months already, going along with the flow of things, never once complaining or refusing to do what the officers or prisoners demanded of him. He felt that he had measured the system and was in control, and that with good behaviour he could get out early. Our presence put his position in jeopardy. They had already managed to get Mark writing a monthly *sixiang huibao* ('thinking report') which had not been asked of him by the authorities but by the Chinese prisoners. When we arrived, he had assumed the mantle of group leader and believed that he was taking a short-cut through the jungle of the so-called reform. When the rest of us found out about the *sixiang huibao*, we were furious. What was a thinking report anyway? We found out later that it should contain not only an outflowing of repentance, remorse and sorrow for your heinous crime, an acknowledgement of guilt and an acceptance of the sentence as being just and correct, but also details of what other prisoners were thinking.

Well, if that was what he had been writing, it was tantamount to treachery. I could not believe that one of our own could do such a thing. Hadn't he been awake during the Cold War? I considered it to be a violation of my rights. Although I loved China and considered many of their techniques successful, I was ideologically opposed to communism. To me this *sixiang huibao* was the first and most serious attempt to play around with my mind. They were not content with handing out harsh sentences, they wanted to brainwash us too. The Germans felt the same and so did Larry.

Some days after we arrived, our luggage turned up. It came in on one of the food trolleys, and was carried up to the third floor by Zhou Wanjia, Sun and a couple of other lackeys known to us already as Silver Teeth (because of his silver crowns) and the Colonel (a former army officer). They proceeded to unpack it all, saying that Captain Yu had instructed them to do so in order to look for contraband and other outlawed items. This made me mad as hell. I had no objection to an officer rooting through my stuff, although that was bad enough, but to have Chinese prisoners doing it was simply too much of a liberty, and I went to complain. Benny looked at me and sneered. This was not the sort of thing that inmates complained about. The prisoners were his workers; they did as he said without question. By the time I had remonstrated for ten minutes, it was all over and I had to go back and pick up my belongings. Zhou Wanjia had thrown them all over the place, happy in the knowledge he was pissing me off.

Webster's obsessive and overbearing manner soon began to wear on everybody. If he couldn't be the star of the show all the time, he became moody and insecure. We watched as his attention-grabbing antics got steadily more perverse. It had all started out innocently enough with a few yarns, but they had turned into tall stories which, when he repeated them, as he did endlessly, had noticeable factual changes. Then he wanted us all to know that he was a child of the 1960s and set about singing his way through the decade. He knew countless songs from that period but nothing at all after 1973. When that lost its appeal, he turned to barnyard impressions, the first rendition of which may have been marginally funny, especially when done by this Ben Gunn lookalike, but its humour waned rapidly.

He moved on to pinching stuff from the number 1's office, things like apples or noodles. His *pièce de résistance* came one day after an argument with the number 1 about sitting in his cell instead of at his desk. When the Chinese went back to work on the other side of the building after lunch, Webster stole into cell 8 and started rooting around, eventually finding the man's enamel eating bowl. Curious to see what he was up to, we gathered round to watch. Webster pulled out his recently herpes-infected penis and wiped its scabby knob all around the inside of the bowl, saying, 'That'll teach the bastard.' The rest of us looked at each other incredulously, unsure whether to laugh or throw up.

It wasn't long before we all noticed that he was being gripped by a terrible paranoia, which unsettled the rest of us as much as it did him. When any two of us were talking alone, he suspected we were talking about him. Without fail he would sneak up and interrupt, saying, 'Sorry, but did I hear you mention my name? I thought I heard you shout Webster.'

'No, you must've made a mistake, we're talking about Stevie Ray Vaughan.'

'I don't make mistakes, pal. Are you trying to make out that I'm a liar, pal?'

Other times, while you were busy writing a letter perhaps, he would come up behind you and peer over your shoulder and say, 'Is that my name you're writing there?'

'No, it's not your name.'

'Well, what are you writing about, then?'

'I don't see that's it's any of your business.'

'It's my fucking business if you're writing about me, pal.'

And so it went on. Constant harassment, day in, day out, and always with violent overtones provoking and waiting for someone to bite. Eventually it got so that I couldn't bear to be in his company, and I was not the only one to feel like that. When he noticed that people were cooling towards him he went in search of someone else to entertain. He found himself a soulmate in the form of Jin Feng, the translator. Little did we realise it at the time, but this relationship would be the cause of an endless catalogue of problems in the future.

Ten days after our arrival, things were on the whole going well. We were getting on well with Benny Goodman. He'd agreed to our requests and had even said he'd go out himself and buy fresh garlic for us. It was lunchtime and we were all in our sheep-pen tucking into some tofu soup when Benny arrived with the garlic. We were just about to thank him when Webster asked me for some pickle. He'd noticed I hadn't eaten my share at breakfast but instead put it in a jar with some soy sauce to see if it would improve the taste.

'Give us some of that pickle, will ya?'

'No, I'm keeping it to see what it tastes like tomorrow when it's soaked up the sauce.'

'Give us the pickle,' he said with noticeable urgency.

'No, I told you, I'm keeping it,' I replied calmly.

'Just give me the fucking pickle!'

'It's not your fucking pickle.'

'Look, I've asked you three fucking times, now give me the fucking pickle!' he said, standing up.

'Sit down and control yourself, you fool,' I retorted, thinking what a petty-minded pillock he was.

That was the final straw for Webster. Grabbing his chopsticks, he lunged at me, shouting, 'I'll poke your fucking eyes out, you bastard!'

The chopsticks missed but the headbutt didn't. It came crashing down on top of my nose with a sickening crunch. Mark managed to drag him off as I contemplated swinging at him, but with the officer standing just two yards away I thought better of it.

What a performance, and right in front of Benny. I couldn't imagine what damage it had done to our cause. Webster was taken into the office with Jin Feng as translator to explain his actions to the captain. He accused me of intimidating him. Well, no matter what I'd said, it hadn't warranted that reaction. Anyway, I was in the clear for not retaliating.

When he was escorted back to the table, it was he who had to apologise, with a weak-hearted 'Sorry.' Looking into his glazed eyes, I knew that this was not over by a long chalk.

As foreigners we had slipped through the normal admission procedure completely. We had come straight into our brigade and started life as prisoners on the first day. We had no uniforms, no haircut and no indoctrination. Mark told me one day how different it was for the Chinese.

'After the photos and fingerprints they are taken to Six Brigade. That is one whole building set aside for new prisoners. They are locked up twenty-four hours a day. They only ever come out when they are being examined about the regulations, and for beatings if they fail to remember the "big fifty-eight". They're in there for at least a month, sometimes longer. It depends if they pass the test or not. The first part of the regs concerns the workplace, and how they've got to reach production quotas and obey, and not pinch stuff or disrupt the work schedule. The second half is about the jail in general, and goes on about not forming gangs, getting involved in fights, trading in food, giving tattoos, smoking and so on. At first they're given a week to learn all fifty-eight articles off by heart. They are then brought out at random and tested by other prisoners whose duty it is to look after the new ones. These are normally old hands and have maybe already served a big piece of their sentence without it being reduced. They are now getting desperate so will do anything to please the authorities. The students who pass the first test are selected to become deputies to the old hands.

'The deputies are told that they have to get their particular team to pass as soon as possible. It is their sole responsibility and they will be blamed if any member of a team should fail, thus causing the whole team to fail. They question their students endlessly, forcing them to sit on little stools and to slap themselves in the face when they get it wrong.

'Anyway, once all that is over, they're assigned to a brigade. If they were a cook on the outside, they'll go to the kitchen, but only if they've been good, of course. The kitchen is a much sought-after position with a lot of trust involved. If they are builders, they go to Five. If they are musicians or artists they go to Two; those experienced in retailing go to Ten where they handle the supplies. If they can repair things, they come here. As to the rest, if they are unqualified they end up in Three or Four, the clothes-manufacturing brigades.

'One Brigade is a special brigade, set aside for death-row prisoners, death sentence with two-year reprieve and lifers, *wuqi tuxing*. The two-year-reprieve prisoners are on the top floor. They have a death sentence, but are given two years to prove that they have changed their ways and reformed. If they fail, they die.'

I listened in awe to this rundown of life in Tilan Qiao and clearly saw it was no holiday camp. I knew I had to get out of there as soon as possible, and the best way to do that was to follow up the *dama zhi* thing. We had been messed about for sure. Larry had had his indictment taken off him in the detention house by his *xun dao* and it was never returned, and therefore he didn't know what he'd been charged with. The Germans and Webster had originally been indicted in November but had had their papers withdrawn on 13 December. When they were finally indicted the second time, the substance had changed from *dama* to *dama zhi*, and Webster's charge had changed from possession to transporting. We discussed this issue over and over again, trying to work out the best course of action. It was decided that we had to write to the court for clarification and ask what was the nature of the drug *dama zhi*, and how it differed from *dama*. It was surely unjust to sentence people for crimes they didn't know the nature of, and that it was the court's duty to explain to us, our families and our governments why and for what substance we were in jail. We knew that because they had changed it back to *dama* in the appeal verdict, whatever answer we were given would be further evidence of their mistake. If they confirmed that there was a difference, how could they change the substance at such a juncture in the proceedings without calling the first trial a mis-trial? Or, if they had to reduce the seriousness of the crime, how come they didn't reduce the sentence accordingly? If they wrote back and said there was no difference, why did they change it and how come the academic study proves it to be ten times more potent than *dama*? The final verdict had confirmed that *dama* was hashish. That meant that *dama zhi* was not hashish. That meant when I had the first trial I was talking about one substance while they were talking about another. How in God's name could that be a fair trial? How could they say that the facts were clear?

Letters were written to the Intermediate Court, and I wrote to my lawyer, asking to see him again. I tried to explain to my consul the discoveries we had made, but was told by Captain Jin Mouling, who officiated, that I was not permitted to discuss my case with visitors, and that if I persisted he would terminate the visit. The consul added, 'It is our job to make sure that you are not being treated any worse than the Chinese prisoners. That's as far as we are allowed to go. We cannot get involved in the legal process.' I got the impression he didn't understand what I was on about and maybe thought I was just trying it on.

There was no response to our letters, so we all wrote again. After another attempt to get my lawyer in to see me, I was called into the office by Jin, who informed me that prisoners were not allowed to see lawyers in jail and that I had no need of a lawyer because my case was over. I had already been given ample opportunity to appeal, and once a case has gone to the Higher People's Court, it was closed. I could write to the lawyer if I wanted, but all letters would be checked, and if there was anything in the contents that the authorities considered harmful to my reform, the letter would be stopped.

It soon became quite obvious that none of our mail was going anywhere. Webster decided to ask Philip Ma for a copy of the academic study he'd made, and instead of having it sent to the prison, asked him to send it to him care of the consul. In this way, at least we'd know if there was a reply or not. In no time at all the consul brought over Ma's answer, but it had to be checked. It looked bad. I believed that there was a good chance they would never hand it over, since this was bound to prove our case.

Webster badgered the guards for his mail every day and finally, after three weeks, he got it. We were all amazed, and even more amazed when we read what the man had discovered. '*Dama zhi* is a chemically prepared esterised cannabinoid derivative.' He claimed that it was pure oil, at least ten times more potent than hashish. Compared to average hash, which has a THC content of somewhere between 10 and 18 per cent, this stuff was 100 per cent pure THC. None of us had ever come across an oil that had been that strong. On average, oil was about 45 per cent THC and was made up in the mountains in little huts, with archaic equipment; to make *dama zhi* you would need a bloody chemical factory like ICI. A hash oil of that purity would be the consistency of sump oil. It would not have been possible to hold it up in court wrapped in clingfilm and tape without it running out all over the place. It would have been pure, not with test results of 'between 7.65 and 10.14 per cent'. This substance simply did not exist in the real world – it was a theoretical product. If anybody smoked it, he'd be on his arse after half a drag. Because it was an oil, though, it meant that it was a Class A drug, up there alongside smack and crack. Hash is a so-called soft drug and nobody has ever died from it. Apparently, a person would need to consume two grams of hash per kilo of body weight to kill him/herself. Like that, a man weighing 80 kilos would have to smoke or eat 160 grams. How? For god's sake. He'd be out of his tits after about 15 grams, incapable of taking any more.

We had the evidence that we'd been gulled in black and white, and now proof that what we were claiming was right, but who would listen to us? The prison authorities were doing nothing to assist us – in fact, it was becoming clearer and clearer that they were obstructing our every move. There had to be a legal way to get justice. I refused to accept that this was the end of the line.

News from Tartary

When one is absentminded, he will neither see what he is looking at,
nor hear what he is listening to, nor judge the taste of what he is
chewing.
The Book of Rites. Great Learning

EVER since we had arrived, Silver Teeth and Zhou Wanjia had been trying to catch us smoking but had failed every time. That was until one lunchtime when Silver Teeth hid in the storeroom and waited until we stoked up next door. Suddenly he was standing there looking at us with his chromium-coated molars glinting in the sunlight, nodding his head in jubilation. He didn't say a word but scuttled off round the corner to tell Captain Yu. That was it, the game was up. A meeting was called and Benny took the chair.

'Since your arrival here,' he began, 'I have been generally very pleased with your performances. You all seem eager to reform yourselves and change your ways. Some of you are making good progress with your studies in Chinese. Others of you are working hard preparing material for the forthcoming Summer Evening Party, the "Cooling Party". This is good and it shows your willingness to reform. But . . .' He paused for effect. 'It has been reported to me that some of you have been not quite as diligent with regards to the regulations as others. When you first came here, I thought I made it clear that it was a rule here that prisoners are forbidden to smoke. It seems that some of you have chosen to disregard that rule. Since you are foreigners, and this is your first infringement, I am willing to regard it as a mistake. But only on one condition. You must all confess to what you have done. Those of you who have been smoking, put your hands up.'

After a few moments of silence and shifty glances at each other, Dieter's hand went up, followed by Werner's, then reluctantly my own and finally Webster's.

'I also want to know from whom you got the cigarettes.'

'From the bin, Captain Yu, sir,' I said.

'From the bin?' he replied incredulously. He couldn't believe we would go to such lengths for a smoke. 'And where did you get the matches to light these things up with?'

Werner handed over his lighter.

'Who gave you this?'

Werner explained that he had bought it in 1990 and that it had been in his pocket all along. Benny looked gutted. It was a system failure, a serious oversight by his minions. He would have to look into it. The meeting was closed with the warning that if anyone should ever again be caught smoking, they would be punished severely.

It was hard to believe. Here we were, China's most notorious drug criminals, getting a bollocking for smoking. What sort of jail was this? All the tales I'd heard about prisons had portrayed them as dens of drugs and violence, where anything was available if you had the money, and here we were being treated like naughty schoolboys. Little did I know, it was only to get worse.

The Chinese, obviously boosted by the success of Silver Teeth who had gained maximum merit points for grassing us up, were now on the lookout for any infringement so that they too could go running to the Goodman with news of our pernicious deeds. It had got to the stage where looking out of the window was a major crime, and since it was a major fascination of mine to watch the female officers go for lunch, I was being ticked off all the time. It was all part of their plan to destroy individuality, and to make the prisoner totally reliant on the system, to take away the capacity for logical thought and replace it with blind obedience.

When the Chinese were around the corner at work it was rare to have any officer watching us – they were too busy playing computer games or watching movies on the televisions that came in for repair. We were normally left in the hands of Zhou Wanjia to get on with whatever we wanted to. Mark, Dieter and I studied Chinese. Werner studied music on a guitar which his consul had bought. Webster had tried studying Chinese but soon became frustrated at his lack of progress and shelved it. Instead he picked up Shanghai dialect swear words from Jin Feng, with whom he now spent more and more time playing cards. Larry studied Chinese history and read issues of *Time, Newsweek* and *Sports Illustrated* which his consul dropped off.

One day the Chinese came back from work early in a very excited mood. They were laughing and sniggering, pointing at us and thrusting their hands down the front of their trousers. I wondered what the hell was the matter with them. They wouldn't tell us, but after a little probing here and there it became clear that they'd been in a meeting around the corner where they'd been shown a video which included news reports about our cases as well as a special documentary about us, which had been shown on Shanghai TV the previous night after lock-up. It showed us in court during our trials as well as humiliating clips of us being strip-searched. To cap it all, they were told never to speak to us, never to divulge China's secrets (which could include the score of a volleyball game against Cuba when they lost), never to do anything for us and to report anything and everything they saw us do, from sitting on the *matong* reading a book to spitting in the sink. We were evil foreign devils who could not be trusted, and it was everyone's duty to protect the Middle Kingdom from such a scourge.

After about two and a half months, our first order of apples, oranges and bananas arrived. As was our habit, we offered to help carry it all up the stairs, but as usual we were told that we were not permitted to cross the line. When Sun, Silver Teeth and Zhou Wanjia brought it up they quickly carried it to the other end of the landing. This was odd, since all other goods were put at the end of our sheep-pen. After about half an hour we were called down to pick up what we had bought. There were two piles of boxes, one large and one small. The three stooges stood in front of the big pile and pointed to the small one, saying, 'That's yours.'

As we looked at the fruit, it became obvious that our boxes were filled with all the defective fruit that these bastards had picked out of the other boxes. The argument that followed nearly brought us to blows, but thankfully we kept control. This was not on, though. This time the complaint had to go beyond

Benny, because it was useless to expect any unbiased response from him. He trusted his three capos – he knew that they would practically die for him – so we had no chance. We stormed out and over the red line down the stairs to find the brigade leader. Zhou Wanjia, fearing he had lost control of us, ran behind, shouting, 'Come back, come back, you can't cross the line! It's not allowed! The captain will be angry and you'll all be punished. Come back!'

As luck would have it, the brigade leader was away, and there was no one superior to Benny to be found. Damn! We had to traipse back up the stairs with our tails between our legs and the wind knocked out of our sails.

Benny met us at the top of the stairs. 'You have been told on more than one occasion that you are not allowed to cross the red line without permission. You cannot just go about the place as you like. We will have to consider this action very seriously.'

'But I wanted to speak with the brigade leader about a very serious matter,' I began. 'If it is not resolved immediately, it will lead to unnecessary conflict between Chinese and foreign prisoners.'

'Well, you can speak to me about it. That's what I'm here for. What is this very serious matter?'

I refused to have Zhou Wanjia as a translator so he called Jin Feng and we went into the office. As I explained what had happened, I could see Zhou Wanjia hovering outside the window trying to listen in. I pleaded with Benny to come and see for himself because, as they say in Chinese, 'It is better to see once than to be told a hundred times.' He seemed to appreciate my use of the idiom and agreed to take a look. When we got down to the bottom end of the landing, there were only our boxes left. The Chinese had already been and collected theirs. On inspection, the fruit inside had miraculously changed into medium-quality stuff that was difficult to complain much about. Sun and Silver Teeth had swapped them back while we had been running around the place. I was left holding a gun with no bullets, and Benny going, 'What's the problem? Your fruit in England is maybe of a higher standard than ours? There is no serious matter here, so I will have to think about what to do about you crossing the line.'

I'd been well and truly set up. The petty little bastards had found a way to wind me up and then get me in the shit. This did not bode well for the future. Now that they knew where the weakness was, they could tweak the same buttons again whenever they wanted. The atmosphere between us and our hosts was thick with hate, but as the days passed everything healed, the same way a stab wound might, and in a matter of days we were back to normal. I hadn't been punished and the Chinese were actually being quite polite towards us for some reason. We were discovering that Tilan Qiao was no different to the China we knew on the outside; it was a place full of contradictions.

Two Brigade was dedicated to providing music and entertainment for the other prisoners. They worked in conjunction with a group of about twenty women from Nine Brigade and were collectively known as the Xing An Song and Dance Troupe. They performed concerts for the inmates on national holidays and other special occasions, and for visitors from the real world who came in to see how we were suffering. They had a small theatre in the Cross Building to practise in and give performances. They had formed traditional and western-style bands and had solo singers of classical and modern Chinese pop, as well as performing dance numbers with a revolutionary flavour. Considering that they were mostly made up of amateurs, they always put on a good show, and for us ordinary prisoners it was a wonderful escape.

Jin Feng was, in many respects, a talented guy. Not only could he speak English quite well in an accent more akin to a public schoolboy's, but he could also paint, write calligraphy, sing, dance the waltz, the tango and the rumba, and play the piano and accordion. He was very keen to be involved in the summer cooling party and introduced the idea to us, saying that it would be very good for our reform. A 'cooling party' was a concert held by a brigade for its own inmates usually in August when the temperature was at its highest and the weather very humid. The dance troupe organised most of it, providing the equipment and applying the necessary technical expertise. They would perform a number of their most popular routines but they also gave the ordinary prisoner the chance to knock out his favourite song or do a gag with a friend.

The Japanese bar-room entertainment of karaoke had become hugely popular in China. Personally, I hated it. I could not see the sense in going to a bar where the prices were hiked to listen to an endless line of untalented people sing tunelessly. Jail was different, though, and we needed as much entertainment as we could get. Karaoke allowed anybody and everybody to be a star for a minute. The officers loved it and always received massively over-the-top adulation from 'their boys'. The most exciting portion of any concert would invariably be the bit when the girls came on to dance and sing. For some prisoners without family it was the only opportunity they'd have to see a woman until the same concert next year. For many country boys it was too much too bear, and it was quite common for there to be the odd accident in the pants as a result.

After Jin Feng had explained the set-up, we agreed to join in. We had Werner's guitar, a borrowed pair of maracas and Jin Feng's tambourine, and decided that we'd fill in the rest with our hands and our voices. The most difficult thing was to select songs that the Chinese liked, because it would be no use singing just to entertain ourselves. We knew that they loved stuff like 'Love me Tender', 'Oh Carol', 'The Last Waltz', 'Ave Maria' and 'By the Rivers of Babylon' and tried to incorporate some of them into our programme. Jin Feng said that if we could sing a Chinese song, it would be even better. There was no chance of that for the time being, or of 'Ave Maria', but eventually it was agreed that I would sing 'Help' and 'Oh Carol', Larry would sing 'In the Summer Time', Webster would do 'Crazy Joe's Café' and Werner would do 'Johnny Be Good', which, using the same rhythm, would mutate into a reggae version of 'By the Rivers of Babylon', at which point I was to take over the vocals. Whoever wasn't singing would provide backing vocals.

After a week of hurried practice in the cells away from the Chinese, we got our chance to make history. As far as we knew, no foreign group had ever played in a Chinese jail, so this was going to be a big moment for us. On 4 July, at six-thirty in the evening, we were called down to the basketball court. The prisoners from the troupe had built a stage from old school desks and covered it with a green tarpaulin sheet. There were two big speakers, music stands, mike stands and chairs for the band. There was a PA system and a mixing console just to the right of the stage. Powerful halogen lights blazed down on the performance area with an almost unbearable heat. The backdrop heralded 'The First Annual Cooling Party of Eight Brigade'. In front, rows of prisoners seated on the little plastic stools they all used for 'education' emitted the collective hum of eager expectation that mixed in well with the feedback and incessant 'one two, one two' of the PA man.

It was hot and very humid, and with everybody bunched up together with no fans I couldn't work out why they called it a cooling party. However, I hadn't expected it to be so well organised, and found it a bit daunting at first. As we walked to our seats, every face in the crowd turned to see. It was a welcome. There were smiles, laughter and the odd '*Ni hao*'. There was a 'Where do you come from?' and a 'What's your name?'. It seemed like we were already big stars in Tilan Qiao. Everyone in the jail had heard about us. They had all seen us on TV and knew that we were the first westerners to be banged up there since the Liberation. Word had got round that we were going to perform and they were obviously all looking forward to it.

We were seated together near the front and watched with interest as the show unfolded. The proceedings were hosted by a girl and a young man from the troupe. He was in a suit and she in a very pretty white cocktail dress. They spoke alternately, each time piling on another layer of excitement, up to the point when they joined in unison, like a simultaneous orgasm, to introduce the show and the first act. This was entertainment.

There was a traditional folk-dance from the girls, where they skipped around in pre-communist peasant attire, waving fake lotus leaves. There was a flute player of an exceptionally high standard and two comedians whose punchline fell on deaf ears. Two prisoners came round and gave everybody an ice-cream. There was a peasant song from Hunan and a revolutionary dance spectacle, paying tribute to the Long March. To liven things up, the band played 'Entrance of the Gladiators' on brass instruments totally out of tune, and then suddenly, without warning, we were on. The place erupted with clapping and cheering so raucous that an officer felt it necessary to stand up and wave a disapproving hand to bring things back to order.

After a brief introduction, I spoke to the crowd: '*Dajia hao ma?*' ('Is everybody all right?')

A loud and enthusiastic '*Hao!*' bounced back.

'*Hao, yi er san!*' ('Good, one, two, three!') and we were away.

Somehow the practising had paid off. We were quite slick and I couldn't believe that we were going down so well. Then, about halfway through the set, it suddenly started to rain heavily and the officers signalled that it was all over. All was not lost, however, as within a fortnight we had another chance and were even better prepared.

This time we dropped 'Help' and replaced it with Bob Marley's 'Three Little Birds'. Werner and I prepared a specially rewritten version of 'By the Rivers of Babylon' with words like 'Well, you can fool some of the people, yeah, some of the time, but ya can't fool all the people, all the time' and 'Stand up for your rights'.

On the stage in front of a horde of officers from all over the jail and about two hundred inmates, we belted out our message with real conviction. Whether they understood it or not didn't matter. They loved it, clapping and cheering as if we were the real thing. In the middle of the applause, an officer led us off the stage and said that they wanted us then to perform straight away in One Brigade. 'Quickly,' he said and quickly it was, as we ran behind him over to the gates and into the basketball yard. The place was full. There must have been six or seven hundred prisoners there, all shouting and whistling like mad men. It was a totally different trip to what we'd just done, and the excitement was infectious. We ran down through the middle of a heaving mass of violent criminal records. There were no officers waving disapproving hands here. Even if they had, no one was listening.

We were introduced and they went nuts. We sang our stuff and they went even more nuts, jumping up and down, shouting and clapping, whistling and screaming. From where we stood on the stage they looked like a horde of crazy animals, with wild starring eyes, long jagged teeth and slavering tongues spitting barks and howls. I vividly recall a shiver running up my spine, and actually felt relieved when it was time to go. We ran out as fast as we'd run in, this time with slaps on the back and outstretched hands.

During the following weeks we got invited to another three gigs in other parts of the jail which at least gave us the chance to have a look around. By then we were calling ourselves 'The Reformers'. The Chinese were blind when it came to sarcasm and thought that it was a great name.

As an interlude to our concert season and a reminder to us of where we were, the mist of the morning of 11 August 1992 lifted to reveal the true nature of Tilan Qiao's approach towards its inhabitants. Looking out of the window, I saw something that froze my blood. Three *kunbang zhe* ('trussed-up prisoners') were being persuaded to stand in line by an officer with a two-foot-long cattle prod. They were not only tied up but shackled by the ankles as well. The rope that tied them was bound tightly around the wrists high behind the back between the shoulder-blades. It then passed up and around the neck a couple of times then was wrapped around the torso before it was knotted at the back to the wrists again. A short length was left which the officer could hold on to, just like a dog lead. If the prisoner didn't at all times keep his arms up as high as he could between his shoulder-blades, the rope around his neck would tighten. Any struggling or relaxation resulted in the prisoner choking himself.

I shouted to Mark and Larry to come over and have a look. By the time they arrived, another six *kunbang zhe* had joined the three originals, and an officer was pinning pieces of paper to their backs. We speculated that it must be either their names or numbers. As we watched, another two of the condemned were manhandled out into the yard. The last man out had only one leg and was being supported by an other inmate. More officers joined the mob, like a band of lynchers in a cowboy movie. They fussed here and there, each trying to look more efficient than other, brandishing electric prods and walkie-talkies almost in a parody of New China's struggle for modernisation.

As far as I could see, the victims were all young boys, the oldest not more than twenty-five. It struck me that if each had the average life expectancy of seventy, the Chinese government was that day extinguishing five hundred years of life from the world. Suddenly, we all noticed that a strange hush had come over the place, as if the whole jail knew what was about to pass. When the labelling was done, and after a sharp crackle of shorting electricity, the procession of walking death disappeared around the corner.

They were destined to be driven through the streets of Shanghai, high up on the back of a truck for all to see. A banner on the front would tell onlookers what heinous and pernicious crimes they had committed, and a sharp mechanical voice shouting through a megaphone would inform the public that these were enemies of the state, and that it was everybody's duty to hate those criminals and exact their death. They were heading for the sports ground and the 'small peanut'.

Playing western rock, pop and reggae in a Chinese jail was a first in itself, and a major penetration of a closed world, but we were about to pierce the last stronghold and enter the darkest corner of the gulag system, namely Nine Brigade, the women's division. Each brigade was run as a separate entity, like a prison within a prison, but the women's brigade was a prison within a prison within a prison. All the windows of Nine were blinkered, not in an attempt to stop the women looking out but to stop the men looking in. The proximity of the women was considered to be a major threat to the reform of male inmates, and everything was done to ensure there was no contact whatsoever.

We were escorted there one balmy night in late August by Captain Yu, Jin Feng and the number 1, Mr Sun, who had managed to convince the officer that he was needed for security. Led in through the door and up the stairs, we headed for the roof. I held back, trying to take in as much of this secret world as I could. Unlike our brigade, Nine was a confusion of dimly lit stairwells and split-level floors. Originally two buildings, they had knocked it into one to house the seven hundred or so women prisoners. The cells were huge but dark and they used electric light every day, all night, summer and winter. With thirty or forty women per cell, it was nothing less than medieval.

The place was deserted, and all the more haunting for being so. The cream of Shanghai's female criminal element were seated wretchedly on their little plastic stools waiting for us to arrive on the rooftop. As we marched down the centre aisle, I tried to scan the faces, but they had been instructed not to look at us, and all eyes were riveted to the floor. Seven hundred women, all with the same basin-style haircut and the same clothes sat there in silence, it was more like a funeral than a concert. They even looked the same size, all bunched up and huddled together.

Without warning, a group of about eighty stood up and burst into song: '*Meiyou Gongchan dang, jiu meiyou Xin Zhonggu*' ('No Communist Party, no New China').

'Fuck me, this is some heavy place,' said Webster.

The discipline was much stricter than anything we'd seen. It was absolute control. Zhou Wanjia had told us that the women were not allowed to buy bananas from the list, and they could only buy sausage if it had been cut up into inch-long lengths first. I felt so sorry for these women. I couldn't believe they had done anything so bad as to warrant the treatment they were getting here. They all looked so harmless, as if butter wouldn't melt in their mouths. The TV and newspapers, however, were apparently full of stories about young women committing murder, crimes of passion and downright sadistic acts of violence, as well as embezzlement, prostitution, theft and selling heroin, no different from the men. We did our set and I believe they enjoyed it, but it was difficult to tell because there was no way these girls were going to start whistling and cheering. A polite clap was the limit of what was permitted.

*

Tilan Qiao was a place of extremes. I was either up on a cloud or down in hell. Contradiction was written into the rules. As the weeks went by it became more and more obvious that the department run by Captain Jin Mouling which handled our mail was not only obstructing our search for justice but also messing around with our private letters. Since the odd reply was trickling through I could easily work out from the postmarks and from what people wrote that letters were not leaving the jail when they were supposed to and that some were not getting out at all. Many sent to me never arrived.

We were being screwed about and denied our only form of contact with our families. Unlike the Chinese, who had monthly visits to look forward to, we only had letters. The Chinese prisoners' letters were posted the day after they were handed over to the officer in charge. Ours were left at the bottom of a drawer in his office for anything up to three weeks or until he could get off his arse and come over to get them. But that didn't ensure they were sent out, though, because they had to be passed on to a translator, who could take anything from a week to a month to put into Chinese what we had written. Then they went back to Jin Mouling, who checked them for 'anti-reform' material. This could easily take another week, with a further week for our officer to go out and post them.

The Chinese received their letters the very same day they arrived – ripped unceremoniously open, of course, but nevertheless as fast as possible. Our incoming letters sat around in Jin Mouling's office for weeks until he could be bothered to get them translated, checked and brought over. Afterwards, we could see them lying around in Benny's office for days. Requests for our mail were answered time and again with '*mintian* – tomorrow'.

The situation was really pissing us off and on more than one occasion we had discussed some form of protest. A hunger strike had been mentioned, but I was against that. Complaints to our consuls had produced nothing other than bad feeling between us and our guards. They resented our protestations to people on the outside and any interference that might come of it. My consul was barely interested, never once confronting the Chinese authorities about what was going on with our mail. I had not helped matters by telling him that the German consul visited every month, not every three months like him, but his answer was certainly not what I'd expected from a British representative. 'Well, if they've got the time to come here every month to see a bunch of criminals, for want of a better expression, then lucky them.' He laughed but it failed to dilute the poison.

One day, out of the blue, I finally got the letter that I'd been waiting nearly ten months for. ShaSha had received my last letter and was in Kashgar staying with her brother. She was all right and obviously free, although there was something that gave me the impression that this had not been the case all along. The letter had been dictated and then translated and written in English by Tahir's French girlfriend Fabienne. ShaSha mentioned that her brother had helped her with a lawyer, but she didn't elaborate. It was obvious that she knew what not to say in a letter in order to guarantee its arrival. She went on to say that she had no money and that she would have to sell some of our carpets and other furniture to raise cash if she was to come to Shanghai to see me. This made me think that she had not received the money I'd left her, or perhaps she'd somehow lost it. But the good news was that she said she loved me. That was everything.

I thought about what she had written twenty-four hours a day, turning it all around in my mind, trying to read hidden messages into the sentences, almost physically wrenching them apart to allow them to grow into all the words I wanted to hear so desperately. Now I knew that she was on her way, it helped me immensely, and I had high hopes that she could do something to sort out the mess and get me the hell out.

My parents were also planning to come and see me, so I thought about trying to get both visits to coincide, and in that way ShaSha could at least meet my mother and father for the first time. Fingers crossed, I set about writing letters to propose the idea.

ShaSha's letter also contained photocopies of some press clippings that she'd managed to get hold of. They were all articles taken from the *South China Morning Post*, one of the most influential and widely read papers in the region. They dated from about the time of my first trial and the verdict:

'HASHISH TRIO FACES HARSHER SENTENCES'

'SHANGHAI POLICE TIE BRITON TO DRUG RING'

'UK DRUG DEALER EXPRESSES REGRET IN SHANGHAI'

'FRIENDS DISPUTE "GODFATHER" TAG FOR WELSH DRUG DEALER'

I didn't know whether to laugh or cry. My God! Reading what had been written about me was weird, and I figured that if the judges had seen all that bullshit, it was no wonder they'd given me eight and a half years.

When I studied what had been said, I spotted a clue as to why we had been stitched up: 'The prosecution in the Shanghai drug trials has presented new evidence which it hopes will provide for harsh sentences to be imposed on the three Europeans tried this week and allow it to press for the maximum penalty against alleged drug kingpin Robert Davies . . . The evidence is based on an extensive investigation into the strength and intensity of hashish by the Ministry of Public Security in Beijing, which concludes that hashish is a far more potent drug than marijuana . . . The Ministry of Public Security in Beijing spent more than a month conducting an in-depth scientific investigation into the properties of hashish in a bid to prove it is a more potent drug than marijuana. The results of the investigation were used extensively by the prosecution in the trials of three other Europeans in Shanghai last week in the hope of winning harsher sentences than the four years' imprisonment given to convicted marijuana smuggler MB last year. All three defendants were accused of smuggling or transporting hashish.'

The two Germans, Larry, Webster and I discussed the issue every day, and it all fell into place. The prosecution had needed to prove that our case was more serious than Mark's to satisfy the critics, so they withdrew the first indictments given to Webster and the two Germans and changed all possession charges to 'transporting'. They changed *dama* to *dama zhi*, making out that a 'scientific investigation' proved that hash was more potent than grass. What a load of old toss. Any scientist worth his litmus paper could do that in one day. What happened, if anything happened at all, that is, was that they could prove nothing, especially if they'd been investigating our 7.6 per cent THC stuff, so they invented 'esterised cannabis'. Mark had been charged with smuggling *dama*. That was an accepted fact. Did not our final verdict also confirm that we also had *dama*?

All this was as clear as day to me and I just could not fathom out why nobody in the west had sussed it. I came to the conclusion that people in Europe naturally assumed that the authorities in any country are to a certain extent efficient and conscientious. They couldn't possibly imagine that a chief prosecutor could put together such a shoddy case as this, which any half-decent lawyer in the west would've shot holes through with a pop gun. The more I thought about it all, the more I despaired. Something had to be done, I needed to put more pressure on the consul to help us find a way to seek justice and resolve the mail problem so that we could send letters to the court. We needed to make formal applications to get permission to see a lawyer, because without one, even a useless one, it would be very difficult indeed.

On 16 September Benny the Fish called a meeting with the foreign unit. Over the previous couple of weeks things had been hotting up. People were getting more and more pissed off. No one had had a response from the court; no one had had a response from a lawyer. The Germans had complained each time they had seen their consul, but nothing had been done.

When the news of the death of his father took three months to come through and the postmark revealed that the letter had arrived in China some ten weeks previously, Werner had had enough. He decided to make a stand by himself and went on hunger strike. At first no one noticed, but by dinner on the first day Zhou Wanjia spotted that one of the containers was still full. On the third day he was called into the office and asked what he was up to. After informing Benny of his grievances, Werner was advised to begin eating again as soon as possible because that sort of behaviour was against the regulations. On the fifth day the brigade leader was informed and he arrived to speak with the German. In a very short time Werner was out of the office and eating again. They had promised to look into the problem about the mail.

The meeting that followed was obviously meant to be some sort of laying down of the law and a warning against further protests. We were gathered around a table halfway down the landing, and Benny sat there with a sour face and his notes before him on the table, waiting for us to be quiet. Jin Feng sat to his right, nervously trying to get us all to shut up.

Eventually, Benny began: 'I should like to make it clear that it is our hope that you can all go home to your families as soon as possible. The majority of you are well behaved and we are very satisfied. However, some of you have had more difficulties settling in than others. Some of you seem confused regarding your position legally. We understand this. But let me explain that if you want to go home at the earliest possible date, you must conform to the requirements of reform. The requirements of this prison are simple. Every prisoner must observe the rules and discipline. Every prisoner is expected to work hard and to study hard. Most importantly, if a prisoner is to receive a reduction in sentence, he must acknowledge his crime and accept his sentence –'

BANG! Down on the table came Larry's fist. 'I will not be forced into accepting my sentence. That is against my rights,' he shouted, immediately getting to his feet and walking back to the sheep-pen.

Benny was thunderstruck. Silence hung over us like a cloud of mustard gas. I wanted to laugh but decided against it, instead kicking Mark to see if I could make him crack. Benny stared ashen-faced out of the window for a good five minutes without a word passing his lips. We waited and waited and waited in expectation of some great words of wisdom, but in the end, his composure shot to hell, he said, 'We will talk again.' Then he got up and stalked off down the length of the landing, deliberately ignoring Larry, who sat in the pen watching him come. The rest of us fell about.

'Is that the long march, then?' I said.

Girls on the Roof

Gua tan li xia – Do not bend to tie your shoes in a melon field.

Chinese saying

MY mother and father were booked into the Peace Hotel in Shanghai. The Justice Bureau had advised them to bring along their marriage certificate and my birth certificate in order to provide evidence that they were who they said they were. The rules prohibited any of my friends from visiting, and if ShaSha had been my common-law wife or even my fiancée, they'd have turned her away. The Justice Bureau contacted the prison authorities and informed them that according to the regulations, only two one-hour visits could be allowed and that they had to be spaced two weeks apart. This should be looked upon as being extremely generous, since in normal circumstances only two half-hour visits were permitted per month. The fact that my parents were going to make an 18,000km round trip counted for nought. (We were later to discover that no such regulations applied to the Chinese. The so-called 'Regulations for Foreign Inmates' was not a government document; it was not even a document sanctioned by the Justice Bureau. It had been arbitrarily knocked up by Jin Mouling in the prison's Education Department.)

On the afternoon of 15 September Captain Jin came by and took me to the visiting room. It was not the same as the one used by the Chinese, mainly because theirs was not geared up to record conversations, and it was not possible to seat the large number of officials who were needed to eavesdrop on every visit.

I had been led to believe that it was the consul who was waiting to see me, so when I turned the corner and entered the visiting room I was astonished. Standing there to greet me were my parents. It had been over four years since I'd seen them. Dad looked like he always did, but my mother looked as if she'd aged fifteen years and had shrunk too. I was full of confused emotions: happiness to see them; grateful that they had come all that way; guilt and shame that I had let them down so badly and caused them so much anguish; pride that they had the balls to make the trip; anger at the Chinese for the poxy one hour and condescending attitude.

There they stood, nervous and unsure, flanked by Sun from the Ministry of Justice, Dong, the head of the Education Department, Mei Linghua, the prison warden, a translator and someone else I didn't recognise. Sitting along the back wall were six other unknown officers. We were allowed a hug and a kiss and a shake of the hand before I was abruptly told to sit down. I immediately ploughed into a fresh pack of Marlboro that my mother had brought along and felt the nicotine rush shoot through my body. A photographer appeared and proceeded to prance around taking shots of the three of us. An officer with a video camera and one of those in-your-face halogen lights showed up, and as they circled around us we could feel the heat from the light adding to the intrusion. I knew they were going to milk the occasion for all it was worth and use it for some serious propaganda. They'd even brought out three bottles of Sprite with straws and placed them artistically on the table between us.

As we began to speak, Captain Jin took notes. Since he didn't speak English, I wondered what exactly he could be writing. Then a woman walked in. She introduced herself in accentless English as another translator. It was astounding. So many people watching and listening. I wanted to scream at them that I really wasn't so bad as to deserve such vigilance. Murderers got less attention.

I could cope all right but I worried how my parents were taking it. China in itself must have been a bloody nightmare, so God knows what was going through their minds at that moment. But they'd made it, and we talked and talked and talked. Then, before we'd hardly started, the whole thing was over. 'Time's up,' said Jin, and that was it. A quick hug and a kiss and I was on my way back to the brigade. I'd never felt so emotionally belaboured in my life. What had we talked about? Had I said the right things? Had I been clear? Had I said sorry? Had I expressed my gratitude?

The weeks between then and the next visit were no less difficult. I was still hoping that ShaSha would make it in time, but I had no control over anything. I tried to work out a way to explain to my parents about the *dama zhi* issue, and that the reason I had received eight and a half years was not because of what I had done or because I was an evil bastard but because I was being used as an example to demonstrate China's willingness to fight the war against drugs and thus appease the America's Drugs Enforcement Agency (DEA) who had recently criticised China for not taking a positive attitude in its anti-drug co-operation with the US.

A copy of *Newsweek* from October 1991 which Larry had got from his consul explained that Mark's four-year sentence was considered very lenient and certainly not sending out the right message to foreign drug criminals operating in China. In response, Qian Qiquan, the Chinese foreign minister, had promised that in future China would clamp down hard on foreigners using the country as a base to export drugs around the world. The US had been blaming China for years for allowing the Golden Triangle's produce to seep out through its borders, and was saying that if China really wanted to join the World Trade Organisation and continue to receive aid and assistance from the DEA, it should prove to the world that it was taking the war on drugs seriously. The official response was that 'foreigners who violate the laws in China will be dealt with in accordance with Chinese laws and in the same manner as Chinese citizens'.

It had taken months to unravel but at last all the pieces fitted together. I knew the plot inside out but how could I explain it all to my parents in a way that was simple enough for them to understand and remember it all so as to inform someone who might be able to help me?

The next visit coincided with my birthday and Mum and Dad brought along a guitar which they had bought in Shanghai. There were also cards, letters and photographs from my friends back home, and a Walkman they had each contributed to. They brought books, pens and clothes and I was so overwhelmed that I forgot about the *dama zhi* thing. Then an officer brought in a birthday cake covered in icing with my name and 'Happy Birthday' written on it. Following tight on his heels came the bloody video crew again. I was grateful but I couldn't help feeling like a puppet in a propaganda circus. I knew they intended to use that footage to cancel out our complaints. What made it worse was that my mother said, 'Oh, aren't they nice. The people we have dealt with have been so friendly.' I wanted to tell her that the smiles on their faces didn't show the hatred in their hearts. They could have spared us the theatrics and just given us the same privileges as the Chinese 'A' class prisoners, who got three-hour contact visits with a meal. They could have taken into account that my parents weren't going to come every month, that in fact this might be their only visit. The excuse about regulations was nonsense. They could rewrite them whenever they wanted. But, of course, they could have refused permission for any visit at all or tied the whole application up in bureaucratic spaghetti for two or three years while waiting for the problem to dissolve and go away on its own.

With five minutes to go, I remembered what I had to do. It was late on enough in the visit not to matter a great deal if they terminated it or not, so, speaking faster than normal, and with a stronger accent to throw the translator off, I began: 'Hey, Dad, I want to tell you something before you go. The reason I'm here for eight years is because of a deliberate cock-up on their part. I did what I did but not what they said I did. The stuff they said I had doesn't even exist. It was a set-up and I have the proof. You need to get a hold of copies of my court papers, particularly the indictment, and especially the Chinese versions. It's there that everything shows up.'

'But how can we read it, if it's all in Chinese?' said my mother, looking quite perplexed.

'Get those papers to my friend John – he'll know someone who can read Chinese and they'll see the discrepancy immediately. You ask John. If it had been a British trial, it would have been called a mis-trial and thrown out of court. I also want you to write and ask the Ministry of Justice here what is the name of the substance I was convicted of trafficking in. And you need the answer in Chinese and English. You must have that right, as my parents, to be informed of the reasons for my conviction.'

'*Shijian daole!* – Time's up!' Jin butted in. One of the other officers had given him the signal to terminate. They'd sussed I was up to something but it was too late. I was pretty sure I'd explained enough of the plot to make my folks realise that all was not as it should be and that they should get my friend to look into it.

I was whisked away in the middle of saying goodbye, and in a flash I was back in the brigade. I was a wreck, my emotions in tatters, a yacht adrift in a storm with its sails shredded by the wind, not knowing when or where land would fall. It had been so good to see my family. It had given me a sense of belonging and the knowledge that I wasn't an outcast for my crimes. I could walk tall down the landing because I had a family who cared, one that was willing to make that extra show when it mattered. All I heard from Dieter was, 'Ach, it's a waste of money, I think, to have my parents come all the way over here to see me. I have already written a letter telling them not to bother.' Very good, I thought, an escape clause, the same as the boys in the detention centre who had written to say that they wanted a divorce before their wives did it.

The days started to go by again but now I had a guitar and lots of books to ease the passage of time. It had always been a major regret of mine that I had never learnt to play a musical instrument. For years I'd said, 'Oh, I'd love to be able to play the guitar, but . . .' In jail I had the time to put that right. It was also a pleasant and restful diversion from studying Chinese.

Werner and I started to write arrangements of old songs in the hope that we could play them in other shows in the future. We also started working on our own songs – I'd write the lyrics and he'd supply the music. It was mostly blues based on the theme of drinking and getting laid. I came up with songs entitled 'Whisky Bar', 'Trespasser', 'Don't Bother No Folk' and 'This Ain't No Hotel'. If the lyrics were too awkward to fit to a tune, I turned them into poems, and filled a little black book up with weird ramblings. One poem which I worked on between August and September that year (completed a year later in August '93) was entitled 'Perfection She Dances'. 'I love you' simply wasn't enough. I needed to express my feelings in a way that ShaSha would know what we had between us was much deeper than that. When it was done, and with Jin Feng's help, I translated it into Chinese and waited for the day when I could give it to her in person.

*

At the beginning of October, and again without warning, I was called out for another visit. As Jin Mouling led me over, he informed me that my wife was waiting to see me. Damn the bloody man! If he had told me just half an hour earlier, I could have had a shave and spruced myself up a bit. What the hell was behind this refusal to tell you anything? It served no purpose except to piss you off.

Instead of going to the visiting room where I'd met Mum and Dad we went into the processing hall. There must have been thirty or more new arrivals there, all milling about waiting for ID cards and to have their photos taken. But there was something else there; I swore I could smell a wisp of perfume in the air, a musky reminder of a night now lost in the clouds of time.

As the crowd parted I saw her, demure as usual, sitting in the far corner on an old wooden bench. Breaking free of Jin's tentative grip on my elbow, I strode towards her as if in a dream. She rose to meet me and we embraced. The kiss was warm, soft and succulent, barely concealing the raw yearning which after only a few seconds of contact was near boiling point.

'Sit down!' shouted Captain Jin. I suddenly realised the whole room had turned in our direction, staring in disbelief at a man and woman in the wild throes of a French kiss. Moreover, she was a blue-eyed Uzbek and I was a foreign devil. What the hell were we doing there? They were all talking at once and the noise was unbelievable, so when ShaSha opened her mouth I couldn't hear what she said. I stood back, looking at her, and began speaking in Uighur.

Jin broke in, all flustered and not knowing what was going on. This was not English and it was not Chinese. 'You must speak in Chinese,' he said. 'We do not have translator, so it is the rules that you must speak in Chinese.'

'But it's very difficult to do that. My Chinese is not good enough,' I remonstrated. 'Why am I not allowed to speak in my own language?'

'You must speak in Chinese or else I will terminate the meeting.'

Damn it! We were wasting time. It was best just to get on with it. We were three people sitting on two benches in the middle of a heaving throng, hemming us in until it was like sitting in a well, staring and passing comment, standing so close I could smell their breath. It was outrageous, but I knew that complaining would only shorten my valuable minutes with ShaSha, so I forced myself to be calm.

'*Ni hao? Qing kuang zheme yang?* How are you? How's things with you then?' I said nervously. I awaited her reaction.

She smiled and said, 'Wow! You can speak Chinese now! I don't believe it. Did someone teach you?'

'No. It was just that there's nothing else to do here. But don't get too complicated, and please speak slowly. Hey, you look well. Where are you staying?'

ShaSha talked and for the first time I could appreciate her eloquence in Mandarin. She spoke the language like I'd never heard it before. She spoke clearly, using distinctive measured syllables that were easy for me to distinguish, and I realised then how slovenly the Shanghainese spoke. They always slipped into dialect if they failed to find the right word in Mandarin and used street slang and swear-words in every sentence.

I wanted to know everything at once, and tell her all that had happened to me at the same time, but it was impossible. Not only wasn't there enough time, but there was an officer listening and writing down every word we said. If he had been a stranger in a café, it would have been bad enough, but this guy was the enemy. He was a part of the machine that had already sunk its teeth into us, and he added substance to the omnipresent implied threat that anything and everything can and will be taken down and used against you.

From the very beginning we were censoring ourselves without even noticing it, editing and holding back from saying the most vital information that we each desperately wanted to know. We quickly learnt to use intimation and suggestion to convey our meanings and use metaphors or the odd word of Uighur or English to conceal the subject. It was not always easy to decode it all on the spot. We had to be patient and by adding each snippet of information to the last, layer upon layer, gradually the picture became clear.

During that first visit I allowed ShaSha to do most of the talking. I was simply overjoyed to look at her and hear her voice. I learnt next to nothing that day about what had happened to her that year. It took me years to find out the whole story but it was here that it started.

After leaving the hotel that day in Urumchi, ShaSha had been told to go to the jeep that was waiting at the end of the road, just out of sight of where I was standing at the window. She was then taken to a *juliu suo* which is a detention house for prisoners who are *not* awaiting trial. Anyone unlucky enough to find themselves locked up in one of these can spend up to two or three years there, and eventually be released without trial or even a charge against them.

Her dingy little room had only enough space for two sets of three bunk-beds and nothing more. The tiny window at the far end was cracked and dirty but still big enough to let in the icy winds that swept down into the city from the mountains. With no fire and temperatures plummeting to -12°C and below, everyone was freezing. Somehow she'd managed to get that message through to me, and I'd sent my leather coat, without which she would probably have frozen to death. Sharing the cell with ShaSha were five other young women from around the region. They all claimed to be innocent.

For the first two weeks, ShaSha was called out for questioning every day in a room not unlike the one where I was to be interrogated later in Shanghai. She had made up her mind to stick to the same story, namely that she was totally unaware of what I was doing. The police tried every tactic but she still denied all knowledge. They got angry, threatening her with ten years in jail regardless of whether she confessed or not, but ShaSha said nothing.

One day, the guards came and told her to get ready to leave. She was overjoyed, thinking that my investigation was over and that most probably they'd fined me and let me go. The police told her that I was waiting for her in Kashgar and that they were taking her back to be reunited with me. Cramped and uncomfortable in a little jeep with three officers, only stopping for food and petrol, it took them two days to cover the 1,500km back to the place of her birth. ShaSha had no idea that I had left her the $3,000, and the officers, seeing an opportunity to take advantage, did not tell her.

As soon as they arrived in Kashgar, ShaSha realised that she wasn't going to be set free at all. Instead she was booked in to the Kashgar Area Jail situated in the compound behind the office for visa extensions and literally a stone's throw from her father's house. Conditions there were barbaric. The cell was at the end of a maze of narrow dark corridors through a five-inch-thick wooden door. There was no window, just a six-inch-square open hole in the roof which allowed in a shaft of light. There was no heating and ShaSha and the five women she shared with all slept on a traditional Uighur *supa*. The jail provided her with just one dirty old moth-eaten blanket, but with temperatures at night plunging down to -20°C, it was nowhere near enough to keep warm. If it wasn't for the fact that all the women had to sleep so close together, ShaSha might well have perished. Her fellow detainees were all girls from ethnic minorities, accused of various crimes from prostitution to dealing in heroin to patricide. Apart from the girl who had killed her father after he had raped her, they all professed innocence. ShaSha knew that she could trust no one, not even the women in her cell, and said nothing.

After about a month, her hopes were fired up again when the police came and said that she was going home. An hour later she was told that it was to witness detectives from the Kashgar Crime Squad dig up our former front room according to the directions I had given the Shanghai cops in order to retrieve the stash I'd confessed to having buried there. The interrogation started again, but ShaSha denied all knowledge, maintaining that she had never been involved with whatever I was supposed to have done. The police got angry and said that because she had married a foreigner, she was a whore. They said that they knew her and that she had a reputation. They told her they would let her go if she had sex with them, but ShaSha replied that she had AIDS. Was she not supposed to be a whore who had been sleeping with a dirty foreigner for the last two years? It was more than enough to make them think again, and they backed off.

They took her back to the jail. Weeks turned into months and still ShaSha languished, not knowing what was to become of her or how long she was going to have to stay in that cell. To pass the long hours the women told stories and sang, and as chance would have it, ShaSha's lilting voice attracted the attention of the young soldiers who patrolled the roof. In the evenings when the police had all gone home, two or three began to come and crouch down by the little skylight and beg ShaSha to sing yet another song for them. She soon realised that the soldiers were good-hearted country boys from Yarkand and Khargalik who might just be able to help her. She was desperate to let someone know where she was being held, and in exchange for songs she got one of the squaddies to supply her with a pencil and a scrap of paper on which she wrote a message to her father. The young soldier agreed to deliver it the following weekend when he was off duty. ShaSha knew that if the boy decided to hand the note over to the police, she would be in deep trouble. She had no choice, though; she had to get help.

The soldier kept his word and at last somebody knew where ShaSha was. Her father showed the letter to Tahir, who immediately responded, promising to do everything he could to get ShaSha out. No one was allowed to visit her, but clothes, food and bedding were sent immediately to the jail with a letter from Tahir concealed in a small pot of cream. When Aunt Aimahan heard the news she began regularly sending big bowls of home-made pilau and half a dozen nan bread in the hope that it would keep ShaSha's strength up.

Tahir went straight to a friend who was a teacher. Together they spent days poring over law books to find out what the score was. Eventually, enlisting the help of a lawyer, they went to the jail to ask for what crime Sharapet was being held. There was no crime, there was no charge, no case against her and so no reason to hold her. The lawyer demanded ShaSha's immediate release, but the prison warden said that he could do nothing without consulting those above. The following day she was released. It was 15 June, ten months and six days after we had been apprehended in Urumchi.

By that time a letter of mine had managed to find its way to ShaSha's father's house and from what I had written it was clear that I had left ShaSha the money. When the local police were asked to return it, they said that it was being retained as a fine for the crimes that I committed in Kashgar. How could that be? I had already been fined by the Shanghai court, so this would mean I was being punished twice for the same crime. ShaSha tried to reason with the officers but it was hopeless. Their only comment was: 'Just content yourself with the fact that we released you. You could still be locked up. What is more important to you – freedom or money?'

For the moment ShaSha was staying with two Belgian friends in Shanghai. It was just a temporary arrangement until she could find a place of her own. She was sorry to have missed my parents, but it had taken three months to raise the money to buy a ticket to get to Shanghai. She'd had to sell most of the carpets we had collected, and it had not been easy. She had taken four or five to the market, but local dealers were less than generous. Luckily, Tahir mentioned ShaSha's predicament to some tourists he'd met and they turned out to be more than willing to buy the carpets at a decent price.

In the remaining five minutes of that first visit, I tried to explain a little about my situation, but it was impossible. If we could have spoken in plain English it would have taken three days, so I aborted that idea and instead made sure that she knew I had hope. I reassured her that everything would be resolved soon. I had a way to put things right, I just needed her help from the outside. 'Whatever happens, we must stick together,' I said earnestly. 'If we part, we are only doing what our enemies want us to do. Together we are strong, and if we survive this one, we will survive forever. Try not to worry too much. I will do everything I can to help you.'

'Time's up,' interrupted Jin Mouling rudely.

I stood up and held open my arms. We held on to each other until we ran out of breath. Then we kissed, our tongues searching for that warmth and slippery wetness that brought back memories.

'Enough, enough!' Jin shouted, trying to part us like a referee stepping between two boxers.

As I was almost pushed out of the room, I looked back and saw the heaving throng of Chinese close in around her for closer inspection. She would have to fight her way through to get out and I wanted to go back and help her, but Jin was already propelling me down the steps and back to Eight Brigade.

A million images flooded my mind. What the hell had the Urumchi and Kashgar detention houses been like? Conditions must have been appalling. What had happened when the police had taken her to our house to watch them dig up the floor? And then another thought dawned on me. What was the date? It was 8 October, one year exactly since we'd seen each other last. Wow! That was weird.

Walking back, I felt incredibly exhilarated, almost on a high, but once I entered our unit I was brought back down to earth with a bang. I'd been human for half an hour and now it was over. I had to put up all the defences again and join in with the performance. Life in the brigade was so false, full of ego-trippers, arse-lickers and backstabbers. You didn't choose your friends, you chose a route. You were stuck in one place with a lot of people you soon grew to hate. Tilan Qiao managed to bring out the worst in everybody. Friendships were coerced or arranged for profit, and when the system encourages every man to inform on his neighbour, the strong are soon ruled by the weak. The scared fall first, then the greedy and then the egotists. Charlatans, con-men, liars and tricksters abound. The place is a minefield of deceit. In every direction there was someone out to fuck you. Rule 1: trust no one.

*

October, and the weather was changing. The sky was taking in water and the nights were getting cooler. It had been a year since my arrest, and although each day had seemed like a week, the whole thing now seemed to have slipped by in the twinkling of an eye. Only seven and a half years to go, I mused. But I could not bring myself to believe that I could possibly stay in Tilan Qiao for that long. Something was bound to happen soon. Once people realised what had happened to us, protests would be made and the Chinese would have to concede that they'd treated us unfairly. I was also beginning to convince myself that we would all go home with Mark when he reached the halfway point of his sentence, which was just six months away. The way I figured it, they could hardly let him out on his own to tell the British media what had happened to the rest of us. Surely they realised that the propaganda had already done its job. They could slip us out the back door quietly now and nothing would be said. Failing that, once the Justice Bureau was forced to inform my parents of the nature of the drug I was originally convicted for, they would either concede that a mistake had been made or at least provide us with further proof.

It was clear that doing things the Chinese way was getting us nowhere. No one was responding to our letters. Requests to see lawyers were refused point-blank. A written request to the captain from us might read as follows:

'Excuse me for giving you additional trouble. I request the honourable captain to notify the prison authorities that I should like permission to employ the services of a lawyer in order to help me clarify certain aspects of my case that I continue to find rather vague. Since I am a foreigner in this land and unsure of the law, I am also in need of professional advice as to which course of action to follow so as to ensure a satisfactory end to this matter. I should like to hire the same lawyer who dealt with my case originally since he is already well acquainted with every aspect of my case. I do hope that the authorities will appreciate that the granting of this permission will prove positive for all parties.

'I await your response. Thank you.

'R.H. Davies, Prisoner 13498.'

All my requests were ignored, so I waited to see the consul to complain about this and numerous other problems that had ripened since the last time I'd seen him. The consul listened to all my complaints, even asking questions and taking notes. But he maintained that his only job was to ensure that I was not being treated worse that the Chinese. He could not involve the consulate in legal matters or question the authority of the prison.

Exercise had been a problem since we'd arrived and seemed to be permitted only when it suited the officers, which was rarely. Not satisfied with this state of affairs, we demanded we be given proper daily exercise as is the basic right of every prisoner. We threatened the guards with the wrath of our consul and after a week or two managed to win two two-hour periods per week, thus satisfying our request for half an hour a day. They arranged that on specified days we could go out at six-thirty in the morning and be watched over by Zhou Wanjia. We must not leave the confines of the basketball ground or speak to any other prisoners. By eight-thirty they wanted us back inside and out of sight, for that was when the day-shift started arriving and female officers from administration began to float about.

We were given a basketball and a deflated football and felt lucky to be able to mess around for while. As the weeks passed, though, it got more difficult to be allowed out. Our captain knew we had permission but none of the others did, and if our boys were off duty (as they often were) we had endless problems convincing those guarding the door that we were allowed out. Zhou Wanjia could have told them and they would have trusted his word because he was an 'A' class prisoner with a 'freedom to roam' badge, an obvious trustee, but he hated watching over us outside in the cold of the early morning and was overjoyed to see us being sent back.

When weeks had turned into months and we had remonstrated with every officer in the building, it finally became generally accepted, and when we asked them to arrange a three-a-side football match between us and the Chinese, they even agreed. It felt as if things were getting better at last, and by playing football together we were getting to be a bit more friendly with the Chinese.

The murderers in One Brigade, whose cells ran parallel to ours the width of a basketball court away, began to intrigue us. We couldn't talk to them but we could see them well enough in their workshops. Dozens of prisoners appeared to be working on what looked like large photographic transparencies on the third floor directly opposite to us, and men cutting lengths of material on the floor below. On the ground floor were boxes. It was not until mid-October that Larry eventually spotted what they were up to. Two middle-aged women had appeared on the scene, wearing white coats. They were obviously civilians working as quality-control inspectors.

'They're making baseball hats!' Larry said to me suddenly one day. 'Tens of thousands of baseball hats. All in different colours and styles.'

'Where are they heading for?' I asked.

'I'll keep watching and let you know. They're bound to make a mistake sooner or later.'

One morning they brought hundreds of boxes out on to the court and proceeded to load them on to a waiting army truck. This had previously always been done at midnight when we were all safely locked up in our cells. Larry could made out the markings on the boxes. 'Speedway USA', it read. There was an address in San Francisco followed by USA again in bold print.

From then on Larry noted down every consignment that left, calculating the production figures. We were to hear later that the quota was twenty-five hats per man per day. So with a workforce of what we estimated to be 120 people, they had to be knocking out three thousand hats a day. The average retail price of a baseball hat in the USA was about ten dollars then, so someone somewhere was raking it in.

These guys were lifers, some of them still under the suspended two-year death sentence. They were working twelve or fourteen hours a day, with no exercise, limited water, cold showers once a month and the knowledge that if they didn't reach the production quota there was no chance of getting out. They were not getting the Yankee dollar, that was for sure. No prisoner in Tilan Qiao, no matter what job he was doing, got more than 25p a week.

By mid-October, relationships within our group had deteriorated badly. It had come to the point where Webster couldn't let a day go by without insulting someone, threatening to 'kick your fucking head in' or 'burn your fucking house down'. He had become completely paranoid that people were talking about him and conspiring against him. The reality was that no one wanted anything to do with him. To conspire against him would have meant thinking about him, and that was the last thing we wanted to do. He should have been given a good hiding, but we had discussed it and realised that as foreigners we couldn't be seen fighting among ourselves. Moreover, knowing Webster to be what he was, it would only make things worse.

It also turned out that Webster and Larry had known each other on the outside, having bumped into one another on numerous occasions in the heyday of the milk runs. Neither had elaborated, but it was quite obvious they were not friends. The tension that lay between them like a ticking bomb finally exploded in a petty argument over the whereabouts of a pot of jam. Webster assaulted Larry in the storeroom when he had his back to him. He also managed to belt Mark in the mouth as he tried to be a hero and break it up.

Webster was fined the equivalent of a fiver. It was a joke, but only he was laughing. Four weeks later, obviously heedless of another fine, he tried to headbutt Larry for using the tape-player for too long. We couldn't go on living under such a threat – it was unbearable. His 'agree with me or I'll beat you up' attitude was beyond endurance and we tried to find a solution. Eventually, on 18 November, after some pressure from the German consul, Webster was removed from our midst. He was given cell 31 on the same landing which put thirty yards between us, and as long as he stayed there it was enough. He was not permitted to enter our sheep-pen or come near us. And, for the moment, that was that.

On 5 December Benny called a meeting. He was in his 'I am your friend' mood, which was a bit disconcerting. 'I know that you all celebrate Christmas in your countries and that this is a very special time of the year for you,' he began. 'Your families are a long way away and must be thinking of you, as you are thinking of them. We here in Eight Brigade would like to help you all pass this special time in the most pleasant way possible.

'Since we are not familiar so much with Christmas, I was hoping that you might have a few suggestions as to how we might arrange things for you. So, tell me what would you like to do.' Was this guy serious or what?

'Go home,' said Webster.

Benny laughed.

'How about we go up on the roof for a little party with some nice food?' suggested Mark.

'Yeah, and we could have the girls over from the art troupe to sing us a song and give us a dance,' said Larry.

'And we could have a few packets of Marlboro floating about and perhaps a bottle of beer each . . . or two,' I added. I doubted if Jin Feng's translation conveyed the derisiveness of my tone, but Benny didn't bat an eyelid.

He continued smiling and then said, 'Well, we'll have to think about that. Tell me what food would you like to eat?'

'How about some smoked duck, some sautéed veal in a truffle-and-Roquefort sauce and perhaps a lobster or two?' I said.

'I want sausage,' said Dieter.

Jin Feng went blank. He knew we were at it and was too frightened to translate. We'd noticed before that if he didn't like something or thought that the captain would disapprove, he'd simply change our words or ignore them completely. He was afraid of being criticised as if the words were his own.

As the meeting dissolved into further nonsense, Jin Mouling appeared and called Mark out. It looked serious. Was he going home? After about twenty minutes he was back, and Jin called me. As Mark and I passed, he whispered, 'It's two British MPs . . .'

So that's why Benny had been so damn nice. He'd been trying to butter us up so we wouldn't say too much. Tough luck. This was the chance we'd been waiting for, regardless of the consequences.

They introduced themselves as Terrence Higgins, MP for Worthing, and Donald Anderson, MP for Swansea East. They explained that they were in Shanghai as part of a business delegation led by Geoffrey Howe, who was deputy prime minister at the time. They began with the usual questions about exercise and food and how many prisoners there were in my cell.

In the previous five months we had been visited by all sorts of people, but they had all been Chinese. We had seen China Radio International, reporters from the *People's Daily*, delegations from the Bureau of Justice, groups from various *dan weis* (work units) and every Wang, Jiang and Mao who wanted to see this freakshow of long-nosed foreign devils. The questions were always the same and were only ever concerned with our living conditions. No one was interested in whether we felt as if we'd received justice or not. Nobody asked if the authorities were assisting us in our search to right the wrongs that had been done, and not one person mentioned anything about the length of the sentences. It was as if they had been told to back off anything to do with the legal process. If that were the case, what was the point in coming?

'Is there anything that you are particularly concerned about, Robert?' said Donald.

'Well, since you ask, there is something.'

I tried to explain the *dama zhi* problem, but as I went on I got the familiar feeling that they had lost the plot. They hid it well, nodding and agreeing, even asking sensible questions. Maybe they did understand but couldn't give a damn either way. Whatever, I had to finish my piece. I said that I was being prevented from seeing a lawyer and that all my attempts to get a response from the court were fruitless. Then, as usual, just as I was getting into the swing of things, the time was up. The visit was over so quickly – just twenty minutes long – but it was made clear that it was a special privilege, and that I should be grateful to the prison authorities for allowing it. The MPs promised to get in touch with my parents and let them know I was in good health, and said they would look into what could be done regarding my case. I felt I had at least given it a good shot, but would anything come of it?

Christmas Day, and Benny kept his word and arranged a little party for us. There were no girls or cigarettes, alas, and instead we were all taken around to the other side of the building where a table had been set especially for the occasion. Looking like Scrooge, Webster was sitting there already. We'd had nothing to do with him for nearly six weeks and it had been wonderful. I imagined it to be similar to the relief a patient gets when a cancerous tumour is removed from the pit of his stomach. Anyway, everybody sat as far away from him as possible and continued as if he didn't exist. As we waited, the video crew arrived and began filming us in Christmas merriment. It must have looked more like the last meal before a hanging. But when Benny suddenly produced all our seasonal mail, the mood did swing and they had us on film with smiles and expressions of gratitude. It was only later, when we examined the postmarks, that we found out the devious bastards had been holding back our letters for the last six weeks in order to look charitable on camera at Christmas.

Then the lads from the kitchen appeared, all dressed in their white uniforms and hats, carrying stainless-steel trays laden with hot, tasty food. They had us again, but this time we were truly floored. It really was a feast. There were fried shrimps, a beef schnitzel, chicken, cauliflower, potato croquettes, a salad of tofu, carrots, peas and peanuts, and a potato-and-cabbage soup. I hadn't seen anything like this for over fifteen months, and I tried to calculate the cost of such a meal in a Chinese restaurant in Britain, but lost interest after twenty-five quid when I bit into a spicy, succulent shrimp.

Jin Mouling arrived on the scene like Father Christmas, carrying a huge salami and a large wedge of cheese. What's he doing? I wondered. He's surely not bought us that for Christmas, has he? I was right, he hadn't. The German consulate had sent it for Dieter who had asked for it in his last meeting with them. Well, if Jin Mouling had a sense of humour, this was when it popped out to say hello to everybody. As Dieter's jaw dropped and fell between his legs in utter disbelief, Jin chopped up the sausage and the cheese into six equal portions, saying that the German consul, a Miss Sievers, had kindly sent the foreign unit a Christmas present.

'Ach, no, it's not for zer foreign unit! It eez mein!' contended Dieter, but by that time it was too late, and we were all given our share. It was so nice that I proposed we say a big thank-you to Miss Sievers, and suggested that Dieter might be able to pass on our gratitude at his next meeting. For some reason he took quite an exception to that idea, and after a quick, hate-filled glance in my direction, spent the rest of the meal pouting.

By then, four of us at least were having quite a jolly time of it, cracking the odd joke and passing the odd remark, as you do. But it was all too much for Webster, and with his plate still half full, he jumped up and stormed off. Benny and Jin Feng, the translator, followed to see what was amiss.

'I was just about to wish him a happy Christmas and all,' said Larry as Webster disappeared around the corner. Five minutes later he could be heard ranting and raving in Benny's office, just behind us, complaining about people not talking to him and joking about him.

As I slipped the last croquet into my mouth, I thought of my mum and dad and ShaSha, and all the cards I'd received from friends and the volunteers of the London-based charity Prisoners Abroad. I hoped they were all able to have a happy Christmas too.

The Enemy Within

There are robbers who persecute all living things, and there are robbers who wound people with secret arrows.

Adventures of Flowers in a Mirror

CHINESE New Year was when the locals could celebrate, and celebrate they did. On our New Year everybody was in bed as usual by half-eight, but we'd had some English-language videos to watch that day so I couldn't really grumble too much. But Chinese New Year was different. Again we'd been given great food, and again they'd let us watch English videos in the afternoon. The evening was set aside for the most-watched New Year programme in the world, Chinese Central TV's special song-and-dance extravaganza from Beijing. We were allowed to stay up until one o'clock to witness it all. It is the one night when the whole country comes together. Stars from every side of Chinese life count down to midnight when every *hutong*, alleyway, doorway, street or bridge erupts with the deafening machine-gun-like explosions of the millions upon millions of firecrackers that are set off to frighten away the evil spirits. The Chinese are notoriously superstitious, especially the peasants in the countryside, and letting off bangers, 'The Festival of the Dead', dragon boat races and *feng shui* are engrained in the Chinese psyche.

Letting us watch this was considered to be a great privilege, but as the show wore on I started to wonder if it were not some form of torture. In 1993 Shanghai had only two TV channels, and both were devoted to the celebration. We had been given a fourteen-inch portable to watch it on in our sheep-pen while the Chinese had a thirty-two-inch monster positioned right outside our cells. Even if we'd wanted to, we couldn't have gone to sleep. They had a peculiar theory that equated decibel level with the number of people watching. This particular evening there were about eighty prisoners hunched up in front of the box, and the volume was such that we couldn't hear our portable even when it was flat out. That sort of noise wears you down after four or five hours, and if like us you were having difficulty understanding the language and the humour, it soon becomes a nightmare. The screams and shrieks of Chinese opera, the high-pitched whine of grown women pretending to be little girls and the obsequious tones of the presenter cut through the nerves like a butcher's cleaver.

This TV had been the cause of a lot of discomfort for months. When the number 1, Mr Sun, was replaced by Cai Zhengguo, we made it a priority to get the situation resolved. Cai had been the secretary of the whole of Eight Brigade but saw being made number 1 of Three Middle as a good step up the ladder. He was very pleased indeed and wanted to prove his leadership skills.

Cai was about thirty, quite good-looking and friendly. He spoke a little English and was keen to practise with us. Doing so not only improved his ability but made him look clever in front of the others. Ever eager to please, he moved the Chinese

TV right down to the other end of the landing, as far away as possible, and we were all exceptionally grateful. This meant that we could continue studying or, when the guards had gone home, slip into the cell early and read a book. I could now hear my Walkman, and didn't have thirty pairs of eyes outside my cell every night charting my every move. Cai's appointment made a big difference to our lives. He wasn't racist in any way. He just wanted to get on with people and be liked.

The strict routine of life on the landing became a joy and a necessity rather than a bind. Anything that threatened to disrupt that routine was not welcomed. As a group, we spoke to each other less and less. Everybody was on his own trip, and we were all pulling in different directions, each thinking the others couldn't see the wood for the trees.

Our status meant that we were not expected to work and we were not included in the 'merit point system' like the Chinese, where points were awarded each month to the prisoners who had shown outstanding progress in reform. We were a separate entity. Those rules did not apply to us. The real prison rules contained fifty-eight articles mostly concerned with conduct in the workshop. Our version, which had been typed up on a bit of paper by Jin Feng, had twenty. All the rules that were obviously gross infringements of rights had been edited out. There was no stamp of approval from any governing body and for all we knew Jin Feng might have made it all up himself.

The most divisive factor within our ranks had of course been Webster, not only due to his piss-poor attitude towards his fellow man, but also because he felt that he'd have more chance of getting a reduction in his sentence if he were treated in the same way as the Chinese. He wanted to work and even volunteered to paint the entire jail single-handedly. He wanted merit points so as to be able to chart his progress, and wrote reports to the authorities asking them to initiate such a scheme. To the rest of us, it was insanity to ask to be treated like the Chinese. It would prevent us from studying, which was the only way we believed that anything good could come out of our imprisonment.

The merit point system was a means of pitting the prisoners against each other. It is one thing to have over a hundred men competing together, but another when it's only six. Such a system would shine a light on us, create more pressure and be far more destructive than constructive.

In addition, if these merit points were going to be awarded, they would be done so by Benny Goodman on the strength of the advice and observation of the number 1 or Zhou Wanjia. To think that my future might lie in the hands of some uneducated, unqualified, xenophobic individual like that made my blood boil. No way.

I was convinced that we were being managed by the Criminal Affairs Department, and that Benny was only a doorman and the merit point system was nothing more than a tool and a trick to maintain discipline. When those in higher places deemed it expedient to do so, they would make the decision to release us, regardless of any points. These differences in opinion were to create untold problems for us, and there formed the division that was our weakness.

The next bone of contention were the *sixiang huibao* or ideological reports, sometimes referred to as 'thinking reports'. No one had asked us to write them or told us that it was a prerequisite to successful reform. Larry, the two Germans and I considered them to be an invasion of the mind. In Turgenev's *Fathers and Sons*, Valentin says to Rubin, 'At least in prison a man has the right to be himself.' Well, not in China he didn't. They want to enter your mind and tell you what to think. They did everything possible to prevent individual thinking. It was a threat to reform. Only blind allegiance to Beijing and its representatives all the way down to the prisoner who was your table leader was allowed.

When they were not working, the Chinese inmates were listening to nightly prison radio broadcasts that instructed them in every aspect of prison life, from how to use the *matong* and keep the uniform clean to how to acknowledge your crime, confess guilt, beg forgiveness and show repentance. It went on and on every evening after dinner, sometimes for two hours or more. Everybody had to take notes in order to show that they were keen and enthusiastic, and be prepared for the questions in the discussion that followed.

From time to time an ordinary member of the prison population would come on to explain to the rest how he had seen the light and embraced the reform system with open arms. Aimed at making even the hardest feel guilty, they would relate pathetically contrite tales in choked, tear-filled voices about how their ninety-seven-year-old mother, who now had no one to look after her, sold hand-embroidered handkerchiefs to raise the money to buy half a dozen apples every month to give to her son on a visit. They would talk about how they realised the wickedness of their criminal acts, and how they now felt that it was their duty to 'advance in reform'. The captains were always their friends, an idea which was totally alien to my mind, especially in face of their blatant methods of control and the severe retribution that was dished out on a daily basis.

In addition to the unrelenting barrage of proselytising from the authorities, the prisoners had to deal with each other. It was a rule that no inmate should ever be left alone in any place or at any time. Movement was monitored closely and a system known as *san lian hao* or 'the three association' had been devised to do just that. Each unit was broken down into groups of three, and each prisoner in the group had to know at all times where the other two were and what they were doing. Sometimes, unknown to the others, a certain member of the group was linked to another group, until the whole brigade resembled the molecular models in a chemistry textbook.

Everybody was snooping on everybody else, trying to increase their merit points. No matter how strong they were, it was a no-win situation. It was always the weak, toady bastards who succumbed to the captain's offer first. In exchange for information, they were given a licence to get away with all sorts of incitement, aggression and bending of the rules, until their behaviour became so unbearable that those who had originally resisted went to the captain for help. For the officer it was then easy to make a convert. Every cadre/prisoner relationship was a 'you scratch my back and I'll scratch yours' situation.

We were not involved in their world and I wanted it to remain like that. The time that stretched out to the horizon of comprehension was enough to cope with. I once asked Jin Feng if he didn't think he was being brainwashed. He replied that he was, but that the word in Chinese did not carry the same negative connotations as it did in English. In China, it was a perfectly acceptable form of education.

I saw 'thinking reports' as the first step down the road to brain invasion. If even one of us wrote them it would indicate that foreigners could adapt, and I wanted to make it clear that we couldn't, that we were different. It was a communist method of rehabilitation, and to expect us to accept it was a violation of our rights. Was the only way out of jail through conversion to Marxism?

The third major dispute within the foreign unit was between the two Germans and myself. Actually, it was between Dieter and me; Werner just went along with what he was told out of loyalty to his friend and countryman. In the first week Werner had apologised to me for giving my name to the police. I respected him immensely for that, and still do. I found out that Dieter had had my image on his bloody video camera getting pissed outside Li Jiangping's and it was that which led to my name being first mentioned. Despite Webster's goading me to exact revenge by stabbing them both in the shower, I was willing to let it slide – we had to live together, after all. I also wanted the three of us to work together to seek justice but Dieter could not believe that I was being genuine. He expected me to hate him and resented my efforts to prove otherwise. He refused to tell anybody what he was doing about the *dama zhi* issue. Everything became a secret to him and he became more and more insular, finding refuge in meticulous routine, order and cleanliness. He couldn't even let anybody have a look at his *Der Spiegel* magazine without a list of conditions. I thought it was all a bit anal myself, and totally counterproductive, and decided he could just go fuck himself.

So, with all of us pulling in different directions and agreeing to disagree, the unit became as strong as its weakest link. The Chinese had us. They had the means to control us and manipulate us at will. They had found out, with out too much hassle, our sensitive areas and could just press the buttons and select the desired effects.

We were all close to becoming as paranoid as Webster at that time, but we had good reason. We suspected that our weakest link was deliberately working against us – but without proof, how could we deal with it? After some time I came across something that gave substance to our suspicions when, purely by accident, I discovered Zhou Wanjia's report book in the bin. It was a diary of our daily movements. The little runt had been watching us for months and had written it all down so that Benny could see what we were up to. The following is an excerpt that survived:

25 March
5.30 All foreigners out of cell except Mark.
5.35 Prisoners clean cells and unit area.
5.40 Mark leaves cell.
6.00 Davies does not eat breakfast. Spends twenty minutes on *matong*, reading book.
6.20 Dieter looks out of window.
6.35 Mark uses water.
6.40 Begin study. Werner plays guitar in cell.
7.00 Larry listens to radio.

And so it went on. The most interesting entry was from 8 April 1993: 'Officer's education. Webster cannot be trusted but he can be used.' The officer in question was of course our 'good man', Benny, and by 'used', he meant used against the rest of us as a tool to hook us and reel us in.

*

In January Larry decided to wage a war for an improvement in the mail system and to put a stop to the racist attitude of the officers and Chinese prisoners. He wrote a letter to the prosecutor complaining about Jin Mouling's mishandling of our letters and the fact that on more than one occasion he had come to our unit drunk and abusive.

After three weeks of waiting, two prosecutors eventually came. Kicking Benny out of his office, they took Larry in to discuss his problems. Benny was forced to stand under the window, listening to the charges levelled against him and Captain Jin. The whole brigade was nervous. The majority of the Chinese had gone to work, but those who remained had stopped their usual babble and sat around as if waiting for an exam result. Every so often Zhou Wanjia would find an excuse to walk past the office to see what he could pick up.

With Jin Feng translating, Larry took about two hours to spell out the reasons for his discontentment. When he emerged, everybody wanted to know what had been said. Benny talked to Zhou Wanjia, and the number 1 collared Jin Feng. Half an hour later, the number 1 was in Benny's office telling him the lot. The code of confidentiality that all translators are supposed to have didn't operate in Tilan Qiao simply because the Chinese could not and would not refuse their captain.

Ten days later Captain Jin showed up and it was quite obvious that he was rat-arsed again. He had not come to have a go at us, however. To everyone's complete amazement, he said that he had come to apologise to Larry for previously insulting him. This I had to see. It was probably the first time in Chinese history that a screw had said sorry to a prisoner. I watched on in amazement as afterwards they shook hands.

Within five minutes, though, he was at it again, telling Larry and Werner to shave their beards off because they were dirty. We'd had enough of hearing that sort of crap from other prisoners who all thought we were unclean. They would even come up and watch you pissing and then point at your dick and tell you it was dirty. Anywhere else in the world that's a free ticket to the hospital, but we all already knew it was best to ignore them. Jin was last seen stumbling across the yard like a man in the desert searching for water.

*

Larry had hurt his leg playing basketball in the autumn, but claimed that when Webster had attacked him in the storeroom he had severely aggravated the injury. He had been limping around for six months, unable to walk very far and certainly not able to play basketball. He believed that it was the prison's responsibility to right the damage because they should have prevented the attack in the first place. The authorities could not deny that they knew of Webster's violent nature – he had, after all, attacked ten people since his arrest. He had never once been punished appropriately, and that had given him a licence to carry out more and more unprovoked attacks. The prison had therefore failed to protect Larry, which was a violation of his rights. The authorities did not agree, unsurprisingly, and after various examinations by different doctors, they informed Larry that he could have an operation, but it would cost him the equivalent of $3,500. They hoped that he would now forget about it. He didn't, and the fight went on.

Larry was also still mad as hell over allegations made in the magazine *Shanghai Tan* which claimed that he had planned his smuggling operations from Karachi and had used Tibetan citizens as conduits. The magazine, according to Larry, had fabricated the whole article and he wanted to 'sue their ass'. For this, of course, he needed a lawyer. He wrote to several to try and arrange a visit. He wrote to courts to ask for clarification of the substance that he had been sentenced for. He wrote to his folks for money and additional evidence to prove he wasn't a smuggler, and to his consul to complain about the way the prison were handling things. Not one letter generated a reply.

Larry went to see Benny on 26 May and accused him and his government of every violation under the sun. Within minutes it turned into a real slanging match which resulted in Larry storming out, vowing to start a hunger strike. Within hours, Mr Sun of the Labour-through-Reform Bureau arrived to talk to him. After two hours of discussion, the jail agreed to call the lawyer of Larry's choice.

Three days later, and against all the odds, Mr Li Guoji, a lawyer, came to the jail to see Larry. He was supposed to have a fierce reputation all over Shanghai. It was the first time that a lawyer had met a prisoner other than one who was going to be shot and wanted to make a will, and all the cadres were clearly quite jumpy about it. (Webster claimed that he'd seen a lawyer back in the winter, but confessed some time later that it was a lie. Why?)

The meeting was conducted in an office downstairs, and after taking nearly half an hour to empty the room of prison guards and Criminal Affairs bodies, Larry and the lawyer got down to business. Within five minutes the door burst open and in came the video crew with lights ablaze. Five minutes later the door opened again and three photographers barged in taking snapshots. When I spoke to Larry later, he was adamant that the room had also been bugged. Every time he'd started explaining a juicy bit, the captains had walked in to ask the lawyer if he'd like some tea or the windows opened.

The contract formalities were agreed on and Li Guoji promised to return the following day. Larry continued with his hunger strike because to his mind nothing had changed – they were still not giving him his mail and they could stop the lawyer from entering the jail at any time. The following day Larry waited well past the appointed hour, but there was no sign of Li Guoji.

The only visit Larry got that day was from Brigade Captain Wang, a hard-line communist who had recently taken over the running of Eight Brigade. He tried to persuade Larry of the harm he was doing to himself and of the pointlessness of it all. He promised that things would improve but that it would take time. He reminded Larry that it was strictly against prison rules to inflict harm upon himself, and that if he didn't start eating soon, the authorities would be forced to take control of the situation and put him in the hospital where he would be force-fed.

'You aren't allowed to do that. It's a violation of human rights,' Larry protested.

The days went by, and there was no sign of the lawyer or of any action by the authorities. On 2 June, the first anniversary of our arrival at Tilan Qiao, Captain

Wang called a meeting for the foreign unit and Webster. Larry refused to attend, staying instead in his cell on his *matong* meditating. Captain Wang proceeded to educate the rest of us about obeying the rules and observing the discipline. Ten minutes into his discourse, the video crew arrived and, tight on their heels, a bunch of six very burly officers I'd never seen before, all with their sleeves rolled up. Bringing up the rear were Captain Jin and Sun with Dong of Criminal Affairs.

Taking no notice of Wang, we watched as Jin asked Larry for the last time to see sense and give up his hunger strike. He refused. Without further ado, three officers entered the cell and grabbed him by the arms and legs. He immediately went limp to make it as difficult as possible for them. As they dragged him out, his injured leg slid through the bars of the door. The officers either didn't see it or didn't care, and continued to pull Larry out of the cell. He started screaming at the top of his voice, but the pulling continued. I got up from the table to go to help, shouting to Jin about the leg, but I was pushed firmly back into my seat and told to mind my own business. Larry was finally wrenched free but it didn't stop his screams.

They dragged him backwards down the landing as Wang went on about the regulations and the administering of punishment to those who persisted in disobedience. We could hear Larry yelling as he was dragged all the way down the stairs and across the yard in the direction of the hospital. They were going to give him a dose of real reform.

With the echoes of Larry's screams finally out of earshot, Wang asked us all in turn for our thoughts about the hunger strike. I told him straight that Larry's grievance was obviously a serious matter otherwise he would not have felt it necessary to embark on such a drastic course of action. I added that the authorities should take his grievances seriously and that they should look into what was gong on with a mind to preventing this sort of thing in the future because we shared the majority of his complaints.

This wasn't what Wang wanted to hear. The problems between the group as a whole and Webster actually stemmed from his and Larry's hatred of one another. Webster believed that because we spoke to Larry, we were in on it. Why had he been ostracised when Larry hadn't? Well, that was easy – Larry had not brought the rest of us into his hatred spectrum.

Webster now saw an opportunity for revenge, telling Wang that Larry was a very bad prisoner and a bad example to the rest of us. Larry did not understand the rules and regulations, he said, and had shown disrespect to the officers. He should be punished and re-educated. Webster explained that he had been bad once, but 'thanks to the teaching of the cadres', he was now able to understand the reform. Reform was a good thing.

The rest of us looked on in disbelief. Well, at least we all knew now without doubt where we stood.

The Young Men's Experimental Brigade

Gu ming si yi – By the name of a thing, one is reminded of its function.
Chinese saying

LARRY had been taken to a single room on the fourth floor of Tilan Qiao's notorious hospital. Nobody wanted to stay there long. Prisoners didn't get well there, they got worse. The place was run by trustees – trusted prisoners – whose aim was to do as little as possible and eat as much as they could. The guards kept well away and the doctors and nurses, who were also officers in the prison system, simply accepted it the way it was.

It was considered a waste of money to feed sick people good food because they weren't working. Every day was cabbage and rice, and if there was ever any meat, it was stolen by the trustees before the patients saw it. Any complaints resulted in the patients being strapped to their beds for days on end with no access to the toilet. They lay in their own shit until their skin was caked in it. Even if it was possible to go to the toilet, no one wanted to. It was filthy, blocked, overflowing and stinking, a breeding ground for flies, cockroaches and mosquitoes.

The stairs to the fifth floor were sealed off with a large, locked metal door, and only the most senior doctors were ever seen to go through it. Rumour had it that it was there that the prison stored body parts from executed criminals. I also heard on more than one occasion that some organs were taken before prisoners were shot, so as to have them as fresh as possible. Such stories came from countless different sources and circulated for as long as we stayed in Tilan Qiao. One prisoner swore that he had seen a pair of eyes in a round stainless-steel container when the doctor accidentally knocked the lid off it. It was a place of mystery and foreboding.

Larry was put in a small ward with four beds. The other three were to be occupied by Zhou Wanjia, Freddy Foghorn and Silver Teeth, the minders who had been ordered to assist in his re-education. Seeing as they were going to force-feed him, it was pointless to continue with the hunger strike, and Larry certainly didn't want that sort of torture. On the second day, the new warden of the whole prison, a megalomaniac called Li, went to visit him and was filmed giving Larry an apple. We'd given Li the nickname Elvis because of his bouffant hairstyle. I had only seen him once, when he gave his inaugural speech on the prison TV. He frightened me. It was as if he had been taught at the Adolf Hitler Nuremberg Rally Speech School. He was ranting and raving and banging the table with his fist saying that all criminals were scum of the earth and that this was not some holiday camp. Prisoners were here to reform whether they liked it or not.

Larry was allowed nothing other than what they gave him to eat and drink. He was not permitted to read books or magazines, write letters, watch TV or listen to music. Every morning at five o'clock he was turfed out of bed and forced to sit on his wooden stool all day until ten at night. All day every day he had to study the prison regulations by writing them out time and time again until he knew them off by heart. They tried to force him to write a self-criticism, but Larry didn't see that he had done anything wrong, and so refused. He had been trying to secure what was his, namely the right to correspond and the right to receive medical treatment.

If Larry did anything at all that he had not been told to do by his watchdogs, they would hold him down and beat him persistently in the ribs and the back. Eventually he wrote a report discussing the contents of the White Paper on Prison Reform that had been published in November 1992, laying particular emphasis on the section concerning the prisoners' right to communication and health. This was not what they wanted, so they beat him up again. After twenty-two days of this torture he was released, but his ordeal was not over yet.

Larry was not returned to our unit. Instead, he was placed in the Young Men's Experimental Brigade or YMX. Situated directly under our landing on the second floor, it housed the most stubborn prisoners, the ones who simply refused to accept the reform in any way. It was here that they received a crash course in discipline. The captain, a sadistic drunk called Ming, encouraged his trustees, all graduates of the unit, to use whatever method they thought best to slap their students into shape. Failure to comply could result in any number of disciplinary measures being taken.

The YMX was under twenty-four-hours-a-day lock-down and they managed to pack in four or five prisoners to each three-metre-square cell – even when vacant cells were available. During the day all prisoners had to sit up properly – if they tilted over or fell asleep, they were poked and beaten with a long stick that was thrust in through the bars. This treatment could continue long into the night and last up to forty-eight hours. To keep the inmates in a state of constant anxiety, any one of them could be beaten up at any time, even for good behaviour.

The *pièce de résistance* of reform therapy was the electric baton. Everyone knew it was lying on the shelf just waiting for that one small mistake or that special someone whom the captain took a dislike to.

The prisoner would be stripped down to his shorts and forced to sit on a small stool with his hands cuffed behind his back. A flannel was jammed into his mouth to stop the screaming and a padded mask was placed over his head to protect it from bruising if he banged it against the concrete floor. Before the baton was applied they poured water over the prisoner's body so as to spread the shock. The genitals were a prime target and prisoners would end up writhing in uncontrollable agony and sheer panic on the floor. It was a near certainty that a victim would piss his pants and quite common that he soiled them too.

Larry had a cell to himself, and after a few days he was allowed out to read and study. Unable to distance himself from such a cruel environment, though, he wrote to the prosecutor, complaining about the violence. Delegations from Amnesty or Asia Watch were never going to see any real corrective punishment on their sanitised tours, so Larry took it upon himself to investigate. His letters somehow got through and even managed to persuade the prosecutor to make an inspection. But the captains found out in advance and removed the nameplates from the doors, took the bruised prisoners into the showers and let the rest out to play basketball. Everything seemed to be in order.

What went on down there in YMX soured the whole place. It became a regular occurrence when walking past the doorway on our way to the basketball court to see prisoners being prepared for the baton. Going down to empty the *matong* on the other side allowed enough time to see the overcrowding. And, as isolated as we were, we still heard all the rumours. Ming's crew would brag about how effective their measures were and after a while it seemed to affect our officers. They too got more aggressive and seemed far more willing to get the stick out than previously. There were regular sessions not twenty metres from where I sat. Even when they did it around the corner, I knew it was happening because the baton caused interference on my radio. It seemed as if humanity was breaking down.

*

ShaSha had been in Shanghai for eight months, and had at last found a little flat in the Pu Dong district. 'Flat' was actually an overstatement, because it didn't sound much bigger than my cell. It was just a box-room in somebody's house; not only that, she had to share it with another girl. Kitchen facilities were also shared with the owners, and in order to wash she had to use the public showers a hour's bicycle ride away.

With so many migrants moving to Shanghai from the countryside, accommodation was scarce. It didn't help that ShaSha was from Xinjiang. Landlords took one look at her and immediately found some excuse to say that the room was no longer available; Xinjiang people are feared because they have a reputation for being on the wrong side of the law and carry knives. At that time Pu Dong was still a mostly rural area, but with the acceleration of Deng Xiaoping's 'Opening and Reform', things were changing fast – so fast that it wasn't long before the landlord was asking ShaSha to leave: the local government were going to demolish the whole village in order to build an office block. Again, with the help of friends, she found another matchbox deep in the *hutongs* behind Wuyi Lu, a largely residential area of the city. It was even smaller than the place she'd just been kicked out of.

That winter was particularly bitter, below freezing for long stretches. With the humid cold of Shanghai, it didn't matter how many clothes you wore, the cold still penetrated right into your bones. ShaSha was freezing. She bought an electric ring on which to boil some water to save disturbing her new landlords, and on the coldest of nights she would leave it on to try and warm up the room a bit. But the little ring could not take it, and it exploded. The landlord thereafter forbade the use of such gadgets in the room and she simply had to wear more clothes.

When he heard about ShaSha's precarious situation, the landlord quickly asked for more money, usually blaming the government for increases in his expenditure as the reason. The official line was that inflation in Shanghai was running at 14 per cent, though according to most it was nearer 18. With each newspaper report that told of an increase in the price of this or that, the landlord demanded an increase in the rent. Inflated charges for water, electricity and gas soon followed. It was time to look for somewhere else.

By then ShaSha had made a number of friends, and thanks to them she managed to find another flat in the same *hutong*. It was no bigger, no cheaper and no more comfortable than before, but she had no choice. I was beginning to wonder if the authorities weren't running her out of town, and my suspicions fell on Jin Mouling. In one meeting with ShaSha in the spring of '93, she had told me in Uighur that he had suggested that if she was willing to pay him, she could have an extra visit every month. I was fuming and had wanted to report the bastard, but I had been intimidated enough by him by that time to realise that it would be me who got the rough end of the stick if I did, so I kept my mouth shut.

ShaSha's new digs were owned by a man with one eye who had a wife who was completely blind. The little house was a one-up-one-down affair with a ladder. The blind folks lived upstairs, and Sharapet downstairs. Across the alley there was a room half the size of a small chicken shed in which they cooked. It had a cold water tap and a bucket which had been converted into a briquette burner. One briquette would burn for about an hour and when the one-eyed man had finished cooking their food, Sharapet had what was left. Many nights ShaSha would be woken by the screams of a woman being beaten by her vindictive little Cyclops of a husband. When the man was away, the wife would he banging and thudding and falling all over the place as she missed the steps of the ladder and dropped things. ShaShas felt sorry for her and gave her clothes and fruit and made tea for her. She soon became her only friend in that dark, miserable life.

Finding a job in Shanghai was also an uphill battle for ShaSha. Being over thirty – and an Uighur to boot – had more stigma attached to it than if she'd had a criminal record. Shops, restaurants and hotels only wanted young women between the ages of eighteen and twenty-six. All this prejudice drove ShaSha to spend more and more time with the foreign community in Shanghai – students, teachers and those working for the ever-increasing number of joint-venture companies that were popping up all over the place.

We had got into the rhythm of writing to each other twice a month without fail. We wrote long meandering *billets-doux*, searching every corner of our hearts in a bid to express a devotion that was immeasurable in time and space. We pledged undying love in a thousand different ways. I would find and translate poems, quotations and passages from the books I read that expressed my every emotion and slip them in before signing off.

In the beginning I would take up to twenty hours to prepare a letter in Chinese, painstakingly searching the dictionaries for the right meaning, cross-referencing time and again, and then carefully scratching out the ideograms with a cheap, leaky fountain pen. It was probably the best way for me to learn the language, and I made good progress, soon being able to write characters with confidence.

One benefit of corresponding in Chinese was that our letters never had to be translated and therefore were not caught up in Jin's postal dragnet. I was treated in the same way as the Chinese. My letters went out in one or two days and the reply was given to me in the same prompt manner. I also soon noticed that if I enclosed a letter in English to my folks and asked ShaSha to post it on, the letter would leave the jail twice as quickly than if I'd written directly. The regulations probably stated that all letters addressed 'to foreign destinations' were to be gone over with a fine-tooth comb. Mine were addressed to Shanghai, and so didn't qualify.

*

Mark had packed his suitcase already and was sure that he was on his way out any day now. The authorities had promised that he would be released after half his sentence, and that time was up. He was so sure of his imminent departure that he refused to buy large amounts of extra food from the prison shop, and when he did, he ate it all up as quickly as possible just in case he had to leave at any moment.

On 26 October we all thought his time had come when we were called out to go to the Cross Building for a 'reduction meeting'. My heart was thumping and the optimist in me believed there was a chance that they were going to let us all go. I was not alone in my optimism either, and as we gripped our stools and marched across the yard in single file under the watchful eye of an empty guard tower, speculation was rife. Mark was so convinced he was on his way to the airport that he'd put on his best clothes and polished his shoes. We had to climb the stairs to the fifth floor, but we did so gleefully because we believed it led to freedom.

The Cross Building was originally built to house the most dangerous criminals but it was now dedicated to the production of clothing. Sewing-machines clattered incessantly from six in the morning until nine at night, pumping out shirts and trousers.

The six of us were ushered into a small hall with a stage at the front. There were about thirty prisoners, all seated in rows on their little blue plastic stools, waiting for the show to begin. For the first time the whole foreign contingent was gathered in one place. There were three Pakistanis, one very old Korean in prison uniform with a long white beard, and us. Two of the Pakistanis I had seen before. One was in uniform but the other two looked as if they were ready to leave like Mark. The Korean was rumoured to have got fifteen years for trying to send a bible to his family. The remaining twenty-six prisoners were human kapok, only there to stop the room looking bare.

I sat there wondering how they were going to handle my release. If I was deported would I be allowed to come back to China to get ShaSha or would I have to wait for her to get a visa? I pondered on the feasibility of acquiring a fake passport in order to come back to rescue her, but decided the risk was too great. I thought it most likely that I'd be sent to Hong Kong, which would suit me fine. Were they going to stick us all on one plane? Would they serve beer? I'd have to send a telegram to let ShaSha know what had happened. Perhaps the jail had already informed her . . . And so it went on, speculation, hope, optimism and maybes.

'All stand.'

In walked three judges wearing crabby expressions and their distinctive blue uniforms with red epaulets. They took their places behind a long table. On the wall behind them hung the emblem of office, something that now always struck fear into me. They were introduced and a rather shaky translator told us that they were a chief judge, a judge and a clerk.

The three Pakistanis, Tahir Amir, Halid Pahan and Parvaz Aktur, had been sentenced to ten years each for trying to pass off just over $15,000 in counterfeit banknotes. The clerk called on Halid to stand. He was about twenty-six and, according to a magazine article I'd come across in prison, he'd led a transient lifestyle around Asia, learning how to drink alcohol and how to cheat. He was always dreaming of one day making it big, and that was why he lived this 'dangerous life'. Halid had recently written a letter to the warden requesting that the authorities educate him. On receiving the letter the warden went in person to visit Halid to praise him for his good attitude, and present him with a Chinese–English dictionary.

Reading from Halid's verdict, the clerk explained his background and then his crime, describing how he had been found guilty and sentenced to ten years in the Intermediate Court. What he said next, in a tone of incredulity and disgust, was this: 'But Halid did not accept his sentence. He thought it was too harsh. Instead, he had the nerve to appeal to the Higher Court.' The clerk paused for a moment before continuing triumphantly: 'But the Higher Court refused his appeal and upheld the original sentence as being correct and appropriate. Ha!'

He had made appealing sound like a crime in itself. If you appealed, he was suggesting, how could you expect the courts to believe later that you accepted the judgment and recognised your crime? It was clear that the sooner you acknowledged everything the way it was, the sooner you'd be eligible for a reduction. How could you possibly think that the Intermediate Court had made a mistake?

He went on, saying that Halid had changed his ways and reformed. He had worked hard in his brigade, studying Chinese and separating cloth. (Hour after hour, day after day, separating scraps of material into individual threads, this was the lowest job in the prison, worse even than cleaning the officers' toilets.) Halid's good behaviour had been recognised by the authorities and a report had been sent to the court suggesting that he be given a reduction. This had been accepted by the Intermediate Court whose representatives were that day to make known their decision. I was certain they intended to deport him and then go through the same rigmarole with each of us in turn. They could easily agree that I had studied hard and helped Jin Feng in his translation work.

'For good behaviour, the Shanghai People's Intermediate Court hereby award Halid Pahan a reduction in sentence of one year.'

'One fucking year!' I thought. 'Are they joking or what?' And then, as it sunk in, 'Oh, well, I suppose it's better than nothing. A year off means I've got only five and a half years to go, and that's only a year to go until half sentence. Yeah, I can live with that.'

I glanced around and everybody looked stunned. But the best was yet to come. We were all told to stand up and, as we did so, the judges got up and walked out. That was it. Mark was devastated and so was Parvaz. As a photographer sneaked round taking shots of our contorted faces, I felt cheated. What had been the purpose of it? Undoubtedly it had been another propaganda exercise to make it look as if there was a system in operation, and at the same time showing us half a carrot.

Doctor Death

Unfortunately they gang up together, shaking their heads and flapping their wings.

Ouyang Xiu, *Fu' of Hatred for Flies*

AFTER each consul visit a report was written regarding the state of my health. That was faxed to the consular department in the Foreign Office in London which was then sent to the family lawyer who passed it on to my mum and dad. In that way they were always well informed about my welfare. But they still regarded seeing me face to face as the best way to put their minds at rest. At the end of November 1993 they were back again, only this time ShaSha was at the airport to meet them and show them around the city. They all came to the jail together but it was the same old ritual as before with a busload of men in green surrounding us during the visit. My mother gave me some hope of an early release when she informed me that the local MP had now become involved and was going to approach the Foreign Office on my parents' behalf. They also told me that Donald Anderson MP had contacted them the year before immediately after his visit and had assured them of my well-being, promising to look into my case. It gave me confidence that wheels were turning somewhere and that I wasn't being left to rot.

*

On Christmas morning the whole brigade was allowed out into the basketball court. The weather was glorious with blue skies and warm sunshine. Everyone sat up against the west wall so as to soak up as much sun as possible. Dieter read his *zeitung* and listened to his Walkman while the rest of us sunbathed. We were not permitted to strip off, but it was still good to feel the warm rays on our faces. Our exercise periods were always in the half-light of dawn and, being on the north side, our landing never caught even a glimpse of the sun during the winter.

Damn it! We'd forgotten the backgammon board. I got permission to re-enter the building to get it. It was nothing fancy, just something that I had knocked together from bits of cardboard and rice glue. We used *go* stones as counters and a pair of dice that a Chinese had given us.

Back in my cell, I grabbed my handiwork and trotted down the stairs to rejoin the sun fest. On the second floor I came face to face with four officers from YMX, one of whom was Ming. The smell of *baijiu* was toxic. Ming was about as drunk as he could be. His cohorts were holding him up as he was obviously too drunk to stand. He spotted me and said, 'What're you looking at, foreign prick? Fuck you, dirty pricks, fuck your mothers. You want to fight me? Come on, I'll give you some education.'

I stood my ground in silence just watching him. His mates pulled him back as he lunged at me, jabbing two fingers into my chest. They were laughing but suddenly seemed to realise that I was actually a foreigner. They immediately apologised and tried to make an excuse for him: 'Oh, he's a bit drunk. Don't worry about him.'

They let me pass as the four of them stumbled about trying to keep Ming upright and away from me. At the bottom of the stairs I could still hear him cursing all foreigners. This incident only confirmed my belief that behind all that smiling and welcoming, the Chinese hated us with a fervour.

In the midst of our celebrations on Boxing Day, as we went down the back stairs to empty the shit buckets, we noticed that Larry's YMXers had been moved to the south side of the building. A gang of welders and brickies had been brought in from Five Brigade and were setting about sealing off the second floor from the rest of the building. At that time you could still walk from the ground floor to the top without any hindrance, but it was clear that when the lads had done their work there would be a series of heavy iron gates to pass through that could only be unlocked by an officer.

It turned out that they were going to move Death Row in its entirety from One Brigade to the landing directly underneath ours. This was fucking eerie. It meant that there was nothing but the thickness of the floor between us and some poor sod who was waiting for a bullet in the back of the head. Somebody had mentioned that the reason for the move was that the proximity of Death Row was upsetting the Death-plus-Two-Years prisoners. But didn't they think that bringing it over here might upset us too?

Within a week it was up and running, and a hundred condemned men were moved in. The authorities got the YMX graduates to run the place. Devoid of any feelings and desperate to gain favour, they were perfect for the job, and if they were a little heavy-handed, so what? A bunch of dead men would never complain. They got no exercise, no hot showers, no special food for Spring Festival, only a talk with a lawyer to dispose of their belongings.

Sometimes in the dead of night I could hear the sobs oozing through the concrete floor of my cell, but I was told by one of the YMXers that on the whole the condemned men were unusually peaceful. Perhaps, as Heidegger wrote, 'When a man knows he is to be hanged in a fortnight, it concentrates his mind wonderfully.' I still believe that each of those condemned men entertained a tiny hope that he would be saved right up until the moment when the bullet entered his brain and the lights went out for the last time.

*

Larry returned from his adventures in the underworld just after Chinese New Year, 1994. He was unrepentant and hell-bent on finding some way to avenge his suffering. We also saw the return of Cai Zhengguo as number 1, which was one hell of a relief. The previous summer he had been caught passing a letter to a girl from the art troupe and was removed. As a number 1 he'd had a free rein to move about as he liked, and found plenty of opportunity to be in the same place as the performers. However, he'd been suspected of being up to something devious and was watched carefully. In the end, the girl was searched and Cai's letter of yearning was discovered. He was stripped of his position and sent to Five Brigade for re-education. In no time at all, though, he had risen through the ranks and we saw him walking freely around the jail again – something that we would never be allowed to do, no matter how well behaved we were.

In the meantime we had been given a new number 1. He was about fifty-five, with liver disease and big black bags under his eyes. I called him Doctor Death. The guy was so racist that you wondered if his mother had been raped by a foreigner; none of us had ever come across such an example of hatred in either real life or fiction, apart from Hitler, of course. But Doctor Death worked overtime to find ways to make our lives a misery. If it was going to piss us off, he would go the extra mile. He enlisted Zhou Wanjia as his sidekick and cultivated the worst in him.

They took the meat out of our food containers; we knew that they had done so because you could see the indentation where the chicken leg or the piece of beef had lain in the cabbage. They took the cake we were given on Sundays; they stole half the bread we had with our soup; and they cut the amount of goods we were able to buy in the prison shop by not adding our orders to the list. They gave us only malfunctioning TVs to watch – ones with just one channel or a broken aerial – when they gave us one at all. They excluded us from festivals where previously we had been welcome. They prevented us from going to the concerts in the Great Hall of the Prisoner. They tried to restrict our use of the washroom by locking the door or leaving only cold water in the tank. They told blatant lies about us to the captains and tried to incite us to respond violently.

I complained time and time again to Benny, but it made no difference – in fact, it seemed to make things worse. We complained to every official who spoke to us. Every time we mentioned the racist treatment. Nothing changed. It was as if what we were saying was so over-the-top that no one believed us. It dawned on me eventually that the fault lay with the translator. He wasn't telling the half of it – leaving chunks out and even adding his own inflection to discredit our words. It was then that I decided to write a report, not in English but in Chinese. I would hand it to the warden personally.

I spent a week writing nine pages of characters, describing every lie, every theft and every violation of our rights committed by those two bastards against us. I wrote that Doctor Death and his puppet had 'created a theatre of hate, that jeopardised the proper running of the brigade'.

I continued: 'As prisoners entrusted with power by the authorities, they thus represent the authorities, and are the face of the people and government of China. With their racist and prejudiced behaviour towards foreign inmates, these prisoners are a festering, malignant growth on that face. They insult their comrades with these actions and are a disgrace to their motherland. I hope that this situation can be resolved as soon as possible, before inmates start taking the law into their own hands. All foreign inmates respect the necessity for discipline but when all avenues to protect individual rights are closed, tell me please what can a man do? I am compelled to inform both the prosecutor and my consul of the present state of affairs, such is the seriousness.'

Ten days later I got my chance. I gave it to the warden, holding my hand up to stop Jin Feng grabbing it, saying, 'It's okay, you won't need a translator. It's all in Chinese. You can read it at your leisure.'

Watching from the corner of the sheep-pen, Death and Zhou Wanjia were incensed. It was out of their hands; there was no way to distort my words or even know what I had said. If questioned, they would have no ready defence. I was taken into the office, where the warden went through each page carefully, looking very serious indeed. I waited for him to say something like, 'Right, let's drag 'em in here, torture 'em and then lock 'em up for six months with no food or water,' but he only nodded his head a bit and finally promised to look into it.

Things did improve after that, but no one was punished and the enmity between the Chinese and us remained until it was time for Death to have the tail of his sentence cut and be sent home – no doubt as a reward for inflicting pain and suffering on us.

We had had one moment of revenge, though, and it was thanks to Webster. In an argument about food or something, Webster had spat at Death, which provoked him enough to hit Webster with a flannel. Webster hit him smack on the nose, breaking it and leaving Death with two black eyes to match the bags below. Webster got thirty days lock-down for it. There was a clear disparity there – if he hit one of us, he got fined the price of a jar of coffee. If he hit a Chinese, they locked him up.

Just as things were getting better, Webster's dream came true and they introduced the dreaded merit point system. He had always blamed that and the lack of work as the main reasons behind his tantrums and violent outbursts. After many an exhausting session with him, the authorities relented and finally allowed him, and him alone, to work. A visiting English-speaking officer had told Mark and I that our consul had agreed to Webster's involvement in physical labour because it was the only way to shut him up. The understanding between the two sides was that foreigners were not to be forced into unpaid physical labour. If we volunteered, that was different, though the work was not to involve any risk of injury, because at the end of the day, who was going to settle the insurance claim if one of us lost an eye or something?

Not knowing what we knew, Webster began working around the other side helping to mend umbrellas, and thinking that he was now on a fast track to reform. The Chinese thought he was a working-man's hero, and started trying to make the rest of us feel guilty. We then became 'lazy foreign pricks' and simply 'bad people'. Webster was good, and got extra food and extra football periods with the Chinese as a reward. He thought that if he complied with the demands of the system they would have to award him the appropriate points, and that once he had accumulated the desired amount they would have to give him a reduction.

My experience told me that there was no 'have to' in Tilan Qiao. I had watched the Chinese points go up on the blackboard every month and had seen nothing to convince me that the system worked that way. I had seen many prisoners achieve high monthly scores all year, only to fall short of the desired total, sometimes by as little as half a point, in the last month. They were told that it was bad luck and that they should not give up but try harder next year. I had seen sometimes twenty or more inmates get enough points to be awarded a reduction but only four or five of them ever get it. Other times a prisoner would get a reduction without even reaching the target.

I realised that if I took it seriously, it would really mess with my mind. From that moment on I did my best to ignore its existence. The Germans and Larry did the same. We went about each day in the same ways we always did. Get up, clean area, exercise in cell, mind own business. Eat breakfast, study and listen to radio, mind own business. Eat lunch, have snooze, drink tea, empty shit buckets, study, mind own business. Eat supper, read book, watch TV, mind own business. Lock up, read book, sleep. Every day without fail. In this way, time passed at an alarming rate – so fast, sometimes, that I wished I could slow it all down. I was getting old too quickly.

The first merit points were posted on 27 April. Webster got 10.3 (say no more), Mark got 5.5, the Germans and I got 4.8, and Larry got 0.

*

On 11 May we had a new arrival in our group, a young man named Dominic. He had been caught with four hundred grams of hash as he got on the boat to Japan and had been sentenced to two and a half years.

Dominic sensed immediately that there was something wrong between us all, but he couldn't put his finger on it. We decided to let him find out for himself why things were as they were. Anyway, I had no need to try and bring a stranger around to my way of thinking. Let him get on with it.

Dominic could play guitar, though, and fitted in with the way of things pretty well. With less than two years remaining, he could forget any reduction in his sentence, so he didn't give a toss and just strummed and sang all day.

*

On 9 September I was called out and told that a judge from the court had come to see me and that he was waiting on the ground floor. Immediately, my heart jumped. Was this it? Was this the day I was going home? Imagining the possibilities, I skipped ahead of my escort all the way down the stairs, thinking about the airport again, and how to inform ShaSha that I was out. Standing there to greet me was Shen Weijia, 'the most frightening man', the judge whom I had met two and a half years before.

I decided I wasn't going home that day but maybe they wanted to interview me to see if I had reformed. Maybe they were going to test me or something. After a handshake, I sat down. Incredible. Shen Weijia still made me shudder. It was as if his voice came from a rolled steel bar that had been kept in a deep freeze for ten years. Actually, if I thought about it, it was Shen Weijia who was the real Doctor Death. How many people had he condemned? How could he sleep at night? Was he married? How could his wife sleep at night?

A group of Chinese prisoners were watching TV at the other end of the hall and trustees flitted by. It was weird, I still expected privacy.

Shen Weijia began by asking about my reform, and I proceeded to give him a statement that I had learned off pat for such situations: 'I work hard in reform. I observe the discipline and abide by the regulations. I do my job and obey the officers. I study the Chinese language diligently, assist an English teacher with his lessons and help the translation department in preparing documents. I join in many activities around the jail, like sports and music. I accept that I committed the crime that I confessed to.'

This was as far as I was prepared to go. They could interpret that how they liked. I had decided that I was never going to say that I acknowledged the crime I was sentenced for, or say that the punishment was correct. I could never do that.

Shen Weijia looked bored. He offered me a cigarette but just as I was about to take it, a prisoner appeared from nowhere and said, 'No smoking in here.' Shit! I wanted a cigarette. What the hell had it got to do with a prisoner?

The judge bent down to pick up an envelope and I heard the clink of pure gold. Ever since my spell at the detention house, I had been asking for the return of my personal effects. I feared that I would never see them again. Most important of all were our unique and irreplaceable wedding rings. I had written to the court at least ten times, and had suggested that if they helped me to retrieve my money from Xinjiang, I could pay off what they said I owed them as a fine. But there was no reply.

Shen tipped the contents of the envelope onto the table and asked if it was all there. I confirmed that it was. 'You were ordered by the court to pay a fine of 10,000rmb and pay back illegal earnings of 4,680rmb,' he said. 'Are you prepared to pay that sum over to the court now?'

I had to think what their game was. If I refused to pay, maybe they wouldn't let me go. However, from somewhere I said, 'The way I see it is, since the Xinjiang police are already in possession of the equivalent of $3,000 of mine, and they are, like yourselves, an organ of the Chinese government, you are actually already in possession of what you say I owe you. May I suggest that your offices contact the Xinjiang police in Kashgar and ask them to hand it over.'

The translator went to work and I watched Shen's face to see how he liked that idea. He didn't so much as blink an eye. It turned out he had no idea what I was talking about, and I was asked to explain. I told him my tale of woe, hoping he would be able to step in and do something.

'I think you had best write to them again,' he said when I finished.

'But my letters don't leave the jail. I've written to Xinjiang and to you countless times and got no answer.'

'What did you write to the court about?' he asked.

'I wrote to ask you to tell me what *dama zhi* is. I have no idea what it is, and I think I should be told exactly what crime it is that I am serving eight and a half years for.'

'But this was rectified in your appeal, I believe,' he retorted.

'But the original sentence was judged on *dama zhi*.'

'I am sorry but we are not here today to discuss this. If you have any legal problems, I suggest you hire a lawyer,' he said, trying to dump the subject.

'But lawyers are not allowed in the jail to discuss criminal cases. Don't you know that?'

'Well, you can write to a lawyer.'

I couldn't believe this conversation. The guy didn't have a clue about what went on in the jail, and he wasn't interested either. I realised that I was getting nowhere, and that if we went on in the same vein I'd lose my temper.

'I would like to return to the subject of your fine,' he continued. 'Seeing as you don't have the money to pay, would you agree to the court selling your gold jewellery to help raise part of the sum owed?'

I looked at him in total disbelief. 'Let me get this right. You are saying that if I don't pay you, you are going to flog our wedding rings to raise the cash?'

'No, only if you cannot pay, this is an option,' replied Shen, looking tired.

'I want to make it 100 per cent clear that this will never be an option. These rings are of great sentimental value. Do you have that in China? And no money in the world can ever replace them. So I want them back.'

'So you are refusing to pay?'

'No, but –'

'When you are ready you can notify us through you consul. You can have your watches now. And once you have paid, we will return the rest.'

The watches were worth nothing.

Scarleg

Colourless green ideas sleep furiously.

Professor Noam Chomsky (1928–)

THE summer of '94 was punctuated by the World Cup, and because Cai also loved football we were able to watch nearly all of it. Mark watched it from the hospital, where he was laid up with TB. He was kept there for nearly two months, and missed the visit to the brigade of our consul, Jackie Barlow, who had replaced Jim Short the year before and was proving to have a much more sympathetic ear than her predecessor.

Other than saying that she'd been there, I couldn't see what purpose the visit served, however. Before she arrived, the prisoners from One Brigade stopped wórking outside and hid everything away in the shed. Then lads from the garden unit in Five Brigade came round with their carts and put out potted flowers all along the intended route right up to our landing and all around our sheep-pen. Next came the removal of name-cards from the cell doors, and in the blink of an eye we lost twenty-three prisoners. Then the merit-point blackboard disappeared. All prisoners who usually worked outside also vanished, and we were told to stay in our pen. Surrounded by an army of officers from various departments, Miss Barlow was allowed to see our cells and that was it. It must have been like going into a forest where they'd hidden all the trees. That's why we called them 'sanitised tours'.

Zhou Wanjia finally went home on 16 September 1994. The double-dealing little rat had been so far up Benny's arse you couldn't even see him. He had been Benny's 'batman', entrusted with the most delicate of duties. Not only did Zhou clean the office, he cleaned Benny's uniform, polished his buttons, washed his civilian clothes (including his underpants and socks), polished his shoes, washed his bath flannel, cleaned his bowl, washed his eating utensils, made his tea, emptied his ashtray and wiped his spit up off the floor. Zhou Li, or Julie as we called her, was the female brigade accountant and suspected of having an adulterous affair with the 'good man' himself. That was backed up by the fact that Zhou Wanjia had been seen on numerous occasions washing her French knickers. A job that made him the envy of many. Zhou was always ready to please and prove that he loved his captain.

Zhou would invent errands when there were none; I'd seen him on countless occasions looking out of the window waiting for Benny to return, then when he could hear him coming up the last flight of stairs, he would throw some rubbish on the floor and start picking it up so that when Benny turned the corner, Zhou was busy. Whenever Benny was required to write a report to his superiors, it was Zhou who wrote it. Benny openly sympathised with Zhou's case, saying that his wife had been 'no better than a whore' and that she 'deserved to be beaten up'.

He was such an obedient and valuable assistant that we all wondered if Zhou Wanjia would ever be released. How could he be replaced? But, as if to illustrate his immeasurable qualities as a sycophant, when he did go after getting a one-year reduction, he was replaced not by one but by two prisoners. One of them was a young man called Wang Jun who had been spotted as a model arse-licker. The other was a half-wit from Zhengzhou in Henan Province whose only qualification was blind obedience. Henan, as we soon called him, dealt with cleaning the floor, the spittoon, the washing of clothes and polishing of shoes, while Wang Jun handled the making of tea and the report-writing.

Wang and Henan had arrived in a big batch of new prisoners in the spring. Wang was the star pupil in the induction course and was rewarded with the post of 'small-table leader', which meant that it was his responsibility to teach the others. He would line his students up on their little stools and ask each in turn to recite verbatim the fifty-eight rules. If a prisoner failed, he was made to slap himself across the face. If Wang didn't think he'd done it hard enough, he had to do it again until Wang was satisfied.

Round about the same time, another new group of relocation prisoners arrived. I had always considered our landing to be just one step up from a mental institution, but when this bunch turned up, I really started to wonder. To describe Three Middle Brigade at that time as being a cross between *One Flew Over the Cuckoo's Nest* and Solzhenitsyn's *First Circle* wouldn't be far off the mark. One of the new arrivals, a man by the name of Dao Guolang, had actually just come from a hospital for the criminally insane. He was about fifty years old, short and with the vestiges of peasant stockiness. His face looked like a relief map of the Himalayas.

Dao's story was one cluttered with misfortune. In his little house out in the countryside, he had woken from a drunken sleep one night to find strangers attacking his wife and children. In a bid to protect his family, he took up a kitchen knife and fought off the attackers. Unfortunately, in the ensuing mêlée, one of the aggressors was mortally wounded and later died in hospital. In the court case that followed, Dao was sentenced to life imprisonment. The shock of such a severe punishment sent him over the edge. He was supposedly sane now but that didn't stop him talking to himself and swiping at imaginary flies. When I met him, he had just finished serving fifteen years in the Chinese equivalent of Broadmoor. Things could only get better for Dao; he only had fifteen years in Tilan Qiao to go.

Dao's friend Liu Gonghua hadn't fared much better. He had been a melon seller and had accidentally killed a customer with his machete. The fact that the customer had tried to steal Liu's takings had been taken into consideration, and he was still given thirty years. A very gentle man, he'd spent eighteen years on a prison farm and in a factory making ball-bearings. He was now close to sixty and hadn't had a sniff of a reduction yet.

The third member of this little band was Gappy. I never found out his real name. He was also short, about forty and with spiky hair. Despite a huge space between his front teeth, he was always smiling. He looked as if he'd just jumped out of a cave in *The Lord of the Rings* where he'd been forging swords for warring dwarves. Gappy had been jailed for fifteen years for knowing and being in the same room as a man who'd accidentally killed another in a fight. I couldn't work out how the hell he remained so happy.

The fourth musketeer was Scarleg. I called him that because his legs were covered in sores and scars from the mosquito bites that he had incessantly scratched away at. About thirty, he was chubby and shuffled around as if he'd been born with shackles on. Scarleg was doing ten years for thieving scrap iron from a government-owned factory. One and a half bricks short of a load, he had a dent the size of an orange in his head, apparently an injury sustained when he fell off the roof of a five-storey building, probably a factory. It was so big, you could actually lose your fist in it. A master at feigning ignorance, an expert at being in the wrong place at the wrong time, perfect at being late and talented at clumsiness, he always had a glimmer of a grin floating over his lips which made you wonder if it was for real or not. He was clearly another no-reduction con.

That summer Cai was sent down for yet another period of re-education and we were put in the capable hands of a wife-murderer named Wei Ji. I had known him for two years already and although we didn't talk much we sort of respected each other. Wei Ji had the captain's ear, he had influence and whatever he heard would find its way back to Benny. Webster immediately moved in to make him his friend and to use him as a conduit for the lies and misinformation he fabricated about the rest of us in his quest to be considered the best reforming foreigner and gain more merit points than the rest of us. He used every opportunity to plant these rotten seeds in Wei Ji's mind and knew full well they would sprout.

*

The guards had some time ago given up patrolling the landing at night, and had got the prisoners to organise it themselves. Two chosen prisoners took it in turns to pace up and down, looking in each cell for violations like attempted suicide, buggery, masturbation or eating. Anything other than sleeping was to be recorded in a book and reported to the captain the following morning.

In the dim light of the thirty-watt bulbs positioned outside every tenth cell, I used my magnifying glass to read until eleven every night. The way I saw it, my cell was my space and not to be invaded. I was reported, of course, and told to change my habits and go to sleep at nine o'clock like everybody else. This I refused to do. They tried to stop me by removing the bulbs, but the night lights were a prison safety regulation and I soon got them put back in.

For some reason they had given Scarleg the chance to gain a few merit points by doing night patrol. They matched him up with a character whom Werner had nicknamed Grumpy. He'd told us that he was doing nine years for duplicating 'yellow movies' or porn videos, but it turned out that he was actually doing twelve for raping his ten-year-old daughter. When someone like Webster caught in possession of seven kilos of hash gets a longer sentence than a incestuous child rapist, you had to wonder how the courts worked out these sentences.

Anyway, on duty one night at about two-thirty, Scarleg found Grumpy asleep and, try as he might, he just could not wake him. He was becoming more and more nervous about being left alone in the dark and didn't know what to do. After about ten minutes, having run out of ideas, Scarleg picked up a wooden stool and hit Grumpy over the head with it. Grumpy didn't wake up. Instead he slumped to the floor with a four-inch gash above his eyebrow oozing blood.

Scarleg was certain he'd killed him and knew that if he was convicted for murder he would without doubt get the death penalty. In sheer panic, he ripped the cover off a nearby electric socket and tried to stuff his fingers into the live wires in a desperate attempt to take his own life. What he didn't realise was that the circuitry of the jail ran at a reduced current; after the initial trickle of juice ran up his arm, he gave it up as a bad idea and proceeded to run around the landing like a man tormented by a swarm of bees. Most of Scarleg's performance had been observed by at least three prisoners who had been woken up by the noise, and it was they who sounded the alarm.

After ten stitches, Grumpy was fine apart from a constant dazed look on his face. Scarleg lasted two more weeks before being sent away on a convict train to some distant destination in the gulag system. It was doubtful if he would ever return home or ever see his family again.

*

On 28 October we were herded over to the officers' dining-room, above the kitchen. We sat in rows on our little stools in front of a line of officers and judges. I waited again to be told that our ordeal was over. What was the use of keeping us in jail any longer? I had done a third of my sentence and had received no disciplinary action, and with Mark on his way out, prepared to spill the beans on this so-called penal system, it was in their best interests to get us all the hell out of there before there was an international outcry.

We sat through a performance where Chinese prisoners' names were called out in groups according to which meritorious award they'd earned, and what reduction they'd got. That day, out of nearly three hundred prisoners, just twenty-five lucky contestants succeeded in reducing their sentence by a total of twenty-one years and eight months, an average of twenty-six days per prisoner. Big deal.

Mark waited with bated breath but nothing happened. We all felt dejected. Then, suddenly, just as they were wrapping up proceedings, an officer called Mark out, and he disappeared through the back door. When the rest of us returned to the landing, he was leaving the building. He did manage to tell us, though, that Jin Mouling had taken him apart in Benny's office, searching everything in his luggage with a fine-tooth comb. He had eventually spotted the indentations of a document hidden in the cover of a magazine. Not readily apparent to the untrained eye, it was miraculously discovered by the ever vigilant (I don't think so) Captain Jin. Someone had grassed him up. Jin threatened to take away Mark's reduction for this outrageous breach of discipline and it had looked for a while as if he was serious and indeed capable of doing so. Thankfully, he wasn't.

Mark had been given a reduction of five months, which we eventually found out was as good as could be expected on a four-year sentence. Usually a 'short sentence' like Mark's didn't get a single day knocked off. It was considered by most of the Chinese to be better to receive a five-year sentence than a four, because then there was the possibility of a reduction.

The reduction system was never explained to us. It was probably an official secret. All we were ever told was: 'Work hard in your reform, and you can be released after half sentence.' It took me three years to realise what that really meant. 'After half sentence' didn't mean *at* half sentence. If they let you go two hours before your time was up, it would still be *after* half sentence, wouldn't it? So where did it leave us? There was no system for us, and as all our attempts to seek justice fizzled out, the light at the end of the tunnel did the same.

It was depressing, but that feeling came around like a woman's menstrual cycle. I would feel fine for three weeks, steadily rising to a day or two when I would feel quite excitable. Then suddenly I would find myself in what I called 'the valley of death'. That lasted barely two days, whereafter I became almost uncontrollably lustful for three or four days.

Webster was running out of ideas, but as part of his on-going plan to be such a nuisance that the prison would be dying to get rid of him, at the end of '94 he decided to pretend he was going mad. With fifteen years hanging over his head, I couldn't blame him for trying every angle to get out, but to use the rest of us in his schemes like stepping-stones was well out of order.

After constant badgering, he'd finally got what he wanted when they allowed him to become the trustee of the boiler and washroom. That gave him all the authority and access he needed to conduct his clandestine activities and gain merit points at the same time.

On 3 March 1995, a meeting had been held where Benny announced that we would no longer be permitted to empty our own shit buckets, because apparently we were using it as a way to get extra exercise. Who could possibly have told him that? The next item on the agenda was the *China Daily*. We were told that we had to read it first and then give it to Webster. Before, he had been given it first so as to make him feel important, but he had seen us cutting out different articles and got paranoid that we were gaining some advantage over him. It was now prohibited to cut clippings, and all papers were to be returned to the captain for inspection.

The last item concerned the use of hot water in the washroom. Not every landing had a boiler-room at the back. In fact, some, like One Brigade, didn't have one at all. The boiler was fuelled down a long pipe by excess steam from the huge rice cookers in the kitchen, and it took an hour and a half to boil 120 gallons of foul-smelling, chlorinated Huang Pu river water so as to make it potable. It was then poured into three insulated forty-five-gallon drums on wheels with a tap on the end. One drum was placed at the end of the landing and, with permission, a prisoner could go and fill his tin mug. Since we had no one to answer to, we went as often as we liked, filling the thermos flasks we'd bought from the prison shop. We steeped tea and noodles in that still chemically redolent fluid, and filled our hot-water bottles on bitterly cold nights.

At the end of every day there was usually at least one tank left over and it was with that surplus that we foreigners and the number 1 and his cronies used to wash with. The rest of the prisoners were sent to the prison showers once a week, a place we all refused to go to. They were like the gas chambers in a Nazi death camp, and with the Chinese prisoners pissing all over your legs and pushing and shoving so as to get under the shower heads, it was a nightmare. Moreover, you had only thirty seconds to wet yourself and a minute and a half to wash the soap off. If you fucked up, you walked out covered in soap. The place stank of piss, was covered in some greasy slime and was dirty beyond belief.

Using the excuse that we exercised every morning, we eventually won the right to wash every day in the boiler-room. One bucket of water and a jug was all that was needed – one jugful to get wet, and the rest to wash off the soap after a good scrub with a flannel. Every morning after an hour of press-ups, sit-ups and running on the spot, we'd troop down to the boiler-room for our wash.

But that area had become Webster's patch, and he wanted us out. Wei Ji reported that we were using drinking water to wash with and, taking his word for it, Benny decided that we were not allowed to take any hot water to wash with. There was no arguing, but we were never going to go back to 'piss parade' and continued to go down to the boiler-room every day to wash in cold water, which we heated up a little with the water from our flasks. Webster's plan hadn't worked and he was fuming.

It was this sort of petty shit that drove you up the wall – not necessarily because of what was being taken away, but because someone had spent the time and effort to make it happen. But it was no use protesting; it was better just to ignore it. However, the winter and spring of '95 turned into a catalogue of disputes and argy-bargy with Wei Ji and his new band of enforcers with Webster scuttling about behind the scenes starting bush fires.

In February, Three Middle Brigade had got a contract to do a job for an outside textile firm. Somebody had informed the officers that Larry and I were out to expose the prison for producing goods for export, so they erected screens to work behind and furtively moved cartons around with cloth draped over them to hide the labels. You couldn't help but take notice.

The first project they embarked on was the manufacture of little green cloth fishing stools for export to Britain. After that, they got a job producing head-rest covers for a Shanghai taxi firm.

Apart from ten or so expert repair men, the rest of our brigade worked ten or twelve hours a day. Benny and his boys were making money at last and he soon came to work on a brand new scooter. All this put a lot of pressure on us. The Chinese, apart from their usual insults like *na lu* ('foreign prick'), started calling us lazy again, and after a few weeks it was really pissing us off.

Soon there were rumours that Webster might actually be on his way to a reduction. We couldn't believe it. It was an outrageous proposition that the most badly behaved prisoner in the entire jail had pulled the wool over the guards' eyes. And, even if he hadn't, they were going to use him to make us go begging to join in the productive labour.

The five of us in the sheep-pen had a meeting to discuss the implications of what was going on and what we could do to turn the tide. We decided that we were quite willing to spend, at most, half the day involved in what the jail termed 'public benefit labour', but we were not going to be used as slaves to line the pockets of racist prison guards or unscrupulous, greedy businessmen on the outside while being blackmailed with 'work hard or you don't get a reduction' and be paid 25p a week and an extra stuffed bun as a bonus for the effort. No way.

We had to have enough time to continue our studies. We were not going to get a job back in the west by being a thread trimmer or an 'experienced umbrella repairman' or 'mop-head maker', were we? We decided to write a group report, in which we volunteered to look after the hygiene on Three Middle Landing and see to the carrying of extra monthly food items up from the ground floor. This way, no one could say we were refusing to work. In order to stop Benny claiming ignorance, we decided to write five copies. One was to go to Benny, one to Wang Da (the brigade leader), one to Captain Jin, one to the warden and one was to be kept and read out in the presence of our consuls. To avoid it being misplaced or messed about with and altered in translation, I wrote it in Chinese and each copy was hand-delivered.

Fast Eddie, the Laughing Horse

I am a Greek to a Greek, and a Roman to a Roman.

St Paul of Tarsus (c.AD3 – c.68)

THE appointment of Captain Ma as the leading captain of the foreign unit signalled a big change in the jail's approach to us. Ma Duizhang actually believed that he could help the prisoners. Most remarkably, he wasn't racist.

Captain Ma was a quite a big guy with a round face and chubby red cheeks. He was about forty-five and wore metal-framed spectacles that made his eyes look porcine. Nevertheless, they were happy eyes. He had one of those soft-grained high-pitched voices and was always laughing in loud bellowing tones. He listened to our grievances and actually took them seriously. He took action and got results. He even told the Chinese prisoners to get off our backs.

His name was Ma, which as well as being a surname, also means 'horse' or 'pony', so he became Eddie the Laughing Horse. Within weeks he was renamed Fast Eddie the Laughing Horse when he single-handedly sorted out all our mail problems. Letters started leaving the prison just three or four days after being handed over, and incoming mail was miraculously arriving in twelve days from Europe. The guy was too good to be true. But Eddie had lots more plans in store for us.

His first move was to appoint me the foreign unit number 1. That was easier said than done, however, and Eddie got his first taste of European obstinacy. I refused. We had decided a long time back that there would be no communist structure within our group. We had to be equal. None of us apart from Webster was willing to do the job, but that was totally out of the question. After lengthy discussions it was eventually agreed that I would take on the job only in order to prevent the alternative. I agreed to be a messenger and no more.

In the spring of that year Larry was beaten up by the Chinese for accusing Wei Ji of accepting Webster's coffee in exchange for merit points. Werner got a dollop of Webster's phlegm in the face and Dieter had been threatened with a mop. They had had enough and complained to their consul. Werner tried to give his consul a list of Webster's violence but it was not permitted and he was told to write a self-criticism and deducted one point. Larry had two points deducted.

Eddie had been going on about teaching us the new prison law as a substitute for the political studies that Chinese received for months, but nothing had come of it and I had put the idea to the back of my mind. I was pretty sure that they'd never try to teach us Chinese politics, as that would have been sure to bring on a torrent of complaints and letters to consuls. When I realised that he was serious, I immediately told him that it wouldn't go down too well. But he insisted, saying that it would be a massive plus for our reduction chances. We considered it to be nothing more than a ruse to get us all into line. We were a disgrace to the Chinese prison system, a loose nut rolling around in the engine, and they'd finally had enough. The mechanism had been put into motion and we were going to have prison law study classes whether we liked it or not.

We began our first class on 21 August. I was given the duty of handing out the English translation of the law and told to inform everybody, including Webster, of the time and place of the class. Eddie wanted to bring Webster back into the fold. He wanted us all to be friends again, because a unit performance earned more credit than an individual effort – which was just another way to get prisoners to police themselves with everyone on the lookout for others' mistakes.

The idea of studying prison law was not a very appetising one but at least it would provide an insight into the Chinese mind – and, as Voltaire said, 'If we do not find anything pleasant, at least we will find something new.'

The first lesson began with 'Karl Marx said that labour purifies the soul'. Oh, shit, what the hell are we doing here? However, it turned out to be not only very interesting but also, thanks to Jin Feng's translation mistakes, extremely amusing too. Every week, on the chosen day at two o'clock in the afternoon, we would all gather and sit around one of the large vacant tables in the Chinese area. Eddie would sit in the middle of us with Jin Feng; and, with a Nescafé jar full of green tea gripped tightly in his right hand, Eddie would proceed to explain the law, article by article.

He read each article from the Chinese version and then, referring to a hand-book, explained the true meaning behind the printed words. We soon realised that the handbook interpreted everything completely differently to the way we read it. On the surface, to an outsider, it seemed to be a fair and just law aimed at protecting the prisoners' rights. In actual fact, it protected the system and the officers and their right to administer punishment arbitrarily. For example:

'Article 7. The criminal's dignity shall not be humiliated, their personal safety, legal property and the rights to defence, appeal, charge and accuse as well as other rights which are not deprived or limited according to law shall be inviolable.

'The criminals must strictly abide by laws, regulations, prison rules and disciplines, obey the administration, accept the education and participate in labour.'

What this actually meant was that as long as a prisoner conforms to the demands of the second paragraph, he can enjoy the luxuries of the first. That is, of course, if you haven't had your rights already taken away from you by the courts in the first place, or if there isn't another law previously in effect that prohibits the extension of such rights. Which brings us to Article 5, which states:

'The activities on administering the prisons, executing punishment, educating and reforming the criminals, which conducted according to law by the officers of prisons, are protected by law.'

What that means is that the guards already have a law relating to the treatment of criminals (most likely with another little explanatory handbook) and that law is protected.

Jin Feng would rattle on about 'procreator-raitors' and 'discipline champagnes', saying, 'He says that ladders must not be left by the walls,' and, 'The prison has walls around it so as to protect the inmates from the public, who may feel like getting their own back on the criminals who stole from them or killed their family members.'

We were told that the prisoners had the right to have rights if (and only if) they obeyed the captains. If the inmate disobeyed, he lost that right to have rights. With regard to work, prisoners were only supposed to work eight hours a day, but if there were special circumstances, such as seasonal production, the prison was allowed to adjust the total amount of hours worked in one day. Seasonal production did not necessarily refer to picking apples or harvesting rice; it was used as an excuse for any type of work.

After each lesson we were given three days to write out each Article in full and explain its meaning and application to 'the real situation'. This was to suffice as a *sixiang huibao* ('thinking report'). Each week we covered an average of six articles and thus it took us a number of months to get to the two badly translated articles that embodied the reform system, Articles 57 and 58.

> Article 57: The prison may give commendation, material award or record meritorious service to the criminals if they are under one of the following circumstances:
> 1. to observe the prison rules and discipline, to study hard, to actively take part in labour and to plead guilt;
> 2. to prevent committing illegal or criminal activities;
> 3. to over-fulfil production tasks;
> 4. to make achievements in economising the raw and processed materials or in protecting the public property;
> 5. to make some progress in technical evolution aspects or disseminating production techniques aspect;
> 6. to make a certain contribution for preventing or eliminating disaster accidents; or
> 7. to make other contribution for state and society.
> The prison may, according to the stipulations, allow the criminals to leave the prison for meeting their family members if they have conducted one of matters listed in the preceding paragraph and already served over one half, always kept good records during serving their sentences and are unlikely to endanger the society outside the prison.
>
> Article 58: The prison may make the warning, the record of the demerit or the confinement to the criminals if the criminals commit one of the behaviours designed to disturb the prison rules:
> 1. to gather a crowd to destroy the prison order;

2. to insult or beat up the officers;

3. to bully and oppress other criminals;

4. to steal, gamble, beat up or to pick a quarrel for making trouble;

5. to refuse to participate in labour with labour capacity or to be slack in work;

6. to be injured or disabled by self for avoiding labour;

7. to be intentional for violating the production operating rule in labour or destroying the productive tools; or

8. to commit other activities in violating the prison rules and discipline.

The confinement to be imposed on the criminals shall be limited within seven to fifteen days according to the preceding paragraph. If the criminal's behaviour mentioned in the above first paragraph constitutes a crime, the crime shall be investigated for the criminal responsibility during serving their sentences.

Of particular importance to me was part 1 of Article 57: 'To observe the prison rules and discipline, to study hard, to actively take part in labour and to plead guilt.' As long as a prisoner fulfilled these four 'obligations', he or she would be eligible for reduction. But that was like saying if you buy a lottery ticket you're eligible to win a million. There was nothing sure.

On 10 November we were given a test. We were all expected to achieve good results and it was almost compulsory to cheat in order to make sure that our captain maintained 'face'. The questions had been leaked to us a week in advance, ample time in which to write out a bundle of crib notes which we stashed up our sleeves. The Chinese had tests and examinations regularly and cheated blatantly. However, there was the odd occasion when the Education Department sent a group of special examination officers around unannounced. These guys would pick on a brigade and proceed to call prisoners out at random to answer questions on the 'big fifty-eight' rules and regs. If they performed poorly, it could result in a 'Hundred Days Rules and Regulation Campaign' where every minute of spare time was employed in studying the rules and sitting tests.

Campaigns were the lifeblood of reform. Prisoners would spend days on end preparing elaborate blackboards which promoted good behaviour and extolled the benefits of strict discipline. These were then placed at the entrance to the unit, so that any visitors could see immediately the sincerity of the prisoners of that particular brigade. When the Chinese had their visit, a blackboard was taken along to the visiting hall with all the merit points chalked up on it, so that the families could chart their loved ones' progress. There was no escape from it all.

*

Remarkably, it had been one of the most peaceful periods since we'd arrived. The partial re-integration of Webster into the group did seem to have had a calming influence on him, but that didn't signify that he had been born again by any means. When Wei Ji went home on 29 November, however, we all breathed a sigh of relief and our situation really did start to improve.

The new number 1 was a guy called Chen Ronghuo, who was doing twelve years for selling three tons of fake monosodium glutamate. He was the most humane of all our number 1s. His main back-ups, though, were Wang Jun and Henan, who thought they were now really big bananas and started to take liberties.

As it happened, Eddie and I were getting on quite well, especially since he had found out that I had an interest in art. He loved paintings, and pushed me to branch out and use oils, and to do more and more. Previously, I'd had a lot of difficulty acquiring the things I needed, often having to raid the bins in search of a brush or some paper. After seeing what I could do, Eddie began supplying me with whatever I wanted. I used a little book of Sisley's paintings that my mother had sent as a course book, and over a period of a year copied or adapted nearly every one.

We soon had an arrangement whereby he took every second picture home to his apartment in the prison officers' housing project in exchange for keeping me supplied with canvas, brushes and paint. It was a wonderful escape for me. After a morning of studying Chinese, I would disappear down the leafy lanes of Louvenciennes and stroll over the bridge at Moret-sur-Loing. I met the people and nodded a polite *bonjour*. It was a breath of fresh air, soothing my nerves and occupying my mind completely.

It wasn't long before I was asked to paint a huge picture of the newly built *Dong fang Minzhu ta*, the Oriental Pearl Tower, which had become the symbol of Shanghai's 'Opening and Reform' policy. They intended to hang the picture at the entrance to our brigade so that everybody would know Eight Brigade supported the Deng Xiaoping theory of 'Development and Opening to the Outside World'. For that project Eddie pulled out all the stops and in one fell swoop supplied me with enough gear to last five years. I estimated that if I'd wanted to buy the same in Britain it would have set me back at least four hundred pounds.

With a more relaxed feeling flowing through the landing, all sorts of changes started to take place. In the previous eighteen months, I had calculated that the Chinese had watched 367 movies on video. The foreign unit had been allowed to watch two. That was all about to change. The video pirates were flooding China with hundreds of thousands of copied tapes, many of which had been filmed in US cinemas and hurriedly made suitable for the Chinese audience with the addition of handwritten subtitles. The quality didn't matter – it gave the average man in the street (or in jail, for that matter) the opportunity to see recently released blockbusters at a fraction of the cost of a cinema ticket. Tapes would circulate through dozens of households, each of whom would put on special video nights for friends and neighbours. The distributors, of course, were going nuts at this blatant infringement of copyright law, but I couldn't see what they were moaning about – it was free advertising, for God's sake. Hollywood was reaching every hole and corner of China, turning the people on and creating the demand for more American movies that the cinemas themselves. We were soon watching movies in Tilan Qiao that had yet to be released in London. We saw *The Mask*, *Leon*, *Batman*, *The Shawshank Redemption* and *Mad Dogs and Englishmen* months before anyone at home had even heard of them.

*

By the time Mum and Dad made their third visit to see me on 15 December, ShaSha had found herself dramatically better accommodation thanks to her network of new friends, and was living in a four-room flat with a balcony in a new development on the outskirts of Shanghai. The unattractive-sounding Nanfang Xincun ('north area new village') was only fifteen minutes' walk from the last stop on the newly completed underground system, which made getting into town comparatively easy.

Cleaning jobs were about all that seemed to be available for a woman closer to forty than thirty, but it was better than nothing and passed the time and put her in contact with a lot of new people. Again, through friends, and thanks to her growing skills in English, ShaSha found a job with an advertising firm. At last she felt as if things might be going her way.

Back in Tilan Qiao, things were still going well with Eddie. It was as if he actually cared not only about prisoners' reform but also about how he was seen as a representative of his government. He wanted to show us that results could be achieved not by adhering to the letter of the law but by keeping within the spirit of the law. It became clear after a while, though, that there was nothing much more Eddie could do for us, but that didn't stop him from taking us on a Christmas shopping trip.

Unfortunately, we were not set for a stroll down Nanjing Lu, Shanghai's most famous commercial street. Instead, we were herded over to the Great Hall of the Prisoner, to the visiting-hall shop. Situated on the lower level was a large hall in which the family members waited to see their criminal relatives, and it was there that the jail ran a small shop for parents and wives to buy their men a few goodies and reduce the burden of carrying it all from home.

For some reason, ShaSha was not permitted to use the visitors' shop and instead she had to trudge around, clambering on buses and tube trains with heavy bags, only to have a swine like Jin Mouling tell her after she'd arrived at the jail that it was not permitted to give me butter or cheese because there wasn't a fridge in our brigade. It didn't seem to matter that in winter the temperature of our landing was four degrees colder than the interior of any fridge.

Anyway, Eddie wanted us to enjoy Christmas, and he allowed us to buy whatever we wanted. It was the first time in over four years that I had been in a shop. It didn't matter that I didn't have any money; it was thrilling to be able to choose things, point at things and run up a bill. Tins of smoked mackerel and fried dace in black bean sauce were favourites of mine, as were tins of tomato purée which I could use to make sauces and tasty accompaniments to the ubiquitous stodgy boiled rice.

And Where Do You Go To, My Lovely?

I bend and I break not.

Jean de la Fontaine (1621–95)

OVER Christmas we were lucky to see a few good movies like *Batman II* and *Doppelganger*, and even got to see a soft-core flick which had somehow slipped through the system. I was told by Chen, the number 1, that the main opposition the Chinese government had to porn was the use of Chinese actresses. It was okay to have foreign women cavorting around naked and getting laid, but they didn't like to see their own women at it on screen. They were a possessive bunch, I knew that from experience. Because Sharapet was officially Chinese, they were jealous that she should choose a foreigner as her husband, but when they found out she was Uighur, they were angry because I had chosen a minority woman and found her more attractive than a Han.

It seemed quite okay for all the young Chinese I spoke to to dream that they could one day bed a foreign woman with huge breasts and blonde hair. Their infatuation with the west didn't stop there; when talking about reincarnation one day, one prisoner expressed his desire to be reborn an American, and if that wasn't possible, a fruit bat would do.

By February things were hotting up in the brigade's workshop. A new contract had come in and it was much bigger than anything they'd ever had before. The Chinese and Webster were working flat out, up to fourteen hours a day, seven days a week, making little printed aprons. Pressure was coming at us from all angles to volunteer, and it wasn't long before Eddie started introducing the subject into the conversation, saying how it would improve our chances of a reduction if we were to join in and cut off a few thread-ends. I got the impression that maybe all the months of nice Eddie, good Eddie, efficient Eddie, fast Eddie were nothing but an attempt to soften us up in preparation for this offensive.

Dieter and I explained the situation to him in simple terms: 'There is no benefit in us participating in this sort of labour. We study, which is what we were told to do when we came here.'

'But it will only be for a few months,' Eddie pleaded.

'No. But don't get us wrong – we are not refusing to work. We have already handed in a proposal for suitable work for us to do, which would be sufficient for us to fulfil our obligations.'

Eddie stopped his diatribe and backed off. But not for long.

By chance we discovered that the aprons were destined for Japan and that they carried the label 'Pierre Balmain, Paris'. We all knew the label thanks to the lyric of the '60s chart-topper 'Where Do You Go To, My Lovely?' by Peter Sarsted, and figured that Tilan Qiao was a long way from Paris, and that the 25p these prisoners were receiving a week was a long way from the fifty bucks recommended retail price that would be asked in Japan. The knowledge gave us all the reason we needed morally to tell Eddie where to go, so when he came back for another sortie

I told him that it was not only a waste of our time, but that it was a matter of social conscience and political belief.

Eddie couldn't understand what the hell I was talking about. To him, it was a matter of getting us to work and nothing more. Another week went by and we hoped that the work would simply dry up, but it didn't, and neither did Eddie. He was soon pestering me again, albeit in friendly fashion, about the advantages and disadvantages of participating in productive labour. But I remained firm. I told him we had given as much as we were going to, and that we as a group had made a fair offer.

Finally it came down to plain and simple blackmail, something the Chinese were quite good at. 'Work and you have a chance of a reduction. Refuse and you have no chance. Webster is working hard every day and will be rewarded. How would it be possible for me to recommend the rest of you alongside him when you have not fulfilled your obligations under Articles 7, 57 and 69 of the new prison law?'

It couldn't get much plainer than that, but why the hell hadn't he said so in the first place? As the group leader I had to go back to the others and explain that we were now not only being pressurised into working on goods for export under slave-labour conditions, but that we were being threatened with the loss of a reduction if we didn't comply. After much discussion, Dieter, Werner and I agreed that continuing to refuse was too great of a risk to take. We were nearing half sentence and every attempt at seeking justice had ended in failure. It looked more and more likely that there was no other way left to get out of the place other than by relying on a reduction. I was certainly not into martyring myself for the sake of a few months' snipping threads – that was a fool's game. I wanted to go home, and if there was a chance of an early release, I wanted it. If I wanted to make a protest about the state of human rights in Chinese prisons, I could do a hell of a better job on the outside. We had been shouting at the top of our voices for the last four years and no one had heard us, so what was the point in languishing in jail cutting off our noses to spite our faces?

It was a turning point. The decision was made. Whether the authorities would live up to their word was another thing, but at least we were going to play the game. The Germans and I agreed to start the following Monday afternoon. We would keep the mornings free for study, do no overtime and rest on Sundays. Larry absolutely refused to have anything to do with it. He felt that after spending all those months in YMX there was nothing he could do that would get him back on the right track in the eyes of the authorities and, as it turned out, he was right. Dominic was due to go home on 10 March and couldn't give a monkey's. He knew he wasn't going to get any reduction, so he continued to play his guitar.

So, on 4 March, we started work. We sat in a circle on our stools, with a bundle of newly manufactured pink aprons in front of us. It was our task to snip off the thread-ends with little scissors. I put my Walkman on full blast and listened to my Beastie Boys and Hole tapes, closing my mind to the world and what I was doing.

Time passed, and Dominic's release was imminent. I was pretty sure that Jackie Barlow, our consul, would see him off at the airport, so I asked him to inform her about everything that had happened and the fact that we were now being bludgeoned into servitude.

About a week after his departure, a meeting was called, and the most irate of Laughing Horses, looking as if the blood was going to spurt from every pore in his face, announced we were being taken off the job. Then he almost screamed, 'I'm not afraid of your consulates and embassies. This prison isn't afraid of anybody. You can tell whatever you want to whoever you want. This is China, we do not listen to anybody!'

The meeting was closed and Eddie stormed off around the corner. We all looked at each other open-mouthed in mock horror. 'If they're not afraid, why have we been taken off the job?' I asked.

While we got over the withdrawal symptoms of the loss of productive labour, Eddie went to work setting things to rights. He dug out the proposal we had given him all those months ago and, after reading through it, approached his superiors for the necessary go-ahead. He asked me to draw up a work schedule, assigning each member of the group an area and a list of essential tasks that needed to be done on a daily basis. When he explained what he wanted, I thought he was off his head. I mean, there were four of us, and all we had to do was mop the floor, clean the windows, wipe the bars of the cells and dust the ceiling. Between us it could be done in an hour, but Eddie wanted it to look as if we were building the Great Wall.

I drew up an elaborate plan, with coloured drawings to indicate assigned areas, and sketched little figures doing the various tasks. He loved it and had it photocopied so he could put it in my records and show other officers how efficient the foreign unit had become. I got the feeling that he'd been sent to us to test his own abilities as an officer, and that our success was in fact his success. Within three days, we started work and every morning we'd make it look as if we were doing the most difficult job in the world. We scrubbed and cleaned every inch of the place, discovering corners that hadn't been touched since the prison had been built back in the good old days of colonial rule. I can say without a word of a lie that that landing was the cleanest prison landing in all of China, and a damn sight cleaner than the hospital.

Eddie was pleased – so pleased, in fact, that he brought the prison photographers around to capture us in action. We were filmed and included in the weekly prison TV broadcast. The foreigners had finally seen the light. Eddie had stopped all the negativity that had originally emanated from Benny's prejudiced mind, and all of a sudden we were heroes. Chinese prisoners now came up to us as we worked and congratulated us on our efforts. I couldn't believe how so little could have so great an effect.

There was one result of all this acclaim that Eddie had overlooked, however. Webster had done the same job for months on his own, and worked overtime in the workshop, and no one had said jack shit about it. Now, all of a sudden, the four of us were being heralded as some sort of success story, and getting the merit points on the board to prove it. He didn't like this at all.

Chen Ronghuo, the number 1, hated Webster. He saw through his act like the rest of us, and any reports that he made told the truth about what Webster was up to. Chen came from a wealthy family and didn't need jars of coffee or any other sort of bribe. It was also no use Webster running to Benny, because he was out of the game. Eddie was our leader, and he had also seen enough of the real Webster to feel disinclined to do him any favours.

Even though the prison law class was over, we continued writing ideological reports every month. None of us had a clue about what we should write and the Chinese wouldn't tell us – it was like some heavily guarded secret. There wasn't even any feedback from Eddie, and I wondered sometimes if he even bothered to read what we submitted. Dominic had experimented with different formats to see if he could raise a response. For example, one month he wrote something like:

'Dear Captain,

'This month I have been thinking about pandas. They are very nice creatures and I am happy that China is doing something to protect them. The panda is the symbol of China and everybody recognises it. Pandas live in Sichuan and eat bamboo. Some of them are taken away to zoos.'

Eddie said nothing, but I knew it wasn't the sort of thing the Chinese wrote. Very soon we were being asked to write quarterly summaries, and then half-yearly ones on top of that and even end-of-year reports. One day when the Chinese were busy writing their quarterlies, I spotted a discarded report. It turned out to be Wang Jun's draft. Now I could see for myself what they really wrote. When I finally translated it all, I was more than surprised.

'Honourable Captain,

'In the month ending 31 May, I followed the discipline and respected the captain. I did not make any mistakes. I recognised my status as a prisoner, acted in accordance with the four permanents and abided by the regulations. I listened to the captain's education, taking notes, and at all times I did my best to apply it to the real situation. I have done my job well, making sure to protect public property and replacing all tools as I found them. I have endeavoured to represent my true and sincere repentance and sorrow for my crime with good actions. I studied hard and embraced the reform wholeheartedly. As small-group leader, I have strengthened my consciousness of supervision and raised my perception of reform goals by entering the Five Standards competition. I have kept close to the government by way of monthly *sixiang huibao* and regular situation reports. At all times, I have upheld the moral order of the unit and protected the honour of the brigade. I acknowledge my guilt and accept that the sentence handed down to me was lenient, fair and correct. I have spent much time in introspection, and realise that the reasons I committed my crime were greediness and laziness. I was weak and easily led. I understand that I am here to atone for my previous perniciousness and learn how to become a law-abiding citizen and useful member of society. With hard work, I hope that I can achieve the earliest possible release, so that I may return to my family who are in need of the contribution that I can make.'

I would never have written a report like that in a million years. This was more than bending over backwards; it was more like cutting yourself open and laying bare your flesh for the communist vultures to piss on. Pride stood firmly in the way of me writing anything like that. It was nevertheless a fact that whatever you wanted had to be requested in a written report. If you felt ill, you wrote a report to ask for permission to lie down. If you wanted one of the tailors to shorten your trousers, you wrote a report.

We had reached the stage where it was clear that there was practically no chance of resolving the Damazhi problem and, if we continued with it, we would exclude ourselves from being eligible for a reduction. Even though I didn't believe that there was a system, I still couldn't afford to discount it totally. If the decision to release us did indeed come from outside the jail, it looked increasingly likely that we would still have to go through the motions of reform. Our firm stance attitude gradually faded. We were told that without constant repentance and expressions of deep remorse at every turn, the judges wouldn't even consider us for a reduction. Eddie's persuasive and convincing patter wore away at my reluctance to dive into the pool of reform, and soon I was beginning to believe that he was simply asking us to go along with the game just for show. It didn't matter if you weren't really sincere, he seemed to be saying, just do it so that he had something to present to the judges. The fact that we were foreigners was no excuse. The judges looked upon every application in the same way. There had to be clear evidence.

I spent many nights contemplating this. People were actually talking about a reduction for us. Although I still had difficulty getting my head around the idea that we could have any sort of influence on our own destiny, I also felt that I couldn't risk being wrong. Eddie was being as straight as he could be with us. After much deliberation, I felt I should at least show willingness.

It dawned on me later that I had been playing a game and sticking to a set of rules that nobody cared or even knew about. The shame and self-disgust I felt at what I saw to be weakness in giving in to the system was in fact a weakness in itself. How could I go on like that? The only principle you needed in jail was to get out as fast as possible. My family were waiting for me so I had a duty to do everything within my power to get released early.

The Chinese behaved the way they were expected to whether they believed it or not. They had no qualms about anything. If an officer told them to cry because it was the anniversary of Mao's death, they cried. It didn't matter if they were sad or not. They all knew it was fake, but it was what was expected.

It had taken nearly four years but the inevitable caught up with us, and, like driftwood in a flood, we lost our grip of the river-bank and were carried away into a torrent of reform.

*

I took Wang Jun's report and adapted it to my own situation. I included some of the new prison law and pushed the servility of it out into regions of absurdity. It became a game between us, to see how over-the-top we could be, testing the line between sincerity and sarcasm to breaking point. The remarkable thing in Tilan Qiao was that they all took it so bloody seriously. If you wrote this sort of stuff in a British jail, the guards would probably beat you up for taking the piss. Anyway, after a few goes, I settled on a format that went something like this:

'Honourable, dignified and generous Captain,

'I hereby submit my monthly ideological report for the month ending ——. This month I was ever-vigilant for weaknesses of character that might creep up on me from behind and force me into anti-reform behaviour. But, thanks to the captain's education, I have learnt how to control such impulses and enjoyed a month where I did nothing wrong at all. I observed the discipline and obeyed the regulations. I have kept close to the government. [This line was a real favourite among us and became an essential part of all our reports.] I have been able to realise that I am a prisoner and the captain is a captain. According to Article 57 of the new prison law, I have fulfilled all my obligations. According to Article 58 of the new prison law, I have not committed any violation. I have done nothing to harm my eligibility for a reduction, and through hard work I have enhanced that eligibility. I have worked hard, perhaps harder than ever, and studied until the lights went out at night, in order to better myself and to give myself a better chance on the outside, whenever that day will be. Through searching deep within myself, I have found that I am able to recognise my crime and accept it as the one that I confessed to. According to my verdict I was given leniency and, looking about, I am beginning to think that it is true. The sentence handed down to me was a good sentence, and one that I thoroughly deserved, in order for me to pay back my debt to all the people of China for the terrible, heinous and pernicious crimes that I committed. I hope that I can go home soon.

Yours, Prisoner 13498.'

I'll never know what effect reports like this had on my chances, but it was the only way I could find to do them and keep my sanity. Apart from the date, every report I wrote from then on was exactly the same, word for word.

The Path Is Clear

> But meanwhile it is flying, irretrievably time is flying.
> Virgil (70–19BC)

THE United Nations Anti-Drugs Day on 26 June was too good an opportunity to miss. Eddie made sure everybody knew how important it would be in providing us with material to show the judges, and he urged us to do a blackboard propaganda show. We decided we could never criticise hash or denounce its use; instead, we would aim to educate the Chinese about the dangers and risks of getting involved with smack and crack.

The simple fact was that they knew nothing about drugs. The Chinese prisoners we'd spoken to had all assumed we were in for heroin because they'd never heard about anything else. The officers didn't have a clue either, and that made me really angry. How could they judge me when they couldn't see the difference between a joint and a syringe? Even Eddie, a relatively clued-up guy, didn't know what the difference was. He said once that hash came from the cocaine tree and that it was made into opium which then made heroin. Others had told us about hash heroin, opium heroin and cocaine heroin. *Dupin* ('drugs') meant smack to them, end of story.

We were each given a blackboard to work on and in our own ways we set about trying to put the story straight. I drew a huge picture of a grass plant with a Rasta rainbow above it like a halo, and by the side of it I wrote a short article about heroin and the ways in which it differed from hash. Webster described the effects of various drugs, Werner and Dieter discussed how hash had become popularised in the west, and Larry did a lengthy piece on the lack of success the Chinese police had had in trying to stop the flow of heroin through their borders, and the fact that if they thought we were 'drug barons', they couldn't really have much of an idea about the real situation.

After three days of toil, each of us dragged his own board down the stairs where they were arranged up against the wall outside. Within minutes, a photographer and the video crew arrived to film us standing by our boards with Eddie proudly alongside. After five minutes, we took them all back indoors and stacked them up.

The next day we put them outside again for the warden to see and then we took them back inside again where they stayed until a few days later when the Chinese snatched them back and washed them all clean. I think about six people in all had seen what we had done, but not one of them had read a single word. We could have written that Mao Zetong had smoked opium and liked to screw young girls, and nobody would have known. However, there was now a clear record of our public repentance and condemnation of heroin abuse. This had to work in our favour, because no one could say we were not reforming now.

The next piece of spin-doctoring Eddie organised was a two-page feature in the prison newsletter about the foreign unit and the amazing transformation it had undergone in the short time since he'd taken over. Two reporters came to interview each of us separately but our replies were irrelevant because it was Eddie who told the reporters what to ask and even what to write.

The finished article was published over two issues, with photographs of us all working, studying, painting pictures, performing at cooling parties and standing with our UN Anti-Drug Day propaganda blackboards. The article set about rewriting the history of the unit. According to the new version, we had all once been very bad but, now, thanks to being educated by the cadres, we realised that reform was our only salvation. We could now acknowledge the perniciousness of our crimes and plead guilt. To prove our sincerity, we worked hard making our actions represent true remorse and repentance. We were pleading with the Chinese people to forgive us for those heinous crimes which had damaged their society so much. We were new men and we had turned over a new leaf.

Rumours abounded. According to all our trusted sources, it was certain that we would be released before very long. I believed because I wanted to believe, but, having been disappointed before, I was unwilling to put all my eggs in that basket. Even Eddie was beginning to hint at it, though, and when he was interviewed by a group of watchdogs who came from the Ministry of Justice in Beijing, he actually stated that it was certain we would all be getting a reduction before the end of the year. Experience had dampened my optimism, however. Unless you had it in your hand, nothing could ever be believed.

That summer had been quite exceptional in terms of heat, overcrowding and the number of vermin about the place. There were cockroaches everywhere and the rats that lived under our desks were running between our legs as we studied. From our landing I could see men sleeping both inside and outside their cells in One Brigade and I was told that there were so many prisoners that some were being forced to sleep in the stairwells. Counting the numbers of food containers leaving the kitchen, I estimated that there were about nine thousand prisoners stashed away in a jail that claimed to have no more than three and a half thousand. Relief came in September when, over a three-day period, thousands were shipped out on buses to the train station where bare carriages lay waiting to haul them to jails in the far west. A week or so before the event, prisoners from other brigades had been around pleading for cast-off clothing for inmates without money who were destined to endure the bitterest of winters in Xinjiang. The jail supplied nothing, because it would be a waste of resources to clothe prisoners who were being shipped out to another region's administration.

We knew the day had come for the evacuation when we were all herded around the corner into the workshop and told to watch a couple of videos. I never could fathom out what it was they didn't want us to see.

Each brigade sent one officer to perform guard duty on such trips. For most, it was the only way they would ever get out of Shanghai and see another part of the country, and for them it was a big party. As always, it would be the trustees who kept control of the prisoners while the guards hung out in the sleeper compartments, drinking *baijiu* and playing cards, whiling away the seven days it took to get to their destination at Korla. After two or three days' rest drinking *baijiu* and playing cards again, they would return to Shanghai, boasting of how intrepid they were.

The months of July and August had been intolerably hot, 38°C with 90 per cent humidity, and Eddie had become more and more angry with Larry's anti-establishment attitude and reluctance to acknowledge his crime. His patience ran out and they were almost at each other's throats. Eddie decided he would show Larry the difference between having an officer on your side and having him as an adversary. It was no skin off Eddie's nose – he simply stopped co-operating. Immediately Larry's mail started disappearing and, while the rest of us had the use of an electric fan, Larry went without. When he asked for the vitamins he'd been prescribed by the doctor to make up for the absence of meat in his diet, he was told that they didn't have any and that the prison could not be held accountable for his decision not to eat meat. When he ordered a new flask to replace a broken one, he was told that it wasn't allowed, even though everybody else had one. All this additional discomfort and pressure resulted in Larry becoming seriously ill. As the days went by, it became obvious that he was suffering more and more, but Eddie thought that he was putting it on and refused to take him to the hospital. Eventually, on 15 October, Larry was physically carried to the hospital and diagnosed as having gallstones.

He had refused to write his *renzui shu* or crime acknowledgement, and now that he was in hospital it meant that he was completely out of the game. Once a prisoner went to hospital, it was classed as leaving the brigade. The prisoner received no merit points and his cadre had nothing to do with him. He belonged to a different management system which did not allow any interference.

*

The other problem Eddie had was Webster. During the last twelve months or so, Webster had reactivated his appeal. All along he had been sending letters out under the wire to enlist the help of his family and the consul in putting it all together. To everybody's surprise, he had managed to get his documents to the right department. It was a major accomplishment and I had to take my hat off to his tenacity and resourcefulness. The problem was, though, that if a prisoner was appealing it meant he was not acknowledging his crime and therefore he was not eligible for a reduction. It was quite obvious that the authorities were in a sticky situation. They couldn't throw it in the bin because too many people knew about it, including our consul. There was only one way to prevent it leaving the jail now, and that was to convince Webster it would not succeed.

Their first line of attack was to make him understand that even if the Supreme Court in Beijing conceded that a grievous mistake had been made, they were not likely to cut his sentence by as much as the reduction that was waiting in the wings. They could even ignore it and thus Webster would lose out on two counts. From experience, a number of us believed that it was in the realms of possibility that the Shanghai Bureau of Justice would agree to give us reductions solely in order to stop Webster's petition leaving their authoritative control. If that appeal, containing clear unequivocal evidence of a set-up, reached the powers in Beijing, there would be hell to pay. There would be too many questions, and someone would get the chop.

Eddie spent days with Webster using Jin Feng as translator, trying to pull him round. When Eddie went home, Jin Feng would continue on his own. Eventually, Webster gave in and agreed to withdraw the appeal. It was so disappointing. Regardless of whether I liked him or not, he had been so close, he'd worked so hard and it was obvious that he had got them worried. After his capitulation, none of us would ever know what might have been.

November had started with the women's brigade being moved to another prison and an earthquake that rattled our cages sufficiently to wake us up. But on the morning of 21 November, the air was full of a different disturbance. Eddie was rushing around doing his best not to look us in the eye, and the Chinese refused to talk. Larry and I were watching ten very young men from Death Row being taken away all trussed up like turkeys when I was suddenly called out together with Werner, Dieter and Webster and taken downstairs.

Webster couldn't control himself and was going on about how he was going to get eighteen months' reduction, I was going to get fourteen and the two Germans twelve. Deep inside I was hoping that they were going to have done with it all, and simply kick us out. I was already planning what I was going to do when ShaSha and I got to the beach in Thailand. My head was so full of thoughts and plans that I was almost dizzy.

We were herded into a back room. Behind a long table sat three judges and a clerk. There were guards running everywhere. As we stood in a row in front of the table, I studied the faces of the men who had come to give me the news I had waited so long for. As our eyes met they made no attempt to conceal the contempt and hatred they felt towards us. For a moment I even entertained the thought that they had found some excuse to increase our sentences.

As I wondered what lay in store, I realised that the proceedings had begun. Webster had been addressed first, and a judge was asking his name. He went on to read out the crime and the punishment handed down. After listing his reform achievements, which for some absurd reason included a merit point for preventing a fight, the judge announced that he was to be rewarded for his hard work with a ten-month reduction.

A gasp escaped into the air and fell like a brick. Without looking, I knew that he was reeling, the very same as if he'd been kicked in the balls. I took comfort in the thought that perhaps the lack of generosity was down to all the aggro he'd caused over the last four years. Maybe things would be better for me.

Dieter was next, and after five minutes which seemed like an hour, he also got ten months. Werner followed and got the same. Right up until the moment when the judge said 'ten months' to me too, I was still thinking it was possible that I could get at least a year.

I was devastated. I turned to Werner and said, 'Well, what a load of fucking bollocks that was.' Poor Werner looked as sick as I felt. I was angry and pissed off. I felt cheated. The way I saw it, I had bent over backwards for their bloody system, and everything I had done – the shame and loss of honour I had endured – had all been ignored. We as a group had done more reform than any Chinese in the whole prison, and we were getting spat in the eye for it. It had never been worth it all for a measly ten months. From there on, I decided they could shove their bloody reform up their arse.

To cap it all, we were then expected to say thank you. Webster managed from somewhere to find the necessary enthusiasm to be as obsequious as usual, and the Germans said that they were very happy. Reluctantly, in a monotone, I said, 'Thank you for the reduction. It's very nice,' which Jin Feng translated more like, 'Oh, thank you so much for rewarding me with such a generous reduction. I vow to continue to work hard.'

'I didn't fucking say that, you old tosser,' I said angrily. But by then we were being pushed out through the door.

Eddie greeted us at the top of the stairs by asking how much we'd got. When we told him, he looked almost as surprised as we had been earlier. He was genuinely shocked and even took me aside later to say he'd thought it was almost certain that we would get a year, because in his report he'd suggested fourteen months. It didn't matter what he'd suggested because it was out of his hands. He was as much of a puppet as we were.

Later that day, calculating my time, I realised that I was looking at 19 June 1999 as a release date. It was just over two and a half years away, but at least I'd make it out for the millennium celebrations. If I could get another ten months off, I'd be out within two years. It all started looking a bit better. Twenty months was nothing. I'd already done five years and was still alive to tell the tale, so what was the sweat?

The following day we attended a post-reduction meeting where each of us was required to read out a statement of gratitude and future intention of continuance of the good work. It looked to me as if the officers who had been asked to preside had declined the offer and we were left with Jin Mouling, Eddie and the drunken psycho from downstairs, Captain Ming, who had nothing at all to do with us. Anyway, as the video camera circled, we did our bit with regurgitated enthusiasm, choking on words like 'reform', 'gratitude' and 'work hard' until there was nothing left to say. We were then lectured about how it was of the utmost importance to continue the good work. Making a mess of it all now could result in terrible consequences. It was not unheard of for prisoners who rested on their laurels to have their reductions rescinded. My God, I thought, no sooner had we got the bloody thing than they were threatening to take it away. 'The path is clear,' said Ming. 'Now that you have graduated to this level of reform, it is but another simple step to attain even greater rewards. We hope you can all go home soon. We realise that you are a long way from your families and that they miss you. Good luck in your reform.'

In the ensuing weeks rumours abounded of imminent release for us and the arrival of more foreigners from the detention house. Everybody I talked to was saying, 'Go home soon, go home soon.' Maybe it wasn't the whole truth but there was definitely something in the air.

When two startled, hairy-looking Pakistanis turned up one day, I realised how used to Tilan Qiao I had become. Things that were normal for me were totally alien to these new guys. Said and Muhtar, who preferred to be known as Sun and Vicki, were doing five and seven years respectively for travellers'-cheque fraud. Both in their late twenties, Sun was short and very muscular from having spent much of his youth as a bodybuilder whereas Vicki was tall and wiry. Both were typical Pakistani wide boys, for some reason embarrassed about their backgrounds and trying to act as western as possible. For example, Vicki wore jeans and a denim jacket and leather boots with brass toes, and swaggered like a cowboy, using every opportunity to try and impress upon us how modern he was. Strangely, both were married to Chinese girls from Hui minority Muslim families and could speak Chinese comparatively well, which was good news to me as it meant I didn't have to translate for them.

Eddie placed them in our sheep-pen with a desk and stool each and asked me to explain the system to them. It was like talking to them in Innuit, and they were not very enthusiastic to say the least, especially about crime acknowledgements and apologies to the court. I soon gave up and told them that if they had any questions they should ask the captain. When I told them that my wife was also from a Muslim family in Xinjiang, and that I had not eaten pork for over seven years, however, they welcomed me as a brother. And when I expressed my interest in Islam and my desire to learn as much as possible about it, they were quite willing to answer my questions. I had always been fascinated by the strength of faith shown by Muslims whether they were the Aga Khan, Malcolm X or the Ayatollah Khomeni. I wanted to know what it was that could make them so devout.

For the moment, though, things were going fine, and when, on the morning of 30 December 1996, we were told to pack our things up, I started to think that for once the rumours were true after all.

The Oriental Express

Don't lend wings to a tiger. If it had wings it would fly to the cities, seize the people and eat them.

Nan Fei, Prince of the State of Han

EDDIE made the announcement. We were not going home. Instead, we were being moved to a new prison out in the countryside, at a place called

Qing Pu. My immediate reaction was one of fear. Better the devil you know.

Fuck these bloody people, I thought. It had taken us five years to reach an established position in Tilan Qiao, where conditions were the most comfortable they'd ever been and we were getting a bit of respect for a change. But now they wanted to send us off to the bloody back of beyond to start all over again. We'd heard that Qing Pu had a full-sized football pitch and that prisoners there were allowed to smoke, but none of that was important to me. I could go without football and I had completely given up smoking thanks to the regulations brought in in '94 which banned smoking throughout Tilan Qiao, even in family visits.

We had no choice, though, but to pack up and clear out. I had thirteen boxes of stuff to take with me. Dieter had about the same, and everybody else about half that. Most of it was food and books that we had accumulated over the years. We were told to take everything, including the buckets we used to wash with and our bedding which we wrapped up and stuffed into large plastic bags. Each box and bag was marked with our number and taken away by Chinese prisoners to a waiting bus parked outside the admissions building.

I filed out of the building with the rest of the gang in the usual disarray that only we as foreigners could get away with, turning briefly to say a quick fuck off to Wang Jun and Henan who were standing by like vultures waiting to swoop in and grab what we had left behind. On the basketball court that had recently been made into a carpark, we waited for the other foreigners to join us. From Three Brigade came Parvaz Aktur and a new Pakistani called Khalid, who was twenty-two and doing three years for travellers'-cheque fraud. From Four Brigade came a Kashmiri known as Butt who had half a five-year sentence to go, also for fraud. Parvaz Aktur's pal Halid had not long gone home, and the other accomplice, Tahir Mir, was in hospital having an operation for gallstones.

There were ten of us, plus Jin Feng who was coming along to act as go-between. We said goodbye to Benny and marched off towards the gate. As we turned the corner, I was compelled to take one last look at the enormity of the tall grey walls to implant in my mind that same sense of awe I'd had the first day.

We were herded onto a real prison bus, with bars on the windows and a separation gate at the front which could be locked. Before that was done we were all handcuffed and told in no uncertain terms by Captain Jin, who was in charge of the evacuation, that any funny business would result in severe punishment. We were to sit quietly facing the front at all times. We were not allowed to look out the window or wave at passers-by.

Eddie, who had been supervising the handcuffing, turned to us and said, 'I wish you all good luck in your future reform. I hope that you can learn from each other and keep up the good work. I am sure you will all go home soon. Goodbye.' As he stepped down from the bus, he gave an almost embarrassed smile and waved. Jin slid the dividing gate shut with a smooth metallic clank and took his place beside five other officers at the front of the vehicle.

The bus pulled out and I felt as if a ghost was leaving my body, as if I had just been exorcised. It was 30 December 1996, and the first time in four and a half years I'd been on the other side of those grey walls. I'd seen glimpses of the streets through holes in the blinds of the boiler-room but this was different. As we sped through the bustling streets of Shanghai, it felt a little bit like freedom, but the knot in the pit of my stomach told me differently. There was still another two and a half years to go, only I couldn't visualise it all yet. There was no way I could even begin to form a picture of what life was going to be like at this new prison. Was it a farm or a factory? Were they going to force us to work in the fields planting rice or to sweat on huge presses making ball-bearings for Chinese tanks?

The Pakistanis lost no time in getting to know each other. Jabbering away in Urdu, it sounded as if they were all talking at once. They quickly established where each one came from, and then found someone they all knew in common. Apart from Parvaz, they seemed fresh and excited. They were not battle-weary like us who had suffered at the hands of Zhou Wanjia, Doctor Death, Wei Ji the wife-killer and Benny the Goodman.

Ignoring the Pakistanis, I stared out through the window at the streets of a city in which I had lived for five years but didn't know at all. Shanghai looked as though it had changed since the last time I'd seen it, though bicycles still crammed the streets and people still crammed the shops. The roads were better; people were dressed better, especially the young women; and the cars were better. New buildings were everywhere, but that didn't mean that the intervening spaces weren't jam-packed with the traditional squalour of any large city in China. Billboards expounded the visionary ideas of Deng Xiaoping. Others advertised Volkswagen, Sony, Dove Chocolate and Marlboro.

We were soon leaving the city behind, and bigger and bigger stretches of countryside came into view. New housing complexes with names like 'Dragon Villas', 'Great Wall Estates' and 'Lotus Pond Developments' were being built everywhere. In the watery winter light, everything looked cold and lifeless. There were fewer mini-skirts now, and the old people were wrapped up warm in padded jackets and trousers, but for some reason they still wore thin green canvas army shoes. Road signs announced the turn-off for the airport, and until we passed it there was always a glimmer of hope that the bus would suddenly switch lanes and take us there.

The airport disappeared into the liquefied horizon of a flat and charmless landscape. There was no plane for us that day. Peasants could be seen tilling the icy soil here and there, and I wondered what they had to live for out here. Driving on, heading in a southerly direction towards Songjiang, I started to wonder how ShaSha was ever going to be able to come and visit me again. Maybe there would be fewer visits but of a longer duration. Maybe they'd even give us one of those conjugal visits that I'd heard prisoners in Beijing got. My mind filled with vivid imaginings of lustful sex in some stark accommodation on the edge of a work farm with guards sitting outside the door, smoking, drinking tea and listening to the effort and exertion of a man and a woman trying to make up for five years of lost love-making. Make a nice scene in a movie, I thought.

After travelling for about an hour down long, straight, featureless roads, over-taking the odd cyclist and passing red-faced peasant work gangs with hoes and shovels on their shoulders, the bus slowed down and turned into a large entranceway with flowerbeds on either side. It could almost have been one of the villa estates that we were about to enter, but the prison guards who emerged from a small building soon dispelled that idea. They circled and peered in, like dogs around a rat hole, passing comment but not daring to come any closer. It was as though we all had some incurable disease they were afraid of catching. Our escorts jumped out and proceeded to hand over a mass of paperwork which was compared to another big pile of paper. When they had convinced each other that we were who we were supposed to be, the giant red oxide-coloured steel door slid open and our bus rolled in.

Welcome to Qing Pu Jail, a reform-through-labour gulag built for the purpose of redirecting the lives of thousands of criminals. The powers-that-be had done a thorough job researching modern institutions the world over before they'd drawn up the plans and started building in 1992. After the completion of the administration buildings, they filled each residential unit as soon as it was finished, to try and ease the terrible over-crowding being experienced in the other jails in the region. Thanks to a series of over-enthusiastic *yan da* or 'strike hard' campaigns by the law-enforcement agencies, thousands of prostitutes, drug dealers, fraudsters and thieves had been arrested in huge raids using hundreds of police officers, and the penal system was close to meltdown.

When we arrived, there were an estimated two thousand prisoners there, housed in large dormitory-style cells in six different blocks. Qing Pu had been built purposely with ample room to expand if necessary, and could in ten years' time house ten thousand or more prisoners.

It was nothing like the dark, oppressive and suffocating Tilan Qiao. Instead, it reminded me of a huge college campus with halls of residence covered with little blue and white tiles and interspersed with green lawns, trees and flowerbeds. As we stood outside the gate of a large compound with a basketball court, we were told that they were going to give us all an X-ray in order to check for lung-related illnesses. Immediately, a cold sweat broke out on my forehead. I didn't believe them and was sure that it was a ruse to look up my arse for my diary which I'd managed to stash there in the morning's confusion. It turned out to be nothing more than what they had said, and I breathed a sigh of relief.

We were then herded into what we were told was the 'subordinate brigade building' near by, and after the usual formalities we were introduced to the man who was to be our new leading captain, Wang Duizhang. He was a mess. Although very authoritative and officious on the surface, his clothes and way of talking suggested he was a right bumpkin. His shoes were dirty, his trousers were too short with stains on the backside, and he picked his nose as he spoke. This man did not give me confidence. At least his deputies were a bit better, two young officers by the names of Wu and Hua. I'd seen them before nosing about Tilan Qiao, no doubt trying to suss us out beforehand.

I felt an almighty feeling of desolation. If Tilan Qiao had been like living in a shoebox in an attic while the party went on downstairs, this felt like the furthest point on the globe from civilisation. Our names were lost on scraps of paper in a bureaucratic nightmare on the narrowest point of land at the far end of the Chinese gulag system. Could there be any return?

The subordinate building was an L-shaped affair with five cells on each of three floors on the long arm. On the short arm were an empty room on the ground, two offices on the second, and another empty room on the third. The whole thing was brand new and totally empty. We were taken to the second floor and shown to the cells that were to be our new home. From the corridor they looked like compartments in a railway carriage, but when I opened the iron gate of the first one and looked in I was immediately taken aback.

I had stayed in hotels that weren't as well appointed as this. Three single beds and a long low cabinet sat in a room four and a half metres long by three metres wide with pale pink walls. Each bed had a small grey desk by its side and there were nice big grey wooden stools to sit on. At the far end were two windows and a thin metal door that led to a four-foot-wide balcony enclosed in a metal cage. That was not a problem as far as I was concerned – this was the Ritz.

Opposite Room 4 was a washroom that contained a urinal, three flushing crouch toilets in cubicles, a large sink and two shower-heads, all done out with white tiles. It was simply too much. At the other end of this Oriental Express was a big iron gate and, opposite that, a guard-room. The way light came in from all sides made it almost like a conservatory. It was great but it wouldn't take us long to realise that the colour of paint makes no difference to a cage.

Everyone was then allocated their rooms and I was placed in Room 2 with, of all people, Webster. Who the hell had organised that, for God's sake? Although we'd been getting on quite well of late, I knew that living with him was out of the question, and that it would only be a matter of time before we started arguing and, most probably, fighting. Still ecstatic about the new quarters, however, I decided to suffer him until I couldn't any longer.

The placing of Jin Feng and two other Chinese prisoners in Room 1 made it clear that the authorities were still not willing to trust us an inch. The two new guys were there to fetch the food and liaise with the cadres. They were there to tell us what to do and how to behave, and to inform the captain when we fell foul of the discipline. Ah Dong, a Qing Pu local who was coming to the end of a five-year stretch for bribery, was made number 1. Although I was glad to lose the mantle, this bugged me no end and I was determined to make sure that his influence over us would be minimal.

The other gofer and spy was a wiry little fellow called Zhou Hui, who had just started a fourteen-year sentence for stealing a car. Stanley, as I christened him, lay awake each night in the knowledge that he had been grassed up by his own brother. He was here to learn the art of translation from Jin Feng.

After rice, braised beef, onions and baby Chinese cabbage, we were allowed a siesta. For the first time in 1,917 days, I lay down on a proper bed. I was glad that it had wooden slats underneath instead of springs because I was used to a hard surface to sleep on by then. Of course, my comfort wasn't the reason the jail had supplied it – they were afraid prisoners might unravel the springs and use them to pick the locks or as weapons to strangle the jailers or each other.

I soon realised that there was one thing I wasn't so glad about: having someone lying opposite me, belching, farting, scratching his bollocks and wanking, and looking to see if I was doing the same. Even though prisoners had patrolled the corridors at night in Tilan Qiao, nobody apart from the odd greenhorn looked in at you. It had felt like privacy, a prized item in the west but almost unheard of in China. It wasn't even night-time and I was missing my old cell already.

In the afternoon Captain Wang called us together for a meeting of welcome and introduction. We sat in the corridor while he, Wu and Hua sat behind a desk just inside the front gate. Jin Feng sat to their left. When Wang had come in, we had made some shoddy semblance of getting to our feet to stand to attention, but it was more like just a shifting of the arse to pull your knickers straight than anything else. He didn't remark on it at the time, but you could see that it had been noted down for a later date.

'First I should like to begin by welcoming you all to Qing Pu,' he said. 'My name is Wang and these are my assistants, Wu and Hua. We shall be directly responsible for your reform here, and we hope that you will work hard in order to gain the earliest possible release.'

'Where have I heard that before?' I thought.

'This is a new, modern and civilised jail with an emphasis on cultural values and employing humanitarian principles. We abide by the theory of reforming the criminal through his participation in productive labour. This is the fundamental principle and no one is permitted to go against it.'

Coughing first, I muttered, 'Well, that sounds humanitarian.'

'As some of you already know, you will all be required to plead guilty and to confess your crime. This is mandatory. I hope that by the regular writing of reports, you can keep close to the authorities, explaining your thinking so that we may assist and guide you through your reform. As cadres, we cannot make you reform yourselves, but we can, when needed, offer help and advice.

'You will at all times obey the cadres. You will abide by the discipline and follow the regulations. You will work to the best of your ability and to the limits of your greatest capacity in order to fulfil the labour task. It will be required of you to perform daily hygiene work and to keep yourselves clean and tidy. You will study hard and be aware of the political reforms going on in China and her place in the new world order. Your self-study periods may include the study of Chinese language and history. These are mandatory obligations. The prison is a dictatorship. There is no negotiation.

'When you have had time to settle in, we intend to introduce a "five good" system of reward and penalty, whereby points will be awarded in the five categories I have just mentioned: crime acknowledgement, regulations and discipline, labour, hygiene and study. Prisoners who achieve top marks in each category will receive a "five good" award. Five "five good" awards will earn you a *biao yang* ['merit']. Two *biao yangs* will earn a *ji gong* ['praise']. Two *ji gongs* means that you will be eligible for a reduction.'

I didn't know whether to laugh or cry. Was he being fucking serious here, or what? At that rate we'd be inside forever, and he only said 'eligible', anyway. Meaningless hogshit.

Wang continued: 'As a new, modern and civilised prison, emphasising cultural values and employing humanitarian principles [not so big of a mouthful in Chinese, which is why he kept repeating it], you will see that we provide you with good food, a bed, windows, toilets and washing facilities.'

'Big deal,' I thought. 'What's the alternative? Bad food, no bed, no windows, no toilets or showers?'

'You should to be grateful to the Chinese authorities for such luxuries, and you are expected to show respect and care at all times. Any damage to prison property will result in serious punishment. In due course you will all be given a schedule of daily activities. It is to be adhered to. You will remain in your allotted cells at all times, unless otherwise stated in the schedule. There is to be no gathering in gangs or secret meetings in other prisoners' rooms. If anyone is caught getting up to activities of this nature, it will be dealt with seriously. After nine o'clock the doors of your cells will be locked. We will provide you with buckets in case anyone needs to use the toilet at night. The balcony at the back of your rooms is intended for periods of unsupervised *fang feng*. You are not allowed to sit there at any other time. If a prisoner is found spending time there other than when shown in the schedule, he will be punished severely.'

I was quickly coming to the conclusion that this guy was a danger to my health. What was the point of calling yourself a new, modern jail which has toilets if they still give you bloody buckets? What was the point of putting us in a room with a bloody balcony if you weren't allowed to use it? That's like giving you water and saying, 'Don't drink it.' As I reflected all this impending horror, Wang continued to spew forth.

'Rooms are to be kept in an orderly fashion and will be checked daily by appointed hygiene inspectors who will award points for cleanliness and neatness. You are required to fold your quilts into a regulation size and shape block which is to be positioned at the foot of your bed.

'As soon as it can be arranged, you will be issued with the prison garb. You will be required to wear it at all times and keep it in an orderly fashion. Clothes will be folded neatly and kept in the cupboards provided. Anyone found with untidy cupboards will be punished. It is not permitted to keep food in your rooms as this may attract vermin. The prison kitchen will provide food to satisfy your tastes as foreigners, and you are expected to eat it. We do not like waste or prisoners hoarding food in their rooms.'

There was more.

'The next item I should like to discuss is manners and other ways of behaving. Whenever a cadre comes into your room, you will stand and say, "*Duizhang hao*" – "Captain good". You will not speak unless you are spoken to and will not sit down until the cadre responds to your politeness and tells you that you may. You must then say, "*Xie xie duizhang*" – "Thank you, Captain". If you meet the cadre in the corridor, you will stop, stand to attention and say, "*Duizhang hao*". If you are working and the cadre comes into the area, you will immediately stop what you are doing, stand to attention and say "*Duizhang hao*". If you wish to make a report to the cadre, you must first seek permission to leave your room from the number 1 prisoner here, Ah Dong. At the line which you can see painted here by the gate, you will stand to attention and say, "*Baoguo duizhang*" – "Report to Captain". You will wait until the cadre beckons and then enter the guard-room with a polite knock. You will make known your position when asked to do so by the cadre. You may not sit or lie down on the bed unless it is indicated on the schedule that it is naptime or bedtime.

'We have decided that participation in drill marching will be a good method to instil discipline into you. We will in due course begin classroom lessons to teach you the commands you need to know in Chinese. We think this will be an enjoyable form of exercise for you and good for your health. When it is convenient for the cadre, you will be allowed to play basketball or football.

'On to the last item now: communications and family visits. You are allowed to receive letters from family and friends. All correspondence will be copied and stored on the prison computer. If any material is discovered to be of an anti-reform nature it will be withheld from you by the authorities for examination. You will be allowed to write two letters to your families per month. The contents will be copied and stored on the prison computer. You may not be rude, tell lies or report rumours, give away prison secrets or accuse falsely and maliciously the prison authorities and government of the People's Republic of China. If correspondence is found to contain such material, it will be retained for examination.

'Family visits will be granted after application is made to the Ministry of Justice. You will be permitted one visit per month, which will be thirty minutes in duration. Visits will be monitored and you will be required to abide by the regulations at all times. If you do not, the visit will be terminated. Prisoners' families may bring a small amount of comestibles and necessary extra clothing. All items will be checked thoroughly, and if it is decided that it is not good for the prisoner's reform, you will not be allowed to receive it.

'If you have any questions, you can write them down in a report or make report to me in person in my office. That is all.'

Ah Dong then ordered us to stand up and say, '*Xie xie duizhang*' – 'Thank you, Captain'. This was done without conviction, in a sort of unintelligible slur. Everybody looked stunned. It was obvious that we were not in for a holiday. I wasn't actually all that worried when I thought about it – after all, it wasn't any different to what I'd heard before, just that we'd got it all in one dose this time. The merit point system was nonsense, so there wasn't any point concerning myself with that. But the idea of being forced to march? Well, that was a direct violation of my rights. The way I saw it, that was army shit, and Red Army shit at that. Another thing that bugged me was the requirement to study Chinese politics. I knew enough already to bluff my way out of that, but I sure as hell was not going to be forced into learning it. The uniform thing was no skin of my nose either. It simply didn't matter to me any more.

But what did matter were the visiting hours. It was going to take ShaSha nearly half a day to come to Qing Pu for a paltry half-hour. That was real bullshit, and I was well cheesed off.

Three of us had Chinese wives and others had family who wanted to visit but they would be put off by having to travel so far for so little. After talking it over with the rest of the guys, we agreed to write a report together, requesting the same visiting hours as A-class Chinese prisoners. After all, we'd had a reduction just six weeks ago which proved we were of the same standard. You had to be an A-class prisoner to get a reduction, so why were we not being given the same visiting hours? Top Chinese prisoners were also allowed to go home at Spring Festival and National Day for up to five days. We suggested that the prison authorities arrange conjugal visits for us to balance out the differences. We were being unfairly treated, it was as simple as that. The report was written and we all signed it.

The fact that we were to be given shit buckets pissed everybody off, especially Sun and the other Pakistanis. According to their religion, it was out of the question to have a shit bucket in the same room you prayed or read the Koran in. Everybody complained and, after some thought, Wang suggested that if a prisoner wanted to use the toilet in the middle of the night he could call the captain on duty to come and open the door. We immediately conspired to call the bastard out every half-hour all through the night and piss them off so much that they would give in and leave our cells unlocked. It was no problem – we couldn't leave the landing anyway.

We also asked if he could include the watching of the English news on Shanghai's International Broadcasting Service on the schedule, as this was a necessary source of information for us, especially for those who didn't understand Chinese. What we didn't say was that we also liked to watch the sexy little Chinese newsreader, Cui Wen, whose English was so cute, and also that by getting this concession there might be a chance that we would also get to watch the English movie which came on after.

For some reason (probably something to do with broadcasting rights and fees or the non-payment of them), the Chinese TV always showed foreign movies in two halves. CCTV broadcast one half on Sunday at five, and the remaining half the following Sunday. IBS showed three a week, half one day and half the next, and two days were set aside for a Chinese movie with English subtitles. It was a strange system but definitely better than nothing. Anyway, Wang gave this request a great deal of thought and eventually agreed.

A few days later, when the schedule was posted, it didn't seem so bad:

6.00	Reveille. Make bed, wash and brush teeth
6.30	Outdoor exercise
7.00	Breakfast
7.30	Hygiene work and inspection
8.30	Self-study/work
10.30	*Fang feng* on balcony
11.00	Lunch
11.30	Self-study
12.30	English news
1.00	Self-study/work
4.00	Recreation
5.00	Dinner
5.30	Self-study
6.30	Chinese TV news
7.30	Free time
8.30	Go to bed
9.00	Lights out

Compared to Wang's speech, this was a walk in the park. What it wasn't, though, was a walk on the balcony. I still couldn't see how they were going to stop us sitting out there when they were off at lunch or in the guard-room. We'd gone five years with just an hour of proper daylight every eight days – and they expected us to look through the window at a balcony which you could sit on simply by pulling back a latch? No way. They'd have to weld it shut to stop us.

The issue of us getting involved in 'productive labour' was postponed due to the severe cold, so we carried on as before. But my God, it was freezing, much colder than Shanghai. People who are free to walk around at will can never know how cold you can get in jail. I can only describe my experience of passing winter in Tilan Qiao as akin to sitting for fifteen hours a day in an empty cattle-shed on the Isle of Skye with the doors open for three months. Qing Pu was worse still; no amount of padded clothing could keep out the cold. At least our beds were warm. Another redeeming factor was that we were surrounded by nature. There were birds singing in the bushes, frogs croaking at night and cicadas chirping. You could smell rotting leaves and the needles on the pine trees out back. We could see stars and the full moon in the sky again. I could watch cloud formations move across the whole sky. How had I been able to live in Tilan Qiao without these simple delights?

The setting-up of the hygiene inspection team was as controversial as any issue. They wanted two people to go round each morning and inspect everybody's rooms for cleanliness and tidiness and to report their findings in a book. No chance! Who amongst us had the right to tell the others that they were dirty and then withhold points which could have a bearing on when you went home? Certainly not me. If the officers wanted to award merit points, they would have to do it themselves.

We finally agreed to go ahead with it when we came up with the idea of rotating the marks so that at the end of every month we all came out equal. After much discussion, it ended up with Webster in charge representing the Europeans and Vicki representing the Pakistanis. Everything went well until one day it dawned on us that there might be a difference between what we were being told by the book-keeper and what was being written down in the book and shown to the captain.

It was the beginning of the end. Tension was growing. Different camps were popping up and the walls started closing in. Vicki revealed himself to be another bloody sociopath and someone to stay well clear of. It wasn't that he was a hard nut – he was simply the most petty, jealous and vindictive shit-stirrer who ever walked the earth. Soon he was being beaten up by his own people and that's when we all embarked upon what turned out to be a never-ending series of room shuffles.

Captain Wang was a pain in the arse, but as long as you played ball with him he would play ball with you. Soon we were out on the balcony and getting to watch English movies, and when he called a meeting suddenly one day I thought we'd also got a result with the visiting hours. Wrong. Instead, he gave us all an almighty rollicking for writing that joint report. In the eyes of the authorities, it was tantamount to a rebellion. We had gathered together. We had held a meeting. We had come to a decision by democratic process. We had challenged the prison authorities as a group. But since this was the first time, and we were foreigners, they were willing to let it go. If it ever happened again, however, they would remember this occasion and severely punish us. If we wanted to petition the authorities on any issue, we were to do it individually. End of meeting.

By the end of January the Oriental Express felt about as big as a telephone box. There was no rest from the incessant chatter of the Pakistanis and with Vicki expounding, bragging and spitting his bullets of venom in the centre of it all, it made you grind your teeth. Things soon came to a head when Webster accused him of cheating at a game of cards. Vicki cursed him and was lucky not to get his face punched in. Webster stashed his anger but when I told him not to be so bloody finicky about everything the following day, we too nearly had a scrap. Apart from the loss of a merit point, it meant that Webster and I were parting company. I couldn't go on living like that and requested a transfer, joining Larry and Khalid in Room 4.

On 19 February, the death of Deng Xiaoping was announced and the foreign press immediately started talking about possible protests and massive changes. Nonsense. They knew nothing. Beijing was in control. Every radio station played non-stop funeral music and the TV showed non-stop commemoration movies. It was dire. We had to watch the funeral on TV. After hours of viewing the funeral cortège and the streets lined with professional weepers, we had to listen to the most over-the-top speech in history by Jiang Zemin. Just when we thought it was all over, we were asked to pay homage by making an individual speech of tribute and talking of China's future 'holding high the banner of Marxism and Leninism, and embracing Chairman Mao's thought and Deng Xiaoping's theory'. What did these people want from us? Some of the Pakistanis didn't even know who Deng Xiaoping was.

In the Name of God

It is the otters that drive the fish into the water, and the hawks that drive the sparrows into the woods.

Li lou, The First Volume. Mencius

NOT long after Deng's death, three new prisoners joined us. The usual excitement about having someone new to talk to was dampened by the fact that their presence meant less space in what was already a very small area.

Mir professed to be from the second-richest Pakistani/Kashmiri/Indian family in Hong Kong. From his family's carpet-trading empire, he had made his own millions by branching out into antiques and gem-cutting. He claimed to have started a company that bought washing-up liquid and turned it into shampoo by adding a little scent. He had flown jet fighters for the Pakistani Air Force, fought in Afghanistan, blown up oil pipelines in Russia, trained Muslim separatists on the Philippine island of Mindanao and had Hong Kong's Governor of Police in his pocket. He'd had forty cars and six wives, three of whom he was still married to. The last wife was from Taiwan and was the daughter of a general. He believed the Chinese thought him a spy, because he had an identity card from the Eighth Army Hospital in Taipei. He also had a birth certificate that said he'd been born in Nairobi, Kenya, the son of a Kashmiri who was an officer in the British Army and a British citizen. He insisted that he was British and that he had two Hong Kong British passports in a briefcase which the prison authorities refused to hand back.

In the eight and a half years he'd already spent banged up in One Brigade of

Tilan Qiao, he had neither received nor sent out a single letter. He maintained that Captain Jin Mouling had taken $1,500 from him for agreeing to post two letters. Mir swore these had never been sent. According to him, his family must by now think he was dead.

Harry was a short sixty-year-old Chinese American who spoke near-perfect English with a voice and accent like Sergeant Bilko's. Originally from Shanghai, his family had taken him to Taiwan at an early age and, with the help of a rich friend of the family, he'd ended up at Harvard, studying business. From his early days selling pretzels on the waterfront at Venice Beach in California, he had risen to become a multi-million-dollar businessman engaged in the recycling of waste paper. He bought seconds and rejects from huge paper manufacturing companies and sent it all to China, where paper quality was poor, for repackaging and subsequent sale. The Chinese authorities had made out that he had tried to smuggle in used syringes and hospital blankets, but according to Harry, the container in question was on its way to the Customs Inspection point to be declared when it was busted, so how could that be deemed smuggling? He suspected he'd pissed off the wrong people in the Shanghai government and that they simply wanted a slice of his pie. Harry wasn't interested in doing a deal so they decided to put him out of action for a while. Ten years. He was furious but also certain that his money, influence and US passport would soon get him out. The Chinese had other ideas.

Latif was a forty-year-old Shi'ite Iranian from Zanjan, a small city north-west of Tehran. He looked like Brutus out of *Popeye*, only he wore a Yasser Arafat scarf around his head. He spoke Persian, Turkish and Uighur but no English. He was devoutly religious and had been on the Haj (pilgrimage) to Mecca. So the Pakistanis put Latif in the 'most favoured person' league. He had been a haulage contractor who made an extra rial or two doing over jeweller's shops in unsuspecting countries. He used the old 'switch the briefcase with the money in it' technique, and had had a good chance of making it but had been caught at the airport. For heisting $200,000 worth of trinkets, and for being the brains behind the scam, Latif got twelve years and was as mad as hell.

My interest in Islam had grown. Thanks to my knowledge of Uighur, I could read a little of the Koran and, with Sun's help, I learnt the prayer ritual and the prayers themselves in Arabic off by heart. He then invited me to join him and Khalid to perform *zohr*, midday prayer on the Muslim Sabbath, or *juma* out on the balcony where we wouldn't be seen – the practising of religion was banned by the prison authorities. I enjoyed the experience no end but decided to take things gradually, and I only joined them on *juma*. If it felt comfortable, I'd start doing more, maybe once a day, just to see.

*

Diary

18 April: The end of Ramadan. Seven of us get busted for group prayer in Latif's room. Mir slaps Webster for trying to take control of handing out the *mantous* in the morning. Khalid loses it completely and smashes up two tables, shouting, 'I come from a political family, I am a dangerous man, I kill people!' Moved to Room 1. Harry joins me and Larry. Peace. Wang tries to lock us all up for bad behaviour. All the Pakistanis go on hunger strike.

19 April: Officers from the Criminal Affairs department arrive to find out why the foreign unit is in such a bloody mess. Doors opened immediately. Everybody interviewed in the office. We blame everything on Wang. Wang sent packing. Caretaker leading captain brought in for interim period. Both Hua and Wu investigated.

28 April: Appointment of a new captain, Qian. He's only about five foot four and has a high-pitched, shrill little voice with a slight warble that echoes down the corridor like a stranded seabird. At least he has a sense of humour, albeit of a sort of sadistic nature. Conditions are better, but prisoner relationships have hit an all-time low.

4 May: First work detail. Two by two to football pitch to pick weeds. Lovely day, good excuse to sit around on the grass taking in some sun. Everybody works really hard for two hours and that's it.

*

Vicki hated the fact that I spent more time with Latif than he did, and started a campaign against me. I was, after all, a Christian by upbringing and still uncircumcised and thus not fit to join them. He would go on and on behind my back enumerating the reasons which he believed prevented me from being a Muslim, and making out that I was a *shaitan* or devil.

I did my best to ignore him, hoping that if the others were as truly religious as they professed, they would act in the way that Allah saw fit. Eventually, after a long discussion with Latif as arbitrator, Vicki agreed to stop his antagonism, and he and I shook hands.

It wasn't long, however, before Vicki reported me to the captain for doing a bad job of cleaning the washroom and toilets. Stanley had come to me and asked me to do it again.

'Who told you to tell me to do it again, Stanley?' I asked in disbelief.

'Captain Qian just told me,' answered Stanley, looking at me warily through his little wire-frame glasses.

'And how would Captain Qian know if these toilets needed cleaning or not? He hasn't been in here today, has he, Stanley?'

Taking a step back, Stanley said, 'Somebody reported you.'

Still leaning over him, I asked slowly and deliberately: 'Who, Stanley?'

'Vicki did.'

Bastard! I was going to fix him now, once and for all. Spotting him, I stormed up the corridor towards him. He tried to put a smile on for me, but his face didn't like the stink and threw it off in a contortion of fear. I raised my hand as if to strike him and he doubled over. 'You fucking bastard! You don't even know the meaning of a handshake, you miserable piece of shit!' I said in an as much of a Clint Eastwood voice as my temper would allow. Walking past him, I presented myself at the Report Line, and said, with a loud and determined resonance: '*Baoguo duizhang.*'

Captain Qian, whom I'd noticed watching through the window, stood up, opened the door and waved me in. I sat down and tried to fix my thoughts. The situation had taken me to the end of my endurance. If it carried on, I was going to do that bastard serious damage. My patience had run dry. But I was also too close to getting another reduction to risk being punished for the sake of that worthless grub. Something had to be done.

As I started to explain what had been going on, in a run-up to requesting Vicki's removal from the unit, the door burst open and in swept the man himself. 'You fucking motherfucker, you!' he chanted in his singsong attempt at malevolence, before kicking me in the shins. (I found out later that he'd gone to his room to change into his brass-toed cowboy boots before storming the office.) He was grabbed by the other cadres and dragged upstairs, screaming and bawling.

Vicki had done my work for me. All I had to do was fill in a few blanks. Upstairs, in what the Chinese called *guanjin bi* ('bang up'), he continued to do us all a favour by slagging off the cadres, the government and the Chinese people in general. He managed to insult every officer in the prison. Over the following days they sent all manner of different officers from Criminal Affairs, the Justice Bureau, the deputy warden and the warden to try and cool him down, and he cursed them all. After about a week he ran out of steam and started to see the error of his ways. The authorities at that point stopped being understanding and set about punishing him.

On 28 June a meeting was held in the corridor. With a glint of vengeance in his eye, Captain Qian proceeded to relate the events of the 18th, and describe the crimes with which Vicki was being charged. Before he read out the punishment, Qian wanted revenge and went on to slag Vicki off for all he was worth. He told us that Vicki was from a backward family where they knew no better than to insult each other, and that Vicki, although talented in some respects, was in general stupid beyond belief. Although I too wanted revenge, I felt that since Vicki wasn't there to defend himself the whole trial was out of order and that the captain was in the end no better than Vicki.

He then announced that Vicki was to be punished with three months' lock-down for insulting the cadres and the Chinese government. He got nothing for kicking me, but that didn't matter as far as I was concerned; he was out of the fucking way at last.

*

Diary
2 July: Replacement gofer arrives, Xu Min. Good English and first one with a sense of humour.
16 July: Parvaz goes home. By tomorrow we'll have forgotten he was ever here.
21 July: ShaSha comes with her mother, my mother-in-law, Erinsa to visit, she couldn't stop crying. I'm glad she has made the trip not only to see me but to give ShaSha support and encouragement. She has not forgotten me or given up on me. She brings good wishes from all the family in Kashgar. They know I don't deserve this sentence, but they know the Chinese. They bring me a big bag of dried figs, apricots, raisins and caramel.
5 August: Simon Featherstone and Sue Perry of the consulate come to visit. Mir has opportunity to explain his predicament in person. British consul has been trying to see him since I informed them of his existence, but prison will not give permission. They have been trying to track him down all over the world but have not as yet been able to find anything that supports his claim to British citizenship.
14 August: Blackboards have been done using Qian's speech, some of the reports written by prisoners and Vicki's own self-criticisms. In an attempt to reduce his lock-up time, Vicki is writing one nearly every day.

2 September: Vicki performs verbal masturbation in public. Reads out self-criticism to the rest of us in a meeting. This is humiliation. He is allowed back to the second floor, but I am not convinced this problem is over yet.

15 September: A Korean, Mr Ho, arrives after spending three years in detention. He's a forty-five-year-old driver for Korean consul, convicted of being involved in heroin distribution. Ten kilos found in the car he was driving. He denies all knowledge of it. Sentenced to ten years all the same.

22 September: During work detail near football pitch, Mir and I witness cadres of Four Brigade whipping the prisoners with their leather belts as an encouragement to march in time. We ask the Party Secretary, who happens to be passing by, why they do this. He refuses to accept what's going on, but afterwards goes and tells them to desist.

31 October: Vicki attacks Larry with a stick.

On the news that day it had been reported that an American fighter had been shot down by Saddam Hussein's forces in Iraq. Hearing this, Vicki laughed and exhaled one of his 'vieeri goowde' remarks. When the following sentence revealed that three Iraqi planes had been shot down in the same incident, both Larry and I replied in unison with another 'vieeri goowde' and then laughed. We got up to return to our room but Vicki tried to block the way. He was shifted aside with a nice shoulder in the chest. The temperature was rising, so much so that I said to Stanley, 'Tell your captain to move that bastard now, or there's going to be a lot of shit.'

An hour later our apple rations arrived and we were called to the gate to collect them. As Larry stooped down to pick up his box, Vicki ran out of Room 2 with a mop handle and went to strike him over the head. Just in time, Mir, who was standing next to him, shouted and raised his hand to deflect the blow to Larry's back. In a flash Mir, Butt and Sun had grabbed hold of Vicki and pushed him back into his room. Larry was stunned and hurt, but was immediately taken to the office to explain what had happened. One by one, everybody who had witnessed the attack was interviewed. Lastly, Captain Qian called for Vicki.

He was still fuming and out of control. Even with the door closed, we could clearly hear him shouting and cursing at Qian and deepening the hole he was already in. When they were finished, the captain announced that once he'd got the necessary authorisation from above, the matter would be dealt with during the next few days. I couldn't believe that they were going wait. I told Qian that he had to move Vicki right there and then or there was bound to be more trouble. He assured me that it was all right and that Vicki would be punished. But it wasn't about punishment – it was about safety. But he couldn't or wouldn't see it.

Vicki was quiet for one day, but the next evening, just as we were all preparing to go to bed, he started swinging a stool around above his head just outside our room. I watched him for a few seconds, wondering what was going to happen next, and then turned away and shut the door in his face. The following morning, as I did my daily run around the basketball court, Vicki was walking back and forth with Sun and Khalid in tow. Each time I passed them, Vicki would stare at me and curse in Urdu and they'd all laugh. Every time I went by he did the same again and I ignored it.

After about twenty minutes of the same wind-up and knowing full well that it would be like lighting a fuse, I said: 'Why don't you just fuck off, Vicki.' As soon as I did it, the three of them stopped in their tracks as if stunned, but then they started to shout 'fuck you this', 'fuck your mother that', and so on. I stopped running and stood in the middle of the court facing them as they approached. Quickly Butt came across, told them to shut up and guided them away.

As I went to sit down for a breather, thinking how close we had come to a punch-up, I suddenly saw Vicki, Sun and Khalid running towards me, shouting and waving their arms as if they were fleeing a herd of elephants. 'Shit, they're going to jump me,' I thought. I waited and watched as they came closer. Vicki was the first to throw a punch but I ducked and he missed, but I immediately felt blows rain down on my shoulders and arms. There was no way that I was going to take this lying down – I'd had a bloody sickener of them and their nonsense. If the captain thought I was just going to let them beat me up so as to gain a bloody merit point for not retaliating, he could think again.

As Webster and Larry arrived on the scene, I twisted my body and saw Khalid looming above me. I gave him a right uppercut to the jaw, and as it landed my left fist was more than halfway to cracking him on the side of his head. Out of the corner of my eye I saw Webster grabbing Vicki by the throat and driving a straight right into his mouth. Larry had caught hold of Sun by the scruff of the neck and was turning him round to get a clear shot at his face. And then suddenly there were Chinese prisoners everywhere, pouring out of Five Brigade in search of extra merit points for breaking up the fight. As they pulled me off the broken Khalid, I saw Vicki running towards the gateway and picking up a brick. Webster was chasing after him, shouting, 'So you wanna play with weapons, you fucking wimp. Here's a fucking weapon!' and he stooped to grab a length of stick, waving it aloft like a broad-sword.

It was utter bedlam. Larry still had hold of Sun, and Khalid was running to save Vicki from Webster's stick, and even though I was being restrained by a Chinese prisoner, I was not done yet. Shrugging him off, I too went after Vicki, but by the time I got to him he was pinned up against the wire fence by about ten of the lads from Five Brigade and, luckily for him, out of my reach. Swivelling around, I saw Khalid coming at me again, and without hesitation I laid into him. As Webster shouted, 'Go on, my son!', I lashed out two swift combinations of three that repaid all the antagonism I'd suffered from the lot of them in the past few months.

As I pulled off, it looked as if it was pretty well all over bar the shouting, so I made my way back inside. Larry joined me, and as we got to the second-floor corridor I spotted Vicki taunting Butt through the window. Without warning, Butt piled into him. Suddenly, Mir, who'd been sitting with the two Germans on the sidelines the whole time just watching, ran in and started punching Butt around the back of the head. Just as I thought about going back out to help, Webster appeared on the scene. He spun Mir around and drove him a beautiful right smack on his jaw, sending him reeling backwards and onto his arse.

Almost as soon as that happened, the officers appeared. But where had they been? Wu, the cadre in charge, hadn't been seen for over half an hour. What had he been doing? Within five minutes, we were all locked in our rooms. But the place was buzzing. Taunts and threats were being shouted up and down the corridor until the concrete echoed with it.

As I paced back and forth in the cell, adrenaline still pumping through my veins at a million miles an hour, I realised that I was as happy as I'd ever been in six years of prison. My patience had finally snapped and I felt on top of the world. I was unscathed and not in the slightest bit worried about any repercussions. Sometimes you've got to stand up and say enough is enough, and that was the day I stood up. It had also been interesting to see that despite the differences between Webster, Larry and me, we had put them aside and joined forces that day.

The investigation that followed what became known as 'The 3 November Incident' was heavy going. There had never had a riot like it before. All the cadres were shamed-faced. They were a disgrace to the prison service. How could they have allowed such a conflagration to develop? Someone would have to be punished. Excuses would have to be found. The blame would have to be shifted and tracks would have to be covered. The investigators came from the administration bureau and we were taken one at a time to the office upstairs to undergo a series of taped interviews.

When it was my turn, they asked me if I had retaliated. 'Look,' I said, 'if you think that I was just going to stand there and let three guys beat the shit out of me, you're wrong. I did what was necessary to protect myself.'

'Who do you think was to blame for the riot – the Pakistanis or the cadres?'

I had not expected to be asked such a reasonable question. They usually just wanted to make you confess and that was it. I took my time and then said: 'The cadres had had ample warning of the approaching storm. Why was Vicki allowed to roam free after he'd attacked Larry with the stick? Captain Qian knew there was a situation brewing and could easily have prevented it.'

Everybody had to write reports which were dumped on Stanley and Jin Feng for translation. After two weeks of investigation it was announced that Vicki was to be removed from the second floor and given an official warning, a demerit of 30 points and the loss of a *biao yang*. Sun and Khalid also lost their *biao yang* and got 15 points' demerit. Webster got a demerit, Mir got a demerit and I lost a *biao yang*.

I was pissed off about that but when I asked Qian why I was getting punished, he said that it was all about diplomacy. He explained that if I had got off scot free, the Pakistanis would have been really mad and lost faith in the government. I looked at him as if to say, 'Who the hell is running this place – you or the Pakistanis?'

'Don't worry,' he reassured me. 'You'll get the *biao yang* next month. It makes no difference whether it's this month or next.' And I believed him.

*

On 22 December we were all ordered down to the ping-pong room. It had just been decorated in readiness for Christmas and was draped with bunting, balloons and a curtain that wished everybody a merry Christmas and a happy new year. This time there were no judges to officiate, just a few officers from the jail and Mr Sun from the Reform-through-Labour department. In a short, blunt meeting, Werner and Dieter were told that in light of their good behaviour they were getting a further nine months' reduction.

There was just enough time for me to say goodbye to Werner and wish him luck. Watching the two of them walk across the yard to the waiting minibus was a strange experience. I was full of contradictory thoughts. I was glad to see them go, because it meant that I would soon follow, but I was also sad because we'd been through so much together. I was pissed off because I didn't see why they should go and I should stay, and I was angry that the authorities hadn't let us all go together. Damn it!

I calculated that as my sentence was six months longer and I'd been arrested three months later, it meant that I had nine more months to go at the very most. It might turn out to be a bit less, but I set my sights on July '98.

The Cattle Prod

He who seeks far and wide for what lies close at hand works hard but to no avail; he who seeks near and handy for what lies after works leisurely but to the end.

The Biography of Zang Gong. The Later Chronicles of the Han Dynasty

WITHOUT the Germans, it was less crowded. Without Vicki, it was a lot more peaceful. Larry and I had been only two to a room for quite some time, and were well able to avoid each other all day – not because we didn't get on, but because that was the way to get on.

My search for enlightenment in Islam had also run its course. I didn't actually need it, because I had another source of power. I had ShaSha. We enjoyed something rare and untouchable, and the trust that we had in each other allowed me to have faith in the future. Many prisoners enjoyed watching others crack up or were glad that their marriages had broken down, because it meant they were not alone in their suffering. The guards also loved to see failure, especially in marriage, because it proved to them that the criminal was indeed a worthless good-for-nothing, and that made their job easier.

*

Diary

5 February: Jin Feng is looking decidedly ill. He doesn't even bother to dye his hair with ink any more. I've heard they're trying to get him parole.

10 March: Hua asks me to write a *renzui shu* – 'crime acknowledgement'. This must be the signal that I'm on my way out. The Germans did one just before they left.

25 March: Qian notifies me that I have received a *biao yang*. That's two now, surely good enough. Have asked my consul to request the jail to take a passport photo of me so that I can apply for a new document. Consul also assures me now that ShaSha will have no difficulty in getting a visa to settle in Britain. I tell consul that it is of the utmost importance that when the day comes, ShaSha and I leave China together. We must start organising this now.

1 May: Weather is already perfect for nude sunbathing on the balcony during lunch-time when the officers are all out. Hope to have a nice tan by the time I get out.

18 May: Our suspicions that the Supply Department are ripping us off are substantiated when they inadvertently leave price tags on a number of items. Reports written to ask for an inquiry.

30 May: Friends in high society send comfort and enlightenment. Take a ride in Timothy's bike. Sart painting the Elixir.

14 June: Two Liberians, Wavi and Eli, arrive from detention house. Devout Christians, here for travellers'-cheque fraud. Put in Room 5 for a month under observation. Only allowed out to fetch their food. No exercise or TV. First time that's happened. They also miss the World Cup.

20 June: Hear that Jin Feng's brother will not agree to vouch for him to go on parole. There's no way he can leave here without a guarantor.

25 June: Building work begins on the new Six Brigade, using about a hundred workers who come in every day from the outside.

5 July: Khalid goes home. Not one day's reduction, but I can understand why.

10 July: Scrap existing merit point system. Want to bring in new system back-dated to this time last year. This means that they can evaluate our behaviour during the last twelve months in accordance with a system that we were not aware of. Moreover, everything we have gained up to this date is now null and void, but everything that has been recorded as a demerit is still on the books.

*

The new system had been knocked up by one of the cadres in admin and sent over to Jin Feng and Stanley for translation. It had taken more than six years for them to devise a system for foreigners. But nothing had really changed: there was no must and will, only can and may. It was there to fuck around with people's minds, play with our hopes and dreams, and as long as one or two prisoners believed in it, it would work.

In all my time, I'd not seen one scrap of evidence to prove their reform system worked. There were too many unanswered questions, too many holes, too many lies. The officers spent all their time trying to convince us of the existence of something that wasn't there. The recommendation for reduction came with the prisoner from the court in his file. It was decided by the court at the time of the trial. If the court thought the prisoner deserved leniency due to his co-operativeness and repentance, they would suggest a realistic term to serve out of the original sentence. The prison would follow those recommendations and nothing else. If a prisoner had not shown willingness in the period of detention or in court, he could forget about in-prison reform and reward. He could work as hard as he liked, obey every rule and regulation to the letter, but he would not be put forward for a reduction. Of course, the authorities could never let this out of the bag or there wouldn't be any reform at all, or any work done.

*

Diary

10 August: I am still here but Jin Feng is gone at last. He died in Tilan Qiao hospital from cancer of the stomach. No wonder he hadn't been eating. Can't blame him for his way of thinking – he was a product of the system. Thirty years of suffering is enough to damage anybody's head. It's just a shame that he never had the chance to see if his dreams would come true. He had written an English phrasebook which I helped him correct that he wanted to publish when he was released, and he often talked about starting up a translation service, convincing himself that one of us would go into business with him. When his brother refused to take him in, I really believe he lost the will to live.

29 August: Stanley, Xu Min, Wavi, Eli, Webster, Sun and I beat Qing Pu Prison seven-a-side champions 5–2. They can't believe it.

10 September: 14 prisoners discovered smoking in Five Brigade at night.

When this happened, the 'new, modern, civilised prison with an emphasis on cultural values and employing humanitarian principles', dropped the pretence and went back to tried and trusted methods of extracting information, namely the electric cattle prod.

The cadres investigating this breach of the rules took the alleged smokers to the kitchen one at a time, where they were stripped naked and handcuffed to a iron gate. They were then subjected to a series of electric shocks until they confessed and named all those involved. Was it their intention to inflict pain? Well, water was splashed over the victims so as to spread the shock, and they used German-made batons because they were more powerful. The screaming, which we could all hear clearly from our unit, went on six hours a day, for seven days. One set of batons was constantly being recharged so as to keep up with the demand.

When all the facts eventually came out, it appeared that one prisoner who had been assigned to the garden detail had purchased a packet of Marlboro from a passing builder for 100 yuan (ten times the real price). He had smoked one a night with various other prisoners until someone inevitably grassed them up.

When everybody had owned up, their heads were shaved and they were relocated to different brigades. They had all been A-class prisoners, some of whom were expecting up to a year and ten months cut, but they lost it all. Even worse, they lost their eligibility for reduction for the next eighteen months. They had also been moved to less lenient brigades where their chances of getting such a big reduction was zero. Some of them were effectively given three and a half years of extra time for taking half a dozen drags on an over-priced Marlboro.

*

Nine months after the release of the two Germans, on the date which left me the same amount of time as their reduction, I was still waiting. It started to dawn on me that the '3 November Incident' had done serious damage to my chances of getting out early. But I couldn't allow myself to dwell on what was out of my control. I had nine months left. That was a fact, although there was always that ounce of suspicion at the back of my mind that they were quite capable of finding some reason to extend the sentence if they felt like it.

When Captain Qian was replaced by Captain Jiang at the end of September, I can't say that I was sad to see him go. Behind his genial mask, he had been a spiteful, vindictive, narrow-minded little coward. By the time he left, he'd made sure that he'd repaid us for every snigger of disrespect. It was rumoured that leading the foreign unit had done nothing to help him in his bid for promotion, and that he was well pissed off. I hoped that the rumour was true, because if they were punishing me for 3 November, it was all his fault. He allowed it to happen.

Captain Jiang was about forty-five but he looked more like sixty. There was a sadness about him, maybe a resignation to life's cruelty. He was the son of a well-known local businessman and could have followed in his father's footsteps but he had decided to devote himself to his country. He didn't have much good to say about the departing Qian either, especially when he discovered there was an ongoing investigation into serious disobedience. In fact he was furious about it because the incident would be recorded and attached to his record, not Qian's, and there was a good chance that he would lose his end-of-year bonus as a result.

One morning early in October, Xu Min simply disappeared. About an hour later, one of the old men from downstairs was seen being escorted across the yard by two heavies from Criminal Affairs. In the afternoon, Captain Wu from admin came and told Harry that he had a consul meeting. Harry put his coat on and went with him. It was to be six weeks before we saw him again.

The following day we were treated to a five-hour-long screaming session emanating from Two Brigade. It turned out that the Electric Inquisition had been convincing Xu Min about the leniency he could receive if he told them the truth. Harry was being held in solitary confinement in the punishment block. He had allegedly been using the old man from downstairs and Xu Min to get letters out 'under the wire'. He had major grievances which centred on a total disregard for his human rights, and was trying to enlist the help of senators and the like in a bid to get released. Using his local knowledge, social standing and dollars, he tried to beat the system, but with informers lurking around every corner he stood no chance of success.

Harry was also accused of giving money to an officer to hire videos from a shop on the outside for us, and I finally understood how for the last year we'd been able to see such good movies so regularly. Damn! That was the end of that, then. The main suspicion floating round the foreign unit was that the investigation had stumbled across all these infractions while following up on a false accusation that had been written in an attempt to get rid of Xu Min. The atmosphere was poisonous and it wouldn't have surprised me if this was exactly what the authorities wanted. They encouraged us to be at each others' throats because then we did their job for them. I felt ashamed to belong to the foreign unit. What an advertisement we were.

Harry was not released from the punishment block for nearly six weeks, which meant that the cadres had obviously not read Article 58 of the Prison Law, the penultimate paragraph of which states, 'confinement to be imposed on the criminals shall be limited within seven to fifteen days according to the preceding paragraph.' Unless, that is, they had decided to call Bill's confinement 'observation', 'under investigation', 'protective custody', or 'separation'.

The one good thing to come out of Harry's confinement was the information that he managed to gather from the other trustees. They had divulged a lot of Qing Pu's secrets willingly because Harry was Chinese and he not only spoke Putong hua but Shanghainese as well, which put them at ease.

We had known for some time that the factory there was making cuddly toys, but we had no idea about which country they were destined for, or the conditions that the prisoners worked under. But when Harry returned from his ordeal, he told us everything we wanted to know. Prisoners were working twelve hours a day pumping out as many toys as they could. It was all done on a daily quota basis, and if prisoners failed repeatedly to reach their targets, they were electrocuted with the prod. In the stifling forty-degree heat of the summer, the factory building itself was a hell hole. With very little ventilation and no fans, the prisoners sat in pools of their own sweat. In winter they froze.

However, the most interesting piece of information came with an actual sample of one of the toys and the label that was attached to it, which read 'S.P. (UK) LTD GT. RUSSEL COURT BRADFORD BD7 1JZ' on one side, and 'BRITISH SAFETY STANDARD' on the other. I wondered how many British mothers knew that when they bought their children cute, fluffy little dogs and bears, they were contributing to a dictatorial regime and the suffering of thousands of prisoners who worked long hours and were threatened daily, not only with an electric cattle prod, but also with loss of remission. The money that was being made in Qing Pu alone through this particular business was rumoured to be in excess of £250,000. Apart from the odd extra bun and a merit point, no prisoner ever benefited. With that sort of money in the coffers you would have thought that they could have provided a decent hospital with proper medicine and facilities to treat people without having to drag them all the way back to Tilan Qiao. But no, it was a bloody shambles full of incompetence, placebo pills and the odd aspirin. There was no dentist and the prisoners had to suffer weeks, sometimes months, of excruciating toothache before the authorities could get themselves together and sort out a mini bus to go back to the City Jail.

Mir told me about one brigade in Tilan Qiao where he had watched in amazement as prisoners stuffed old steamed bread buns into the toe end of cuddly slippers. He also said that many prisoners, due to the water rationing, never washed their hands after going to the toilet: the majority were suffering from skin diseases brought on by the heat, so the toys were full of scabs and dried pus.

The Race

I am truly happy to have discovered that suffering need not destroy: it can be creative.

Terry Waite, *Taken on Trust*

AFTER Mark left he sent a few letters disguised as if from someone else, but they soon dried up. Dominic had been better, sending books and the odd postcard from India, and Werner had written to tell us about his new life living in a recording studio putting seven years of song writing and new talent down on tape. No one, as far as I knew, had ever followed up the Damazhi issue.

After so many years of being stonewalled you have to change tactics, and that's what we all did. It was not like Britain where there are procedures in place to allow a convicted man a legal avenue to seek justice. China had nothing. After the second trial, that was it. Accept it and and shut the fuck up. The only way out was to conform and wait.

Those that had queried our convictions had been fobbed off with blunt retorts from minions who knew only to protect their motherland. Damazhi had been well and truly swept under the red carpet of the Chinese Justice Department. But althougth we spoke less and less about it, it could never be forgotten.

Christmas Day 1998 and everybody was herded over to the Great Hall for a meeting. The hall was full and there must have been about a thousand prisoners in all from Two and Five Brigades. Twenty or thirty officers sat at the back drinking tea, while another dozen took their places on the stage behind a long table stacked with microphones, red thermos flasks and tea-cups. The warden and his two deputies sat in the middle. To one side sat the secretary of the Communist Party, the captain from the Education Department and the captain of Two Brigade. On the other side sat the captains from admin, Criminal Affairs and Five Brigade. Trustees scuttled about nervously topping up the tea and trying to make the PA system come to life. Above the stage a red banner declared: 'End of Year Appraisal Meeting'.

All this meant was long, boring speeches about the meaning of reform, reform goals and reform achievements. It was the same old jargon every time they opened their mouths. Three hours later, barely able to keep my eyes open, we at last came to the interesting bit, the bit which applied to me, and the bit which could mean that I was going to get a reduction or not. Thanks to the odd rumour, my optimism had been rekindled, and I thought there might just be a chance that they would kick me out as they had done with the Germans the year before. Maybe Christmas was the time to release foreigners as a seasonal gesture.

I sat waiting, listening to the names of Chinese prisoners being read out, hoping the vice-warden would say my name and add, 'Go home.' As the minutes ticked by, it looked increasingly likely that they'd left us off the party invites again. But then, in the middle of a long list, like finding a gold ring in a bucket of worms, I heard my name. '*Lobota Haw Dai wis, gai zao ji ji fen zi.*' Reform Activist award. Bloody hell, that was something. That meant I was almost certain to be on my way. They wouldn't bother to give me such an award otherwise. As I thought about it, I realised that I was more than likely the first European ever to receive a *gai zao ji ji fen zi*, so that was a result in itself.

Returning to the unit afterwards, I half expected the officer to tell me to pack my bags, but it never happened. Two days later I was given a little red card with gold writing on the front which said, 'Shanghai City Qing Pu Prison Reform Activist Certificate.' On the inside an inscription read, 'Criminal RHD in light of excellent achievements in reform while serving sentence is judged to be a Reform Activist. Special encouragement, Shanghai City, Qing Pu Prison. 1998–12–18.' It had the prison seal with the five-point star in the centre.

*

Diary

10 January: A magazine called *The High Wall* carries an article which states that 'a foreign prisoner called Amir should be commended for reporting another foreign prisoner, Latif, for receiving dollars hidden in the packaging of parcels sent by his family'. The beauty of this place is that as soon as two people know something, it is no longer a secret, and if anyone decides to get up to something devious, they must expect that it will quickly become common knowledge. There is only one way to play it here, and that is straight. We see each other every day and I know how each person behaves. If someone does something differently, I notice it immediately and then take a closer look to see what is wrong. I am not the only one who notices these discrepancies. Everybody is watching everybody. There are no secrets.

21 January: Mir goes home ten years to the day. Not one day's reduction.

*

Spring Festival 1999 featured an all-comers sports competition. Included were basketball, football, tug-of-war, 400m relay and a 1,500m race. Our Captain Jiang was confident that I could win the 1,500, and entered me for it whether I wanted to or not. Compared to the way I'd been for the previous fifteen years, I was pretty fit, but I couldn't see me out-running those nimble little Chinese guys nearly half my age. Nevertheless I decided I'd have a go.

It was a beautiful spring day and competitors from all over the jail were there taking part. Prisoners sat in rows on the inside of the bends ready to cheer on their mates and slag off their enemies. There were about twenty of us on the starting line, all jostling for position, and I was nervous as hell. I knew from my schooldays that I couldn't just shoot off at full pelt because that would mean I wouldn't have anything left for the end. I planned that for the first few laps I would just stay back a bit, keep the leaders in sight and wait until they were flagging before making a move.

Almost before I was ready, the starting gun cracked and off we went. Straight away, about eight Chinese shot off as fast as they could and left me way behind. I could never match that sort of pace and had no intention of trying. As they continued, doubts crept into my mind that maybe I wasn't as fit as I thought after all. But then, on the second lap, after overtaking a couple of lads whose legs had died, I passed the early leader lying on the ground, gasping for air. He had completely exhausted himself and looked as if he was about to be sick. I was finding my rhythm by then and felt quite comfortable, but I knew that I was running at the limit of my ability.

On the bend I passed another four who had all but come to a halt and were puffing like cows after a stampede. As I looked ahead I could see at last that there was only one guy left in front of me, and I was gaining on him fast. After seven hundred metres I was in the lead. Damn it, that wasn't what I'd planned. It was too early and I was running too fast. Feeling the strain, I gritted my teeth and dug my heels in, but there was no way I could go any faster. I dared not look round to see where my nearest rival was – it might lose me valuable seconds – so I just concentrated on the rhythm and ran.

On the last lap, coming up the back straight, I couldn't believe that I was still in front. Suddenly I heard Webster shouting that somebody was catching up. I knew that I had been slowing down because Larry had been calling out my lap times as I passed. If I was going to win, I had to search for that little bit more to get me over the line. I tried and tried to find a kick but it simply wasn't there.

Suddenly, the finishing line was there in front of me, and I more than expected some Chinese kid to tear me behind up me and leave me standing five metres from glory, but he never came, and I crossed the line to the cheers and applause of both Chinese and foreigners. Turning back to see where my rivals were, I was surprised to see the guy in second place still had at least two hundred metres to go.

When Larry told me my time, I couldn't believe it. It was 4 minutes 26 seconds. I felt as good as I'd ever felt. I was even glad that I was still in jail and had had the opportunity to prove to myself that I had the will to do it. I'd always thought that I had made my time in jail work for me, and that I had achieved something worth while from what could have been idle years, but this was the ultimate. It was my reply to those who had tried to shoot me down over the years, and like way, there was no bragging or big talk, just plain and simple action.

I won a bottle of Pantene shampoo worth about a quid, and gave it to ShaSha when she visited that month. When I told her about my victory, she was pleased but she could never fully appreciate what it had been like for me. She was more concerned about my release or the absence of it. We had been busy for months trying to arrange her visa for settlement in the UK and still didn't know what was going to happen. I had actually started arranging our departure two years before, in an attempt to make sure there were no cock-ups like before. We had thought it might be necessary for Sharapet to go to Beijing for an interview, but at the end of '98 the consulate in Shanghai opened a visa section, so there was no need.

This time ShaSha was applying for a settlement visa, and in response to my constant requests the consul had brought along the chief of the visa section so that he could conduct my part of the interview to evaluate our relationship, future accommodation and finances so as to make his recommendation. As it happened, he was just going through the motions in order to fulfil the requirements. Unlike before, we had everything that was necessary, like letters of invitation from my parents, guarantees of accommodation and financial support, and it wasn't as if they didn't know us, was it? The consul knew ShaSha well because she had been there often to ask for advice and pick up the mail that was sometimes posted there for me.

I was anxious about every detail, and tried to make the consul understand that it was imperative she get the Chinese authorities to inform her at least two weeks in advance of my release so she could let ShaSha know and then she could get the visa. I was told this was not a problem, and that the prison would have to let her know in advance so that she could purchase my plane ticket. 'Please buy two tickets,' I asked her, 'because I don't want ShaSha on one plane and me on another. And I want us side by side, not at different ends of the plane. So that's two one-way tickets to London, non-smoking by the window because I want ShaSha to have a view.' The consul assured me that she would do her best, and I was certain she meant it. ShaSha's visa could be issued in twenty-four hours if necessary so it looked as though it was all systems go. Even though seven years of experience told me never to count my chickens, I was starting to feel a little bit more confident that things might just work out.

I had no regrets about all my optimism. It had been a great help along the way and a safety-net that had stopped me falling into the deep dark pits of despair. Looking back at how I had coped, I realised I had done it all in sections, and I never felt as if I had to serve more than two years at a time.

When I went into Tilan Qiao, I had convinced myself that I was going to go home with Mark, but when that didn't work out I had looked at half sentence as a certain date of release. When that day passed without incident, I decided that two-thirds would be quite convenient. When I got the reduction, I was sure that I wouldn't spend another eighteen months inside, and now finally there was less than three months to go. Somehow I had made it. If I had honestly thought in the beginning that I was going to do over seven and a half years, I would have cracked up. But it's impossible to see that far ahead – it's almost as though the brain has a fail-safe switch called hope in its circuitry.

On 14 April Captain Jiang called me into Harry's room for a chat and, after the usual polite nonsense, told me he had been informed that I was going home the following day. He wasn't supposed to tell me this, but he thought he'd do me a favour and give me a bit longer to pack my bags. I didn't tell him that I had been on red alert for nearly a year already, and that I could be ready within minutes if need be, which is not a very long time after seven and a half years, is it?

I went back to my room, still not believing it, but I told Larry all the same. His response was about as much as I could expect from someone with another six years left to serve. 'Umm . . . yeah . . . good.'

The next morning I knew that the day had come. I could feel it in the air. At about half past eight Captain Liu from the Education Department came to the cell and told me to put on my civilian clothes, wrap up my four sets of prison garb and bring it with my belongings up to the office for inspection. After a hot shower, out came the pair of trousers I'd kept clean and pressed for the last four years, and my favourite black T-shirt that I hadn't worn since the day I was busted. It felt good. I was a new man all of a sudden. Reformed? Definitely, but not in the way they had intended.

I had enough time to say goodbye to my cheeseplants, to Larry, Harry and Mr Ho before I was led up to the admin office. It was full of officers all trying to look as busy as possible. I sat down on the sofa like I was told and listened intently as a little man read from a document. In light of my receiving the Reform Activist award and my general good behaviour, the prison had seen fit to apply to the court for a reduction. The court had accepted the recommendation and now rewarded me with a reduction of two months and three days. 'How bloody tight can you get?' I thought.

After I had signed the release paper, another officer handed me back my personal effects. My heart beating faster with every breath, I quickly took a look inside, and to my relief saw that our wedding rings were still there, albeit a little tarnished. I decided to leave them in the envelope for the time being so that we would have the replacing ceremony later on the plane – that was, of course, if ShaSha was waiting for me at the airport. Did she know? Had the consul been able to contact her in time? Had there been enough warning to issue her visa? It would be so easy for all that planning to go wrong.

But this was the moment I'd been waiting over 2,700 days for. I had to try and take it all in. At last it was coming true – I really was leaving. I had decided years before that any celebrations would be left until I was clear of Chinese air-space, when I planned to order a bottle of something nice.

All my fears of their baggage inspection were gradually dispelled as I watched the officer half-heartedly rummage through my belongings. They were going through the motions, that was all. I could have put anything in there and it wouldn't have mattered. But I was still glad that I had taken the precaution that morning of swallowing my diary and other documents that I wanted to take home. Other sensitive material had been hidden in two parcels of books that I'd sent out with the consul back in the summer of '98, and I knew that they were safe. The authorities were so scared of the slightest piece of information leaving the prison, it was laughable. They tried everything to prevent it happening but we had plenty of time to think up ways of evading their rules and, anyway, what did they expect from a bunch of smugglers?

When the formalities were done, I picked up my bags and followed the officers down the stairs. Stanley was at the bottom. 'Zaijian Stanley,' I said to him, 'it's been a pleasure meeting you.' And it had been. Stanley was one of the very few Chinese prisoners I'd met during my time inside whom I can truly say I liked. He had been straight with me, honest; a principle which he had regarded highly. He had taught me how to play *go* and during lengthy sessions answered my questions about China and the Chinese. Thanks to him, too, I was leaving with a very neat collection of Chinese calligraphy.

It was a beautiful spring morning. The sun was already halfway up the sky and the birds were singing their heads off. There was a cool edge to the air. and there was a smell of new life all around. Walking across the yard, I wanted to look back but forced myself not to. Who was watching me go? Who was cursing my back? Who dared not look? Who'd already forgotten that I'd even been there? Who cared?

No sooner than I'd hopped in the mini-bus, we were off, and I just managed to see Larry waving from the window behind the TV set before the bus lurched up towards the gate. This time the officers had release orders, which were studied long and hard before the guards on the gate gave them the stamp of approval. All I can remember from then on is the bus zooming down a long straight road with the siren blaring as we passed the odd donkey, a few bikes and lots of little vans. I could read all the signs this time, and felt as if I was a part of country around me. I knew China like no other foreigner could ever do. I had more than scratched the surface on this mysterious eastern world. I had seen it from within.

We passed nice two-storey houses, shops, supermarkets, factories, housing developments, golf clubs, Toyota dealerships, Volkswagen service stations, Coca-Cola billboards and directions for Carrefour supermarkets. The place had changed as much in the last two and a half years as it had done in the previous five. It was incredible. They had built another city from scratch with everything in it. For a country that professed so much poverty, where had the money come from?

The dragon was spitting me out at last. Maybe I had digested it more than it had me. Seven and a half years had been a long time, but it had passed. It was strange: I wasn't really bitter, but I would never stop feeling that I had been cheated, and that the day I was sent down justice had been away on holiday. But I was comforted by the knowledge that I had not wasted those years. From the very beginning I'd made the effort to seize the opportunity to fill in all the gaps in my life and become a more complete person. ShaSha and I still had our marriage and our love not just intact but deeper and stronger than it could ever have become without going through this ordeal. We had said things to each other that might never have been said had I not learnt to speak and write Chinese. The same sentence in a British jail would, I'm sure, have been a disaster with very little gained, but in China every day was a revelation. For all their faults, dirty tricks, lies, intimidation and disregard for people's rights, they did at least allow me the time to educate myself. Oh, and the food was brilliant, especially the tofu.

Driving down the road that day, though, I knew that it was not all over yet. Would ShaSha be waiting at the airport for me? I ran that question through my head a thousand times. It would totally be in keeping with the way they had done everything to screw us up at the last moment. I was almost beginning to expect it. Would she be there?

Perfection

Po jing chong yuan – A broken mirror is joined together.

Of course she was there.

Perfection she dances,
Holds me with blue eyes,
Songs of streams and mountains,
And a love that never dies.

A tapestry, a garden,
A silver bangle two,
My summer breeze, my soft caress,
My early-morning dew.

Beauty crowns her mistress,
With nature pure in time,
Oh rose cloud bathe my body,
With your golden lotus wine.

No image tells the story,
No word can paint the truth,
The nights of blood and tears,
That lifts the veil of youth.

From the dawn of our creation,
I've known you all my life,
And the rest of time's not long enough,
To spend with you, my wife.

Epilogue

AFTER a seventeen-hour flight, ShaSha and I finally arrived in London. It had been nine years in all since we had first attempted to make this trip, and now that we were here, China seemed like a dream. While I went to look for a hotel, ShaSha sat in Paddington Station keeping an eye on our luggage. She saw drunks stagger by with carrier bags begging for the price of another drink, down-and-outs with their shopping trolleys full of cardboard looking for a suitable doorway to doss in, punks with Mohican hairstyles, and men with pink hair and a multitude of grotesque facial piercings. Not really the right ingredients for a favourable first impression.

I had always feared that when I dropped the barriers I had created to protect myself on the inside, I might well end up close to the edge. But I felt fine. Once back in my home town, the only problem I encountered was recognising people that I supposedly knew well. ShaSha's main problems were the lousy, unpredictable weather, the fact that every meal came with peas and carrots, and the incredible price of things apart from baked beans and spaghetti hoops.

After discussion, I soon realised that all attempts made by my family and friends to clarify the Damazhi issue had been fruitless, Most enquries were never answered. Those that were answered brought replies which simply off-loaded responsibility onto some other department.

I have written to Larry and sent him books on numerous occasions, but I have not once received a letter in return. This, I am sure, is not through his not trying to do so. The prison continues to restrict the free flow of mail out of fear that some violation of a prisoner's rights might be disclosed, or that a prison secret might be given away. Like the officers' ID numbers for example.

Captain 'Benny Goodman' Yu 3101427
Captain Jim Mouling 3101044
Captain Ming 3101505
Captain Li (Warden) 3101001

Je ne regrette rien.